2004

The
Psychological Assessment
of Political Leaders

THE

PSYCHOLOGICAL ASSESSMENT

OF POLITICAL LEADERS

With Profiles of

SADDAM HUSSEIN AND BILL CLINTON

Edited by Jerrold M. Post, MD

THE UNIVERSITY OF MICHIGAN PRESS
Ann Arbor

Copyright © by the University of Michigan 2003
All rights reserved
Published in the United States of America by
The University of Michigan Press
Manufactured in the United States of America
⊗ Printed on acid-free paper

2006   2005   2004   2003   4   3

A CIP catalog record for this book is available from the British Library.

Library of Congress Cataloging-in-Publication Data

The psychological assessment of political leaders : with profiles
of Saddam Hussein and Bill Clinton / edited by Jerrold M. Post.
p.   cm.
Includes bibliographical references and index.
ISBN 0-472-09838-1 (cloth : alk. paper)
1. Political leadership—Psychological aspects.
2. Politicians—Psychology.   3. Heads of state—Psychology.
4. Hussein, Saddam, 1937-—Psychology.   5. Clinton, Bill, 1946-—
Psychology.   I. Post, Jerrold M.

JC330.3 .P79   2003
320'.01'9—dc21   2002153616

To Alexander George, a dear friend
and admired mentor, whose gentle wisdom
and clarity of vision have illuminated
the path for so many.

Contents

Contents

Contents

Preface

Jerrold M. Post

With the wisdom of hindsight, many of life's most consequential decisions are often a matter of happenstance. In the spring of 1965, I was in Washington, DC, completing my second year as a Clinical Associate of the National Institute of Mental Health before I was to return to Boston for a planned career in academic psychiatry, when a friend from medical school approached me to discuss "an unusual job opportunity." Despite having secured a position on the faculty of Harvard Medical School, I could not resist this provocative invitation. We met for lunch, and he offered me the opportunity to develop a pilot program for assessing at a distance the personality and political behavior of foreign leaders for senior U.S. government officials. A service of common concern, the unit would be administratively based in the Central Intelligence Agency. I thought it would be an interesting divertissement and decided to delay for two years my entering the groves of academe.

In what was to be a marvelous intellectual odyssey, the planned two-year diversion lasted twenty-one years. On assuming my position at the Central Intelligence Agency, it was immediately clear that my training in clinical psychiatry, while useful, was clearly insufficient for the complex and daunting requirements of the challenging task ahead. The clinical case study was designed to establish a diagnosis in a patient suffering with mental illness, but the large majority of political leaders are psychologically normal. Indeed, severe mental illness would be incompatible with sustained leadership. Yet political leaders from different political cultures differ profoundly, and understanding those differences would be of inestimable value to our senior leaders both in negotiating with them and in dealing with them in politico-military crises. But what elements of leadership should be delineated?

When the pilot program was institutionalized, I sought out leading figures in the emerging discipline of political psychology and developed a senior advisory panel to ensure that state-of-the-art knowledge and methodologies were applied. Serving on the panel were two of the contributors to this volume who specialized in the psychological evaluation of political leaders at a distance: Margaret Hermann, professor of psychology and political science at the Mershon Center of Ohio State University, and David Winter, professor of social psychology at Wesleyan University. The ranks of the core group of profilers were augmented by Steve Walker, professor of political science at Arizona State University, and Walter Weintraub, a research psychiatrist at the University of Maryland, who had applied a method of psycholinguistic analysis he had originally developed working with patient populations to political personalities in his analysis of the Watergate tapes transcripts.

Over the years at the annual scientific meetings of the International Society of Political Psychology, it was rare when a panel of profilers did not consider presidential candidates or the new Soviet Party chairman. The Gulf crisis again highlighted the importance of leadership psychology. I had the opportunity to testify twice before congressional committees holding hearings on the Gulf crisis—the House Armed Services Committee under Les Aspin and the House Foreign Affairs Committee under Lee Hamilton—to present my assessment of the personality and political behavior of Saddam Hussein.

In 1991 Stanley A. Renshon, professor of political science and director of the political psychology program at the City University of New York, convened a conference on the political psychology of the Gulf crisis, which became the foundation of an edited volume (S. A. Renshon, ed., *The Political Psychology of the Gulf War: Leaders, Publics, and the Process of Conflict* [Pittsburgh: University of Pittsburgh Press, 1993]). At the conference, I remarked to my long-standing colleagues Hermann, Walker, Weintraub, and Winter that a book bringing these methods for the psychological assessment of political leaders together was long overdue. The group seized upon the idea, and the notion of an edited volume, in which each methodologist would first describe his or her method and then apply the method, was born. Indeed, a unique feature of the book, chosen by its contributors, is to illustrate these methods using two leaders from radically different societies, William Jefferson Clinton for a democratic society and Saddam Hussein for a closed totalitarian system, showing how personality manifests itself in such different systems. Renshon and Peter Suedfeld, professor of social psychology at the University of British Columbia, both major figures in the field of at-a-distance personality assessment, were also invited to contribute.

This book represents the fulfillment of a long-cherished dream: to bring together within the covers of one volume the specialized methods for psychologically evaluating the personality and political behavior of world leaders pioneered by a small group of specialists, many of whom I have been working with for nearly thirty years.

1. Profiling Political Leaders: An Introduction

Jerrold M. Post, Stephen G. Walker,
and David G. Winter

The influence of a leader's personality upon the course of political events has been the subject of lively debate. The "great man" view of history, of which Thomas Carlyle was a prominent proponent, has often conveyed the march of history in terms of leading political actors. In the spirit of Carlyle, we often view a nation's foreign policy in terms of the personalities of its leaders. Thus George III and Lord North are said to have lost Great Britain's American colonies by virtue of their stupidity and arrogance. (If only the elder Pitt had continued in power after 1767!) In 1919, Woodrow Wilson won the war but lost the peace because he negotiated ineptly, confused rhetoric with substance, and refused to compromise. Two decades later, Adolf Hitler set Europe aflame with a foreign policy that seemed to be rooted in his personal pathology. Perhaps the appeal of these familiar examples reflects our human tendency to reduce complexity to simplicity, attributing the causes of other people's behavior to their internal dispositions rather than to their situations (Jones and Nisbett 1972). Certainly in reviewing the history of the twentieth century, it would be difficult to portray the major events as simply a consequence of historical and political forces, ignoring the impact of such giant figures as Woodrow Wilson, Franklin Delano Roosevelt, Winston Churchill, Josef Stalin, Adolf Hitler, and Mao Ze-dong.

Set against these personality interpretations is the counterargument that foreign policy decision makers generally respond to realistic appraisals of situations and act within the available constraints and opportunities. Thus given American reluctance to maintain troops in Europe after 1918 and to submit national sovereignty to a supranational league, Wilson's weakness was one of position rather than personality. Even in the case of Hitler, the historian A. J. P. Taylor (1961) argues, his foreign policy

> was that of his predecessors, of the professional diplomats at the foreign ministry, and indeed of virtually all Germans . . . to free Germany from the restrictions of the peace treaty, to restore a great German army; and then to make Germany the greatest power in Europe from her natural weight. (97)

The scholarly terrain is defined by these two boundaries: on the one hand is the naive view of political outcomes as merely the projection of leaders' personalities, and on the other hand is the equally simplistic view that individual personalities have no effect.

Charting a course between these extremes, Greenstein (1969, chap. 2) suggests that a leader's personality may be especially important under four conditions: when the actor occupies a strategic location, when the situation is ambiguous or unstable, when there are no clear precedents or routine role requirements, and when spontaneous or especially effortful behavior is required. These conditions stress the importance of the context in which the actor is operating, observing that the impact of leader personality increases to the degree that the environment admits of restructuring.

Among the many fields of politics, these conditions are perhaps most often met in the arena of foreign policy. Included in the circumstances that Hermann (1976) has identified in which leader personality is most apt to affect foreign policy are the following: (1) in proportion to the general interest of the head of state in foreign policy; (2) when the means of assuming power are dramatic; (3) when the head of state is charismatic; (4) when the head of state has great authority over foreign policy; (5) when the foreign policy organization of the nation is less developed and differentiated; (6) in a crisis; and (7) when the external national situation is perceived to be ambiguous.

During the relatively stable era of the superpower rivalry, it often seemed that the powerful forces of the rival Western and Eastern blocs significantly reduced and constrained the capacity of individual leaders to affect the course of events in the arena of foreign policy. Yet few would doubt that the leadership actions of John F. Kennedy, Fidel Castro, and Nikita Khrushchev in October 1962; of Richard Nixon in China; of Jimmy Carter at Camp David; and of Ronald Reagan, Mikhail Gorbachev, and Boris Yeltsin in the twilight of the cold war made a difference.

The History of Leader Profiling: Two Historical Strands

In reviewing the historical development of the psychological assessment of political leaders, one is confronted with two strands: developments within the academic interdiscipline of political psychology and applications in support of policy within the government. The two efforts developed from different disciplinary perspectives and had quite different goals. Within the academic community the goal was to expand knowledge concerning the psychology of leadership; within the government the goal was to assist in high-level negotiations and during politico-military crises. Initially, leading academic scholars came principally from the disciplines of social psychology and political science, while clinically trained psychiatrists played a leading role in developing the government program. The academic approach focused more on individual traits or trait constellations leading to the development of rigorous quantitative methodologies to assess leader traits; the applied strand emphasized a more comprehensive approach, integrating psychobiography and psychodynamic psychology, producing qualitative case studies. To be sure, the strands did not develop in hygienic isolation, and the government efforts in applied political psychology were enriched by contributions from academic political psychology. Other disciplines, such as cultural anthropology, clinical psychology, political sociology, and history, usefully augmented the perspective of the core disciplines and contributed to the advance of the field in both settings. Having said that, the paths of development were in fact quite different.

Part 1 of this volume contains two historical overviews representing these two strands: the development of quantitative methods in the academic community and the development of the qualitative case study method in government.

4

The review of academic research in chapter 2 shows that scholars outside the government tended historically to focus on only some aspects of each individual, such as key beliefs or prominent personality traits. This focus on a few important characteristics rather than on the whole person is often accompanied by attempts to observe trait manifestations with quantitative methods. This methodological strategy has led to the standardization of measurement techniques and the possibility of controlled experimental or statistical comparisons of several individuals. Predictions of likely behavior under different contingencies are based on comparisons of several individuals who share these characteristics in different degrees and whose behavior varies accordingly in response to the same stimulus—often in laboratory rather than real-world settings.

The majority of these scholars have studied different dimensions of cognition, ignoring for the most part the domain of affect and drives. If the terrain of political cognition has been thoroughly explored, and the terrain of affect has had some preliminary forays, the conjoint terrain of cognition and affect is for the most part terra incognita. A small number of intrepid explorers, represented in this volume, have ventured into this perilous territory. David D. Winter has explored the relationship between cognition and motives, exploring particularly the need for power, the need for achievement, and the need for affiliation, as well as the ratio among these needs. In addition to systematically measuring the needs for power, achievement, and affiliation, Margaret G. Hermann has also studied the traits of ethnocentricity, suspiciousness, self-confidence, and cognitive complexity. By studying the relationships among these needs and traits, she has been able to elaborate six foreign policy orientations, which in effect represent a typology of political personalities. These personality types represent patterns she has identified in the political world but are not related to traditional clinical personality types. Stephen G. Walker's work has also been concerned with the relationship between motivations and beliefs, as exemplified by his work on the motivational foundations of a typology of political belief systems. George Marcus has made major contributions in explicating the relationship between affect and political leadership as well, emphasizing the role of affect and its impact on political judgment and decision making (Marcus, Neuman, and MacKuen 2000).

As the historical overview of qualitative case studies in government in chapter 3 demonstrates, psychobiographic and descriptive studies of leaders, such as Adolf Hitler and Nikita Khrushchev, set the stage for the development of the comprehensive approach illustrated by the Camp David profiles of Menachem Begin and Anwar Sadat, in which the analysis of the leader's personality was the basis for a diagnosis of likely behavior under different contingencies. The goal was to identify how the leader's political personality affected such dimensions of leadership behavior as negotiating behavior and crisis and strategic decision making. These studies are informed by psychodynamic theory, so that they characteristically develop a psychobiographic portrait to serve as the foundation for the assessment of political personality. There is an emphasis on providing an account of the cultural/historical/political context in which the leader's personality was formed and the political context in which he or she operates. A goal is to identify recurrent patterns of behavior, so that predictions of future behavior are often based on observations of the individual's past responses under similar circumstances.

Broadly speaking, three types of psychological evaluations of political leaders are described in this volume—cognitive, personality traits, and comprehensive qualitative case studies integrating psychobiographic analysis with a psychodynamic analysis of character and personality structure. The methods for developing these kinds of assessments are the subjects of the chapters in part 2 of this volume. The contributors present detailed descriptions of the methodologies they have developed and employed.

Comprehensive evaluations drawn from the clinical case study approach integrate psychogenetic, psychodynamic, and phenomenological perspectives. In the psychobiographic analysis, they delineate important events in shaping the leader's psychology and then assess the dimensions of political personality, attempting to identify the basic personality/character structure. They attempt to discern which public actions are driven by private motives and to detect recurrent patterns of political behavior. In chapter 4, Jerrold M. Post describes the applied method he developed in the government setting that drew upon his training as a clinical psychiatrist. The method emphasized the integration of psychobiography with the political personality study, drawing implications for negotiations, leadership style, and crisis and strategic decision making. In chapter 5, Stanley A. Renshon, a political scientist trained in psychoanalysis, presents his method with a model emphasizing three key aspects of character: ambition, integrity, and relatedness.

Studies of personality traits also combine strategies of manifest and latent content analysis. Analyses of overt motivational imagery in the prepared speeches of leaders can identify needs that indicate a leader's propensity for strategies of cooperation or conflict and risk-taking orientation. Classification of the grammar and syntax of more spontaneous utterances in interviews illustrates the use of latent content analysis to detect politically relevant personality traits. In chapter 6, the research psychiatrist Walter Weintraub presents his method for assessing key personality traits, drawing on grammatical and syntactical analysis, a method originally drawn from a psychiatric patient population and subsequently modified for application to political leaders. The social psychologists David D. Winter and Margaret G. Hermann both have developed methods for the analysis of motivational imagery. In chapter 7, Winter discusses his method for analyzing the need for power, the need for achievement, and the need for affiliation. In chapter 8, Hermann presents her methods for analyzing these needs, as well as a complex of other traits she has determined to be of importance in influencing political behavior.

Studies of cognitive content—belief systems and cognitive maps—employ manifest content analysis to identify the leader's beliefs about political life. From these overt surface features in public or private statements inferences are made about the likely impact of leaders' beliefs on their behavior in the world. In chapter 9, Stephen G. Walker, Mark Schafer, and Michael D. Young present a discussion of the method of the Operational Code, which analyzes both the leader's beliefs about the nature of the political universe and the rules for the conduct of political life. Other studies of cognitive style—integrative complexity and causal attribution—employ latent content analysis to identify the structure of a leader's thought patterns. From these more covert features inferences are drawn about a leader's underlying optimism and pessimism and a competitive versus cooperative approach to problem solving in different situations. In chapter 10, Peter Suedfeld, Karen Guttieri, and Phillip E.

Tetlock present a discussion of integrative cognitive complexity as it relates to a leader's behavior.

Part 3 of this volume is divided into two sections containing a series of psychological assessments of two leaders: William Jefferson Clinton and Saddam Hussein. For each leader, a comprehensive qualitative case study evaluation combining a psychobiographic analysis and a character analysis is first presented. Drawing on his Neustadt Award–winning analysis of President Clinton, *High Hopes,* Stanley A. Renshon presents in section A a psychoanalytically oriented portrait of Clinton. In section B, drawing on the political psychology profile of Saddam Hussein he offered in testimony during hearings on the Gulf crisis before the House Armed Services Committee and the House Foreign Affairs Committee, Jerrold M. Post presents a psychodynamic portrait of Saddam Hussein. Following these comprehensive qualitative assessments are chapters in which the personality traits, leadership style, beliefs, and cognitive style of each leader are addressed, employing manifest and latent strategies of quantitative content analysis. They offer complementary analyses of these leaders and illustrate the possible uses of different assessment tools.

Each of the leaders presents a different type of problem for assessment, inference, and prediction. President Clinton is the leader of a democratic regime operating in a complex institutional setting where political power is fragmented among powerful bureaucratic agencies and shared by different branches of government responsive to different constituencies. In contrast, Saddam Hussein is a relatively autonomous leader with political power residing primarily in his hands within the context of an authoritarian regime. The contributors discuss how their profiles of Clinton and Hussein illustrate the use of sources and the types of cases encountered in doing this kind of research.

Collectively, the authors and cases in this volume represent the current state of the art in profiling political leaders. In the conclusion in part 4, there is a review of the prospects for further progress and the need for more research in this area of political psychology. While the prospects for reducing the psychological assessment of leaders under a single approach are not imminent, this discussion does identify possible strategies for integrating results, methods, and research problems.

Part I. Leader Personality Assessment in Government and Academia

2. Assessing Leaders' Personalities: A Historical Survey of Academic Research Studies

David G. Winter

This chapter is a review of the main developments and landmarks in the study of political leaders by academic and research psychologists, setting the stage for the following chapters that illustrate several modern techniques in their latest form.

As described in the next chapter, "Leader Personality Assessments in Support of Goverment Policy," Langer, Wedge, and Post were commissioned to profile living foreign leaders. Usually their work was urgently required and drawn on as guides for government policy in times of change, threats, conflicts, and opportunities.[1] In contrast, academic political psychologists are driven more by intellectual curiosity and questions of historical interest than by the requirements of government policy. They often have better access to a wider range of information, as well as the leisure to speculate, discuss, and rearrange their data and interpretations. This is especially true when working on profiles of leaders from the past: historians and political scientists are certainly interested in working out the puzzling personality dynamics of a Woodrow Wilson, an Adolf Hitler, or a Nikita Khrushchev, but there are no longer pressing policy reasons for rushing the job. And now, long after their deaths, we are likely to have more information of all kinds available about these leaders than we had when they were alive and in power. In the case of Hitler, for example, we can now add to Langer's (1972) original wartime analysis later studies by Binion (1976), Erikson (1942, [1950] 1963),

Fromm (1973), and Waite (1977), as well as the comprehensive review of Hitler biographies and psychobiographies by Rosenbaum (1998), Kershaw (1999), and Langer (1999). Compared to their colleagues working in government, academic profilers have it easy.

Academic political psychologists have also had the scholarly leisure and resources to reflect about what they are doing when they try to assess the personalities of political leaders they have never met. As a result, they have formulated canons of principle and procedure for studying personality at a distance. This chapter reviews the academic side to profiling leaders' personalities. It begins with the academic development, elaboration, and critique of psychobiography and related techniques that are similar to how clinicians (psychiatrists or clinical psychologists) would assess someone if they had direct access (via therapy, interviews, and so forth). It then moves on to discuss the development of objective and valid techniques for *measuring,* at a distance, specific personality variables and syndromes.

Perhaps the first attempt to relate a leader's foreign policy to that leader's personality factors was the brief interpretation of a dream of the nineteenth-century German chancellor Otto von Bismarck by the psychoanalyst Hanns Sachs (1913). (Freud reprinted the paper in later editions of *The Interpretation of Dreams* [1901] 1953, 378–81.) In 1863, Sachs noted, Bismarck had dreamed that he was at an impasse on a narrow Alpine mountain path. With his riding whip, he struck a rock, which crumbled to reveal an easy, broad path down to a forest valley in Austria, where there were Prussian troops with banners. According to Sachs's interpretation, the dream suggested that beneath the *conscious political plans* of Bismarck the statesman— to provoke a war with Austria to achieve German unification (represented in the dream by the presence of Prussian soldiers in Austria)—were *unconscious personal fantasies* of infantile masturbation (handling the whip), erotic conquest (the broad path through the mountains), and even an identification with the Biblical Moses (striking the rock).

Doing Psychobiography

What is a psychobiography or clinical at-a-distance assessment? One useful definition, based on Glad 1973, is that psychobiography involves the systematic application of psychological theory or concepts—usually (but not always) drawn from psychoanalysis or some other variant of personality theory and research—to the explanation of certain known biographical "facts." Which facts? Some psychobiographers focus on constructing a portrait of their "subject's" overall personality—that is, describing "what kind of person they are." Other psychobiographers set themselves a more limited goal of explaining certain puzzling "facts" of patterns that cannot easily be explained (or explained fully) by ordinary explanations such as rational self-interest, the logic of the situation, or social roles and expectations. A psychobiography, then, is different from a complete biography of the ordinary kind: it may not necessarily tell the whole story but rather focuses especially on behavior that is at odds with conscious goals and appropriate means, actions that are, in Freud's words, "unusual, abnormal or pathological" ([1936] 1964, 239).

The Three Tasks of Psychobiography

How should a psychologist, psychiatrist, or historian go about constructing a psychobiography? Greenstein (1969, chap. 3) has identified three separate components of the process. The starting point is a simple description of what is to be explained—the surprising and unusual behaviors or, in Greenstein's terms, the "identifying phenomenology." (A psychiatrist might use the term "presenting symptoms.") As previously suggested, the phenomenology may involve the person's entire life course, or it may involve only a part of the person's life (sometimes a few acts or even a single act). For example, George and George (1956) explored a wide range of behaviors over the entire course of Woodrow Wilson's adult life (especially his presidency). In contrast, Runyan's (1981) study of the Dutch painter Vincent Van Gogh focused on a specific question: "Why did Van Gogh cut off his ear?" Cutting off one's ear is the phenomenology, the action to be explained by concepts and theories of psychology. Notice that we turn to psychology for explanation because Van Gogh's action was *unusual*. If most people (or at least most nineteenth-century Dutch painters) cut off an ear, then we would probably look elsewhere than psychology—perhaps to history or anthropology—for an explanation. It is usually possible to get fairly good agreement about this first step in the psychobiography process.

Having identified what is to be explained, the psychobiographer then constructs a psychological explanation—in Greenstein's terms, "the dynamics." That is, what combination of assumed psychological concepts (motives, defenses, cognitions, traits) can transform the phenomenology from something that is "surprising and unusual" to something that is understandable, reasonable, or "normal." Here there is more likely to be disagreement. For example, Runyan mentions thirteen different theories that attempt to explain Van Gogh's action.

Runyan (1981) then goes on to suggest some criteria by which we can evaluate alternative psychobiography explanations or dynamics: comprehensiveness, consistency with other known biographical facts, parsimony, and the ability to predict (or "retrodict") additional behaviors. The problem, of course, is to avoid circular explanations in which the validity of the explanation is no more than the behavior that the explanation was constructed to explain. It advances our understanding very little if we explain Woodrow Wilson's unwillingness to compromise as due to his obsessive-compulsive personality and then attempt to validate our explanation by citing his unwillingness to compromise. At the very least, we need to adduce further supporting biographical evidence for our interpretation; better still, we should try to develop some independent measure of the postulated psychological dynamics.

Finally, some psychobiographers try to trace the origins, or genesis, of the presumed dynamics in the childhood, early experience, or development of their subject. This third task is optional: an account of the origins of a psychological characteristic may bolster our confidence in the correctness of the analysis, but it is by no means necessary. In fact, such accounts are often quite controversial, for independent supporting evidence that the relevant trauma, experience, or events actually happened is usually quite hard to uncover from historical sources, which are usually more meager in their coverage of childhood years. As a result, many psychobiographers are thrown back upon unsatisfying circular explanations that involve speculative phrases such as "X must have felt that . . ." or "most children react to this by developing . . ."

Psychobiography Illustrated: The Case of Woodrow Wilson

We can illustrate Greenstein's three tasks by referring to psychobiographical interpretations of Woodrow Wilson, the twenty-eighth president of the United States. The study by Alexander George and Juliette George, *Woodrow Wilson and Colonel House: A Personality Study* (1956), has become a classic of psychobiographical method that has helped to define the field. A later publication by the same authors (1998) summarizes their interpretation (chap. 2) and method (chaps. 1 and 3), as well as updating their conclusions in the light of scholarly discussion and debate (chap. 4).

Wilson's Phenomenology

If ever there was a leader whose performance in office called for psychological interpretation, surely it is Woodrow Wilson. There is general agreement on what needs to be explained. From his presidency of Princeton University through his participation in the Versailles Peace Conference to his final speaking campaign urging Senate ratification of the Versailles Treaty and the League of Nations, Wilson showed a consistent pattern in which he seemed to undercut his remarkable leadership skills and defeat or undo his considerable accomplishments. In its fullest manifestations, this pattern included the following elements: (1) Wilson articulated visionary goals in the sweeping language of moralistic oratory. (2) When faced with opposition, however, he would not compromise, even when compromise would clearly further his ultimate goals. (3) On the other hand, he also refused to play hardball and fight back directly and aggressively. (4) Rather, he counterattacked with renewed and exhausting speechmaking campaigns. (5) In the process, Wilson often became suspicious of people who had been close supporters, even aggressively turning against them. (6) In the end, his original goals were often lost in the scrimmages of politics. (7) Even victory usually brought him little sense of satisfaction. Put simply: Wilson defeated himself, again and again.

Wilson's behavior during and after the Versailles Peace Conference illustrates most of the elements of this sequence. First, he was reluctant to use American economic and military power to overturn the Allied war aims and secret treaties and thereby bring about his goal of a "just peace." Instead, he poured his energy into writing and refining the visionary language of the League of Nations Covenant. Advice to compromise, given by his close aide Colonel House, only led to rupture of their relationship. Later, when Republicans led by

Senator Lodge blocked his campaign for ratification of the treaty, Wilson refused any alteration or compromise, despite the urgings of the staunchest supporters of the League, including Edward Gray (the former British foreign minister) and even his own wife. In the course of a frenzied national speaking tour on behalf of the treaty, Wilson suffered a massive stroke that effectively ended his political career. Table 2.1 illustrates these themes, along with some of the personality explanations and interpretations of them suggested by George and George, as well as two other psychological analyses of Wilson that will be discussed briefly later.

The Dynamics of Wilson's Self-Defeating Pattern

In formulating their analysis of the dynamics of Wilson's behavior, the Georges drew on the classic theories of Alfred Adler and on Lasswell's (1948, 44–49) formulation of power-seeking behavior as compensation for inner doubts and low self-esteem (see also George 1968).[2] The Georges argued that the main dynamic or motive underlying Wilson's phenomenology was a *compulsive drive for power and domination*—a "deep-seated, unconscious interest in imposing orderly systems upon others as a means of achieving a sense of power" (1998, 38). Drawing on a variety of psychodynamic theories, they described the workings of this dynamic in ways that certainly seem to fit the Wilson pattern:

> In the spheres of activity in which they seek power gratifications, compulsives are sensitive to interference. They may take advice badly. . . . Often they exhibit difficulties in deputing work to others, being convinced . . . that they can do everything . . . better than others. This conviction is sometimes exaggerated to the point that they believe they are unique. Negativeness, secretiveness and vindictiveness are traits often displayed by compulsives. (33)

In elaborating their description of this dynamic, the Georges suggested that Wilson's power drive actually concealed a "more basic need for self-esteem, or security" (1998, 33). Thus their full dynamic explanation, with psychological concepts emphasized, would be as follows: Wilson was driven by (1) the *need to dominate,* which developed out of the need to restore and protect his (2) *damaged self-esteem,*

TABLE 2.1. FOREIGN POLICY BEHAVIORAL CHARACTERISTICS ("PHENOMENOLOGY") OF WOODROW WILSON, AS EXPLAINED BY DIFFERENT INTERPRETATIONS

	George and George	Freud and Bullitt	Weinstein
Visionary oratory	Need to dominate, as a result of low self-esteem	Identification with father and Jesus, resulting in a refusal to fight	
Refusal to compromise	Compulsiveness		Stubbornness
Refusal to fight	Insatiable achievement aspirations	Passivity toward father	
	Need for approval and respect; anxiety at prospect of opposition		
	Reaction-formation against aggression		
Rhetorical counterattack	Irritability	Repressed aggression toward father, displaced onto symbolic "younger brothers"	
		Protection of threatened self-esteem	
		Denial and distorted perception	
		Overconfidence	
Turning against supporters			Suspiciousness
Little satisfaction		Identification with mother	

Source: Data from Freud and Bullitt 1967; George 1971; George and George 1956, chap. 7 and 317–22; and Weinstein 1970; 1981.

and was further tempered by (3) *needs for approval and respect.* Often he succeeded, especially when he was moving along the path to power. When this combination aroused (4) a *reaction-formation against aggression* and (5) disruptive *anxiety* at the prospect of opposition, however, he avoided a fight. When an issue had become emotionally charged, however, his (6) insatiable *achievement aspirations* and (7) *compulsive stubbornness* led to (8) *denial* and *distorted perception.* When this happened, he usually failed.

Genesis of Wilson's Personality Dynamics

The Georges trace the origins of Wilson's inner doubts and low self-esteem to his conflicted relationship with his father, Joseph Ruggles Wilson, a towering presence of a Presbyterian preacher, who made perfectionist demands on those about him, including his children, and reacted to errors with scorn and sarcasm. The Georges' thesis is that these paternal demands created anxiety and resentment in the young Woodrow Wilson. Furthermore, they suggest, he repressed negative feelings and adopted his father's standards as his own, trying to reduce anxiety by pleasing his father through high achievement.

Given the paucity of records and information about father-child dynamics in the Wilson household, it is not surprising that the Georges' reconstruction of the genesis of Wilson's personality has met with some controversy from historians and Wilson biographers (Schulte Nordholt 1991; Weinstein, Anderson, and Link 1978–79; the scholarly debate is summarized in a series of articles in *Political Psychology* introduced by Post 1983a, 1983b).

Alternative Interpretations of Wilson's Personality

Interpretation by Bullitt and Freud

The two right-hand columns of table 2.1 give brief presentations of two alternative assessments of the dynamics behind Wilson's phenomenology. Each is controversial, and each has major methodological faults. The jointly written analysis by Sigmund Freud and William C. Bullitt (a former U.S. diplomat), published in 1967 but completed in the 1930s, is marred by the authors' hostilities toward their subject as well as a rather crudely mechanical style of interpretation.[3] Like the Georges, Freud and Bullitt focused on the prominent role of Wilson's father. Woodrow, they argued, "never solved the major dilemma of the Oedipus complex" (306). As a result, he both identified strongly with his father (resulting in a harsh superego) and yet had repressed aggression toward his father, which he typically displaced onto associates who were symbolic "younger brothers." More latent was his passivity, the result of a latent identification with his mother.

Interpretation by Weinstein

Weinstein (1970, 1981, 1983) and his colleagues (Weinstein, Anderson, and Link 1978–79) were very clear about the underlying cause of Wilson's foreign policy behavior: he was, they argue, suffering from cerebral vascular disease, manifested in periodic strokes and culminating in the final, massive stroke of 1919. These medical conditions, Weinstein (1981, esp. chaps. 10, 20, and 21) argues, precipitated a series of personality changes that contributed to Wilson's self-defeating pattern: euphoric overconfidence, stubbornness and irritability, suspiciousness, and delusions.

From the available biographical evidence it is clear that Wilson suffered from a variety of vaguely described physical complaints throughout his life. However, as Post (1983b) observed, we lack the kind of detailed medical records that could definitively prove many of the details of Weinstein's hypotheses—hypotheses that Weinstein treated as established facts. On the basis of an independent review of the available evidence, a number of medical experts doubted Weinstein's diagnosis (e.g., Marmor 1982, 1983; Monroe n.d., cited by George and George 1998, 5–6, see also 10–11; Post 1983b). Others have argued that even if Weinstein was correct, the medical conditions he attributed to Wilson do not adequately explain what Weinstein thought they explained (see George and George 1981–82, 1983; Post 1983b; Ross 1982).

Summary Characterization of Single Case Study Psychobiographies

Like all psychobiographies, the George and George analysis of Woodrow Wilson relies on a sensitive understanding of the available evidence—perhaps especially the written words—of the person being studied. To do this well, psychobiographers must have both empathy and detachment, as well as an awareness of their own emotional reactions to their subject (George and George 1998, 1). After immersion in these "data," psychobiographers then employ all their mental faculties to work over the data.

> All this mass of material the biographer lets flow freely into him. He is the medium through whom the chaotic raw data [are] digested, ultimately to be rendered back in an orderly verbal re-creation of an intelligible human being . . . what kind of person [he] was, what his characteristic attitudes and defenses were and how they developed, what made him anxious, what gratified him, what goals and values he adopted, how he went about pursuing them. (George and George 1998, 17–18)

This process often involves a repeated cycling back and forth from biographical fact to theoretical concept. Of necessity, it engages every mental faculty of the psychobiographer: curiosity and sensitivity to "facts," the capacity for logical thought, a fine-tuned awareness of feelings, and a mobile, even playful intuition (see George and George 1998, chaps. 1 and 3). Finally, successful psychobiographers must have an appreciation for complexity, realizing that the personality of any political actor is always expressed in a context—that is, in "institutional variables, situational variables, and those aspects of political culture that the leader has internalized during the course of his or her political socialization or that affect his or her performance even if not internalized" (67). In this connection, psychobiographies that offer a longitudinal perspective are particularly valuable, because they help us understand how previous life experiences shape present political behavior and help us distinguish political behaviors that are merely the result of *role* from those that reflect strong *personality* influences engaged by political circumstances.

Several books and articles contain lists of psychobiographical studies (Cocks and Crosby 1987, esp. 217–22; Crosby and Crosby 1981; Elms 1994; Friedman 1994; Glad 1973; Greenstein 1969, esp. 72; Howe 1997; McAdams and Ochberg 1988; Runyan 1983, 1984, 1988a, 1988b, 1990, 1997; Simonton 1999; Stone and Schaffner 1988) that provide a good survey of this literature.

Developing Objective at-a-Distance Measures
of Single Personality Variables

Some psychologists would argue that a sophisticated and vivid case study is a work of art that could only be degraded by the "improvements" of psychological science. On the other hand, the controversy about the dynamics of Woodrow Wilson's personality previously described suggests the importance of well-defined variables and objective measures. If only we could measure Wilson's self-esteem or superego strength and determine whether he did indeed score below and above average, respectively. If only we had well-validated measures of the "psychological effects of stroke" (whatever they may be), so that we could calculate Wilson's scores over time and see whether they follow the pattern demanded by the claims of Weinstein et al. In an effort to resolve controversies of this kind about evidence and inference, and to introduce objective standards of scientific measurement into the process of doing psychobiography and personality assessments of leaders, political psychologists have in recent years developed several methods of measuring personality variables at a distance. As with any scientific measurement, the methodological credentials of these at-a-distance measures are established by two of their characteristics—the objectivity with which they can be applied and the validity that has been established through previous replicable research.

Objective Measurement at a Distance

Most personality variables are operationally defined in terms of tests or other procedures that cannot be used with political leaders, because researchers lack direct access. That is, most prominent contemporary leaders[4] usually cannot be tested, and even when they can, ethical considerations would usually make it difficult to disclose the results. Leaders of the past present an even greater problem: they are dead and (to adapt a quotation from Glad 1973) by their deaths have taken their personality characteristics—their Oedipus complexes, authoritarianism, or power motivation—with them. Hence the need for personality measures that can be used at a distance, without direct access or contact. Because *words* are a resource that generally exists in great abundance, both for living and dead leaders, many at-

21

a-distance measures involve some kind of content analysis of written or verbal material.[5] Typically, these measures are carefully designed, with examples and training procedures, to enable previously inexperienced scorers to apply them with high reliability (percent agreement and correlation .85). A detailed discussion of issues and methods of psychological content analysis can be found in Holsti 1969; Schafer 2000; Walker 2000; Winter 1992a, 1992b; and Winter and Stewart 1977a.

Validated Variables

At-a-distance researchers typically use operationally defined personality variables, the validity of which has been established through systematic research. Elms (1986), for example, analyzed the personalities and public behavior of four key twentieth-century U.S. foreign policy advisers (House, Dulles, Kissinger, and Haig) in terms of Machiavellianism, ego idealism, and authoritarianism—three variables with well-established, research-based validity credentials. Compared to the vagaries of ordinary language that are inherent in words such as *stubbornness* (as in the case of Wilson discussed previously), these three terms have relatively precise, operationally defined, and delimited meanings.

The sections that follow review research relating political behavior and outcomes to various single personality variables. For convenience, the basic elements of personality can be grouped under three broad headings (see also Schafer 2000, 516–18).

> *Motives:* the different classes of goals toward which people
> direct their behavior. Power, achievement, and affiliation
> are among the most frequently studied motives. Since many
> motives or wishes involve conflict and are therefore
> defended against or transformed, measures of defense mech-
> anisms could also be included here.
> *Cognitions and beliefs:* specific beliefs, attitudes, and values, as
> well as more general cognitive styles.
> *Temperament and interpersonal traits:* consistent individual dif-
> ferences in style features, such as energy level, sociability,
> impulse control, emotional stability, and styles of relating
> to others.

Human Motives and Their Measurement

Major Dimensions of Motivation

Psychobiographical studies often invoke a wide variety of different motives, "goals," or other dynamic processes—sometimes constructed ad hoc, sometimes drawn from psychological theory—to explain leaders' behavior and political outcomes. Psychologists have proposed a variety of typologies or dimensions of motivation or goals. (*Motive* and *goal* are used interchangeably to indicate behavior that shows direction and persistence.) Freud, for example, grouped all human motives into two broad categories: *libidinal* or love motives (also called the "life instincts") and *aggressive* or death instincts (Freud [1940] 1964; see also Winter 1996, chap. 3). Traces of these groupings can be seen in the paired motivational concepts of *communion* and *agency* used by later theorists (Bakan 1966; see also Leonard 1997), as well as more recent concepts of attachment and narcissism.

Murray and his associates (Murray 1938) proposed a very different method of identifying fundamental human motives. On the basis of an intensive study of fifty-one male college students and other young adults, they developed a list of twenty basic motives or "needs" that they believed necessary to give an adequate account of the young men's important goals and strivings. These, in turn, can be grouped or organized into two fundamental dimensions—interpersonal harmony seeking and individual assertive striving—that bear close resemblance to the dualisms of Freud, Bakan, and others (see Wicker et al. 1984). For the sake of simplicity and uniform terminology, these two dimensions will be referred to as affiliation and power, respectively.

Cross-cultural research also confirms the generality of *affiliation* and *power* as motivational dimensions (Kornadt, Eckensberger, and Emminghaus 1980). Such a convergence of theory, empirical research, and cultural evidence suggests that affiliation and power are nearly universal ways of arranging and describing goals.

Measuring Motives

For Freud, free association and the interpretation of dreams was the "royal road" to an understanding of people's motives, since anxiety and the operation of defense are likely to block their own awareness of their true motives. In later years, psychologists have also added social desirability, impression management, and simple inaccessibility of implicit mental processes (Greenwald and Banaji 1995; Nisbett and Wilson 1977) as factors that severely limit the validity of self-reports about motives. To measure motives, therefore, many psychologists have turned to indirect means. Many such methods are based on the Thematic Apperception Test (TAT), developed by Morgan and Murray (1935; see also Murray 1938), in which people tell stories to a series of vague or ambiguous pictures. (*Apperception* means assigning meaning to a stimulus, in contrast to *perception,* which refers to sensing and labeling the stimulus.)

TAT-Based Measures

Since the experimentally derived technique for scoring motives in the TAT developed by McClelland and his associates (McClelland et al. 1953; Smith 1992; Winter 1998a) has been the basis for most of the objective measurement of motives at a distance in political psychology, including chapters 7 (Winter) and 8 (Hermann) in this volume, its essential features can be briefly described here. To develop a measure of any particular motive, that motive is first aroused, preferably through several different experimental procedures. For example, the power motive has been aroused by testing candidates for student government while votes were being counted, by showing a film of President John F. Kennedy's inauguration, and by role-playing a protest group about to confront the police (Winter 1973, chap. 3). TAT stories written by people under these different motive-arousing conditions are then compared to TAT stories written by people in a neutral, nonaroused group. After considerable reworking and refinement, the differences between the two groups of stories become the basis of the scoring system. Experimentally derived scoring systems of this type have been developed for the two fundamental dimensions of affiliation and power motivation, as well as a third dimension of achievement motivation. Political psychology researchers have adapted these TAT scoring systems to score motive imagery in a wide variety of other kinds of verbal material, including speeches, interviews, popular literature, diplomatic documents, dream reports, folktales, and even television programs (Winter

1991; see also Hermann 1979, 1980a, 1980b, which use only the affiliation and power measures). These motive imagery scores are usually unrelated to people's conscious beliefs or statements about their goals (see Weinberger and McClelland 1990). Among politicians, moreover, motive imagery scores are usually unrelated to policy statements: in other words, it is possible to speak or write for or against any particular political goal or program, with or without using achievement, affiliation, and/or power imagery.

Political leaders studied with this technique include U.S. presidents and Supreme Court justices; leaders from several countries and factions in sub-Saharan and southern Africa during the mid-1970s; general secretaries of the Communist party of the Soviet Union, as well as members of the Politburo of the Party's Central Committee; and various groups of significant world leaders. Systematic and objective motive imagery content analysis has also been used as part of the psychobiographical study of individual leaders, ranging from U.S. presidents Woodrow Wilson and Richard Nixon to former Soviet leader Mikhail Gorbachev and former Italian leader Benito Mussolini.

Psychoanalytic Measures

Using a quite different theoretical and methodological approach, Luck (1974) developed a priori objective measures of certain basic psychoanalytic motivational concepts (such as orality and anal-sadism) and carried out a comparative study of Hitler, Stalin, Mao Zedong, and Liu Shao-ch'i (Liu Shaoqi).

Cognitions and Cognitive Style

Specific Cognitive Beliefs

Hermann (1980a, 1984) developed at-a-distance measures of several specific beliefs and interpersonal style variables that have been extensively studied in personality research. Nationalism (or *ethnocentrism*) as a cognitive belief and distrust as an aspect of interpersonal style are two aspects of a broader *authoritarianism* (see Brown 1965, chap. 10; Winter 1996, chap. 7). Among heads of state, these two variables are associated with expressions of strong, negative affect toward other nations and with low levels of resource commitment in foreign relations (i.e., keeping one's options open). Although Hermann did not directly measure war and peace outcomes as such, we would certainly expect that in many situations these two personality characteristics, by heightening an international climate of hostility, would predispose leaders toward war. These variables are further discussed in chapter 7 of this book.

The belief that one can control events reflects the traditional personality variable of *locus of control* or *attributional style* (see Strickland 1977). Leaders with this belief tend to avoid resource commitment and keep their foreign policy options open, perhaps on the theory that they maintain their own control thereby. (The locus of control concept has been elaborated into the more general concept of attributional style or explanatory style, which is discussed under the heading *cognitive style*.) Hermann's list of variables includes a measure of self-confidence that reflects both self-esteem (see Rosenberg 1979) and self-efficacy or perceived sense of competence and control of the environment (see White 1959; Bandura 1982).

Using techniques of evaluation assertion analysis, Holsti (1967) observed a belief pattern of *inherent bad faith* in the public statements of John Foster Dulles about the USSR over a period of several years. Holsti found consistent negative relationships between Dulles's perceptions of Soviet strength and his view of Soviet friendship; thus Dulles attributed friendly Soviet behavior to Soviet weakness rather than to Soviet friendship. As a personality or cognitive construct, inherent bad faith may be at the base of Jervis's (1976, chap. 3) notion of the "deterrence" model of international relations and conflict.

Operational Codes

In his classic study of the premises of Soviet thinking, Leites (1951) introduced the concept of "operational code" to refer to the set of axioms, postulates, and premises that appear to constitute the foundation of more specific beliefs and practices. In Leites's work, operational codes were intuitively extracted from political writings. In later years, George (1969), Holsti (1970, 1977), and Walker (1983, 1990) have refined the operational code concept, suggesting several standard dimensions or typologies of issues around which operational codes of specific individuals could be constructed. Two classes of beliefs have been refined and elaborated: those concerned with the leader's philosophical beliefs about the nature of the political universe and those concerned with the leader's choices and instrumental tactics (George 1969).

As originally formulated, operational codes are like portraits: at their best, they faithfully reflect the individual being portrayed, but different portraits of different leaders cannot readily be compared. Thus Walker (1986) reconstructed an operational code for Woodrow Wilson, confirming some of Post's (1983a, 1983b) analyses based on more traditional psychobiographical methods. More recently, Walker and his colleagues (e.g., Walker, Schafer, and Young 1998) have developed objective quantitative methods for assessing operational codes. These have been used in studies of several U. S. presidents from the latter half of the twentieth century (Schafer 2000; see also chapter 20 of this volume for a general discussion of operational codes).

Cognitive Style

Cognitive Complexity

In personality theory and research, cognitive complexity is generally associated with more sophisticated and better adaptive behavior, especially in ambiguous or confusing situations. Hermann (1980a) measured cognitive complexity at a distance by calculating the ratio of certain words and phrases identified as high complexity to words and phrases designated as low complexity. Among heads of government, cognitive complexity defined in this way is associated with expressing positive affect toward other nations and receiving positive feedback from other nations.

Working with a two-stage theory of cognitive complexity that involves first differentiation and then integration, Suedfeld and his colleagues (e.g., Suedfeld and Tetlock 1977) have adapted a laboratory measure of integrative complexity for at-a-distance research. (While this *integrative complexity* is conceptually related to Hermann's measure, to date no research has explored the intercorrelation or discriminant validity of the two measures.)

Several studies have demonstrated that integrative complexity is related to peaceful resolution (versus escalation) of international conflicts. For example, Tetlock (1979) found significantly lower levels of integrative complexity in speeches and public statements of U.S. leaders during three crises showing Janis's (1972) "groupthink" pattern that escalated to armed conflict (the Bay of Pigs, crossing the 38th parallel in 1950, and escalating the Vietnam War), as compared to two of Janis's "non-groupthink" crises, where conflict was controlled (the Marshall Plan and the Cuban Missile Crisis).

Suedfeld and Tetlock (1977) compared communications and statements from two crises that ended in war (1914 and the 1950 outbreak of the Korean War) and three peacefully resolved crises (the 1911 Morocco crisis, the 1948 Berlin airlift crisis, and the 1962 Cuban Missile Crisis). As expected, they found higher levels of integrative complexity when war was avoided. Suedfeld, Tetlock, and Ramirez (1977) studied United Nations (UN) speeches on the Middle East over thirty years and found significant decreases in integrative complexity during periods just before the outbreak of wars in 1948, 1956, 1967, and 1973. (On the other hand, integrative complexity also dropped during 1976, when no war followed.) While the post–World War II Berlin situation never led to a shooting war, Raphael (1982) found a similar negative relationship between integrative complexity in speeches and statements about the Berlin issue and levels of tension over the status of Berlin.

One study, however, does not support the presumed relationship between integrative complexity and war. Scoring both Japanese intragovernmental documents and formal diplomatic communications from Japan to the United States, Levi and Tetlock (1980) found no tendency for levels of integrative complexity to decrease during the last months of 1941, just prior to the Pearl Harbor attack.

In a further study of communications from Pearl Harbor and eight other "surprise attacks," however, Suedfeld and Bluck (1988) found that the "attackers" showed a drop in integrative complexity between three months and several weeks before the attack, while the "to-be-attacked" nations showed increases during the month before the attack (with a dramatic drop just after the attack). Suedfeld and Bluck suggest that, as the attacking nation hardens its negotiating position (low integrative complexity), the to-be-attacked nation tries even harder to be flexible and to understand the other side (high integrative complexity). After the attack, however, integrative complexity in the attacked nation quickly declines to war levels.

An alternative theory of cognitive complexity, involving the four processes of shaping, reflective articulation, extrapolation, and system transformation, has been developed by Jaques (1986; Jaques and Cason 1994). However, to date this conception has not been employed in the at-a-distance assessment of political leaders.

Cognitive Mapping

The technique of cognitive mapping (Axelrod 1976) is a way of representing the structure of causal beliefs or assertions of individual political leaders, particularly as they involve relationships between policies, goals, and outcomes or effects. Maps of different leaders can be evaluated and compared in terms of characteristics such as density (the number of causal links), balance, links between peripheral and policy variables, and so forth. Hart (1977) used this technique to study Latin American leaders, and Hart and Greenstein (1977) analyzed the cognitive maps of U.S. presidents Wilson and Eisenhower. Bonham (1993) cites applications of cognitive mapping to the analysis of diplomatic events such as the 1919 Versailles Peace Conference and the 1970s arms reduction negotiations. Walker and Watson (1992) discussed the relationship between cognitive mapping and various measures of cognitive complexity in a study of British leaders during the crises of 1938–39.

Explanatory Style

The concept of explanatory style grows out of decades of research on variables such as internal versus external locus of control and patterns of causal attribution. An optimistic explanatory style involves explaining "bad" events by external, specific, and temporary factors. It is related to feelings of zest, persistence, and good performance. (In contrast, the pessimistic style, where bad events are seen as the result of internal, global, and enduring factors, leads to depression, avoidance, and failure.)

Zullow et al. (1988) found that Lyndon Johnson showed a highly optimistic explanatory style during the Gulf of Tonkin incident and subsequent American military Vietnam War buildup. During the

1968 Tet Offensive, however, the limits of American success and power became clear and Johnson decided not to seek reelection. At this time, his explanatory style score moved down into the pessimistic or depressive range. These results are intriguing, but only further research can determine whether optimism leads to a specifically aggressive foreign policy or merely to a zestful and persistent pursuit of any foreign policy.

Studies of several world leaders (Churchill, Hitler, Franklin Roosevelt, Stalin, George H. W. Bush, and Saddam Hussein) by Satterfield (1998; see also Satterfield and Seligman 1994) suggest that an optimistic explanatory style, especially if combined with low integrative complexity, is associated with risky, aggressive policies, actions, and events.

Mental Functioning and the Rorschach Test

While the Rorschach inkblot test has often been claimed to measure all sorts of psychological characteristics, including even ends or goals or motives (Zillmer et al. 1995, 60), most psychologists would argue that it reflects the *structure* of the mind or a wide variety of processes of mental functioning: complexity, accuracy, abstraction and integration, conventionality, capacity for fantasy and inner reflection, anxiety, introspection, and emotional regulation (73–74). While the best methods of administration and interpretation of the Rorschach test are debated, and while the test has not been used often in assessing political leaders, the Rorschach-based study of Nazi leaders (carried out at Nürnberg in 1945–46 but not fully reported until several decades later; see Zillmer et al. 1995) is a noteworthy study that illustrates considerable variation in intelligence and mental functioning among different Nazi leaders.

A further study of Rudolf Hoess, the first commandant of the Auschwitz extermination camp, combines Rorschach interpretation with a novel technique of proxy administration of a personality test (see Ritzler and Singer 1998). In this instance, two psychologists thoroughly familiar with the details of Hoess's life took the Minnesota Multiphasic Personality Inventory (MMPI-2) as if they were Hoess (see also the study by Rubenzer, Faschingbauer, and Ones 2000, discussed later).

Traits and Temperament

The domain of traits refers to the public, visible, stylistic (or adverbial) aspects of personality.[6] In recent years, personality psychologists have reached some consensus on the importance of five trait factors or dimensions: extraversion (or surgency), agreeableness, conscientiousness, emotional stability, and openness to experience (see John and Srivastava 1999). Rubenzer, Faschingbauer, and Ones (2000) measured these five trait dimensions among all forty-one U.S. presidents from Washington through Clinton by asking 115 authors of presidential biographies (both historians and public figures) to fill out three different standard instruments (a questionnaire, an adjective checklist, and a Q-sort). They discussed the trait profiles of Washington and Lincoln and reported moderate correlations, among all presidents, between the "openness to experience" dimension and ratings of presidential performance.

Simonton (1986, 1988) also measured a variety of trait factors of U.S. presidents, in this case by asking student raters, who had read brief personality descriptions excerpted from presidential biographies (with identifying information removed), to fill out adjective checklists or lists of trait phrases.

Several researchers have studied particular traits of various groups of political leaders. Etheredge (1978) used questionnaires and standard personality tests to measure traits directly in a study of over two hundred male United States foreign service officers, military officers, and domestic affairs specialists. He found that men who scored high on the traits of *dominance* and *competitiveness* were (when the research was carried out, in 1971–72) more likely to view Soviet foreign policy as "active," "powerful," and "menacing." Consistent with these perceptions, they were also more likely to advocate the use of force across a series of different scenarios involving hypothetical international unrest or Soviet "expansion." In contrast, men who scored high on *interpersonal trust* and *self-esteem* (variables that also involve cognitive beliefs) were against the use of force.

Etheredge then confirmed these results with an at-a-distance study of twentieth-century American presidents and foreign policy advisers. Traits were rated by judges who read excerpts of standard biographies (with names of persons and other identifying details concealed). In examining a series of foreign policy disagreements between 1898 and 1968, Etheredge found that those leaders judged to be high in dominance argued in favor of using force (threats, ultimata, military intervention, and war) and opposed arbitration and disarmament. Leaders judged to be high in extraversion supported cooperation with the Soviet Union, while more introverted leaders argued against cooperation.

Hermann's (1984a) interpersonal style variable of *task versus interpersonal emphasis,* derived from Bales's (1958) description of two kinds of group leaders, may involve a variety of traits such as extraversion, agreeableness, and conscientiousness. As might be expected, task-oriented leaders tend to be active in foreign policy, but Hermann's results further suggest that this activity can be directed into either an expansionist or merely a self-reliant foreign policy, depending on the influence of other variables (discussed later).

Weintraub (1981) developed content analysis measures of several traits (including anger, anxiety, depression, and emotional expressiveness), as well as several different kinds of decision-making styles (e.g., decisive, dogmatic, impulsive, paranoid, and obsessive). He later applied these measures to the analysis of press conference responses of U.S. presidents Eisenhower through Reagan (Weintraub 1989).

Summary of Single-Variable Research Findings

What do we know about the effect of particular personality variables on foreign policy? Table 2.2 suggests some conclusions that can be drawn from the research literature cited in this chapter. To facilitate comparison and integration of results, foreign policy behaviors are loosely grouped into two broad categories: (1) *war disposition* (actual war, advocacy of force, hostility, perceiving enemy as a threat, and "independent" foreign policy orientation) and (2) *peace disposition* (cooperation, positive affect, arms limitation, and "interdependent" foreign policy orientation).

From the table, it seems clear that having power goals and a dominant behavioral style, along with simplistic cognitive structures that involve nationalistic beliefs and distrust, is associated with a war disposition in foreign policy. Peace dispositions, in contrast, result from having affiliative goals and a trusting, extraverted behavioral style, along with cognitive complexity and self-esteem.

Personality Orientations and Multivariate Strategies

The results summarized in table 2.2 suggest that predictions of political behavior are likely to be better if they are made using *combinations* of variables, preferably drawn from different elements or levels of analysis. However, personality is not a mere agglomeration of discrete and isolated individual variables but rather a complex and integrated whole. For example, extraversion may have very different effects when combined with power goals and distrust, as opposed to affiliation goals and trust (see Winter et al. 1998). While personality research is still looking for the ideal research strategy to deal with such complexity, Hermann has developed some methods for doing integrated, multivariate profiles.

Toward an Integrative Model of Personality and Foreign Policy

First, Hermann (1987b) worked out a series of six personality orientations, each consisting of different combinations of the eight motives, cognitions, and traits that she had previously studied as separate variables. Table 2.3 lists these orientations along with their component variables. While these particular orientations were derived from a specific political psychology literature—involving conceptions of national role as related to foreign policy—they can also be seen as metaphors for some common personality types in political life generally.

TABLE 2.2. PERSONALITY VARIABLES ASSOCIATED WITH VARIOUS FOREIGN POLICY OUTCOMES

	War Disposition	Peace Disposition
Motives	Power motive	Affiliation motive
Cognitive beliefs	Nationalism Self-confidence	Self-esteem
Cognitive style	Low integrative complexity Optimistic explanatory style	High integrative complexity
Temperament and interpersonal traits	Dominance Competitiveness Distrust	Extraversion Trust

Source: Data from Winter 1992b.

Hermann also expanded the traditional foreign policy outcome variable of aggression, or war versus peace (e.g., as used in table 2.2), into a much more differentiated and elaborate series of alternative foreign policy behaviors and outcomes that could be predicted from personality. Each orientation is assumed to have its own characteristic worldview, style, and level of tolerance for disagreement. Leaders of different orientations have different ways of searching for information, picking advisers, and dealing with opposition.

TABLE 2.3. PERSONALITY ORIENTATIONS AND THEIR COMPONENT PERSONALITY VARIABLES

	Definition	Component Variables
Expansionist	Interest in gaining control over more territory, resources, or people	Power motivation Nationalism Belief in ability to control events Self-confidence Distrust Task orientation
Active/ independent	Interest in participating in the international community, but on one's own terms and without engendering a dependent relationship with another country	Affiliation motivation Nationalism Belief in ability to control events Cognitive complexity Self-confidence Task orientation
Influential	Interest in having an impact on other nations' foreign policy behavior, in playing a leadership role in regional or international affairs	Power motivation Belief in ability to control events Cognitive complexity Self-confidence Interpersonal orientation
Mediator/ integrator	Concern with reconciling differences between other nations, with resolving problems in the international arena	Affiliation motivation Belief in ability to control events Cognitive complexity Interpersonal orientation
Opportunist	Interest in taking advantage of present circumstances, in dealing effectively with the demands and opportunities of the moment, in being expedient	Cognitive complexity Interpersonal orientation
Developmental	Commitment to the continued improvement of one's own nation with the best help available from other countries or international organizations	Affiliation motivation Nationalism Cognitive complexity Self-confidence Interpersonal orientation

Source: Data from Hermann 1987b, 170–73.

Personality Assessment and the Situationist Challenge

Over the past twenty-five years, some theorists (e.g., Mischel 1968, 1984) have debated the relative contribution of personality and situational factors to the explanations of behavior. Clearly, situational stimuli (to the extent the person notices and takes account of them) often override the influence of "deeper" personality factors. In addition, the limitations and opportunities of particular locations in formal and informal structures and institutions set limits to the effects of personality.

Along with her emphasis on combinations and interactions of discrete personality variables, Hermann also suggested a series of other factors, including situational variables, that mediate or "filter" the effects of personality on foreign policy behavior. For example, a strong interest in foreign policy is likely to amplify the effects of personality, while training and previous experience (situational or learning factors) and sensitivity to the environment (probably a personality disposition) are likely to diminish those effects.

Hermann (1987b) has applied this model in an intensive study of twelve leaders from sub-Saharan Africa, as well as in individual case studies of U.S. presidents Ronald Reagan (1983) and George H. W. Bush (1989a), Soviet president Gorbachev (1989b; see also Winter et al. 1991a, 1991b), and Syrian president Hafez al-Assad (1988a). On the basis of his scores on the eight component variables, for example, Reagan showed aspects of both the "expansionist" orientation (recall the invasion of Grenada and the unrelenting pressure on the Sandinista regime in Nicaragua) and the "developmental" orientation (recall his attempts to build up American economic and military strength using available ties with NATO and "help" from other Western leaders). Bush, in contrast, was viewed as more of a mediator or integrator (literally extending his inaugural hand to the Congress, in pursuit of a "kinder, gentler" nation). Gorbachev's pattern of scores classified him as a "developmental" leader, willing to use any means and draw upon any help to improve his country. In the end, of course, the Soviet Union proved not to be a viable political entity, despite Gorbachev's best (and most radical) efforts.

Hermann's model, combining as it does the interactive effects of eight objectively defined, major personality variables with these filters of interest, learning, and situation, reflects some of the most sophisticated and advanced trends of modern personality theory and research applied to the interpretation and understanding of foreign policy behavior. The striking confirmation of this model in the Reagan, Bush, and Gorbachev cases should encourage its further development and application.

The at-a-Distance Assessment

We must recognize that even with the best psychobiographical portraits or at-a-distance measures, predictions of leaders' behavior must always be phrased in contingent or conditional "if/then" terms (Wright and Mischel 1987a, 1987b). That is, the effects of leaders' personalities will always depend on the situations in which they find themselves—and personality profiling can never predict those exact situations. On the other hand, by developing complex ways to represent the interaction of personality elements with each other, and with the situation and environment, we should be able to make both academic progress and useful contributions to the formation of policy. In their follow-up to an earlier analysis of Bush and Gorbachev, Winter et al. (1991b) illustrated the way in which predictions made on the basis of a profile of the leader's personality must be "conditionally hedged" in the presence of unpredictable changes in the situation. That is, although their original profile of George H. W. Bush had described him as a "peacemaker, concerned with development and not prone to seek political ends through violence and war" (Winter et al. 1991a, 237), they also noted his impulsivity and tendency to react defensively, with anger, when threatened by someone perceived as dissimilar, as happened when Saddam Hussein's armed forces invaded Kuwait in 1990. Bush went on to fight the Gulf War in ways that were consistent with his overall profile. Even in the face of situational uncertainties and surprises, Winter et al. concluded, personality profiles can still provide useful "if/then" guides to understanding the behavior of leaders.

The last few decades have seen great progress in academic research and practice for profiling and assessing political leaders, both by means of psychobiographical portraits and by systematic and objective at-a-distance measures. Later chapters of this book provide more detailed descriptions of these methods, and examples of applications of this work to two leaders from strikingly different political settings, William Jefferson Clinton and Saddam Hussein.

Notes

This chapter draws significantly on Winter 1992b. The reviews of literatures are intended to be illustrative rather than exhaustive.

1. Even journalists sometimes feel the need for assistance from psychology (at least retrospectively). For example, in reviewing two biographies of Mao Zedong, Burns (2000) confessed that "For myself, I wish now that in covering China, South Africa under apartheid, the Soviet Union and wars in Afghanistan and the former Yugoslavia, among other places—scars, all, on the conscience of the 20th century—I had made fuller allowance for, or understood better, the role of wounded psyches in producing the Maos, Stalins, Vorsters, Najibullahs, Karadzics and Arkans I wrote about along the way" (7).

2. While Lasswell's formulation is a popular and widely cited interpretation of power strivings, there are alternative interpretations that emphasize the role of direct early reinforcement of power behaviors rather than perceived weakness or inferiority (see Winter 1999).

3. Most psychoanalysts are embarrassed by the crudeness and hostility of the Freud and Bullitt interpretation (see, e.g., Erikson 1967); many have questioned whether Freud actually contributed much to the interpretation or writing. In his preface, Bullitt wrote that he and Freud worked on the book for over ten years, finally completing a manuscript in 1932, but with subsequent revisions in 1938. According to Freud's biographer, Ernest Jones, who read the book in manuscript, the book was written in 1930–31 and "although a joint work it is not hard to distinguish the analytical contributions of the one author [Freud] from the political contributions of the other [Bullitt]" (1953–57, 3:160, see also 3:173).

4. Some researchers have been able to administer tests and questionnaires to leaders as high as the level of members of state legislatures (Altemeyer 1996) or members of national parliaments (DiRenzo 1967), although of course they did not report the scores of named individuals. One major exception to this generalization are the psychological tests given to Nazi leaders at Nürnberg (see Zillmer et al. 1995), but of course they were prisoners at the time.

5. Of course, most documents and speeches that bear the name of a major political leader are actually written by one or more speechwriters, and even "spontaneous" press conference responses to questions and "informal" comments may be highly scripted. Thus one may ask whether a content analysis of such materials produces personality estimates of the leader or of the speech writers. Suedfeld (1994) and Winter (1995) discuss this issue and conclude that because leaders select speech writers and review their drafts, and speech writers "know" their clients, personality scores based on content analysis (at least of major

speeches) can be taken as a valid indicator of the personality and psychological state of the leader—a claim that has generally been validated by research with such scores.

6. Many psychologists use the term *traits* much more loosely, and imprecisely, to refer to all personality variables (see Buss 1989)—a practice that is regrettable because it confuses fundamentally different kinds of personality characteristics, such as motives and cognitive representations, with true traits (see Winter 1996, chaps. 1 and 11).

3. Leader Personality Assessments in Support of Government Policy

Jerrold M. Post

The provenance of the U.S. government effort to apply at-a-distance leader personality assessment in support of policy can be traced to the studies of Adolf Hitler. The very word *studies* (plural) will perplex most readers, since until recently the only notable, and presumed first, such study was that prepared by the psychoanalyst Walter Langer, brother of the noted historian William Langer (Langer 1972). Declassified in 1969, the study has been published under the title *The Mind of Adolf Hitler.* Commissioned in the spring of 1943 by "Wild Bill" Donovan, director of the Office of Strategic Services (OSS), the predecessor of the Central Intelligence Agency (CIA), the study was completed in December of that year.

But this was not the first study of Hitler commissioned by the OSS. An earlier study, simply titled *Adolf Hitler,* the author or authors of which are unspecified, was completed a year earlier, on December 3, 1942. It was only recently declassified, on May 18, 2000, under the provisions of the War Crimes Disclosure Act of 2000.

In contrast to the later study, *The Mind of Adolf Hitler,* the first study, *Adolf Hitler,* is for the most part descriptive and not analytic. Indeed, it is rather incoherent, jumping back and forth from description to analysis, with no apparent rhyme or reason; it would not be clear to a policy official what to make of this study or how to employ it. That may be the reason for commissioning the later study by Langer, who was apparently not aware of or privy to the earlier study. Because *Adolf Hitler* has not previously been published, as a matter of historical interest I will summarize it in this chapter. Despite the disorganization, it does convey a measure of understanding of Hitler that augments the understanding derived from the later Langer study.

Adolf Hitler

Background

The sixty-eight page document is introduced by a remarkably brief (three-page) background note, which describes the unhappy marriage of his parents and documents that his father, Alois Schickelgruber, was physically sadistic, "in the habit of beating his dog until the dog wet the carpet." Twenty-three years older than his wife, Clara, Hitler's mother, Hitler's father was fifty-two years old when Adolf Hitler was born in 1889. It was a marriage between a hated sadistic father and a suppressed mother, who "quite possibly enjoyed this treatment." As an adolescent, Hitler was "constitutionally opposed to his father" (cf. *Mein Kampf*); the result of this domestic situation on Hitler was a mixture of Narcissus and Oedipus complexes. The author goes on to emphasize the important influence of his mother upon his life, quoting Hitler on the occasion of her death, when he was twenty: "The greatest loss I ever had."

Education

Hitler's education is only briefly addressed in the study, with the observation that "Hitler always despised education, having had so little himself." Under this general heading, the study comments upon Hitler's writing, reading, concentration, and conversation. The author observes that "it is obvious that Hitler only reads to confirm his own ideas." He is described as attracted to works that offer outstanding examples of rhetoric and historic epigrams, being drawn, among others, to Solon, Alexander the Great, Brutus, Caesar, Henry VIII, Frederick the Great, Jesus Christ, Mohammed, Moses, Luther, Cromwell, Napoleon, Richard Wagner, and Bismarck. His reading of these figures is confined to the "demagogic, propagandistic and militaristic side." One good phrase or catchword, which could be used in a later speech, is described as being worth much more to him than "cartloads of dry exposition and theory." His world is "one of action, not contemplation."

Under the subject of conversation, the author observes Hitler's tendency to present long monologues in social settings—episodes of his own life, such as "When I was in Vienna" or "When I was in prison," as well as rhapsodic monologues on Richard Wagner. Notable by its absence was any mention of colleagues or friends in his reminiscences.

Physique

In this section, the report considers Hitler's personal appearance, cleanliness, endurance, exercise, sight, voice, sleep, and reactions. Observing Hitler's meticulous concern with his physical appearance, the report cites his reaction to his physician's attempt to get him to extend the width of his moustache: "Do not worry about my mustache. If it is not the fashion now, it will be later because I wear it!" His endurance was described as remarkable, putting in twenty-hour days with his staff for weeks at end in 1932. It was noted that he slept very badly following his imprisonment at Landsberg, taking "some sleeping draft every night." He often was unable to sleep until dawn. Under the subject of reactions, he was characterized as "a mixture between a fox and a wolf. He plays the fox as long as possible and sometimes even a lamb, but in the end the wolf is always ready to emerge." He was described as "astonishingly brave," as someone who could remain "calm and collected even in emergencies."

The next four sections—diet, personal protection, entertainment, and information—briefly address these various elements of Hitler's persona. The author notes that Hitler gave up beer and wine following his imprisonment in Landsberg. The report also notes that, after an accidental injury incurred by one of his aides in which a nearby physician by prompt intervention saved his life, Hitler insisted on having a private doctor near him at all times. Personal security became increasingly more important to Adolf Hitler: "guarding of his person has become such an important problem that he is virtually a prisoner and he knows it." The protection of his motor vehicle procession was modeled after that afforded to President Woodrow Wilson. When Hitler went out on walks, five or six armed guards in civilian clothes in front and five or six behind accompanied him. Armed patrols would cover the flanks.

Although the entertainment section addresses the full spectrum of music, dancing, theater, vaudeville, and the circus, it is Hitler's fascination with music, in particular Wagner, and the circus that captures the most attention. The effect of music on Hitler is described as follows: "Tristan acts as a dope to him. If he is facing an unpleasant situation, he likes to have Meistersinger played to him. Sometimes he would recite entire passages from the Lohengrin text." Hitler was fascinated by American football marches, which he "adored"; the "Seig Heil!" used in political rallies was copied from the technique used by American cheerleaders. He also loved the circus and was particularly enthralled with tightrope acts and trapeze artists, people who risked their lives. After his release from prison, he said to his physician's wife, "Now we'll have to try all over again, but this time you can be certain that I won't fall from the tightrope!"

Religion

Hitler was profoundly influenced by the Catholic Church, which, in his view, according to the author, "knows how to build up a mental world, by a constant repetition throughout the Church year of certain passages in the Scriptures," which "leads to these chapters assuming a slogan-like concentration in the brains of the hearers." Hitler eloquently used this method in developing his mass influence upon the Hitler youth.

After this detailed description of Hitler and his proclivities, the study moves again into a biographic mode, first treating the Landsberg Prison experience.

Metamorphosis in Landsberg

Hitler was released from Landsberg Prison in 1924 after serving a term for political agitation. His time in prison was a powerful shaping experience according to the author of the study. While in prison, Hitler was deeply influenced by Rudolph Hess. After his release in 1926, despite having developed a personal relationship while in prison, Hess always referred to Hitler as "Mein Fuhrer." The author suggests that the affinity with Hess might have bordered on the sexual, confirmed for the author when he learned that in 1934 Hess attended homosexual balls dressed in women's attire. It was also during Hitler's time in prison that he developed a great admiration for the Italian leader Benito Mussolini.

Sexual Life

In this section, the author considers the Vienna period, which began in 1909, when Hitler was twenty years old. The author develops two significant issues in this section. First is the observation by the author that, by reading between the lines of *Mein Kampf,* one can speculate that Hitler became infected with a venereal disease after spending time with a Jewish prostitute. Second, there is some discussion of Hitler's involvement in homosexual circles.

In analyzing this period, the author observes that Hitler's "sex life is as dual as is his political outlook. He is both homosexual and heterosexual; both Socialist and fervent Nationalist; both man and woman." Inferring that what Hitler sought was "half mother and half sweetheart," the author suggests that the frustration Hitler experienced as a result of not finding the woman he needed led him to escape into "brooding isolation and artificially dramatized public life." When asked by his physician why he did not marry, Hitler responded: "Marriage is not for me and never will be. My only bride is my Motherland."

In discussions with a beautiful blonde married woman with whom he was temporarily infatuated, Hitler spoke of his reaction of disgust to the "wanton display and the Jewish materialism" that he experienced in Berlin, adding, "I nearly imagined myself to be Jesus Christ when he came to his Father's Temple." The author sees this as the first indication of the "Messiah complex" that is believed to have increasingly consumed Hitler. Ridiculed by the German and Continental press that spoke of Hitler as the "vest-pocket Mussolini," his failure to march on Berlin led Hitler to see himself "in the role of the Messiah with a scourge marching on that Babel of sin [Berlin] at the head of a small gang of desperados who would inevitably be followed by more and more of the dissatisfied elements throughout the Reich."

Self-Identification Patterns

This section is concerned with "the important role of auto-suggestion in the career of Hitler." In the fall of 1918, while the soldier Hitler was recovering in the infirmary, "he received a command from another world above to save his unhappy country. This vocation reached Hitler in the form of a supernatural vision. He decided to become a politician then and there. He felt that his mission was to free Germany."

Among the self-identifications he used in fulfilling that mission were the following:

a. The drummer: At a number of meetings, Hitler referred to himself as "the drummer, marching ahead of a great movement of liberation to come." He varied "the drummer" message with one of self-identification with John the Baptist, calling himself a voice crying in the wilderness.

b. Messiah: Starting in the early 1920s, the deification of Hitler was seen to be progressing steadily. In denying a rumor in the spring of 1923 that he was engaged to his physician's daughter, Hitler told the doctor: "I authorize you hereby to tell the press that I shall never engage myself to a woman nor marry a woman. The only true bride for me is and always will be the German People." This would remind those familiar with Christian literature that Christ's only true bride was the Church.

c. Cromwell: Hitler particularly admired Cromwell and often referred to him as an enemy of Parliamentarianism, of the universal franchise, of communism, and of Catholicism. Hitler particularly admired Cromwell as a self-appointed dictator and was fascinated by Cromwell's beheading of Charles I, no doubt an influence in Hitler's 1930 theme, "Heads will roll."

d. Frederick the Great: The early period of Frederick's life, in which he was in violent opposition to his stern father, fascinated Hitler, with the parallel biographic features obvious. But the author notes that Hitler apparently identified with Frederick's father, who would have "beheaded his own son to ensure discipline. That is how all German youth will have to be brought up one day. That is the way German justice should be handled. Either acquittal or beheading."

e. Bleucher: The driving force against Napoleon and a symbol of German faith and courage, General Bleucher, also known as "Marshall Vorwaerts," was an inspiration to Hitler. It was Bleucher's technique of perpetual attack that in Hitler's judgment led Napoleon to lose his nerve.

f. Napoleon: Napoleon was the figure in European history of greatest interest to Hitler. Hitler was clearly intrigued by, and sought to emulate, Napoleon: "Napoleon the Jacobin, Napoleon the soldier, the propagandist, the coiner of phrases, the tyrant, the Imperator." Hitler modeled his own leadership style after Napoleon, who demanded that his people follow his model, such that "Napoleon became France and France Napoleon." Like Napoleon, Hitler particularly directed his appeal to the youth of the nation. While deprecating the aged and the rich, Hitler built his followership of "little Hitlers." Both leaders, being mediums of the inner wishes of their respective nations, were "like avalanches." Napoleon considered himself the "flagellum Dei" while Hitler saw himself as "the scourging Messiah."

Speechmaking Technique

Listed under the final heading of "speechmaking technique" were the following topics: preparation of speech, entrance, interruptions, speech, posture, oratory, end of speech, avoidance of names and personages, and exit technique.

Recognizing the power of his oratory, Hitler was meticulous in the preparation of his speeches, working on each one for four to six hours and using cues on ten or twelve foolscap sheets. The notes were for cuing only; he would never read a speech, recognizing that to do so would lose spontaneity. He was extremely concerned with audience reaction, so each aspect of his speech—the entrance, the exit, the martial music—was carefully orchestrated. The average length of a speech was two and one-half to three hours, during which time he was not concerned with applause but instead sought to convert the audience to his ideas. There was a rhythm to his speeches, with the first two-thirds in march time. Often questioning his own ideas, he would masterfully demolish the questions he had raised. In the last one-third of the speech, "he [swept] from exhortation, promise, dedication to the rhapsodic finale." In the last eight to ten minutes, Hitler's oratory "resemble[d] an orgasm of words. It is like the throbbing fulfillment of a love drama. . . . Liebestod."

Comment

Much of this material is quite interesting, particularly Hitler's preoccupation with himself as political actor, with meticulous concern for his self-presentation, and his increasing Messiah complex, his identification with himself as the savior of the German people. And while the policymaker reading this assessment may feel that he better understands Hitler after this account, how to translate these understandings into policy prescriptions is not at all clear, which was perhaps the reason for commissioning the Langer study.

Langer's Study: *The Mind of Adolf Hitler*

What has generally been considered the pioneering effort of at-a-distance leader personality assessment in support of U.S. government policy was the assessment of Adolf Hitler prepared by the psychoanalyst Walter Langer. Intrigued by psychoanalysis,"Wild Bill" Donovan of the OSS had asked Langer to set up a Psychoanalytic Field Unit to help in understanding the morale of the American people and the psychology of the German people.

The dramatic nature of Hitler's leadership compelled attention to his personality, and in the spring of 1943 Donovan informed Langer that they needed "a realistic appraisal of the German situation." Donovan asked, "If Hitler is running the show, what kind of a man is he? What are his ambitions? How does he appear to the German people? What is he like with his associates? What is his background? And most of all, we want to know as much as possible about his psychological make-up—the things that make him tick. In addition we ought to know what he might do if things begin to go against him" (Langer 1972).

It was clear to Langer at the onset that Hitler was more than the crazy paperhanger depicted in popular media. How, he puzzled, could this shiftless ne'er-do-well, who had never been promoted above the rank of lance corporal, "in the course of a relatively few years talk his way into the highest political offices, hoodwink the experienced leaders of the major powers, turn millions of highly civilized people into barbarians, order the extermination of a large segment of the population, build and control the mightiest war machine ever known, and plunge the world into history's most devastating war?" (Langer 1972, 11). With the aid of three psychoanalytically trained researchers in New York, who reviewed the literature on file in the New York Public Library, Langer scoured the United States and Canada for persons who had had contact with Hitler and personally interviewed each of them. Under immense time pressure, Langer prepared a study that was disseminated within government circles in the fall of 1943 but was not declassified until 1969. Psychobiographic in approach, the study examines the formative events in Hitler's life and how they shaped his emerging personality, positing the powerful psychodynamic forces that were to play out so destructively upon the political stage.

The design of Langer's study is instructive. The first section, "Hitler as He Believes Himself to Be," is followed by "Hitler as the German People Know Him," "Hitler as His Associates Know Him," and "Hitler as He Knows Himself." It is only after examination of Hitler through these four lenses that Langer depicts "Hitler, Psychological Analysis and Reconstruction," ending with "Hitler, His Probable Behavior in the Future."

In presenting the section "Hitler as He Knows Himself," Langer selected language from Hitler's writings and commentary to his associates. The selection was guided by Langer's psychoanalytic framework. He observed that Hitler's sense of his own destiny was remarkable. When early in Hitler's career during a policy discussion Strasser suggested that Hitler was mistaken, Hitler responded: "I cannot be mistaken. What I say and do is historical" (Langer 1972, 30). His exalted self-image, Langer observed, was not confined to his role as statesman. On the field of battle, Hitler believed he had special gifts as well. "I do not play at war. I do not allow the generals' to give me orders. The war is conducted by me." And he considered himself supremely gifted as a jurist. "For the last twenty-four hours, *I* was the supreme court of the German people" (original emphasis). Commenting on Hitler's exalted belief in his own powers, Rauschning observed, "He feels no one in German history is as equipped as he is to bring the Germans to the positions of supremacy which all German statesmen have felt they deserved but were unable to achieve." Langer observed that, in addition to his great abilities, Hitler prided himself on his hardness and brutality: "I am one of the hardest men Germany has had for decades, perhaps for centuries, equipped with the greatest authority of any German leader . . . but above all I believe in my success. I believe in it unconditionally."

In his messianic leadership, Hitler associated himself with Christ, but his pride in his hardness stood in conflict with Christ's gentle, loving nature. He handled this by redefining Christ's nature: "My feeling as a Christian points to my Lord and Savior as a fighter. . . . It points to the man who recognized the Jews for what they were and summoned men to fight against them and who, God's truth! was greatest not as a sufferer but as a fighter. . . . I read through the passage which tells of us how the lord rose at last in His might and seized the scourge to drive out of the Temple the rod of vipers and adders. How terrific was the fight for the world against the Jewish poison!" (Langer 1972, 36). Langer concluded that Hitler increasingly conceived of himself as a second Christ. He glowed with pride when addressed with the salutation "Heil Hitler, our Savior." Confirming his sense of his own role in history and his identification with the Messiah, Hitler's propaganda machine painted the following message on a hillside: "We believe in Holy Germany. Holy Germany is Hitler! We believe in Holy Hitler!" (56).

Langer cites the reports of Hitler's preoccupation with his mausoleum, which was to be the mecca of Germany after his death. Planning a monument seven hundred feet high, which would have a great psychological effect, Hitler declared, "I know how to keep my hold on people after I have passed on. I shall be the Fuhrer they look up at and go home to talk of and remember. My life shall not end in the mere form of death. It will, on the contrary, begin then" (Langer 1972, 37–38).

A diplomat commented that Hitler was convinced of his own infallibility and success. This in turn was associated with a resistance to criticism, which angered him. "To contradict him in his eyes is a crime. . . . [O]pposition to his plans, from whatever side it may come, is a definite sacrilege, to which the only reply is an immediate and striking display of his omnipotence." Thus Langer asserted that

Hitler was convinced of his own greatness, a conviction bolstered by the response to his fiery rhetoric.

Hitler was described as attuned to his audience in a remarkable fashion. "Hitler responds to the vibration of the human heart with the delicacy of a seismograph . . . enabling him with a certainty with which no conscious gift could endow him to act as a loudspeaker proclaiming the most secret desires, the least permissible instinct, the sufferings and personal revolts of the whole nation" (Strasser, quoted in langer 1972, 46). In *Mein Kampf*, Langer observed, Hitler focused on mass psychology, emphasizing that "the mass prefers to submit to the strong rather than to the weakling; the mass, too, prefers the ruler to a pleader" (47).

His fiery oratory stirred the masses into a frenzy. "His oratory used to wilt his collar, unglue his forelock, glaze his eyes; he was like a man hypnotized, repeating himself into a frenzy." He was, another observer declared, "in the presence of a miracle. He was a man transformed and possessed." His hypnotic self-presentation was echoed in the German propaganda machine, which depicted him as "the acme of German honor and purity; the Resurrection of the German family and home. He is the greatest architect of all time; the greatest military genius in all history. He has an inexhaustible fount of knowledge. He is a man of action and the creator of new social values. He is . . . the paragon of all virtues" (Langer 1972, 53).

In this longitudinal psychobiographic study, Langer was to examine the psychological underpinnings of Hitler's conviction of his own greatness. Langer persuasively depicts the inner emptiness that underlay and drove the messianic self-concept and public role. In describing the illegitimacy of Hitler's father, Alois, Langer noted the data suggesting that the real father of Alois may have been one of the Rothchilds, a Jewish family for which Hitler's grandmother was a maid. Langer observed that the salient question was, What did Hitler believe and fear? (This theme was later to be stressed in Waite's *The Psychopathic God*.)

Langer then describes the bleak early years and the extended period during Hitler's adolescence when he was lost psychologically and was in a period of identity diffusion, the equivalent of a street person, unemployed, moving from flophouse to flophouse. World War I provided the exit pass from this extended period, and Hitler found himself fighting for Germany, again to be plunged into despair by the military defeat and the peace terms he was to define as traitorous. Identifying external "reasons" for this bleak period in Germany's and his own life characterizes Hitler's rhetoric during this period. Three themes were to dominate Hitler's speechmaking before he came to power: (1) the treason of the November criminals; (2) breaking the rule of the Marxists; and (3) the world domination of the Jews. The Jew as the focus of his hostility, the "reason" for Germany's weakness, was increasingly to become the focus of his mesmerizing rhetoric.

The purpose of this discussion of Langer's study is not to psychologically analyze Hitler but rather to describe the analytic approach taken in this pioneering study. Langer studied Hitler in the same way he tried to understand the patients on his psychoanalytic couch. Without further detailing the life history of Hitler elaborated by Langer, suffice it so say that Langer integrates in *The Mind of Adolf Hitler* a psychobiographic analysis, a psychodynamic profile, and a depiction of the public man, discriminating between those aspects of the public persona that are contrived for public consumption and those that are powerfully psychologically driven to compensate for the inner void.

Though it is a powerful and persuasive study, Langer acknowledges that it is not clear to him the degree to which decision makers relied upon his work. He does report that Lord Chalfont of Great Britain, on meeting him quickly, identified him as the author of the Hitler study, making it clear that the work had been shared with U.S. allies.

While the degree of influence of this study upon the conduct of the war is not clear, as the prototype of the psychodynamically oriented clinically informed assessment of a foreign leader at a distance, it is of great importance, for it was to become the model of subsequent endeavors in support of government policy.

Khrushchev at a Distance

When Nikita Khrushchev burst on the political scene in 1953, his political persona differed dramatically from that of his predecessor, Josef Stalin. The CIA convened a conference in 1960 for the specific purpose of assessing this complicated leader for the Kennedy administration. The CIA had amassed a great deal of open material, including films as well as interviews and articles. The panel of some twenty psychiatrists, psychologists, and internal medicine specialists immersed themselves in the films, speeches, and interviews and developed assessments of his political personality and health.

In 1961, when President Kennedy was to meet with First Party secretary Khrushchev in Vienna in a major summit meeting, Bryant Wedge, a psychoanalytically trained psychiatrist who was a member of the panel, wrote Kennedy a memo summarizing the conference findings, with emphasis on implications for negotiations.[1]

Khrushchev was described as a stable hypomanic character, which Wedge characterized as a chronic optimistic opportunist. Yet his impulsivity was noted too. While it was opined that Khrushchev could tolerate disagreement, there was no point in trying to persuade or convince him of it. Wedge also advanced recommendations for dealing with him when he was being thoroughly unreasonable. He also emphasized the fundamental differences between Khrushchev and Stalin.

It is important to observe that the conference of clinicians concluded that Khrushchev had a recognizable clinical character type, based on what was essentially a phenomenological analysis. The clear personality type on which they consensually agreed has important implications for negotiations. Unlike the Langer study of Hitler, which was heavily psychobiographic in approach and combined with a phenomenological portrait to infer the psychological conflicts driving political behavior, the Khrushchev study was a detailed description of Khrushchev's personality style based on intensive study of his present-day leadership functioning. Wedge observes that he does not know who read his memo or to what uses it was put.

The Establishment of the Center for the Analysis of Personality and Political Behavior

Started in 1965, the pilot program to assess leader personality at a distance was initially based in the Psychiatric Staff of the CIA's Office of Medical Services. Because the products of this experimental effort were well received by senior U.S. government officials, it was determined that the effort should be formally incorporated within the Directorate of Intelligence, which provided finished intelligence to intelligence consumers throughout the government. This transition led to the establishment of the Center for the Analysis of Personality and Political Behavior (CAPPB), an interdisciplinary behavioral science unit with lead analysts at the doctoral level trained in cultural anthropology, political sociology, political science with a specialty in leadership studies, history, organizational, social, and clinical psychology, and psychiatry.[2] A senior advisory panel of nationally prominent political psychologists representing diverse disciplines was recruited.

To ensure that studies of personality and political behavior were designed in a manner that would be optimally useful to senior consumers, the lead analysts worked closely with the senior panel to develop an intellectual framework for the studies. For senior consumers—in particular the president, secretary of state, secretary of defense—there was an intense interest in understanding "what made this leader tick?" These senior consumers well understood that politics *is* people. They wanted to learn about the life experiences that had shaped the leader's attitudes, the issues of particular concern. For this purpose, the psychobiographic analysis that was a major component of the clinical case study to mental illness was adapted to focus not on the early life experience that led to vulnerability to mental illness but rather on the key events that shaped a future leader. Moreover, one of the purposes of assessing the individual in the context of his or her past history is that the individual's past responses under similar circumstances are, other things being equal, the best basis for predictions of future behavior.

But the qualitative data necessary to develop a detailed psychobiography often were not initially available, particularly with what came to be known as "pop-up" leaders, that is, leaders who suddenly emerged as the consequence of a coup d'etat or other dramatic event whose actions required an immediate response. Sometimes for such leaders the only data available were speeches or a press conference. Here the sophisticated content-analytic methodologies of members of the senior panel proved of inestimable value in providing the first approximation of leader personality and mental maps. At times these techniques were employed prospectively to avoid a predictable surprise. An interesting example was provided by a comparative analysis conducted by Margaret Hermann (1980b) of possible successors to Communist party chairman Leonid Brezhnev at a time when the succession was by no means clear. This analysis permitted identifying and distinguishing the candidate who was apt to be most rigid and ideological from the one apt to be most flexible and adaptable.

But for summit meetings and other high-level negotiations, senior consumers preferred comprehensive in-depth political personality profiles that placed the leader in his or her longitudinal context and provided insights on the historical forces that shaped the leader's political personality. Such an occasion was provided by the Camp David negotiations of 1978.

The Camp David Profiles

If the degree of influence of the Langer study of Hitler and of the assessment of Krushchev is not clear, it is clear that the psychological portraits of Anwar Sadat and Menachem Begin, the Camp David profiles, significantly informed and influenced President Jimmy Carter's understanding of the protagonists and the strategy he developed for the conduct of the negotiations. Indeed, according to Carter, they were among the most important influences upon the strategy and tactics of his personal diplomacy with Begin and Sadat.

In his presidential memoirs *Keeping Faith* (1983), Carter spoke of the intensity of his study of the backgrounds and personalities of these remarkably different leaders. In August 1978, just prior to the historic Camp David negotiations, Carter took a vacation to Jackson Hole, Wyoming, to relax before what he knew would be an arduous and testing challenge. After a day of fly fishing for cutthroat trout in the Snake River, Carter immersed himself in psychological analyses of Begin and Sadat.[3]

Ours would be a new approach, perhaps unprecedented in history. Three leaders of nations would be isolated from the outside world. An intensely personal effort would be required of us. *I had to understand these men!* I was poring over psychological analyses of two of the protagonists which had been prepared by a team of experts within our intelligence community. This team could write definitive biographies of any important world leader, using information derived from a detailed scrutiny of events, public statements, writings, known medical histories, and interviews with personal acquaintances of the leaders under study. I wanted to know all about Begin and Sadat. What had made them national leaders? What was the root of their ambition? What were their most important goals in life? What events during past years had helped to shape their characters? What were their religious beliefs? Family relations? State of their health? Political beliefs and constraints? Relations with other leaders? Likely reaction to pressure in a time of crisis? Strengths and weaknesses? Commitments to political constituencies? Attitudes towards me and the United States? Whom did they really trust? What was their attitude toward one another? . . .

From time to time I paused to consider the negotiating strategy I would follow at Camp David; I made careful detailed notes. These few evenings away from Washington were an ideal time for me to concentrate almost exclusively on a single major challenge—peace in the Middle East. During the coming days at Camp David, my studies at the foot of the Grand Tetons were to pay rich dividends. (Carter 1983, 319–20; original emphasis)

The recent declassification of the article "Personality Profiles in Support of the Camp David Summit" (Post 1979) permits discussion of the personality profiles sent to Carter. The history of the Camp David profiles is discussed in detail because of their historic significance. This is the first time a detailed consideration of the development and use of the profiles has been presented.

On a visit to CIA Headquarters in August 1978, President Carter interrupted a briefing to ask the assembled analysts and intelligence managers how they could help him with the forthcoming summit, which had only recently been announced. In particular, he wanted to be "steeped in the personalities of Begin and Sadat" (Post 1979).

In response to this request, the CIA's CAPPB prepared three political personality profiles: a profile of Menachem Begin, which called attention to the increasing trend of oppositionism and rigidity in his personality; a profile of Anwar Sadat entitled "Sadat's Nobel Prize Complex," which stressed his increasing preoccupation with his role in history and the leverage it could provide in negotiations; and a paper that discussed the implications for negotiations of the contrasting intellectual styles of Begin and Sadat. The profiles were based on the detailed psychological studies of the personality and political behavior of Begin and Sadat prepared in 1977.

In the CAPPB there was often a request for "instant magic" when a coup, assassination, or election upset brings to the fore a leader previously not well known to the foreign policy community, and an in-depth personality assessment of the leader was requested immediately. In order to anticipate the needs of the community, the CAPPB had regularly surveyed key intelligence consumers, including the National Security Council, the secretary of state, and the secretary of defense, to identify leaders of special interest. Usually this survey would reveal considerable diversity. The survey completed in the summer of 1976 revealed for the first time across-the-board highest priority interest in one world leader, President Anwar Sadat of Egypt.

In developing personality studies for various leaders, the CAPPB would review a broad range of data. Official and unofficial biographies often provided key background materials and insights, as did television, newspaper, and magazine profiles. While many would discard the authorized biography as being exaggeratedly biased in a positive direction, in fact the contrast between the authorized and unauthorized biographies was found to be instructive: the contrast between the idealized leader as he wished to be seen and the more realistic flesh-and-blood leader, with all his warts, blemishes, and psychological sensitivities. When there were significant holes in the data or unresolvable conflicts, requirements would be sent to the field. Often psychologically relevant material was readily available in response to the questions sent to the field, questions that previously had not been asked. Particularly rich information was derived by debriefing senior officials who had had extended contact with the leader in question. Ambassadors and others who had dealt with the leader over time usually had regularly reported on substantive matters, such as economic plans or weapons procurement programs, but rarely had reported on the personality, attitudes, and negotiating style of the leader—knowledge that was subsequently often lost in the transition between administrations.

By integrating interview impressions of officials who had dealt with Sadat with psychobiographic analysis, several important themes emerged. Sadat's concern with his role in history and his pre-occupation with "the big picture," coupled with his abhorrence of details, were regularly mentioned. By appealing to Sadat's long-range goals, Secretary of State Henry Kissinger was often able to overcome negotiating impasses over technical details.

The American ambassador to Egypt, Herman Eilts, related an amusing and charming anecdote that epitomized this quality, an anecdote that would rarely be reported but one we in the CAPPB found quite telling (Post 1979, 3). The occasion was a luncheon hosted by President Sadat just after a breakthrough in negotiations. The two negotiating teams—the Egyptians and Israelis—had been at an impasse, wrangling over such issues as the number and position of troops and the placement of sensors. Responding to Kissinger's skillful urgings to rise above this petty dispute for the sake of history, Sadat had made a grand compromise, overriding the objections of his advisers.

Present at the luncheon were President Sadat; Madame Sadat, an outspoken woman in her own right; Secretary of State Kissinger; and Ambassador Eilts. "Your excellency," said Secretary Kissinger, raising his glass, "without your broad vison of history and your refusal to be bogged down by petty detail, we never would have come to this day." "No, Henry," replied President Sadat, "it was your negotiating skills which brought us to this day." "Oh, no, your Excellency," replied Kissinger, "it was your ability to think in strategic terms that . . ." At this point, Madame Sadat interrupted with a loud sigh to Ambassador Eilts, "Oh, no, here we go again."

A major conclusion of the study "Personality Profiles in Support of the Camp David Summit" addressed the manner in which Sadat's special view of himself and this "big picture" mentality interacted.

Sadat's self-confidence and special view of himself has been instrumental in development of his innovative foreign policy, as have his flexibility and his capacity for moving out of the cultural insularity of the Arab world. He sees himself as a grand strategist and will make tactical concessions if he is persuaded that his over-all goals will be achieved. . . . His self-confidence has permitted him to make bold initiatives, often overriding his advisers' objections. (Post 1979, 3)

So prominent was Sadat's special sense of self that the major study of Sadat that CAPPB produced was entitled "Sadat's Messiah Complex." Sadat's creative diplomacy in November and December 1977, highlighted by his historic visit to Jerusalem in which he overrode his advisers' objections, emphasized this central personality quality. When Sadat became the object of intense media attention, giving major interviews to the likes of Walter Cronkite, John Chancellor, and Barbara Walters, it was an explosion of narcissistic supplies, and his extreme self-confidence was magnified to grandiose extremes, a phenomenon initially dubbed by the CAPPB as "the Barbara Walters syndrome."

Over the succeeding months, his grandiosity magnified exponentially. One of the most interesting changes had to do with the sharp increase in his use of the first-person singular pronoun. No longer did Sadat speak of the problems with Egypt's economy. Rather, he spoke of "my economy." There were accounts suggesting that Sadat would be angered by and would refuse to believe reports that his goals for Egypt and himself were in trouble. This led to a shrinkage of his leadership circle to sycophants who only told Sadat what he wanted to hear, leading him to be increasingly out of touch with political reality. Sadat's grandiosity became so pronounced that the profile prepared by the CAPPB for Carter was entitled "Sadat's Nobel Prize Complex." In his memoirs, Carter indicated that this aspect of Sadat's personality was in the forefront of his thinking.

> Sadat was strong and bold, very much aware of world public opinion and of his role as the most important leader among the Arabs. I always had the impression that he looked on himself as inheriting the mantle of authority from the great pharaohs, and was convinced that he was a man of destiny. (Carter 1983, 328)

In contrast to Sadat, who was well known to a succession of American diplomats, when Menachem Begin came to power in a stunning election upset, he was a virtual unknown with whom there had been little official contact. But there was a rich source of information in the open literature, for in two autobiographical works, *White Nights* and *The Revolt,* Begin had detailed the experiences that had shaped his personality and political attitudes. He emphasized the seminal role of the Holocaust, which was to be captured in his well-known phrase, "Never again!" Begin as leader frequently gave voice to provocative statements, often precipitated by a reporter's questions, losing sight of the context and of the negative political fallout from the statement. Indeed, this trait was reflected throughout his career. In *White Nights,* Begin's autobiographic account of his political exile in Siberia, he proudly recounts the frequent debates with his Soviet jailers over details of Soviet law in which he regularly bested his captors with his superior knowledge of their law. However, this was quite counterproductive in terms of his own welfare. His focus on detail and legalisms was emphasized in the profile, as was his tendency toward oppositionism related to his vow "never again" to yield to superior force.

In *Keeping Faith,* Carter indicated how steeped he was in Begin's background. Believing that Begin, like Sadat, saw himself as a man of destiny, Carter saw Begin as a student of the Bible who insisted on using biblical names, such as Judea and Samaria, for disputed territories to emphasize Israel's historic entitlement to the land of Israel.

The prominence of the personality differences of Sadat and Begin led to a proposal by the CAPPB to devote one of the dinner symposia periodically hosted by Admiral Stansfield Turner, director of the CIA, to the role of personality in the Middle East conflict. Participants in this dinner seminar, held in the spring of 1978, included a number of senior individuals who had been intimately involved in Middle East negotiations: Ambassador-at-large Alfred Atherton, Ambassador to Egypt Herman Eilts, Assistant Secretary of State for Near East Affairs Harold Saunders, and Dr. William Quandt, the National Security Council's senior Near East specialist. The discussion was purposefully free of discussion of policy and substantive differences, focusing only on the striking differences in the personalities of the two protagonists and how they would affect the negotiating process.

How could two individuals constructed so differently psychologically participate in simultaneous negotiations? This was the subject of the third paper prepared by the CAPPB for Carter concerned with the problematic implications for simultaneous negotiations of the contrasting cognitive styles of Sadat, the "big picture" man with an abhorrence for detail, and Begin, the legalistic wordsmith consumed with detail and precision, who had a tendency to become embroiled in power struggles.

This paper informed and influenced the middleman role Carter played in these intensely personal negotiations, while minimizing direct contact between the two protagonists, and the manner in which he worked at narrowing the gap between Sadat and Begin. Carter indicated that he was concerned that Begin's "preoccupation with language, names, and terms could severely impede free-flowing talk" (1983, 330). On one occasion, he cleverly put his own concern with Begin's penchant for details and with the gap between Sadat's and Begin's style into Sadat's mouth.

> As [Begin] was preparing to leave after our stilted and some-what superficial discussion, I told him that Sadat had expressed a concern about Begin's preoccupation with details at the expense of the major issues. Begin looked up quickly and said, "I can handle both." (330)

After his diplomatic triumph, President Carter conveyed his appreciation to the CIA for the intelligence support provided him and singled out the personality profiles for special praise: "After spending 13 days with the two principals, I wouldn't change a word" (Post 1979, 1). The Camp David profiles highlighted the value of leader personality assessment in support of government policy, emphasizing their special value in summit negotiations.

The Institutionalization of Political Personality Profiling

Certainly the recognition given by President Carter of the value of the Camp David profiles of Menachem Begin and Anwar Sadat was a transformational event for the CAPPB. No longer would the in-depth studies they prepared be considered avant garde. Now they would be considered a requisite for each summit meeting and a required resource for managing politico-military crises.

Because of the lead time required to develop in-depth political personality profiles, the CAPPB regularly surveyed senior officials at the Department of State, Department of Defense, and the National

Security Council to identify leaders of priority interest. The results of the surveys were an important factor in establishing priorities for the CAPPB's program, although politico-military crises and other unexpected international events often led to crash requirements for an assessment of a political leader. Much embassy reporting would be concerned with political, economic, or military matters, but little attention was paid to leader personality. Yet there was often substantial untapped knowledge concerning the leaders of concern. Because biographic files typically began with the leader's ascension to power, the very background features important to a political psychologist were often missing. But these gaps could often be filled with queries to the embassy. Similarly, a search of open source material often produced a rich lode of material from local periodicals. The opportunity to meet with senior embassy officials who had had contact with the individual of concern was particularly valuable, for these sources were often gifted observers who had never been debriefed from the perspective of political psychology.

As the academic interdiscipline of political psychology emerged, the name of the CAPPB was changed to the Political Psychology Center, and subsequently to the Political Psychology Division. The analytic approach of the division was systematically examined and refined with the assistance of a senior panel of prominent academic political psychologists to ensure that the needs of senior policy consumers were being met by the studies.

An important aspect of the approach was the continuing emphasis on ensuring that the subjects analyzed were appropriately anchored within their respective societies. This was accomplished by regularly teaming a psychologist or psychiatrist with an area expert. Thus in assessing a leader from sub-Saharan Africa, for example, a cultural anthropologist with particular expertise in culture and personality would be a core member of the analytic team; similarly, for the study of a South Asian leader, a political sociologist with particular expertise in the region would be a core member of the analytic team.

The dissolution of the Soviet empire and the end of the cold war led to a major reduction in the intelligence budget, especially resources devoted to human intelligence in comparison to technological intelligence. With this cutback, the scope of the resources devoted to developing in-depth political personality profiles was significantly reduced. In recent years, however, there have been a number of intelligence "surprises," including the failure to predict nuclear testing by India and Pakistan and major terrorist events— the bombings of the U.S. embassies in Kenya and Tanzania and the suicide hijackings of September 11, which resulted in the destruction of the World Trade Center and the crash into the Pentagon by al Qaeda, Osama bin Laden's terrorist organization. After the nuclear testing by India and Pakistan, the Rumsfeld Commission was established to examine this intelligence failure. A major conclusion was that there was an overreliance on technological intelligence and insufficient human intelligence and analysis of leadership. At the time of his confirmation hearings, Secretary of Defense Donald Rumsfeld identified as his leading nightmare not understanding the intentions of dangerous adversaries. Accentuated by some of the recent intelligence "surprises," the need to have a robust applied political psychology capability has been highlighted and increased resources are currently being applied to human intelligence and to the study of the personality and political behavior of foreign leaders, both national leaders and terrorist leaders.

Notes

1. The assessment prepared by the panel was classified as "secret," but Wedge elected to publish it in the *Washington Post* in 1967, and it was subsequently republished in Wedge 1968. Wedge explained that since Kennedy was dead and Krushchev was retired he believed the original classification was no longer valid.

2. The editor of this volume had the honor and challenge of founding and leading CAPPB for twenty-one years. An interdisciplinary behavioral sciences analytic unit, CAPPB produced assessments of the personality and political behavior of key foreign leaders for three purposes: (1) to assist the president and senior cabinet officials in summit meetings and other high-level negotiations, (2) to assist in crisis situations, and (3) to assist in estimative intelligence.

3. Carter had been critical of the strategy briefing books prepared for him by the State Department and the National Security staff, whose expressed goals for Camp David had been very modest, and set his goals on a written agreement for peace between Egypt and Israel. But he knew that to succeed in achieving this ambitious goal would require an understanding of the psychology and attitudes of the principals in depth.

Part II. Methods for Assessing Leader Personalities: An Introduction

The Search for Causal Mechanisms

Stephen G. Walker and Jerrold M. Post

We noted in chapter 1 the distinction between qualitative and quantitative methods of leadership assessment generated by the contributors to this volume. In part 2, the qualitative methods employed by Post (chap. 4) and Renshon (chap. 5) identify the structure of the individual's personality and character. The quantitative methods used by Weintraub (chap. 6), Winter (chap. 7), and Suedfeld, Guttieri, and Tetlock (chap. 10) provide an expanded analysis of different parts of a leader's personality, including beliefs, cognitive style, and other personality traits. Hermann (chap. 8) and Walker, Schafer, and Young (chap. 9) embed their respective assessments of leaders in a typology defined by a particular constellation of beliefs, motivations, or traits. All of these analyses specify procedures for detecting different causal mechanisms, defined as processes operating inside the individual and connecting environment and outcomes, as indicated in the graphic that follows (adapted from Hedstrom and Swedberg 1998, 9; see also Bunge 1967).

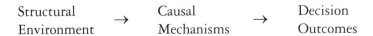

| Structural Environment | → | Causal Mechanisms | → | Decision Outcomes |

Structural theorists of world politics often assume (a) the causal mechanisms of agency are transparently "thin" models of rational choice responding to environmental conditions, and (b) these mechanisms are not autonomous in their effects, explaining very little of the variation in outcomes across situations. Decision-making theorists have long argued that these mechanisms are not rational processes endogenous to structural conditions and may have an important autonomous impact on decisions and outcomes. Assessing the conditions under which "personality" as a causal mechanism becomes more important is necessary to determine the fit between a structural theory and a particular case under analysis. At this point, the objective is precisely to determine whether the case in question conforms to the covering-law generalization from a structural theory about a universe of cases or deviates from it due to the operation of intervening causal mechanisms between structural conditions and decision outcomes.

The causal mechanism may operate either endogenously within the theory so that the generalization is valid in some cases or autonomously to make the generalization invalid in other cases. A weak claim for the importance of the latter possibility is that causal mechanisms occasionally operate to disrupt the effects of structural conditions located at macrolevels of analysis (Holsti 1976; Greenstein 1987; Hermann 1976; George 1979). A strong claim is to argue that such disruptions are more likely to be the rule rather than the exception (Jervis 1976, 1997; Little 1998). The latter position is a critique of the inherent underspecification of simple structural models, especially for the analysis of individual cases. Greenstein's (1987) conditions of "action dispensability" and "actor dispensability" are efforts to resolve this dispute regarding when the causal mechanisms of personality—beliefs, traits, and psychodynamic processes—are likely to have an autonomous effect on outcomes.

In the following chapters, the authors probe the microfoundations of political behavior by analyzing a variety of causal mechanisms with different methods of content analysis. These methods operate at different layers of analysis within the leader's personality. Collectively, the authors cover the cognitive states, affective traits, and characterological structure of the leader's personality and the corresponding mechanisms of object appraisal, mediation of self-other relationships, externalization, and ego defense (Greenstein 1987; see also Smith 1968).

The first two chapters by Post and by Renshon explore the processes of externalization and ego defense generated by the deep structure of a leader's personality and how they reflect the impact of psychobiographical experiences on the development of the leader's personality (Smith 1968). The next three chapters by Weintraub, Winter, and Hermann, respectively, probe more deeply into parts of the leader's personality by focusing on motivational and affective traits that operate as mechanisms mediating the relationship between self and others. The final two chapters by Walker, Schafer, and Young and by Suedfeld, Guttieri, and Tetlock are cognitive analyses of the process of object appraisal, which reveal how beliefs orient the leader toward action in the political universe and how aspects of the leader's cognitive style influence the leader's thinking and decision making.

While it is possible to postulate a simple linear model of causation in which the deep structure of the personality shapes and constrains the operation of motivational, affective, and cognitive mechanisms, the authors of these chapters do not all make this assumption in their analyses. The comprehensive analyses by Post and Renshon attempt to identify pattern and shaping influences, but the authors are always mindful of the complex interaction with the environment. Nor do the analyses by the other contributors postulate a simple linear model of causation. Rather they tend to be agnostic about this possibility in varying degrees, depending on how comprehensive and explicit their models of personality are regarding linkages among beliefs, motivations, and character. We shall return to a discussion of the possibilities for integrating these analyses in the conclusion.

A. Integrated Personality Study

4. Assessing Leaders at a Distance: The Political Personality Profile

Jerrold M. Post

The political personality profile was developed to provide senior policymakers with a comprehensive psychological representation of the leader in context, not only describing the life course of the leader that shaped key attitudes but also specifying particular aspects of leadership behavior especially relevant to policymakers dealing with the leader. Thus in addition to traditional elements of clinical psychological assessment, the elements reviewed in assessing political personality include management style, negotiating style, strategic decision making, crisis decision making, rhetorical style, cognitive style, and leadership style. Each of these aspects of political leadership is of course shaped by the cultural and political context, but the core leader personality influences each of these leadership characteristics.

The term *personality* connotes a systematic pattern of functioning that is consistent over a range of behaviors and over time. In the political personality profile, we attempt to characterize the core political personality, identifying the deeply ingrained patterns that are coherent and accordingly have powerful predictive implications. But it is important to emphasize that not all political situations engage the political personality, and an important goal of the political personality profile is to identify which political issues and decisions are especially salient for the leader's personality. Put more colloquially, the task is to identify which issues "hook" the leader's political personality and differentiate them from those that do not.

To be able to specify what those issue areas are and to identify deeply ingrained patterns that are consistent over time, it is essential to integrate the life experiences that shaped and gave form to that political personality. As Brewster-Smith (1968) has emphasized, that goes beyond the family environment and must encompass the historical, political, and cultural context as well. This emphasis on the life course and the entirety of the political personality, integrating longitudinal life course analysis with the cross-sectional analysis of personality, stands in contrast to the approaches of political psychology scholars who have focused on particular elements of political personality, such as political cognition, political drives and motives, and other traits.

The Methodology for Developing Political Personality Profiles

The method for developing political personality profiles is drawn from the clinical case study methodology, also known as the anamnesis, which integrates a longitudinal and cross-sectional approach. In the longitudinal consideration, the life course of the subject is reviewed, constructing a psychobiography. The cross-sectional approach analyzes the subject's cognition, affect, and interpersonal relationships, attempting to define the nature of the basic personality.

But in applying this approach to political figures, the method developed necessarily goes well beyond clinical case studies, focusing on life course and personality features that bear particularly on political leadership. In contrast to the psychobiographic reconstruction of the clinical case study of the psychiatric patient, in which the primary task is to analyze the traumatic events in the life course that predisposed to the present illness, in the psychobiographic reconstruction of the life course of a political leader, the goal is to understand shaping life events that influenced core attitudes, political personality, leadership, and political behavior. Similarly, in the cross-sectional personality study of a political leader, the goal is not to specify dimensions of psychopathology but rather to identify characteristic adaptive styles and those aspects of cognition, attitudes, affect, and interpersonal relations that bear on specific elements of leadership functioning, such as leadership style, crisis decision making, negotiating style, as well as the identification of those political issues that are especially salient for the subjects' psychology. An outline of the longitudinal and cross-sectional elements considered in constructing a political personality profile can be found at the conclusion of this chapter.

The Leader in Context

Drawing on Brewster-Smith's elegant map of personality and politics, and as modified in Stone and Schaffner (1988), the leader is envisaged as residing within a series of fields, the cultural, political, and historical context of his country, the specific aspects of the leader's background that shaped the individual, and the nature of the current political situation (see Figs. 4.1 and 4.2). The importance of that political and cultural context cannot be overestimated. Greenstein (1987) has observed in his seminal discussion of *action dispensability* that the degree to which leader personality affects political behavior is in part a function of the nature and flexibility of the political system. There is a profound difference in how personality will affect political behavior between a leader functioning in a collective leadership and a dictator functioning in a closed system. The manner in which the culture shapes expectations of the leader also shapes the formation and selection of the leader. The political figure who violates cultural norms will not survive long. In constructing a political personality profile, the degree of constraint upon the political behavior of the leader by his role and by the culture and nature of the political system is regularly examined.

The psychoanalytic framework of Erik Erikson ([1950] 1963), which relates personality development to the cultural context, is extremely helpful as a model. It emphasizes the intimate dynamic relationship between the developing personality and the environment and undergirds Brewster-Smith's emphasis on the cultural, political, and historical context in which the leader develops. Leader personality does not exist in vacuo; it is the leader in context that is our focus, the context that shaped the leader's development, the contemporary context that continues to shape and influence leader behavior and decision making. Before even considering the particular circumstances surrounding the development of the future leader, however, one must understand thoroughly the culture, especially the political culture, in which the leader's family was embedded. In these regards, the works of Pye (2000) and Kellerman (1991) are especially instructive.

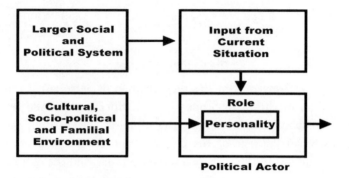

Fig. 4.1. Variables relevant to the study of personality and politics. (Also see Brewster-Smith 1968.)

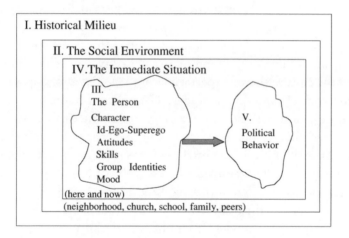

Fig. 4.2. Stone and Schaffner: Field model

The Life Course of Political Leaders: The Psychobiography

In developing the psychobiographic section of the political personality profile, the primary focus is on shaping events. It may be that several years can be captured in one sentence, while the details of a key afternoon may require several pages to depict and analyze. Thus the psychobiographic profile is envisaged as collapsing and expanding, by no means a merely linear and chronological depiction of life events. Early leadership successes and failures are particularly important to identify and analyze in detail, as they are often endowed with exaggerated importance in guiding future events. The manner of writing the psychobiography should prepare the reader for the detailed description of the political personality and analysis of leadership to follow.

In the psychobiographic reconstruction, particular attention is given to specifying the sources of political identity. Erikson's ([1950] 1963) emphasis on the formation and vicissitudes of personal identity is especially helpful in reconstructing the lives of political leaders, for as personal identity is consolidating so too is political identity. This requires careful research in the preceding generations. Thus the influence of King Abdullah, the grandfather of King Hussein of Jordan, on the development of Hussein as a leader was profound. A charismatic man of towering political stature, Abdullah was ashamed of his son Talal, who suffered from chronic paranoid schizophrenia. He early selected his grandson to play a special role in the history of Jordan and started shaping him to the role of future king. The boy was fifteen and at his grandfather's side on the steps of the Al Aqsa Mosque when his grandfather was struck down by an assassin's bullet. Young Hussein too was struck by a bullet but was reportedly saved from death by the medal on his chest that his grandfather had given him earlier that day—probably a powerful determinant of Hussein's sense of destiny (Snow 1972).

A psychobiographic nugget from which we can infer the degree to which a political leader was shaped to fulfill a parent's own ambitions is provided by the mother of David Hawke, former prime minister of Australia. When she looked in the crib after her newborn son was brought to her, she reported that she realized some day her son would be prime minister. Her prophecy was to be fulfilled, powerful confirmation of a mother's shaping her son to fulfill her own narcissistic dreams (Post 1986). Indira Gandhi recounted in her autobiography the influence of her grandfather, Motilal Nehru, twice president of India and prominent nationalist leader, and her father, Jawaharlal Nehru, four times president of India, who continued his father's struggle for Indian independence (Gandhi 1982). When her parents were away in prison, as they often were during her politically tumultuous childhood when they were struggling for independence, Indira Gandhi indicated she did not play with dolls but rather with toy metal soldiers. At the head of the column of soldiers was one with a white shield on which there was a red cross, suggesting her identification with Joan of Arc. She marched the soldiers into a fire again and again, suggesting the early foundation of her career long bent for conflict, perhaps presaging her ultimate martyr's death in her assassination by Sikh bodyguards in the Golden Temple. It is instructive to observe that she was characterized as "the goddess of destruction" by her political opponents and was seen as a leader who regularly promoted political conflict, lacking her parents' conciliatory skills.

Key Life Transitions

Erikson follows the course of personality over the life cycle, identifying the major crisis associated with each developmental epoch. Drawing on Erikson, Dan Levinson's (1978) work on the life course is instructive in focusing on the three major life transitions—the young adult transition, the mid-life transition, and the late adult transition. Levinson emphasizes that the successful negotiation of each life transition requires successfully weathering the challenges of the previous life transition. Levinson's work has important implications for the influences of the life cycle on the leader's political behavior (Post 1980, 1984). His emphasis on the role of what he calls the Dream and the importance of the mentor during youth is particularly important in understanding the influence of key life experiences in shaping political personality.

Foundations of the Dream: Childhood Heroes and Models

It is important to search for the foundation of political ambition—the Dream—the crystallization of political ambition that for some can serve as a lode star. Childhood heroes and models are important to identify. Young Anwar Sadat, for example, as a boy identified with Mohandas Gandhi and would cloak himself in a sheet, leading his goat around while on a self-imposed fast, the germs of his later role as peacemaker between Egypt and Israel that won him the Nobel Peace Prize.

The Dream, formed in adolescence, may be the spur to future greatness, a quest that can be accelerated when confronting major illness. Both King Hussein and Palestinian chairman Yasir Arafat had survived over the years by carefully assessing political risks. Hussein had never broken from major Arab constituencies; nor had Arafat, in his quest for an independent Palestinian nation, been willing to break from the radical absolutists in the Palestinian movement. But both leaders took major risks for peace in the wake of confronting their mortality, which emphasized that their time was limited to accomplish their goals. It was only after Arafat's helicopter crashed in the Libyan desert, killing the pilot and resulting six weeks later in a medical evacuation to the King Hussein Hospital in Amman for emergency brain surgery to remove blood clots on the brain, that he broke with the radical rejectionists and agreed to participate in the Oslo negotiations, leading to the remarkable handshake with Prime Minister Yitzakh Rabin of Israel in the Rose Garden and to the Nobel Peace Prize. Several weeks later, King Hussein was hospitalized in the same hospital to remove a cancerous kidney. Subsequently he entered into independent peace negotiations with Israel, his attempt to remove the stain on his historical record of losing custody over the holy sites in Jerusalem in the 1967 Arab-Israeli War and to fulfill his historic destiny. To be sure, his grandfather, Motalil, who had held meetings with Israeli Palestinian Jews in an effort to achieve peace, provided a positive model for such efforts, but the timing, coming as it did in the wake of his confrontation with mortality, suggests that this provided an impetus to abandon his customary caution and boldly strike out individually as he faced the ebbing of his life. From a distance, of course, we never can know to a certainty what drives and influences a leader, but, as this example makes clear, the more solidly we understand the foundations of the leader's identify and ambitions, the more confidently we can infer psychological influences on political behavior.

But reactions to frustrated dreams of glory have led to intemperate acts that have been destabilizing as well. The Shah of Iran had written of his mission for his country, what had been termed the White Revolution, his goal of transforming Iran into a modernizing Middle Eastern nation. When he was informed by his French physicians in 1973 that he was ill with a slowly developing malignancy, he accelerated dramatically the pace of his efforts. Breaking with the Organization of Petroleum Exporting Countries (OPEC), he quadrupled the oil revenues pouring into Iran, which had a poorly developed infrastructure. This led to a tidal wave of rising expectations, which destabilized the social structure, leading to profound discontent and setting the stage for Ayatollah Khomeini's Islamic revolution. In his rush to accomplish his dreams before he died, the Shah superimposed his personal timetable on the political timetable.

The Role of the Mentor

The role of the mentor in determining a leader's political behavior is extremely consequential, and it is important to subject it to careful analysis. Young Iosif Dzhugashvili (who was not to assume the pseudonym Stalin until twenty years later), oppressed by the rigors of the Orthodox seminary in Tbilisi, rebelled by smuggling in the works of Karl Marx and Vladimir Lenin. He came particularly to admire, indeed idealize, Lenin through his revolutionary writings and left the seminary to serve the cause of the revolution and assist his idealized mentor in pursuing that dream. But the contrast between Lenin as idealized model at a distance and Lenin as personal mentor was striking. A mentor is both a role model for political behavior, the source of important political ideas, and a teacher of the practice of politics, but a mentor also can be seen as an impediment to achieving power. Initially a loyal protégé, increasingly Stalin became restive under Lenin's leadership, seeking power and authority for himself, which led to a powerful confrontation between Stalin and his mentor when Stalin was in his early forties. Lenin subsequently suffered a disabling stroke, and Stalin went on to consolidate his power.

Another example of lifelong effects of a positive role model, although not as intense a relationship as that of Stalin to Lenin, is provided by Menachem Begin, who early came to admire the Zionist pioneer Vladimir Jabotinsky, whose dreams of a secure Jewish homeland were deeply influential and became consolidated within Begin as a core aspect of his political personality.

The Influence of Early Experiences

Autobiographic memoirs are a particularly rich source of material for determining the political behavior of leaders. With Menachem Begin we were fortunate to have not one but two memoirs: *White Nights,* which detailed his years in political exile in Siberia, and *The Revolt,* the story of his leadership of the underground resistance group Irgun in the struggle for Israeli independence. Begin recounts being seared by the experience of losing many of his family in the Holocaust, leading him to vow "Never Again," a psychological pledge that was to shape his oppositional political style. Prime Minister Felipe Gonzalez of Spain recounted the impact on him as a boy of living in the shadow of a political prison in the Franco years.

Psychologically Salient Issues

Referring again to figure 4.1, it is important to distinguish between those political behaviors that derive from the leader's role and those that engage his political personality. Discriminating which issues can be considered objectively and which strike deep psychological chords is crucial. Chiang Ching-kuo, president of the Republic of China, was judicious and objective in his considerations of economic policy for Taiwan, selecting world-class economists as his advisers and helping create the economic miracle of Taiwan. His primary political mentor, however, was his father, Chiang Kai-shek, which meant that the issue of relationships with mainland China could never be considered with the same rational objectivity and that progress toward ameliorating that conflictual relationship would have to await his death. As this example illustrates, it is important to identify which issues are salient for the leader's political psychology. However intense the family influences, the leader is exposed to the vicissitudes of the political environment to which he must react and adapt. The leader who cannot adapt to external realities because he rigidly adheres to an internally programmed life script has, in Laswellian terms, displaced his private needs upon the state and has rationalized it in the public good. Inevitably the gap between the private needs and the public needs becomes the source of ineffective and/or conflicted leadership.

The Political Personality Study

In the cross-sectional analysis, the political personality study, the goal is to identify and characterize the nature of the subject's personality, with particular reference to the political personality. Personality implies a *patterned relationship* among cognition, affect, and interpersonal relationships. Accordingly, *the organizing concept of personality implies a linkage among belief systems, value systems, attitudes, leadership style, and other personality features.* Put differently, *the nature of person-*

ality puts constraints upon information processing, the range of beliefs and attitudes, and the nature of relationships with the leadership circle, including who is chosen to serve in the inner circle, all of which influence political decision making.

Again, as with the longitudinal analysis and psychobiographic reconstruction in the previous section, careful attention is given to all of the traditional elements considered in the clinical case study,[1] but additional elements particular to political leadership are examined as well. Traditional elements of particular importance to political personality include intelligence; knowledge; drives and affects, including anxiety, aggression, hostility, activity and passivity, and shame and guilt; evaluation of reality; judgment; interpersonal relations, including capacity for empathy; identity and ambivalence; and characteristic ego defenses.[2] The additional elements applicable to political leaders include health (energy level, working hours, drinking, drugs); cognitive/intellectual style; and the drives for power, achievement, and affiliation. The latter are important in attempting to identify whether the leaders sought their leadership role in order to wield power, to be recorded on the pages of history, or merely to occupy the seat of power with the attendant place in the limelight.

Ego Defenses and Personality Types

It is particularly important to identify the characteristic pattern of ego defenses, for it is this repetitive manner of mediating between the subject's internal and external worlds that is at the heart of personality, the basis of the structure of character. The identification of patterns of ego defenses is a matter not of intuition but of pattern recognition. Well-trained clinicians will reliably identify the same characteristic ego defenses, but it does not require clinical training to be sensitive to and identify these patterns.

Clinicians and students of personality development have identified particular personality types, each of which has a characteristic array of ego defenses mediating between inner drives and the external world, each of which has its own cognitive, affective, and interpersonal style. In evaluating ego defenses, it is useful to discriminate a hierarchy of defenses, from the most primitive through the mature defenses.[3] Defenses do tend to aggregate, as exemplified by the so-called psychotic triad of denial, distortion, and delusional projection. This primitive, most seriously disordered pattern is associated with paranoid psychoses and severe paranoid disorders. In contrast, the obsessive-compulsive personality pattern, which will be described in detail shortly, is associated with a much healthier array of ego defenses, the neurotic (intermediate) defenses, which include dissociation, displacement, isolation (or intellectualization), repression, and reaction formation.

Identifying a characteristic pattern of ego defenses is especially helpful in predicting behavior under stress, for it is under stress that these coping mechanisms not only come into play but can become exaggerated. This is particularly true in the face of serious illness (Post and Robins 1993) and with increasing age (Post 1973). As people grow older, they do not mellow but become more like themselves, a veritable self-caricature. Thus the somewhat compulsive individual whose decision making was unimpaired in the early and middle decades can become paralyzed by indecision in the later years. This is apt to be particularly problematic in the face of a crisis, when, searching for certainty, an individual is required to make a decision in the face of ambiguous or conflicting information. The suspicious individual can become frankly paranoid under stress. Lavrenti Pavlovich Beria, the Soviet secret-police chief, was able to manipulate Stalin's paranoid tendencies to advantage himself by eliminating rivals. As with the case of Stalin and Beria, personality significantly colors interpersonal relationships and thus can significantly distort relationships within the leadership circle. The fragile narcissist whose ego is intolerant of criticism may be impelled to surround himself with sycophants who can significantly distort his appreciation of political reality.

In exaggerated caricatured form, each of these patterns of personality organization can be psychologically disabling, at which time they would be considered *personality disorders.* The essential features of personality disorders, according to the standard psychiatric diagnostic reference,

> are deeply ingrained, inflexible, maladaptive patterns of relating to, perceiving and thinking about the environment and oneself that are of sufficient severity to cause either significant impairment in adaptive functioning or subjective distress. Thus they are pervasive personality traits and are exhibited in a

wide range of important social and personal contexts. (APA 1994, 630).

Most of the major personality disorders, such as the avoidant personality, the dependent personality, and the schizoid personality, are clearly inconsistent with sustained political leadership; a leader exhibiting the characteristics of these disorders would not last long in the seat of power. On the other hand, other personality patterns, such as the narcissistic personality and the obsessive-compulsive personality, are disproportionately represented among political leaders. Though the paranoid personality is not common in the ranks of political leaders, when it occurs it can have catastrophic consequences for international relations. As previously noted, severe personality disorders are inconsistent with sustained political leadership, at least in democracies, but under the stress of crisis decision making, each of the discrete personality patterns can at least temporarily show features of the disorder, and prominent examples of leaders with the full-blown disorders are found in the pages of history, particularly in closed societies led by dictators. The stable pattern of defenses is also known as *character,* or the character armor (Reich 1933). The personality disorders referred to in this discussion are also called character disorders.

The Linkage between Personality Types, Belief Systems, and Leadership Styles

Particular personality types tend to be associated with particular belief systems and particular leadership styles.[4] A major element of personality—emotional needs and drives—will often constrain the range of beliefs (or the types of belief system) that individual will ultimately develop. Paranoid individuals consumed by fear of enemies will not develop an optimistic and benign worldview. Accordingly, discussions of cognitive factors should pay greater attention to the emotional determinants of beliefs and to the manner in which personality style affects decision rules and information processing. One can identify the cognitive approaches typically associated with particular personality types and emotional needs. Some previous political science studies of emotional factors have focused narrowly on only a few traits or needs rather than on larger stable constellations of related traits and needs, that is, personality types.

The differentiation among personality types described in this chapter provides a means of explaining an empirical conclusion that has dogged belief system approaches for some time; namely, that some individuals seem to be able to tolerate a great deal of inconsistency in their statements, espoused beliefs, and actions without any apparent ill effects from cognitive dissonance. For a personality type frequently encountered in political leaders, the narcissistic personality, it is extremely hazardous to infer core determinant political beliefs from public statements, so that the measurement of their expressed beliefs will demonstrate greater "ambiguity tolerance." To an extent much greater than for other personality types, the narcissistic individual often, indeed characteristically, publicly espouses beliefs only for immediate instrumental purposes, that is, for the immediate political or personal utility derived from their public association with these beliefs. Methodologically, it is important to treat the public expressions of beliefs of these individuals in a much different fashion than one would treat statements of individuals more inclined to consistency.

Misperceptions and distorted, apparently irrational, decisions can be produced by "motivated" biases, that is, those driven by emotional drives, or "unmotivated information-processing factors" or some combination of these. While certain types will be more prone to misperceptions and miscalculations than other types, nevertheless all types will have vulnerabilities under certain circumstances to particular types of suboptimal decision-making behavior. For example, the individual with a paranoid personality, for a variety of primarily emotional reasons, has a strong need to maintain his belief system intact. He had a particular disposition to see hostile intentions in his adversaries. The paranoid personality will be the most prone to motivated biases, the most prone to disregard information inconsistent with this belief system, and the least willing to reexamine past policies in light of new evidence. On the other hand, the obsessive-compulsive personality may engage in suboptimal decision-making behavior due to a somewhat more complex interaction of emotional needs and cognitive factors.

Knowledge concerning these personality types has not been sufficiently applied to the analysis of political leaders. Two of these personality types—the narcissistic personality and the obsessive-compulsive personality—are frequently encountered among political and military leaders. The third type, the paranoid personality, while rarer, can have major political consequences. These three personality types will be described in greater depth, and special aspects of their associated styles with implications for political functioning will be explored.

Personality and Political Behavior: Linkages among Cognitive Beliefs, Information Processing Styles, Organizational Propensities, and Political Preferences

In this section, each of the three personality types—narcissistic personality, obsessive-compulsive personality, and paranoid personality—will be discussed in relationship to two groups of factors important to political functioning. First, certain *cognitive factors* associated with each general personality type will be identified. Two different cognitive factors will be examined: cognitive beliefs and cognitive processes. Second, this section will look at certain *organizational propensities and policy preferences,* which would tend to flow from each of the personality types. Examination of the belief system in relationship to personality types will include the image of the adversary (e.g., George 1969, 1979), the beliefs about the role of conflict and the image of the international system (George 1979; Holsti 1977), and the beliefs about the manner in which war might start in a crisis. In some cases, associations between a particular personality type and an operational code belief system (Holsti 1977; Walker 1990) will also be made.

Cognitive beliefs are closely tied to other personality elements; affective needs and emotional drives can constrain the particular form of cognitive belief system that develops. Moreover, the presumption is that the stronger and more rigid the personality characteristics, the more frequently one would see systematic distortions that affect information processing associated with particular leader personality types. For illustrative purposes, crisis behavior will be the particular form of policy preference examined here. Crisis behavior would include such matters as the types of general approach to international crisis bargaining, the inclination toward the use of force in a crisis, and the negotiating style of that personality type in that crisis.

The Narcissist in Power

It is probably not an exaggeration to state that if narcissistic characters were stripped from the ranks of public figures, the ranks would
be significantly thinned.[5] The label *narcissism* covers a broad range of
behaviors. At the healthiest end of the narcissistic spectrum are ego-
tistical individuals with extreme self-confidence. But primitive narcissism, so-called malignant narcissism, represents an extremely
severe and dangerous personality disorder, which, in addition to
extreme self-absorption with an incapacity to empathize with others,
is characterized by a paranoid outlook, absence of conscience, and
willingness to use whatever aggression is necessary to accomplish
personal goals.

The following information summarizes the clinical description of
the narcissistic personality disorder as delineated in DSM-IV, the
Diagnostic and Statistical Manual of Mental Disorders (APA 1994). A
number of the features described have obvious relevance to the decision making and behavior of political leaders.

The essential features of the narcissistic personality disorder are
the following: a grandiose sense of self-importance or uniqueness;
preoccupation with fantasies of unlimited success; exhibitionistic
need for constant attention and admiration; characteristic responses
to threats to self-esteem; and characteristic disturbances in interpersonal relationships, such as lack of empathy, entitlement, interpersonal exploitiveness, and relationships that vacillate between the
extremes of overidealization and devaluation.

The exaggerated sense of self-importance tends to be manifested
as extreme self-centeredness, egocentricity, and self-absorption.
Abilities and achievements tend to be unrealistically overestimated,
but minor setbacks can give a sense of special unworthiness.

There is a preoccupation with fantasies involving unrealistic
goals. These goals may include achieving unlimited power, wealth,
brilliance, beauty, or fame. These fantasies frequently substitute for
realistic activity in pursuit of success. Even when the goals are
satisfied, it is usually not enough; there is a driven quality to the
ambitions that cannot be satisfied.

There is a constant search for admiration and attention and more
concern with appearance than substance. This quality too is insa-

tiable, so there is a constant need for reassurance, a constant concern for how well he is doing, how well others think of him, and an exaggerated response to criticism or defeat, which can lead to feelings of rage, inferiority, shame, humiliation, or emptiness.

Interpersonal relationships are regularly disturbed. Because these individuals are so self-absorbed, there is a failure of ability to empathize with others. Indeed, others are seen as extensions of the self and are there only to supply admiration and gratification, such that when an individual is no longer perceived as psychologically useful, he or she can be dropped suddenly. There is often an exploitative quality to interpersonal relationships. These individuals, who can be extremely charming, are often described as "sharks."

An aspect of the "special" quality of these individuals is the feeling of entitlement they convey. They expect special treatment from others, expect others to do what they want, and will be angered when others fail to live up to their unreasonable demands. They regularly ignore the rights and needs of others. There is accordingly a major inability to sustain loyal relationships over time.

There are a number of apparent contradictions in the narcissistic personality, because for each of the dimensions there is both an overt and covert aspect (Akhtar and Anderson 1982). Thus the overt picture of haughty grandiosity overlies feelings of inferiority, which helps explain the narcissist's continuous search for fame and glory. There is a hunger for acclaim and a tendency to change meanings of reality when self-esteem is threatened. The overt picture of zealous morality overlies a corruptible conscience.

The Narcissistic Personality: Implications for Leadership

The following discussion amplifies the characteristics described previously in order to highlight the manner in which narcissistic personality features influence the conduct of leadership. A notable aspect of the narcissist in power is the manner in which the narcissistic personality seeks to gratify his or her psychological needs through the exercise of leadership. Despite the apparent sustained devotion of their energies to socially productive endeavors, and the selfless rationales, the primary goal of the self-oriented narcissist is actually to gain recognition, fame, and glory. This search for recognition and adulation that drives these individuals springs from their excessive self-absorption, their intense ambition, and their grandiose fantasies. But underlying and impelling this quest is an inner empti- ness and uncertainty about identity. Helen Tartakoff, for example, has written of the Nobel Prize complex, the search for acclaim by intellectually gifted narcissists (Tartakoff 1966).

The interpersonal relationships of narcissists are regularly and characteristically disturbed. There is a quality of personal exploitive- ness, with a disregard for the feelings and needs of others. The nar- cissist surrounds himself with admirers and requires a constant stream of adulation from them. Yet it is a one-way street, and when the loyal followers are no longer useful to the psychological economy of the narcissist, they can be dropped suddenly without a backward glance. This precipitous fall from grace will frequently be bewilder- ing to the individuals dropped, who mistakenly believed they were highly valued by their hero. Indeed, their provision of psychological supplies of adulation was valued, but they had not been seen as sep- arate individuals, with needs of their own, but rather as an extension of the narcissist. The narcissist is often extremely charming and delightful to be with, contributing to the false spell cast over his intimates. Thus there is a characteristic difficulty in sustaining loyal relationships over time.

The mirror image of the quest for adulation is sensitivity to slight and criticism. The narcissist is vulnerable, easily hurt, and goes through complicated maneuvers to avoid being hurt. The narcissist can put on a mask of cold indifference and can envelop himself in what Volkan (1980) has called "the glass bubble." Like the Little Prince, the narcissists feel they live by themselves in splendid isola- tion, a glorious but lonely existence, enclosed by an impervious but transparent protection.

Because narcissists are so vulnerable to injury psychologically, they cannot afford to acknowledge ignorance. This in turn leads to major difficulties with learning, for the learning process carries with it an implicit assumption of lack of knowledge and it inhibits pro- foundly the acceptance of constructive criticism. Dogmatic certainty with no foundation of knowledge is a posture frequently struck by the narcissist. This discomfort with learning is related to the sensitivity to constructive criticism. If the narcissist's self-concept of perfection and brilliance is to be sustained, no one can give him new knowledge and no aspect of his understanding is to be faulted.

Volkan has emphasized that the narcissist in power has special psychological advantages in terms of sustaining his grandiose self-image. He can actually restructure his reality by devaluing or even eliminating those who threaten his fragile self-esteem. This leads to a tendency for the narcissistic leader to be surrounded by sycophants who sense their leader's need for uncritical adulation and agreement and who have been sensitized by the abrupt departure of advisers who dared to criticize or brought unpleasant news. Thus the narcissistic leader can be in touch with reality psychologically but by dint of surrounding himself with anxious sycophants can be totally out of touch with political reality. The savvy adviser in such circumstances will learn to provide recommendations to the narcissist in such a way that the leader believes it is his own idea, for example, "I agree with your suggestion that . . ."

The conscience of the narcissist is dominated by self-interest. Unlike the sociopath, who is without an internal beacon, without an internalized body of scruples and principles, the narcissist does indeed have a conscience, but it is a flexible conscience. He sincerely believes himself to be highly principled but can change positions and commitments rapidly as "circumstances change." The righteous indignation with which he stands in judgment of the moral failure of others often stands in striking contrast to his own self-concerned behavior. The sincerity of his beliefs is communicated in such a way that the unwary may be completely persuaded of the sincerity of the narcissist; and indeed, *at that moment,* he is sincere.

It is hard to identify the narcissistic personality with any consistent beliefs about the world, the adversary, and so forth, because these beliefs tend to shift. In addition, more than any other personality types, what the narcissistic personality says should be viewed as calculated for effect. Accordingly, to place great weight on the analysis of core determining beliefs from speeches when dealing with a narcissistic personality is apt to lead the unwary political analyst far astray. Words do not convey deeply held beliefs for the narcissist. Their only use is instrumental, to enhance his personal position and gain admiration and support. *The only central and stable belief of the narcissist is the centrality of the self. What is good for him is good for his country.* The interesting point here is that this attitude goes beyond "naked" self-interest. The individual comes to believe that the national interest and national security are in fact crucially contingent upon his reelection or reappointment.

The central tendency has interesting implications for the narcissist's image of the adversary. For one thing, the narcissistic personality has a profound inability to empathize or to understand different points of view, interests, or perspectives. Perhaps even more important, the narcissist tends to greatly exaggerate the degree of influence one can have on the internal politics or external actions of other nations. By far the most important cognitive heuristic for the narcissistic personality in trying to understand the world is with reference to his own personal experiences.

These characteristics of the narcissist make for certain serious problems in information processing and problem solving. Unlike the paranoid, who imagines problems that don't exist, or the obsessive-compulsive, who responds to real problems but in a futile, counterproductive manner, the narcissistic responds to a totally different sort of agenda. For the narcissist, the problems are not "What are the threats to our nation?" and "What can be done to meet these threats?" but "How can I use this situation to either preserve or enhance my own reputation?" Information search is undertaken in as public a manner as possible with a view toward eliciting public admiration and making the leader "look good."

Generally speaking, the narcissistic personality would show a preference for a style of management in which he or she is at the center and there is a heavy emphasis on support and teamwork from group members. Because of the narcissist's sensitivity to slight and the underlying fragility of his or her self-esteem, there would be strong pressure to avoid dissension to help meet this person's need for reassurance and to prevent the narcissist in power from looking bad. Moreover, because of the narcissist's need to be omniscient, to know everything, it is hard to present the consummate narcissist with new information. Such action would indicate his ignorance, which is unacceptable. The purpose of the group is not to generate new options or to provide additional cognitive capacity for evaluating these options and not even primarily for reasons of division of labor—its purpose is but to serve as a means for reassurance and supporting the personal needs for attention of the narcissistic individual. Yet if the followers of the narcissist are able to convey ideas to him or her in such a way that they seem to be embellishments of his or her own ideas, this can be effective, as long as they do not try to take credit themselves for the ideas. Bright individuals seeking to shine themselves do not last long in the circle of the narcissist. The narcissist in subtle fashion often plays one adviser against another to ensure that he is the supreme leader, the major domo. The narcissist in power is particularly apt to stimulate the collective decision-making malady of groupthink.

The Obsessive-Compulsive Personality in Power

The obsessive-compulsive (O-C) personality is frequently encountered in government and business executives, scientists and engineers, academic scholars, and military leaders. The strengths of this personality style—organizational ability, attention to detail, emphasis on rational process—all can contribute to significant professional success. But when these traits become exaggerated, the strengths can become disabilities. This extremity comprises the O-C personality disorder. The O-C personality places heavy reliance on the ego defense of intellectualization, emphasizing rationality and abhorring emotionality, which implies lack of control.

In summary form, the essential features of the O-C personality disorder are the following: preoccupation with matters of rules, order, organization, efficiency, and detail, with a loss of ability to focus on "the big picture"; indecisiveness; insistence that others submit to his or her way of doing things; excessive devotion to work and productivity to the exclusion of pleasure; serious and formal relationships with others; and restricted ability to express warm and tender emotions. These features will be described in detail to shed caricatured light on qualities that, in more subtle form, can systematically influence decision making and can adversely affect crisis decision making.

Although maximal efficiency and perfection are the idealized goal, they are, of course, never attained. Time is regularly poorly allocated, with the most important tasks left to the last moment. There is an inappropriate preoccupation with trivial details, causing the individual to lose perspective of the overall picture "not seeing the forest for the trees."

Decision making is either avoided, postponed, or protracted. This springs from an inordinate fear of making a mistake, for the overweaning goal of the O-C personality is to leave no room for error, to not make mistakes, to achieve perfection.

The O-C personality places a major positive value on work and productivity, to the exclusion of pleasure and the value of interpersonal relationships. When pleasure is contemplated, such as a vacation, it requires a great deal of planning and must be worked for. It is not uncommon for such individuals to keep postponing activities that are supposed to be pleasurable. The ranks of workaholics are heavily populated with O-C characters. But while there is intense preoccupation with work, it is often busywork, because of the tendency to become preoccupied with details. Thus an individual may spend hours locating a misplaced list rather than recreate the list from memory in a few minutes.

Frequently such individuals are excessively conscientious, moralistic, scrupulous, and judgmental of self and of others. Location in the interpersonal hierarchy is of great importance to individuals with this character type, and they are preoccupied with their relative status in dominant-submissive relationships. Although oppositional when subjected to the will of others, they stubbornly insist that others submit to their way of doing things and are unaware of the resentment their behavior induces in others.

These individuals have considerable difficulty showing warm and tender feelings and are stingy both with their emotions and with their material possessions. Their everyday relationships tend to be serious, formal, and conventional, lacking charm, grace, spontaneity, and humor. Wilhelm Reich (1933) has described these individuals as "living machines."

In his classic *Neurotic Styles,* David Shapiro (1967) focuses on three particular aspects of O-C cognitive style: rigidity, autonomy, and loss of reality. The rigidity of the compulsive character leads them to be described as dogmatic or opinionated. Such individuals are perceived as uninfluenceable. It is not that they oppose contrasting views; rather, they actively disattend to them in the service of persevering with their own views. The O-C will have a sharp focus, will indeed in examining the situation get the facts, but in getting the facts will not get the picture. As noted earlier, the individual "loses the forest for the trees."

The preoccupation with productivity and concentration imparts a special cast to the cognitive style and life-style of these individuals. They are immensely productive and show impressive abilities to concentrate on their work, often cranking out huge volumes of work, especially in technical areas. But everything seems laborious, determined, tense, and deliberate; there is a quality of effortfulness, leading to the frequent characterization of the O-C as "driven." Yet, as Shapiro notes, if the individual is driven, then he or she is the driver, for the O-C very much marches to his or her own drummer, is his or her own harsh taskmaster. The O-C is dominated by *shoulds* and *oughts*. These individuals regularly tell themselves (and others) what they should do; the language of "wants" is alien. There is a necessity to maintain a rigid and continuous state of purposeful activity.

The O-Cs then are not free men. While these directives, to which the O-C is subjected, are on the one hand burdensome, they also provide clear guidelines for behavior. These individuals do not feel comfortable with any nonpurposive activity. To relax for the sake of relaxation is unthinkable, indeed anxiety producing—thus the gravity with which leisure time activity is planned. The guarded state of attention, the inability to relax, the preoccupation with "should" are all in the service of avoiding the loss of control. There is a tight lid on feelings, an avoidance of impulse or whim.

The O-C personality has major consequences for decision making. The preoccupation with doing what is "right" places a premium on avoiding mistakes. O-Cs accordingly often have difficulty coming to decisional closure, searching for additional evidence to ensure they are not making a mistake. But they live in a world of ambivalence and mixed feelings, and their decision making is like that of the "fiddler on the roof"—"on the one hand, on the other hand." To travel through a decision-making process with a thoroughgoing O-C is an exhausting journey. And just as they apparently are coming to a decision, all of the doubts rush up to question, and often undo, the conclusion.

This decisional agony can be forestalled if there is a rule that can be applied. Thus if the elements of a situation fit a psychological template that is well established for the individual— "When one is in situation a, the right thing to do is b"—he or she can without thinking apply the formula. If there is no formula, however, the O-C will become quite anxious. Thus new and unanticipated situations are particularly threatening.

The preoccupation with detail can lead to a distortion of reality. Preoccupied with formulas, the O-C, as Shapiro (1967) notes, is concerned with what "fits" rather than what is. He gives the example of the obsessive man who said of the girl he planned to marry, "I must be in love with her—she has all the qualities I want in a wife."

As long as the formula fits, certain details and even major facts can be excluded from attention and ignored. This leads to the dogmatism noted earlier but can also lead to significant distortion of the capacity to evaluate reality.

The Obsessive-Compulsive Personality: Implications for Leadership

The O-C personality will typically take much longer to develop cognitive beliefs and will be much more uncertain as to the validity of these beliefs than the narcissistic personality. While the O-C personality might still ultimately develop a few fixed, black-and-white beliefs, more typically the O-C personality tends to see a world that is characterized by shades of gray. In fact, the world is seen as so complex and foreign policy is seen as so subtle that the O-C personality often despairs of his or her inability to make clear choices. The image of the adversary tends to be mixed, therefore. One is always in some state of uncertainty.

For the O-C personality, the drive in life is to achieve certainty, to try to put a modicum of order in a chaotic world. This perspective colors the O-C's view of the origin and nature of international conflict. International conflict is due first of all to lack of order in the international system; that is, international anarchy is at the root of international conflict. There may be other causes as well (e.g., aggressive motivations of some nations)—one never knows—but the anarchy is always a necessary contributing factor. As long as anarchy exists, conflict will persist.

The O-C is characterized more by rigidity in cognitive processes rather than by rigidity in cognitive beliefs. (This is in sharp contrast with the paranoid personality, whose beliefs are fixed.) The exact nature of these processes may vary from individual to individual; nevertheless, one can identify some commonalities among all O-Cs. One commonality is the decisional imperative: "Act only after gathering as much information as possible." Another related imperative is to "Preserve one's options as long as possible." Like the paranoid individual, the O-C individual will want to receive raw data. However, both the scope and the magnitude of these information requests are much greater in the O-C. The O-C will want to see the minutiae about almost everything. The strong preference here is to act later rather than sooner, preferring procrastination rather than the dangers of hasty action or "premature closure." Due to this lack of certainty, the O-C will have a strong tendency to opt, by default, for the status quo or perhaps make incremental change. The O-C has a strong bias for satisficing rather than optimizing.

The O-C personality will have a tendency to focus on concrete and quantifiable data rather than the abstract, nonquantifiable dimensions. This is an ironic development for the personality type, which more than any other tends to recognize the complexity of the world and tends to want to avoid "simplistic" understandings of issues. It is important to understand that the process the O-C adopts is counterproductive. When confronted with uncertainty (essentially, when faced with any policy decision), the O-C responds by becoming immersed in as many details as possible in a quixotic quest to somehow "fully understand" the issue. What happens is that this drive is so obsessive, and the data search and immersion in minutiae so extensive, that the O-C begins to lose perspective. Paradoxically, in the drive to understand the subtleties of the situations, the O-C is forced, unconsciously, to place a heavy reliance on very simplistic cognitive shortcuts, most particularly, to focus on concrete and quantifiable data rather than on abstract data. Eventually, he simply becomes overwhelmed with minutiae and raw data, and he begins to think of issues in terms of data. The use of quantifiable indices becomes a convenient and readily available shorthand for understanding the issue. Unlike the paranoid, who is more belief driven, the O-C is more data driven. The absence of definitive data is extremely anxiety producing.

Most O-Cs tend to prefer a formalistic style of management. This management style is most compatible with their strong need for order and regularity. Because of their strong need for raw data, however, many O-Cs would not be content with the summaries and general policy analysis of their immediate advisers. Instead, they would request—following normal channels—much of the raw data and subanalyses that went into these reports. Thus they have a great deal of difficulty delegating and relying upon subordinates, who, after all, might make a mistake.

The inclination of the O-C is to wait in a crisis rather than to take immediate, dramatic action. The O-C decides by default often to go with the status quo. As a natural consequence of their tendency toward procrastination and incremental responses, O-C personalities will tend to feel (probably accurately) that they are always "behind the power curve," that as much as they try, they can never seem to be quite on top of crises (and events in general). When a decision is forced, there is a strong imperative to adopt a middle or mixed course—one that preserves one's options as long as possible. In bargaining terms, the O-C personality would favor both the "carrot and the stick" rather than one or the other, or he or she would have a carefully prescribed sequence for introducing one and then the other. If escalation were to occur, it would be measured or incremental in nature; it would tend not to be dramatic. The O-C would be adverse to dramatic political-diplomatic solutions, as well as to major military escalation, because these might narrow one's options. In military actions or diplomatic activities, there is a tendency to elevate process over substance. The O-C personality may, for example, begin to see diplomacy as exclusively the procedures and the process.

Dominated by a strong conscience, the O-C personality is a "man of his word." When he has made a commitment in negotiations, he can be relied upon, in contrast to the narcissistic personality, who can reverse commitments as circumstances dictate. Moreover, to the extent that the O-C has committed to writing policy goals and preferences, these can be taken as a reliable map of intentions.

The Paranoid Personality

The essential features of the paranoid personality disorder are a pervasive and long-standing suspiciousness and mistrust of people in general. Individuals with this disorder are hypersensitive and easily slighted. They continually scan the environment for clues that validate their original prejudicial ideas, attitudes, or biases. Their affective experience is severely limited.

In *Neurotic Styles,* Shapiro (1967) describes in detail formal features of suspicious thinking, the sine qua non of the paranoid personality. A striking quality is pervasive rigidity. Suspicious people have something on their mind, and they search repetitively, and only, for confirmation of it. Suspicious people do not ignore new data but examine them extremely carefully. The goal of the examination is to find confirmation of their suppositions, dismissing evidence that disconfirms their fearful views and seizing upon what apparently confirms them.

In many life circumstances, being suspicious and on guard is both appropriate and adaptive. However, psychologically healthy individuals can abandon their suspicions when they are presented with convincing contradictory evidence. Paranoid individuals, in contrast, have a firm conclusion in search of evidence. Hostile, stubborn, and defensive, they will reject evidence that disproves their suspicions. Indeed, well-meaning attempts to reassure them or reason with them will usually provoke anger, and the "helpful one" may become the object of suspicions as well. Paranoids are hypervigilant, ever alert to a hostile interpersonal environment, always expecting plots and betrayal. They have a readiness to see themselves alone, surrounded by enemies. This explains why paranoia is the most political of mental disorders, because of the requirement for enemies.[6]

Paranoids tend to be rigid and unwilling to compromise. In a new situation, they intensely and narrowly search for confirmation of their bias with a loss of appreciation of the total context. They usually find what they anticipated finding. Theirs is a world of hidden motives and special meanings. They have a readiness to counterattack against a perceived threat and can become excited over small matters, "making mountains out of molehills."

Priding themselves on always being objective, unemotional, and rational, they are uncomfortable with passive, soft, sentimental, and tender feelings. They avoid intimacy except with those they absolutely trust, a minute population. They show an exaggerated need to be self-sufficient, relying on no one. They avoid participating in a group setting unless they are in a dominant position. Keenly aware of rank and power and superiority or inferiority, they are often jealous of and rivalrous with people in power. Their wary hypervigilance and readiness to retaliate often generate fear and uneasiness in others. One treads carefully around a paranoid, "walks on eggshells," lest he or she become upset.

Thus pervasive suspiciousness is at the core of paranoid individuals and colors every aspect of their behavior and thinking. The suspicious cognitive style of the paranoid has a number of formal characteristics, of which Shapiro (1967) considers *rigidity* the most fundamental one. Paranoids look at the world with fixed expectations. They know the Truth in advance and accordingly know what they are looking for. They will examine data extremely carefully, "seeing through" what does not confirm their expectations and seizing on the elements of the data that confirm their fixed beliefs. This rigidity, as Shapiro notes, has the quality of *directedness.* Their ideas are not the mere product of an overactive imagination but are the result of disproportionate attention to confirmatory details that are the result of intense and penetrating observation. What is the underlying premise that is being confirmed by this directed attention? It is the premise of *external danger.* Thus the essential cognitive feature of the paranoid is *a rigid, intentional search for external danger.* Because the premise of external danger is a fixed conclusion in search of confirmatory evidence, there is at the same time *intentional disregard of disconfirming evidence.*

In addition to the qualities of *rigidity* and *intentionality,* another key quality of paranoid individuals that influences their cognitive style is *hyperalertness and hypersensitivity.* Always on the alert for danger, their antennae constantly sweeping the horizon for signs of threat, paranoids will mobilize their rigid intentional cognitive mode in the face of anything unusual or out of the ordinary. Thus anything surprising is extremely distressing to an individual with this mind-set. Their world has been disturbed, their structure undone. A goal of the searching that is mobilized is to bring that which was out of control under control.

Clearly, insofar as paranoid individuals intentionally seek out only data that confirm their premise of external danger and systematically exclude evidence to the contrary, their evaluation of reality is often skewed. In effect, their views of external reality are distorted by their internal needs. In searching for details, paranoid individuals do not accurately place events in the totality of their context. The search for a particular kind of tree regularly has them not apprehending the quality of the landscape, be it forest or meadow.

The primary basis of the paranoid style's characteristic suspiciousness is an overreliance on the ego defense of *projection—the attribution to external figures of internal motivation, drives, or other feelings that are intolerable and hence repudiated in oneself.* Projection, as Shapiro notes, distorts the significance of apparent reality; it is an autistic interpretive distortion of external reality. It is regularly observed that there is usually a core of reality in a paranoid notion, that "projection is a compromise with reality," that "the paranoid meets reality halfway."

An important characteristic of the paranoid that has significant implications for leadership style but also affects cognitive style is the exaggerated need for autonomy. Paranoids are constantly seeking evidence that dangerous others are out to control them or to betray them. The only defense in such a dangerous world is to rely on no one, to exaggeratedly emphasize independence and autonomy.

Paranoid individuals guard against losing control of their feelings, especially warm, soft, tender, and passive feelings. This is in the service of avoiding submission, of yielding to another. There can be no yielding to pressure or authority. This exaggerated fear of submission is a reaction to a strong wish to submit, a wish that is unacceptable to the paranoid and must be avoided at all costs. Being on guard at all times against one's feelings blocks all spontaneity. There can be no humor or playfulness, and, absent spontaneity, there is clearly a major inhibition of creative expression. Shapiro (1967) has characterized this constant state of internal surveillance as "an internal police state." Like an army, the paranoid is constantly on alert, mobilized to counterattack against the ever-present danger.

Thus paranoids are simultaneously defending themselves against external danger and internal impulses, a burdensome and exhausting psychological war on two fronts. As internal tension builds, suspiciousness grows, and through the process of projection an external *and more manageable* threat is constructed. The individual then has a state of heightened alertness, a state of continuous, alert guardedness against the now external danger.

It is evident that individuals who view the world through a suspicious lens and are continually seeking to confirm their core premise of external danger, against which they must defend themselves, have significant constraints on their interpretation of the political world and their manner of dealing with it.

It is clear from the foregoing discussion that there are many similarities between the O-C personality and the paranoid personality. For both, there is a focus on detail, an emphasis on autonomy, and a guarded rigidity. But these qualities have significant differences too. The O-C fixes on details, while the paranoid searches for clues. The O-C is searching for certainty, while the paranoid is searching for confirmation of a fixed conclusion of danger. While the O-C is stubborn and obstinate, the paranoid is touchy and guarded. The O-C is dominated by conscience, by what he or she should do, whereas the paranoid is dominated by fear and is in a constant state of perceived external danger. There are many points of continuity, but the paranoid style is more extreme, more unstable, and more psychologically primitive.

The Paranoid in Power: Implications for Political Behavior

The paranoid personality tends to hold very strong, rigidly entrenched cognitive beliefs. Of all the personality types, this type is the one most motivated to seek to maintain internal consistency among cognitive beliefs—often at the expense of an "objective" examination of incoming information. The paranoid personality typically includes a belief system with a vivid and central image of the adversary. As one might suspect, the adversary is seen as inherently and pervasively evil and a major and incorrigible threat to one's own personal/national interest. There is little doubt that the adversary will respond to conciliatory goals by taking advantage of them. The paranoid personality, by definition, sees adversaries everywhere. Therefore, the individual sees the world in polarized terms. The paranoid's world is a Manichean universe, divided into two camps— allies and adversaries; neutrals are impossible. "If you are not strongly for me—you must be against me."

There is a powerful tendency to exaggerate greatly not only the hostile nature of the adversary's intentions but the adversary's political and military skill and ability to take threatening actions relatively unconstrained by logistical, chronological, or informational constraints. The paranoid personality tends to view the adversary as highly rational, highly unified, in total control of all his or her actions. People or nations are never compelled to do things by virtue of circumstances. Rather, their actions are always a product of their negative adversarial qualities. For example, there is no such thing as a "defensive" action by the adversary taken solely to protect their own security—all actions of one's adversary are necessarily "aggressive." The attitude toward the adversary's military capabilities is oddly mixed. On the one hand, there is a tendency to exaggerate the adversary's military capabilities as to the degree to which they threaten one's own interests—the paranoid assumes that they do. One can never safely assume that the adversary's military *potential* is so small that it will never become a threat, even if it isn't one now. On the other hand, the paranoid personality often exaggerates his or her own capability to temporarily (though never permanently) thwart the capabilities of this adversary.

The world is a conflictual place, and the source of conflict is the evil nature or character of other nations or people. War would never emerge in a crisis for inadvertent reasons; war occurs because of the nefarious, aggressive motivations of the adversary. Under no circumstances is international conflict attributed to anarchy or even to an absence of balance between forces in the system.

The information-processing style and cognitive heuristics of the paranoid personality are closely associated with the belief system described previously. There is often a heavy and very simplistic over-reliance on historical analogies that reinforce this black-and-white view of the world. In other words, when confronted with a new situation in world politics, the paranoid personality, like the narcissistic personality, would tend to say, "This is like what happened to me."

Precisely because of the rigidity of the beliefs and the central importance of the adversary image in the paranoid's worldview, this individual is heavily biased in favor of worst-case analysis of almost any incoming information. In fact, the information search pattern will be exclusively tactical in nature because the long-term objectives of the adversary are already known. The paranoid individual will seek information on the probable military or political ploys this adversary is likely to employ in this instance and the various counters to these ploys. An important related topic of interest will be information relating to the "enemy within" or "fifth column activity." The adversary is believed to be very creative and devious in this sort of covert subversion, and people of one's own nation who do not fully share the views of the paranoid leader are believed to be either suspect themselves or, at best, naive, unwitting dupes.

Faced with the need to make a decision, the paranoid personality will manifest a strong tendency to act sooner rather than to procrastinate, out of fear that "he who hesitates is lost."

The paranoid personality will gravitate toward one of two management styles described by Alexander George (1991). The paranoid in power will adopt either a competitive style or a formalistic style. The decision will be made largely on the basis of whether that individual can identify a few individuals that he or she can trust. If he or she can, there will often be a propensity for a formalistic style with all information and contacts funneled through these few (often one or two—and certainly no more than a handful) uniquely trusted individuals. More often, however, the paranoid will adopt a management style that is closer to the competitive model described by George. The assumption is that one can't trust any one source of information or any one concentration of power. So to garner diverse information and, most important, to prevent the rise of any potential internal threats, the paranoid leader adopts a management style that seeks to play one adviser or one bureaucracy off another one. Paranoid political decision makers, especially those with a competitive management style, will often manifest an almost insatiable desire for raw data. They will typically not be satisfied with the analyses and conclusions of people working under them. The manipulative subordinate can take advantage of the paranoid leader's suspiciousness to plant suspicions concerning bureaucratic rivals, as did Beria with Stalin.

Because of the paranoid's image of the world as very conflictual and because of the image of the adversary as incorrigibly aggressive and politically devious, the paranoid leader has a strong preference for the use of force over persuasion. In other words, the leader would prefer a fait accompli that directly affects the capabilities of the adversary to a coercive threat that tries to affect the willingness of the adversary to threaten. The point is to alter leadership or capabilities of adversaries rather than try to "persuade" the adversaries not to do something or to alter their behavior. In a crisis, there is a strong preference for what is seen as preemptive action. The paranoid may even initiate a crisis or a war out of the belief that preventive action against the adversary is necessary and that one might as well "strike while the iron is hot"; that is, since the adversary is preparing to act, it is preferable to act first while the military balance is more in one's favor.

In those instances when the use of brute force is not seen as practically feasible, then coercion through threat of military retaliation (deterrence or compellance) becomes the preferred method of crisis bargaining. A preponderance of force is preferable to a balance of force or to rough equivalence to help one achieve this coercion. This preponderance has no practical limits because the paranoid can never be satisfied that he or she has attained enough arms or military capability. Negotiations and diplomacy may be viewed as either largely efforts that ratify the military status quo or exercises in Machiavellian deception and counterdeception. Accommodation is used only to lull the adversary into lowering his guard.

Having described these pure character types in detail for illustrative purposes, it is important to emphasize that most individuals, and most leaders, possess a broad array of characteristics that do not fit one pure type. Rather, it is the predominance of one style over another that affects outcomes.

The healthy leader personality has characteristics that contribute to effective leadership, to sound decision making, to accurate diagnosis of the environment, and to effective work with a leadership circle chosen for their expertise and wisdom and from whom the self-confident leader can learn and take wise counsel.

Concluding Thoughts

What the single case studies provide that is particularly valuable is a longitudinal perspective that offers a framework for understanding the manner in which previous life experiences help shape and influence political behavior and help distinguish between political behaviors that are role dependent and those that reflect strong personality influences, where leader personality is particularly engaged by the political circumstances. A key aspect linking the psychobiographic and psychodynamic approaches is understanding psychological themes ingrained during adolescence that psychologically continue to influence throughout the life cycle. As has been emphasized, dreams die hard, and pursuit of the dreams of glory formed during adolescence can drive a leader throughout his lifetime, having special force at the midlife transition and during the later years' transition.

A significant emphasis of the approach described for developing the political personality profile is identifying stable and enduring aspects of leader personality, including cognitive, affective, and interpersonal elements. Implying a linkage between belief systems, attitudes, and leadership style, the nature of personality puts constraints upon information processing and the nature of relationships with the leadership circle. Leader personality importantly influences negotiating behavior as well as crisis decision making. Because personality is stable over time, the longitudinal approach helps identify enduring patterns of behavior.

Three important leader personality types—the narcissist, the obsessive-compulsive, and the paranoid—and their implications for political behavior have been described at length to illustrate this important principle. These patterns are deeply ingrained and, when present, permeate all aspects of political behavior—crisis decision making, strategic decision making, negotiating behavior, worldview, and relationships with the leadership circle. The centrality of the self for the narcissist influences all aspects of political behavior. The narcissist's sensitivity to slight and need to be seen as all knowing and perfect tends to lead to a sycophantic leadership circle. The flexible conscience makes the narcissist's use of words instrumental, with no organized belief system, and commitments can change as circumstances change. For the obsessive-compulsive, there is a tendency to get lost in details. The search for certainty can be particularly troubling in crisis situations, leading to procrastination and indecisiveness. The centrality of intellectual processes and the strong conscience of the obsessive-compulsive have important implications for negotiations, as well as the ability to identify central beliefs from language. The dominance of paranoid individuals' conviction that enemies surround them colors not only their view of political adversaries but also interferes with their capacity to trust their own advisers. Because these personality patterns are so deeply ingrained, they can be detected early in a political career and can reliably be predicted to continue to affect leadership behavior throughout the political career and become intensified with stress. These personality qualities do not mellow with age. Indeed, these characteristics tend to become intensified with the passage of years.

Appendix: Conceptual Framework and Organization Design for an Integrated Political Personality Profile

Jerrold Post

PART I. Psychobiographic Discussion: The Development of the Individual in the Context of the Nation's History (*use parallel time lines*)[a]

1. Cultural and historical background. Describe constraints of the political culture on the role of leader.
2. Family origins and early years
   a. Family constellation—grandparents, parents, siblings; relationships—politics of family
   b. Heroes and models
3. Education and Socialization
   a. Climate in country
   b. Student years, examples of leadership
4. Professional career
   a. Mentors
   b. Early career
   c. Successes and failures
5. The subject as leader
   a. Key events
   b. Crises
   c. Key political relationships, influences
6. Family and friends

PART II. Personality

1. General personal description
   a. Appearance and personal characteristics (include description of lifestyle, work/personal life balance, working hours, hobbies, recreation)
   b. Health (include energy level, drinking, drug use)
2. Intellectual capacity and style
   a. Intelligence

---

[a] The analyst is required to develop two time lines, one indicating key events in the life of the subject, the second indicating key events in the nation's history. By moving these lines parallel, a visual representation is created of the impact of historical events on individual development.

    b. Judgment
    c. Knowledge
    d. Cognitive complexity
3. Emotional reactions
    a. Moods, mood variability
    b. Impulses and impulse control
4. Drives and character structure
    a. Identify personality type (if possible)
    b. Psychodynamics
        i. Self-concept/self-esteem
        ii. Basic identification
        iii. Neurotic conflicts
    c. Reality (sense of/testing/adaptation to)
    d. Ego defense mechanisms
    e. Conscience and scruples
    f. Psychological drives, needs, motives (discriminate to degree possible among drive for power, for achievement, for affiliation)
    g. Motivation for seeking leadership role (to wield power, to occupy seat of power, to achieve place in history)
5. Interpersonal relationships
    a. Identify key relationships and characterize nature of relationships
        i. Inner circle, including unofficial advisors, "kitchen cabinet"
        ii. Superiors
        iii. Political subordinates
        iv. Political allies, domestic and international
        v. Political rivalries, international adversaries

PART III. Worldview
1. Perceptions of political reality (include cultural influences/biases)
2. Core beliefs (include concept of leadership, power)
3. Political philosophy, ideology, goals, and policy views (domestic, foreign, and economic policy views and view of U.S. Include discussion of which issues most interest the leader, in which issue areas his or her experience lies, and which issues are particularly salient for the leader's political psychology). Note that not all leaders have a core political philosophy or body of governing political ideas.
4. Nationalism and identification with country

PART IV. Leadership Style
1. General characteristics (include discussion of the role expectations—both general public and elite—placed on the individual, emphasizing the leader's political and cultural determinants and skill in fulfilling them)
    a. How subject defines his or her role
    b. Relationship with public
    c. Oratorical skill and rhetoric

2. Strategy and tactics—goal-directed behavior
3. Decision making and decision implementation style
   a. Strategic decision making
   b. Crisis decision making
   c. How does leader use staff/inner circle? Does the leader vet decisions or use them only for information? How collegial? Does the leader surround himself or herself with sycophants or choose strong self-confident subordinates?
   d. Dealing with formal and informal negotiating style

PART V. Outlook
   1. Note particularly political behavior closely related to personality issues. Relate personality to key issues, emphasizing in which direction the psychological factors point. Estimate drives, values, and characteristics that are the most influential.
   2. Attempt to predict how the individual will interact with other political figures, including opposition leaders and other key foreign leaders.

Notes

1. Traditional elements include appearance; level of activity; speech and language; intelligence; knowledge; memory; thought content and delusions; drives and affects, including anxiety, aggression, hostility, sexuality, activity and passivity, shame and guilt, and depression; evaluation of reality; judgment; interpersonal relations, including capacity for empathy; identity and ambivalence; and characteristic ego defenses.

2. For an excellent example of the systematic application of the traditional elements of psychiatric diagnosis applied to a historical figure, see the psychopathological assessment of Adolph Hitler in Redlich1998.

3. Drawing on the works of early neo-Freudian Elvin Semrad, Vaillant (1992) has identified four levels of defensive organization. He identifies the psychotic triad of denial, distortion, and delusional projection as representing the most primitive level of psychological organization. The immature defenses include projection, passive aggression, acting out, and fantasy. The neurotic (intermediate) defenses include dissociation, displacement, isolation (or intellectualization), repression, and reaction formation. Mature defenses include suppression, sublimation, and altruism.

4. This discussion of the relationship among three key personality types, leadership style, and worldview draws on Post and Rogers 1988.

5. This section draws significantly on Post 1992.

6. See Robins and Post 1997. This volume offers an extended treatment of the political manifestations of paranoia. A number of the key points expanded at length in Robins and Post 1997 are summarized in a preliminary article (Robins and Post 1987).

5. Psychoanalytic Assessments of Character and Performance in Presidents and Candidates: Some Observations on Theory and Method

Stanley A. Renshon

Modern democracies place individuals at their helm with access to immense power and, of necessity, grant them enormous discretion in its use. Therefore, the competence and integrity in exercising the authority with which the leaders of democracies are entrusted is no minor matter. Leaders who corruptly or ineptly use the awesome means at their disposal endanger not only the success of the policies they propose but the fabric of trust and hopeful expectation that binds citizens to each other and their institutions. In short, the psychology of presidents matters enormously. Their ambition, values, integrity, and ways of dealing with the issues they face make a profound difference in the success or failure of their time in office.

Understandably, Americans have become increasingly interested over the last four decades in trying to learn something about the personal characteristics of their leaders. This interest has, however, been repeatedly frustrated and in some cases thwarted. What are the personal and professional standards by which one can reasonably evaluate presidential candidates? Is every personal characteristic of a candidate a matter of political concern, and, if not, which ones are and why? Finally, even if we agree that certain personal qualities do have important implications for how presidents approach and carry out their responsibilities, the question remains, How are we to discern these qualities without relying on candidates' views of themselves?

After all, as the public has become more concerned with the personal qualities of its leaders, they in turn have become increasingly sophisticated in presenting themselves as they would prefer to be seen rather than as they are.

Any answer to the question of what personal qualities are important in a president necessarily directs to psychology to help answer the question. However, as Greenstein (1969) pointed out some years ago in his seminal consideration of the dilemmas that political scientists face in turning to psychology, they more often find rival theories and unanswered questions than easily borrowed solutions. Moreover, deciding which psychological theory or theories to use does not fully resolve all the issues involved in such an effort. One needs not only a theory of psychology but a theory of leadership performance with which to link it.

Presidential Performance: Which Psychology?

Let us begin with trait psychology. Americans have, for many years, routinely evaluated leaders on their personal and political traits, for example, integrity, leadership, and even intelligence (cf. Krosnick and Kinder 1990). The use of traits to evaluate presidential candidates has much to recommend it. Traits seem distinct and specific and, from the standpoint of assessment, amenable to measurement at a distance. We can generally tell if a candidate appears well informed, at ease under pressure, or charismatic.

Moreover, in some instances, the relationship between a trait and a desirable political capacity seems self-evident. It is easy, for example, to see why a candidate's honesty is important when citizens are often asked to accept a president's statements about policy actions and the reasons for it. So, too, a concern with a candidate's intelligence would seem to be related, if not always directly, to an ability to grasp and perhaps resolve complex public problems.

As intuitively appealing as trait evaluations might be, however, there are a number of substantial problems in using isolated traits as the primary tool of candidate assessment. For example, a singular focus on intelligence as IQ may obscure other personal or cognitive skills that might inform skillful presidential decision making or judgment. Moreover, a focus on intelligence as an isolated trait neglects to ask the purposes to which intelligence is put. That, of necessity, involves us in a consideration of an individual's motivations.

Rather than considering traits in isolation, it is useful to consider a theory of psychological functioning that focuses on broad patterns of motivation and the more specific patterns of personality and behavior that develop from it. One advantage of such a theory is that it provides a theoretical link by which any particular personality trait might be more firmly anchored in a deeper understanding of its role in the person's overall psychology. In doing so, it provides some insight into the ways in which particular traits, viewed in the context of a person's overall psychology, affect or might be more usefully viewed in relationship to responsibilities of office. A strong intelligence embedded in and shaped by a strong motivation to do what is "right" will differ from one embedded in a motivation structure dominated by self-interest.

An obvious candidate for such a theory is psychoanalytic theory. Early psychoanalytic theory and its more sophisticated successors provide a broad view of human motivation and psychological functioning. It is also a framework whose theoretical source is found in everyday behavior. As a result, it is a theory rich in possibilities for understanding the responsibilities and performance of political leaders.

However, like every other theory, it has several drawbacks as well. Although all psychoanalysts accept the existence of unconscious motivation, the importance of early experience as a foundation of an individual's psychology, and the view that individuals develop stable and understandable patterns of adult functioning that reflect how they have been able to integrate their experiences, skills, and circumstances, there is no single psychoanalytic theory. Some focus on the primacy of childhood; others stress adulthood. Some focus on the internalization of object representations; others stress the importance of interpersonal relations. Some view motivation through the prism of instinctual drives; others view it through the prism of what it takes to develop and maintain a coherent, vital sense of self. Greenstein's (1969) well-taken point is as relevant for different kinds of psychoanalytic theory as it is more generally for theories of psychological functioning. The theoretically sophisticated and contextually sensitive analysis by the Georges (1956) of the impact of Woodrow Wilson's formative childhood and adult experiences on his substantial political accomplishments is an exemplar of such analysis.

Derived from psychoanalytic theory, the present framework for the analysis of presidential candidates and others leaders (developed in Renshon 1996a, 1996b) is guided by several considerations. Among these is the consideration to develop a framework for analyzing character psychology (1) that focuses on a character's nature and specific content rather than argues its importance primarily on its dynamic functioning; (2) that does not require information only available, if at all, in a psychotherapeutic setting; and (3) in which the theory of character and psychological functioning could be directly and plausibly linked with the analysis of leadership performance.

Character as a Framework for the Analysis of Presidential Performance

The term *character* is derived from the Greek word χαρακτηρ, which means "engraving." Allport (1961, 2–3), in his classic work on personality theory, defines character as "a person's patterns of traits or his lifestyle." He distinguishes the term *character* from *personality*. According to Allport, personality denotes "appearance, visible behavior, surface quality," while character implies "deep (perhaps inborn), fixed and basic structure." Baudry reaffirms that the term *character* refers to

> the broadest grouping of stable, typical traits by which we recognize a particular person. Our concept of character is made necessary that we find in individuals reoccurring clusters of trait with a degree of consistency suggesting that some underlying principles govern the selection, ordering and relations of these traits to one another. (1989, 656)

The early understanding of character reflected three basic clinical observations: (1) it was central to an individual's psychological and social functioning, (2) its consequences could be observed in stable patterns of public behavior, and (3) it was present and observable in diverse circumstances, though, contrary to the views of some "situational psychologists," each character element is not required to be equally present in all circumstances. Situations may call forth character elements or alternatively may inhibit them. Some situations might be more highly resonant with a person's history or needs than others and thus be more likely to engage character elements. Unfortunately, the early understanding of character grew out of clinical practice with its emphasis on disturbance of function. The view of character as essentially the sum of a person's defensive mechanisms or his or her deficient resolution of psychological or developmental dilemmas does not provide a useful guide for the analysis of character in our political leaders, who are not prone to reveal their innermost fears and characteristics and who indeed strive to present themselves in the best light possible. Moreover, focusing as it does on explaining deficiencies and disruptions of psychological functioning, this view of character does not provide much help, as most leaders have substantial character strengths and skills.

How then can we better conceptualize character? We begin by pointing out that character differs from other psychological features in that it is pervasive across time, circumstance, and interior psychology, including belief systems, information processes, and all the other elements that orient individuals for work. Beliefs, attitudes, and even neuroses typically represent only small parts of the total personality system. Each may be relevant to, and therefore engaged only in, limited areas of functioning. Character, on the other hand, stands at the core of the personality system and is the basic foundation upon which personality structures develop and operate. The development and operation of character shape beliefs, information processing, and ultimately styles of behavior. Character is, therefore, deeply embedded in the most basic and important foundation of psychological functioning.

From this perspective, character is not conceptualized as a leader's supreme virtue or failing but rather as a set of psychological patterns that he or she brings to every circumstance. Character, in this sense, is the answer to the question of how we can best understand a leader's psychology. It is the foundation of one's stance toward the world. It reflects the fundamental elements at the core of people—their basic ambitions, the ideals and values by which they live, and their relationships with others. Although character runs deep, knowledge of it does not necessarily require leaders to expose themselves to psychoanalytic inquiry. We get to know a person's character in the presidency, as in ordinary life, by paying attention to the steady accumulation of choices we see him make, both in and away from the public spotlight. Character is reflected as much in a president's observable behavior as it is in the deepest recesses of his psyche.

The Character-Performance Framework

The framework developed in Renshon 1996b and applied to President Clinton (Renshon 1996a) and later to Republican presidential candidate Robert Dole (Renshon 1998a) draws on a theory of character with three major elements. *Ambition* is the domain of a person's aspirations and the skills that he or she has developed to realize them. We must all figure out what we want to do in life and refine the skills that help us realize these ambitions, if we are to be successful.

Character integrity is the domain of a person's ideals and values—the moral, ethical, and motivational principles that provide a true-to-self compass through choices. Every person must develop principles for navigating life's inevitable, but often unclear or difficult, choices. Some will aspire to high ideals but will fail to put them into practice. Others will be guided primarily by self-interest but will present their choices as if they are in the public's interests. A smaller number will struggle to remain faithful to their ideals, even when it is difficult to do so.

Relatedness refers to the domain of our interpersonal relationships, the nature and quality of our relationships with others. Every person exists and lives in an ocean of others. Others are our friends and our enemies, our allies and our competitors, and our most trusted and intimate relations; we may move toward, away, or against others, or stand apart from them, but we cannot avoid them (Horney 1937). They are as central to our emotional lives as oxygen is to our physical ones.

It is important to underscore that these three elements of character serve as a framework for analysis. They reflect a theory hinging on the proposition that the three elements are essential and interrelated. However, unlike Barber's ([1972] 1992) theory of presidential character or Lasswell's (1930) theory of democratic or political character types, this framework has no pretensions to exhaustive, mutually exclusive categorizations. Rather, from the perspective of this framework, it remains to be determined in each particular case just how each of the character elements is related, individually and in combination, to the essential elements of leadership performance. With this framework, each element requires the reality of data to give it meaning, and any particular package of elements represented by an individual's psychology is a matter that emerges from the data, not from placement in a category.

The framework also does not make or require a priori assumptions about the way(s), if any, each or several of the character elements are related to the twin pillars of presidential performance, judgment in decision making and political leadership.

Applying the Framework

The theory underlying the framework of analysis developed in *The Psychological Assessment of Presidential Candidates* (Renshon 1996b) focuses on selecting American presidents. Yet, as noted in the book, it was not intended to be a theory of presidential character. The framework consists of two parts: a theory of character and a theory of presidential role performance.

Let us first consider the importance of ambition in presidential candidates. The book argues that the nature of the modern presidency and what was needed to obtain it made high ambition more of a given than a variable. That is, almost all candidates could be assumed to have strong ambition since the investment necessary to try and obtain the office would mitigate against those who didn't "really want it." Even Ronald Reagan, whose somewhat passive executive style in the presidency has been much commented on, spent many years and much time reaching for that office.

Of course, the fact that most modern presidential candidates are highly ambitious still leaves open the questions of what their skills are and whether these skills support or impede the candidate's ambition. It is possible that one's skills support the level of one's ambitions, are greater than one's ambitions, or don't measure up to one's ambitions. Also, the assumption of high ambition in the presidency leaves open the issue of the relationship between skills and ambition on the one hand and political performance on the other.

The uniformly high ambition of modern presidential candidates results in focusing more attention on the other two character elements as possible sources of useful distinctions. Certainly, specific ideals and values would seem to be a more variable and therefore more useful tool to differentiate among candidates, as would capacity for remaining faithful to ideals and values.

This brings us to a second important point about the framework. The relationship of its two major elements, character and performance, is contingent. Character is a constant. Ambition, character integrity, and relatedness are central parts of anyone's interior psychology, regardless of the political roles being analyzed. Yet, the reverse is not true.

Different roles call on character psychology differentially. One of Bill Clinton's ambition-supporting skills was his verbal facility, certainly important for a political career and particularly important to the leadership performance dimension of the modern presidency. Bob Dole, on the other hand, had a number of skills to support his ambition, but being articulate was not among them. In a governing context in which "going public" is one key tool of presidential leadership, to be inarticulate is a terminal disability. Yet, public verbal facility as an ambition-supporting skill was clearly less important in Dole's role as Senate minority/majority leader than it was for his attempt to gain the presidency.

The framework begins with the view that essential performance characteristics of different political roles are different for each role. The two chief dimensions of presidential performance are judgment and leadership. Are these two dimensions equally important for judges and members of Congress? That remains to be seen. One might argue that leadership, or judgment, is important in both these public roles and perhaps others as well. However, judicial or congressional leadership would seem to differ from each other, and both differ from leadership in the presidency. Just as each character element requires understanding in the context of a specific individual, so too does each element of performance to which it is tied.

Finally, there is the question of whether this framework is useful cross-culturally. Would the three elements of character help us to understand political roles in, for example, India or Brazil? The focus on character arises from the fact that performance measures of role enactment are always dependent on the particular nature of the role in its historical, political, and cultural context.

The problem can be illustrated with a question: How does one gauge the degree of ambition in Japan? In that culture, the direct expression of self-interest, and the desire to stand out at the expense of others, is taboo. How, then, would one assess the relationship between ambition and political performance there? What does political leadership mean in such a cultural context? These and related questions will have to be addressed and resolved before the framework can be usefully applied outside of the context for which it was developed.

Theory and Evidence: Some General Considerations and Concerns

The interplay between theory and evidence in applying psychoanalytic theory to biography is complex. Psychoanalytic theory, especially as it has developed since Freud first formulated it, is a powerful tool for understanding the interior psychology and public behavior of those in political life. The psychoanalytically framed analysis of political leaders and leadership has benefited from the extraordinary accomplishments of some of its early pioneers, such as Harold Lasswell, Alexander and Juliette George, Erik Erikson, and others. But, in the hands of some of its more enthusiastic though less thoughtful practitioners, psychoanalytically oriented psychobiography is prone to errors of reductionism in its various forms.

Reductionism is the error of attributing too much to too little. It is a form of theoretical grandiosity and is reflected in several patterns of analysis:

- a tendency to give too much causal weight to a person's psychology and too little to role and circumstances;
- a tendency to reduce a person's psychology to one or a few conflicted elements with little weight given to the skills and areas of psychology that have brought the person to high political office;
- a tendency to think that an analyst can intuit the unconscious motivation of others' behavior; and
- a tendency to explain large-scale social or historical events by terms describing individual psychology.

The common defect in all these errors is the failure to treat an individual's psychology as part of a composite explanation in which the causal weight to be assigned to any particular element is a matter to be determined.

Some psychoanalytically inclined analysts add to these theoretical errors others of a more personal nature. Character psychology and its relationship to leadership performance is complex. Those who undertake such analyses should be comprehensively trained in the theory and practice of the disciplines they purport to apply. Reading Freud alone no more prepares one to undertake a psychoanalytically informed analysis of a leader at a distance than does being able to read musical notes prepare one to conduct a symphony.

One further difficulty that needs to be addressed here is the tendency for some practitioners, both trained and untrained, to make use of unconscious motivation in their analyses. Recently, one well-known analyst and his collaborator (Lifton and Mitchell 1996) "explained" the unconscious conflicts that led President Truman to drop two atomic bombs on Japan. Another (Volkan, Itzkowitz, and Dodd 1997) thought it possible to make us privy to the unconscious thoughts that Richard Nixon's mother had about her son early in her marriage.

By definition, unconscious motivation is not known to the person motivated by it. Less appreciated is that, even in a psychotherapeutic context, solid information about the unconscious motivation emerges slowly and tentatively and is often subject to revision in light of new material. The unconscious underpinnings of behavior originate, and then develop, through a complex and ongoing process. The fact that an event happened that is considered important in one or another version of psychoanalytic theory does not automatically bestow causal significance upon it.

Consider a presidential candidate with a cold and distant father or mother. Many have grown up with such experiences, but they do not necessarily result in uniform outcomes. Along with knowing that events have happened, it is important to understand what their meaning was to the person involved, the ongoing context in which they occurred, as well as any mitigating factors that may be relevant.

In psychoanalytic psychotherapy, the meaning of these early experiences is varied and complex. Meaning emerges with some clarity, if at all, only after a period of sustained analysis and reflection on the experiences, often from a number of vantage points. Through this process, the meaning of these experiences *to the patient* gradually becomes clear, as does the role of the experiences in the patient's development and the ways in which they have become a part of, but not synonymous with, adult behavior. In the absence of any real capacity to meticulously trace events and their subjective meaning to the person, the analysis of unconscious motivation is speculative.

Evidence for a Psychoanalytic Analysis of a Political Leader

An analyst developing a psychologically framed biographical analysis or profile of a president or candidate operates at three different levels.[1] First, he or she operates at the level of historical fact. What are the key events? What evidence is there that the event(s) took place and as described? Did Democratic candidate Al Gore really learn to plow fields as a young boy? He did. Did Bill Clinton really grow up in the harsh economic circumstances that his stories about an outhouse on the family property suggest? He did not. Establishing the authenticity of facts that are relevant to the analysis is critical.

Second, the analyst operates at the level of interpretation and meaning. What does it mean that George W. Bush's father was president or that both he and Al Gore come from families with generations of high-level public service behind them? What were the psychological consequences of Bob Dole's severe war wounds? What are we to make of Al Gore's bifurcated childhood growing up both in rural Tennessee and at the posh Mayflower Hotel in Washington?

Third, the analyst operates at the level of theory. How shall we understand and explain the facts that we find? Do we use, as many have, the theory of the psychological dynamics of the adult children of alcoholics to explain major elements of Bill Clinton's character? Or, focusing on his mother's early and prolonged absence from her young child to study nursing in New Orleans, would the theory of attachment (and its darker side, abandonment) be more appropriate?

The first level of analysis is the foundation for the others. Therefore, the analyst must sample a wide range of behavior across both similar and different circumstances. What makes data more (or less) useful for analysis? At the level of factual information, the analyst relies on the density of information, the authority of the source(s), and their accord with other known facts. Some, but by no means all, facts about many candidates and presidents are easily ascertained and validated by the density of recollections of the person by family, friends, and associates. Still, there are many pitfalls awaiting the unwary.

Public Data

The raw information used to support the analysis of character elements and their relationship to presidential performance is all "public data." That being the case, the term deserves some attention.

Public data is simply information that is available to any interested person and that resides in the public domain. Included are multiple, cross-checked news accounts of events; multiple, cross-checked biographical accounts; the words of the candidates themselves; and those of others about them. Each kind of public data is used in a specific way for a limited purpose with recognition of each source's biases, advantages, and limitations. I characterize the approach to that information as "psychologically informed events analysis."

Newspaper and other journalistic accounts are primarily used as documentation of the major facts concerning a particular event; for example, a presidential candidate made a particular pledge, a particular event took place within a certain sequence of events, and so on. The accounts themselves are, for the most part, concerned with *describing* events and the circumstances surrounding them.[2] This material is an important part of the attempt to use specific contexts and circumstances in a theoretically useful way. In attempting to answer the question of what happened (as a prelude to trying to answer why), a presidential researcher depends on many types of data, including presidential news conferences and interviews, interviews with major actors, documentary evidence, and so on.

None of these sources is without flaws. However, each can be viewed as a form of commentary designed to influence the framing and understanding of particular narrative lines or incidents. Thus, a presidential press conference can be viewed as the president's narrative of his behavior and the reasons behind it. Likewise, interviews with other actors provide their own narrative perspective. Even the release of what seems to be less subjective data, such as a report released by the White House (or its opponents) on the number of welfare mothers given help to find employment, is part of a narrative with a particular definition of work and of success.

Another important source of data for psychologically informed events and case analysis is the experience and understanding of the events as expressed by the leaders themselves. Therefore, a key source of supplementary evidence to accounts of events is the (now often transcribed) words of the candidates themselves. These include unstructured (but not necessarily unrehearsed) interviews, press conferences, and other spontaneously recorded transactions that are a part of every campaign and presidency.[3]

It is obvious that candidates and presidents have private understandings or motivations that they don't reveal (and may not even be aware of). Even so, it would be a mistake to totally discard as unimportant analysis of their publicly stated views and behavior. Why? First, candidates' publicly stated views and behavior may be very useful in revealing, sometimes quite starkly, what they wish to convey about themselves to others. When Al Gore stresses his childhood roots in Tennessee (and not Washington), he is inviting us to see him as a candidate who has not been part of the Washington establishment (via his father) and who has grown up with core American values. When Democratic presidential candidate Bill Bradley stresses his upbringing in a small rural town, he too is inviting us to see him as the product of a way of life nostalgically remembered as reflecting a better time and place.

My point is not that these invitations are fraudulent. Both cases do reflect *aspects* of the candidates' experiences. However, the role of the analyst is to learn enough to identify the extent to which they are representative. In Al Gore's case, he spent only summers at the family farm in Tennessee, and in Bradley's case he came from a well-off family that traveled widely when he was a child, including trips to Europe. Neither of these facts necessarily means that small town virtues were not part of either's childhood experience; rather, it just means that inferring psychology from large sociological concepts (e.g., "small town values") is best done carefully.

Candidates' views of themselves also provide an important basis for comparison to a candidate's behavior in other less public circumstances. Consider the 2000 presidential campaign, when Republican presidential candidate John McCain ran on a platform in which his honor, integrity, and role as a "truth teller" were critical to his success in the early rounds of the nomination process. His cornerstone and signature campaign issue, building on this persona, was campaign finance reform. This he defined as the elimination of the role that money from large campaign contributors played in elections and policy-making.

Yet, a news account presented documentary evidence (in the form of letters) that McCain had twice written to demand that a regulatory agency that he oversaw as chairman of an important Senate committee make a ruling on a proposal that would benefit a major campaign contributor. Moreover, the letters were sent shortly after he and his aides met with the contributors and had received more than twenty thousand dollars from them (Labaton 2000a). A subsequent story noted that McCain had written many such letters for campaign contributors in his role as chair of the Senate Commerce Committee. As the headline delicately put it, "Issue for McCain Is Matching Record with His Rhetoric" (Labaton 2000b).

The public statements and overt behavior of leaders may actually reflect what they really think and how they are really attempting to shape or respond to circumstances. This point is often lost sight of in discussions of methodology and critiques of case studies. The key reason for making use of these data elements is to uncover and assemble a pattern of behaviors with which to construct a theoretically useful framework for explanation and analysis.

One question that often comes up is whether the psychologically minded researcher has conducted an interview with the president or candidate being analyzed. Behind that question is a very naive assumption, namely, that an interview produces better data than that which is available in the public record. Contrary to some views, a psychologically trained interviewer does not possess the emotional equivalent of X-ray vision. The psychologically trained interviewer will not be able to cut through the sometimes decade-long practiced answers and evasions to get to the psychological essence of the person. This is an unwarranted and foolish assumption. People rarely have a single psychological essence, and, if they do, no known type of psychological training can discover it in a brief interview, especially with an unwilling informant.

Usually, a psychologically minded political analyst will want to know something about the family circumstances within which a leader grew up and came of age. It is a fact of modern life that leaders running for high office attract the attention of reporters and writers anxious to discover who they are. Almost every major modern presidential candidate has generated at least one major biography and often more.

Moreover, in spite of laments about campaign coverage, at least two of the nation's national newspapers (the *Washington Post* and the *New York Times*) have produced major series tracing the biographies and careers of the major presidential candidates, and excellent biographical material is often available in local papers from a candidate's home state (e.g., Baker 1999 or the reporting on John McCain's temper in the *Arizona Republic*).

Candidate autobiographies are also becoming a staple of political campaigns. Sometimes these are written by the candidate and a chosen "helper," as in the case of George W. Bush's (1999) and Bob Dole's (1988) autobiographies. Sometimes the autobiographies are written (for the most part) by the candidates themselves, as appears to be the case with 2000 Democratic presidential candidate Bill Bradley. These documents must be treated like any other element of information used to assemble an understanding of a leader; and, though often criticized as idealized, they can provide information and descriptions that can be used to develop an understanding of the person. While George W. Bush's autobiography has been characterized as little more than a campaign vehicle (which, of course, it is), in it his real love of flying jets as an Air National Guard pilot and his real attachment to his wife are clearly evident.

A second use of such information is to convey the leader's understanding of the events and people that shaped him. Clearly, campaign autobiographies are written for a purpose and often reflect strategy as well as candor, nonsense as well as insight. It is only in relation to other sources that particular elements can be judged. What other sources might these be? Surprisingly, books and interviews by close family members provide a range of useful information. No one who wants to explore the family circumstances in which Republican presidential candidate George W. Bush grew up can afford not to read his mother's memoir (Bush 1994). That can be supplemented with interviews given to major news shows by his mother and wife (Bush and Bush 1999). Similarly, anyone who wants to understand the circumstances that gave rise to President

Clinton's psychology cannot avoid reading his mother's autobiography (Kelley 1994a). These can be supplemented with interviews she gave on national news shows (Kelley 1992, 1994b).

Another major source of information on leaders comes from their own words. Psychologically minded political analysts have an unprecedented amount of this kind of primary material available to them. Transcripts of debates, of interviews, and of comments made during varied appearances are all routinely available to researchers with access to Lexis-Nexis or other data retrieval programs.

And, of course, when a news story breaks across the country, the researcher no longer has to rely on secondhand accounts. The analyst can go right to the source. When John McCain began to gain prominence in the Republican primary race, a major (but not national) newspaper in his home state published an editorial and a long article about the senator's locally well-known temper. That story was treated as a major item by several national newspapers, which gave *their* interpretation of the information (e.g., Broder 1999). One might have been content in the past to rely on that secondary analysis, but, with the resources available on the World Wide Web, it is no longer necessary to do so.

Behind-the-Scenes Accounts

My (1996a) psychologically framed biography of Bill Clinton made use of yet another good source for the political psychology of leaders: the behind-the-scenes account. Several (Drew 1994; Woodward 1994) such accounts became available early in his presidency as the book was being written. These accounts and similar ones generally rely on intensive and extensive interviews with high- (and more modest-) ranking members of the White House staff, including those with daily and direct access to the president. They are primarily descriptive. As Drew says of her book,

> This is a genre of middle-distance journalism, intended to catch events and people's involvement in them or reactions to them while they are still fresh and before they have been fuzzed over, and retouched, in recollection. *It is intended to offer the analysis and perspective of someone close to the events, seeing them unfiltered."* (1994, 438, emphasis added)

Sullivan (1994, 11), reviewing Woodward's book, faulted it for "showing little sense of history and [being] unable to relate a narrative to a larger argument," and for reflecting the "journalism of mere process." On the other hand, as Lehmann-Haupt (1994, C18) points out, "Readers with a solid background in Presidential politics will probably find Mr. Woodward's book invaluable." These inside accounts provide a crucial complementary set of data to supplement and deepen our understanding of the public record and to cross-check against it.

In examining political leaders, much benefit can be gained from insiders' memoirs, if one is careful. Memoirs by or interviews with major insiders about past events in which they were involved are shaped by memories and views, but, above all, motives. In that respect, there is something to be said for the freshness of contemporaneous accounts, when the actors are in the middle of their efforts. In many memoirs, the real story is often how the author struggled to wage the good fight against impossible odds (Reich 1997) or the author's centrality to someone else's presidency (Morris 1996, 1997), or both (Stephanopoulos 1999). However, in these cases, and with any other partial account of a president's behavior, you cannot evaluate the "what" without knowing more about the "who."

CAVEAT EXPLICATOR: KNOW YOUR SOURCES

The psychoanalytically oriented analyst of a president's psychology and performance can expect to have available a wide range of public behavior for analysis. These data provide a very large pool of information from which an analyst can develop a good understanding of a president's psychology and assist in inferring the patterns that underlie it. However, these sources can also be a swamp of misinformation, politically and personally motivated biases, and hidden factual dangers. It is no place for the factually ill-informed. It is imperative for anyone doing such work to know the players involved and their personal and political relationships to the subject. However, even a determined effort to place the players may not always work, if the real relationships are hidden and emerge only in retrospect. For example, the political journalist Sidney Blumenthal (1993a, 1993b, 1994) wrote a series of very positive articles about then candidate Clinton and very negative ones about the Republican candidate

Robert Dole in the *New Republic* and the *New Yorker.* His later appointment and conduct as a top personal aide to President Clinton cast some doubt on his objectivity and independence during the campaign.

It is important as well to know more about who the candidate or leader selects to represent or advocate his interests. For example, it is useful to know that Al Gore's campaign manager, Donna Brazile, was fired from her role in the 1988 Dukakis campaign for spreading rumors about then President Bush's extramarital affairs. Knowing this information helps in uncovering what appears to be a pattern of harsh rhetoric and questionable judgment. This pattern in turn raises questions about the judgment and strategy of the candidate who selected her. It is also instructive, once the analyst uncovers such a pattern and it becomes a public issue (Mitchell 2000), to see what the candidate does in response.[4]

In short, there is no substitute for immersion in the facts of circumstances and relationships when gathering and evaluating the information that forms the basis of psychoanalytically formed analysis.

Anecdotal Evidence

Biography and other forms of history, like the insider political histories noted previously, often rely on the accumulation of narrative incidents. The person in question may tell of the incident; a friend or someone who was present at the time may do so; or a person may even report what others say they have seen or heard. The weight of these accumulated narrative stories can often be used to usefully contribute to a psychologically framed portrait or analysis.

Such materials have played an important but controversial role in the psychological analysis of presidents and their presidencies. Some critics object that such narratives are merely anecdotal. The implication of the "anecdotal" label is that such data are inherently suspect. Psychoanalytically oriented analysts who make use of anecdotal case material must, like their statistical data–oriented counterparts, address the issue of the quality of the data. There are essentially four areas of concern raised by the use of such material: validity, degree of representation, consequence, and meaning.

An anecdote is a story put forward to support a characterization. The first question that must be addressed is whether the story is true.

But establishing that a particular event did take place is only the first step. Who is telling the story? Were they there, or are they repeating what they have heard elsewhere? What is the relationship of the person telling the story to the person about whom it is told? What is his or her motivation for telling the story?

The next question is how representative the incident is and of what? Consider in this regard the various stories regarding President Clinton's anger. Woodward reports a number of instances of Clinton's anger (1994, 33, 54, 133, 255, 278). So does Drew (1994, 96, 218). When one totals up these incidents and adds to them other public displays of temper, including the outburst of rage and indignation during the *Rolling Stone* interview (Wenner and Greider 1993) that took place during the campaign, it seems clear that this *is* an element in Clinton's psychology that warrants attention and explanation. The density of the anecdotal material supports the view that there is indeed something present to be explained. The question then arises as to whether the element is consequential, and if so what does it mean?

The Origins and Development of a President's Psychology

Psychoanalytic theory is synonymous in many people's minds with a focus on the childhood and adolescent origins of adult behavior. To some degree, this perception is both accurate and, from the standpoint of psychoanalytic theory, important. How else would we know how adult psychology has developed and why?

Less appreciated is the fact that, strictly speaking, understanding why a person acts as he or she does is different than, and not necessarily dependent on, understanding how that set of characteristics developed. As Alexander George (1971, 85) points out in his classic essay:

> In making use of available knowledge of the compulsive personality for purposes of political biography, an answer to the causal question is not essential. What creates a given personal dynamism, the dynamism itself—which is what interests the biographer most—can be fairly readily identified in accounts of the subject's behavior.

Generally, the psychoanalytically oriented analyst trying to construct an understanding of a president's early years must rely on several sources that are unlikely to be wholly satisfactory. The analyst can gain some information from what the now grown child says of his parent(s), but this is limited by emotional attachments, discretion, and even political needs. The analyst would also, ideally, like to draw on a president's family for their views. However, here too it would be foolish to believe that such recollections would not be colored by the wishes and motives of family members to put themselves and their child in the best light. It is an appreciation of the parents' psychology, not necessarily their recollections of their children's early years, that is perhaps of most use to the analyst.

For example, Virginia Kelley's autobiography reveals far more than she intended, much of which does not reflect well on her. It also raises troubling questions regarding her son, Bill Clinton. This creates certain issues for the psychoanalyst. It is obvious from her autobiography that her behavior, as a parent, had a decisive influence on her son's psychology, not always for the best. Her impact is not the salutary one that both she and her son describe. What should an analyst do in such circumstances?

Her autobiography is, of course, a public document, made so by Kelley and her son, who reviewed the manuscript before publication (Kelley 1994a, 285). In doing so, they presumably stand by her account as presented. Still, the material that emerges from the autobiography is damaging to the image that both held publicly of each other. The only path an analyst can follow under these circumstances is to frame the material as carefully as possible, noting its limitations and, where plausible, presenting alternative explanations.

By revealing herself, Kelley also allowed others access to the heretofore very private and carefully presented world of Clinton's developmental experiences. These experiences often do not coincide with what Clinton has said about them. In many ways Kelley's book reveals more problems than her son has either been aware of or has chosen to reveal. His mother's book therefore has the effect of helping to undercut the Clinton family myth and, in doing so, reveals much about the gravity of the emotional issues Clinton faced.

At the same time, the analyst of presidential performance has another responsibility, and that is to trace the public consequences of what he uncovers. One can appreciate and empathize with the problems Clinton faced, and one can appreciate and certainly respect his efforts to surmount them. However, the emphasis in assessing a president's performance cannot lie in appreciating the distance he has traveled to become president but what he actually did once he got there.

Constructing Psychological Understandings

Once the analyst has assembled anecdotes, biographical information, news reports, or other material that points to something that suspects psychologically driven political behavior, the second phase of the analysis, the formulation of psychological meaning, begins. Establishing the *meaning* of the psychological elements revealed in the data is critical to the analysis. This means trying to formulate how the element functions, what psychological purposes it serves, and what role it plays in the subject's overall psychology.

There is, of course, a theoretical and conceptual paradox in such work. Evidence of any psychological element, including character and personality, is found in behavior, but it is also behavior that we seek to understand and explain. The analyst cannot use the very same behavior to both extract by inference and cross-validate an element that is then used to explain that same behavior. What the analyst must do in these circumstances is examine a range of behaviors in order to strengthen such psychological inferences. These must then be cross-validated by reference to both other psychological characteristics that are theoretically linked as well as behaviors other than those used to make the original inferences.

This does not require the analyst to pierce the deepest recesses of a president's psychology. The psychoanalytically trained observer of candidates and presidents can often find some insight into the meanings of their behavior by observing behavior in a variety of contexts to gain some understanding of their most important behavioral preferences. The analyst can then seek out clues to the pattern of such behaviors. These patterns, which form the basis of psychological inference, need to be tested against other, different behaviors for consistency with theoretical understanding and an understanding of the contexts in which these behaviors took place.

The psychologically minded analyst of political leadership faces a number of dilemmas in formulating dynamic understandings. The first involves uncovering and establishing the psychological elements with which he or she works. The second is to develop a plausible case for their actual importance to what leaders do. The third is to then establish how an element operates within the more general frames of that person's psychology. And last, the analyst must make some attempt to locate that element and its dynamic relationships in the person's developmental history. In others words, a dynamic theoretical explanation of an element of a candidate's or president's behavior and an accounting of its origins are separate enterprises. One has not provided a dynamic explanation of an adult characteristic by giving an accounting of its origins.

Consider the characterological element of ambition. Analysts have not completed their task when they are able to bring forward enough evidence to support the existence of high (or low) ambition in a candidate or president. Many questions that are important for addressing the role this element plays in presidential performance remain. How is ambition connected with the individual's sense of accomplishment? Is it uniform across circumstances? If not, what accounts for differences? With what other psychological and behavioral elements does it appear to be associated?

High levels of ambition, for example, can spring from a number of psychological sources, including the wish to achieve, the wish to bolster one's sense of worth in the face of doubts expressed by others, the wish to please a demanding parent, and so on. Examining the contemporaneous dynamics of such an element (what other elements it is associated with, when and why) can help us in distinguishing its origins as well as clarifying its theoretical dynamics.

Analyst and Subject

Psychological analysis involves inferences about behavior. This being true, explicitness about the process of inference construction is critical. Inferences begin with a pattern of facts. The concept of pattern is critical in evaluating these facts. The questions regarding facts are, How many are there and how consistent are they? Identifying patterns is, therefore, a complex process in which there are many potential pitfalls.

At least since Freud's analysis of Woodrow Wilson it has been clear that the analyst's own political preferences and views can play an important and distorting role in assessing leader psychology.[5]

This can happen because the analyst either admires or dislikes, or has some other set of feelings about, his or her subject. Beyond such basic biases, and less appreciated, is the role that the analyst's own psychology, for good or ill, can play in distorting the analysis, just as a psychoanalyst's own unresolved conflicts can distort the treatment of his or her patients.

The analyst, especially one who makes use of and is trained in psychoanalytic psychology, has a particular obligation to be clear in these matters. That is why I revealed that I had voted for Bill Clinton and my basis for doing so in the course of my biographic analysis of him (1996a, 318). No analyst can avoid personal reactions to the materials with which he or she constructs an analysis, but one can try to be as explicit as possible about one's own potential biases. In that explicitness lies at least a partial solution to unintended or, worse, systematic bias.

In the end, the analyst's work must stand on its merits, not the feelings it evokes in political partisans. Ultimately what matters is not the analyst's stance toward his or her subject, examined or not. Rather, what matters is the following: Does the analytic framework of analysis put forward appear to cover the most important aspects of what needs to be explained psychologically? Is the evidence for putting forward those categories of analysis persuasive? And, finally, are the implications drawn regarding these characteristics found in the real world of the president's actual behavior?

Theory Validation and the Prediction of Presidential Behavior: Gold Standard or Pyrite?

In the physical sciences, prediction is the "gold standard" of theory validation, and for good reason. However, for the social sciences, prediction may be more useful as an ideal than as a model. Why? Because no physical science must navigate the complexities of individual choice and perception.

Theory validation has been an even more perplexing and difficult problem for scholars with interests in life histories (Runyan 1984, 121–91). Among these problems are (1) a tendency to over emphasize psychology at the expense of external circumstances—after all, insofar as the leader must always be analyzed in context, the contextual variables will always be there to influence the leader's decision making—and (2) a tendency to infer too much from too little data and a tendency to rely on psychological theory that is not well developed or explicated in the study.

Even among those united by their use of psychoanalytically framed theory and biographical history to analyze the performance of presidents there is disagreement about whether prediction is possible. In his study of then president Richard Nixon, Mazlish (1972, 162) gives an example of true prediction: "If, as in the natural sciences, the psychohistorian could predict with utter certainty that Nixon's personality would compel him to keep Agnew as his Vice-President in 1972, that would be a 'true prediction.'" "Utter certainty" is a high standard. Not surprisingly, Mazlish concludes (1972, 162, 165) that such a prediction is not possible and that the fusion of psychology and contemporary historical analysis "cannot give us the sort of certainty involved in true prediction. Above all it cannot predict a specific act, such as visiting Peking. . . . psychohistory is basically a retrospective enterprise."

Barber ([1972] 1992), on the other hand, subtitles his book "Predicting Performance in the White House." His view, not a particularly radical one, is that if we can trace the pattern of a person's life before he enters the oval office, we are better able to estimate his likely patterns once in it (2). He acknowledges, rightly, that such predictions are "not easy" and will require "some sharp tools and close attention to their use" (3, 4). Yet, he thinks them worth the risk both because the questions they address (the quality of those in our highest office) are critical and because the theories that attempt to answer them can best be refined through practice. But to estimate a likely pattern or tendency is much softer than hard prediction.

The fundamental basis of psychological prediction is the consistency of behavior. A prediction is a test of our understanding of three areas: the psychology that underlies a person's behavior, the circumstances that will affect it, and the relationship between them.

Unlike a person's attitudes or personality traits, character reflects a person's basic and habitual ways of relating to circumstance. So, to the extent that a person's character has become psychologically consolidated, we can expect significant consistency in his or her behavior. It is this consistency that provides the basis for any confidence in our expectations about how someone will act.[6]

Predictions of individuals require a knowledge of the psychological frames into which this person might best fit. However, it also requires knowledge of the unique constellation of elements, the characterological and psychological strengths and weakness, that define *this* person. Individuals with substantial levels of ambition and the necessarily talent, along with the focused persistence to reach the top, are more likely to be successful. And, having achieved success *because* of their past behavior, they are more likely to persist in the patterns they have developed.

However, predicting the behavior of shrewd, intelligent, and highly functioning individuals, who are acutely aware of their circumstances and what may be needed to surmount them, is a very tricky undertaking. It is possible that, in spite of their own psychological inclinations, such persons will overcome any adverse impulses, if not alone, then certainly with the help of many advisers whose only occupational purpose is to help the leader succeed. This just adds one more layer to the hurdles that must be overcome if character or type is to carry the burden of prediction.

Lasswell (1930, 38–64) argues that building political typologies is a useful route for developing and refining theories of political leadership. But Barber's (Barber [1972] 1992) efforts suggest the limits of these efforts for predicting the behavior of presidents.[7]

If we compare the logic of political typologies to the more specific formulations of individual leaders we can discern some paradoxical features. By sacrificing specificity for generalization, a focus on the former undercuts their rationale vis-à-vis the latter. That is, more but not wholly accurate generalization may wind up being purchased at the expense of better understanding and thus, in the particular case, better prediction.

The Analysis of Consistency

Psychoanalytically framed studies of presidential biography and performance face daunting problems in trying to develop confidence in their theories and procedures. Many strategies available in the social sciences more generally are not possible for them. They cannot, for example, make use of large or multiple samples for establishing reliable probability estimates. The confidence that psychoanalytic formulations earn is ultimately a function of their being critical in examining evidence, inferences, and conclusions (Runyan 1982, 144).

As argued previously, prediction is a precarious, though not impossible, task. However, in addition to the excellent suggestions contained in Runyan's (1982, 121–91) seminal treatment of case study and ideographic approaches to biographical analysis, there is one further step that can be taken. It shares some similarities with, and some advantages of, prediction, but it is not wholly retrospective. Yet, of necessity, it makes much use of the past in developing causal links to a president's future. I characterize this strategy as the *analysis of consistency.* The basic and uncomplicated idea behind this approach is to compare the degree to which one's theoretical understanding of a president or candidate at time one is consistent with his behavior at time two.[8]

Conclusion

The psychological analysis of presidents and other leaders is likely to persist, in spite of all of its controversies and difficulties, for two very fundamental and important reasons. First, the underlying psychology that motivates how presidents see and try to shape the world is related to their exercise of power. If we want to understand what they do, we had better have useful theories of why they do it. Second, variations in the psychology that presidents and leaders bring to their positions affect what they will, won't, or can't do. In short, there is an enormous practical set of implications to leaders' levels of ambition and the skills (or lack thereof) that accompany them; their ideals and values, along with their capacity to remain faithful to them; and how the leaders truly feel about the many kinds of relationships with which they must contend.

It is hard to imagine that any theoretical stance that does not require of its practitioner that he or she be immersed in the details of a leader's ongoing life will bring the level of confidence in the theoretical understanding or validity required by this critical task. Sixty years ago Lasswell (1930, 1) observed, "political science without biography is a form of taxidermy."

Since Lasswell wrote those words, developments in psychoanalytic theory and its increasingly sophisticated application in a variety of settings have brought us to the point where we might well add the following statement to Lasswell's observation: Analyzing presidential performance without the tools of modern psychoanalytic theory is like assessing the performance of a grand prix race car designed without wheels. It can be done, but it is unlikely to result in much theoretical or substantive mileage.

Notes

I would like to thank Alonzo Z. Hamby, Alexander L. George, Fred I. Greenstein, and Jerrold M. Post for their helpful comments on an earlier draft of this chapter.

1. Recall Greenstein's (1969) distinctions between three levels of analysis: phenomonology, dynamics, and development. The first consists of the facts (a) "as they are," (b) as they are seen, and (c) as they are organized. It is clear that theory plays some role in these processes, especially those (e.g., b and c) that require some sorting or construction exercise on the part of the analyst. The second, the dynamic level, consists of theoretically informed hypotheses or tentative explanations that try to account for the facts as they have been seen and constructed. The third, the developmental level, seeks to account both for the origin and evolution of the characteristics that are put forward to explain the pattern of facts and for their social and psychological explanations.

2. News accounts provide at least five kinds of important information for the analyst. First, they can be used to establish the basic existence of an event, that is, that the event has taken place. Second, the nature of the event and its place in a sequence of events can often provide an analyst with important information with which to help construct an understanding of the meaning of the events. Third, news accounts can also be used to help establish some of the circumstances surrounding an event. These details, while most likely incomplete, do help to deepen appreciation of the context. Related to this is the fourth purpose of news accounts, which is to convey some sense of an actor's understandings of these events as reflected in his or her public discussions or actions. Fifth, and very important, by following such accounts over time one can use later accounts and *outcomes* to cross-check the validity of earlier accounts. Differences between public portrayals and the emergence into public discourse of what had been private knowledge can be important data for the analyst. They can reveal elements of presidential psychology and style that the analysts must take into theoretical account.

Of course, news accounts, even when cross-checked, have at least three limitations that must be kept in mind. First, reporters may report events accurately but may miss important aspects of an event, either because it is not evident at the time, because they did not have access to all that went on, or because they simply didn't appreciate the implications of what they were reporting. Second, reporters often piece together their understanding of events in the form of a "story," and this subtext can be shaped either by a reporter's attitudes or view or by decisions (strategic or unconscious) of the person(s) on whom the reporter relies. Third, stories on occasion can simply be in error. This is a special difficulty when covering presidents, but it also occurs when covering candidates. Both presidents and candidates (and their staffs) try to put the best frame on events. For all these reasons, events data must be *one* of a number of data sources that an analyst uses.

3. Unstructured interviews, while in some ways more revealing of the candidate, are often not completely spontaneous. It is a fact of political life that candidates and presidents spend much time behind the scenes considering how they should approach or respond to pubic issues or events. The amount of uncalculated information that is reflected in the give-and-take of a question and answer format depends in large part on the nature of the format. General questions from supportive, or for other reasons, uncritical audiences allow a candidate or president more opportunity to respond in preselected ways than if the format was a real debate.

4. Al Gore let it be known that he had been in contact with General Powell. However, he refused to say whether he had apologized to General Powell. On the *Today Show,* Gore said, "That was the spirit of the call. That word wasn't used. But I regretted the way *he heard* Donna's comments" (Seelye 2000, A1, emphasis added).

5. Freud acknowledged that his study of Wilson "did not originate without strong emotions," that he found Wilson "unsympathetic," and that "this aversion increased in the course of years the more I learned about him and the more severely we suffered from the consequences of his intrusion into our destiny" (1967, xiii, xvi). However, Freud went on to say these feelings had "underwent a thorough subjugation" (xvi) to a mixture of "sympathy, but sympathy of a special sort mixed with pity" (xv). This is hardly an auspicious vantage point from which to conduct such an analysis, and it has led some observers like Elms to make the very sensible suggestion that the analyst will "choose a subject towards whom he feels considerable ambivalence rather than harsh antagonism or uncritical adulation" (1976, 179).

6. Even then, a person may become aware that there are dangers lurking in their psychology and will try to avoid them. George and George (1956, 321) report that Woodrow Wilson told his closest advisor of reoccurring nightmares that he might repeat the pattern of success then failure that had plagued him as president of Princeton. The Georges argue that he "was casting about for ways to avoid a repetition of his highly distressing experience as a reformer at Princeton." He failed in doing so.

7. A major problem is that different variables will lead to the construction of different typologies. However, a bigger problem is that people rarely fully fit the categories to which the typologists would like to assign them. Barber's Nixon,

an active-negative, confounds one of the basic characteristics of the type by being ideologically flexible. Eisenhower is a passive-negative, although Barber ([1972] 1992, 179) admits "this case presents certain difficulties."

8. The analysis of consistency does not ask whether, and certainly does not require that, the feature in question is the *sole* or *primary* cause but only whether it provides support for the original formulation. In Clinton's case, one might compare the theoretical formulations put forward in *High Hopes* (Renshon 1996a) with the president's behavior in the period after the book was published. Such analysis might take the following form: Is the president's decision to become involved with a White House intern consistent with the theoretical formulation of Clinton as a man who dislikes boundaries and chafes under the rules to which others must ordinarily adhere?

B. Trait Analyses

6. Verbal Behavior and Personality Assessment

Walter Weintraub

Speech can be studied from a variety of viewpoints. The language component can be divided into the disciplines of (1) phonology, which describes how sounds are put together to form words; (2) syntax, which describes how sentences are formed from words; (3) semantics, which deals with the interpretations of the meaning of words; and (4) pragmatics, which describes how we participate in conversations. Nonverbal phenomena include such variables as rate, pauses, amplitude, and pitch.

Of the speech data available for analysis, syntactic and certain paralinguistic variables are most suitable for the study of personality traits. Semantic variables, on the other hand, have only limited usefulness for the identification of habitual behavioral responses. Speakers do differ in their choice of vocabulary, but such preferences are influenced by certain situational variables, notably the topic of conversation (Laffal 1965, 93). Other investigators have stressed the slow rate of change of a number of syntactic measures and their suitability for the study of characteristic behavior. Steingart and Freedman (1972), for example, have written:

> Common sense argues that what a person says is much more influenced by transient situational characteristics than how he says it. . . . grammar would appear *a priori* to possess certain advantages for the exploration of . . . personality constructs. (135)

Systems of verbal analysis that depend upon the measurement of meaning demand the exercise of subtle judgment by scorers. Syntactic structures, being independent of meaning, can be easily recognized and scored (Chomsky 1957, 17). A speaker's choice of grammatical forms is subject to little conscious manipulation.

We assume that styles of speaking reflect characteristic nonverbal behavior. But how do we go about identifying grammatical structures that are associated with personality traits? Two examples will help demonstrate the method.

The first illustration concerns a man with problems of impulse control. He acts without considering the consequences of his behavior. As a result, he often finds himself regretting his actions and trying to undo their harmful consequences. How might this impulsive trait be reflected in our subject's speech? We would expect him to blurt out ill-considered remarks and then attempt to take them back or qualify them in some way. How would this tendency be mirrored in his grammatical choices? We would expect our subject to make frequent use of adversative expressions, such as *but, nevertheless,* and *however.* A number of years ago, a colleague, Dr. H. Aronson, and I published a report showing that a group of hospitalized, impulse-ridden psychiatric patients did use significantly more adversative expressions than a group of normal control subjects (Weintraub and Aronson 1964). Similar results were later obtained from a group of binge eaters, individuals who impulsively consume large quantities of food and then try to undo the consequences of their overeating (Weintraub and Aronson 1969).

Let us take as our second example an individual with compulsive, ritualistic behavior. Such a person feels compelled to perform repetitive, apparently senseless acts, such as washing his hands over and over again or checking repeatedly to see if his door is locked before retiring for the night. If our subject attempts to resist his compulsion, he becomes anxious and cannot long maintain his resolve. Since compulsive patients are logical to a fault, they must provide themselves and others with reasons to justify their repetitive acts. We would, therefore, expect their speech to contain numerous explanatory expressions, such as *because, therefore,* and *in order to.* A study Dr. Aronson and I published confirmed this expectation. A group of compulsive psychiatric patients did, in fact, use significantly more explanatory expressions than a normal control group (Weintraub and Aronson 1974). Similar results were obtained with a group of delusional patients who demonstrated a need to justify unconventional beliefs (Weintraub and Aronson 1965).

While reading these clinical illustrations, the reader may have been struck by the similarity of the grammatical structures studied to defense or coping mechanisms described in the psychoanalytic literature. Adversative expressions seem to reflect the mechanism of "undoing," while explanatory expressions seem to reflect the mechanism of "rationalization." In fact, almost all the categories used in our verbal analyses have been described by clinicians as reflecting important ways of dealing with psychological stress.

We do not assume that every use of an adversative or causative expression reflects impulsivity or rationalization, respectively, only that individuals with impulsive and compulsive tendencies will choose such structures more frequently than persons not so disposed. Adversative and causative conjunctions and phrases are examples of grammatical structures that are easily recognized. Naive judges can be taught to identify and score them with little training.

Our method of verbal behavior analysis rests upon three assumptions: (1) patterns of thinking and behaving are reflected in styles of speaking; (2) under stress, a speaker's choice of grammatical structures will mirror characteristic coping mechanisms; and (3) personality traits are revealed by grammatical structures having a slow rate of change.

Transformational Grammar and Verbal Style

Why do different people use different grammatical structures to convey the same message? "John loved Mary" and "Mary was loved by John" are two correct ways of saying the same thing. Transformational grammarians would say that they constitute different surface structures derived from a common deep structure. Every language is considered to have transformational rules that allow its speakers to say the same thing in different ways. Although in our example the two sentences are identical in meaning, they differ noticeably in style. When verbal styles of different individuals are compared, we are, in a way, comparing preferences for transformational rules. Why a particular person chooses one rather than another grammatical structure is related, in our view, to personality factors. The sentence "John loved Mary" may be too assertive for certain people who prefer the more passive and softer "Mary was loved by John." In fact, some of our previous work indicates that inactive or helpless psychiatric patients do have a preference for certain passive grammatical structures.

Collecting Verbal Data

If verbal mannerisms are to be used as a way of determining how an individual copes with stress, it is important to gather samples of speech under moderately stressful conditions. Subjects exposed to minimal or extreme levels of stress will not provide us with the verbal data we are seeking. An example will illustrate this point. Suppose we wished to test a baseball player's ability to catch fly balls. We would not hit balls beyond his reach since nobody, not even the most skillful player, could meet such a challenge. Nor would we hit balls directly to our player since almost anyone could catch them. To properly test a player's catching skills, we would hit difficult but catchable fly balls. Requiring a subject to speak uninterruptedly for ten minutes on any subject or subjects he wishes is a difficult but manageable task for most people between the ages of five and eighty-five. Normal as well as emotionally disturbed people can speak uninterruptedly for ten minutes. Researchers use the term *free speech* to refer to verbal data gathered under the experimental conditions just described.

When dealing with the remarks of public figures from a distance, it is necessary to modify the data collection method. To obtain spontaneous speech samples, transcribed news conferences and personal interviews are used. Their use is based upon the assumption that the stress generated by such encounters is roughly comparable to what subjects experience when speaking without interruption for ten minutes. To make the interview data as comparable as possible to the subjects' ten-minute monologues, only responses to questions that exceed thirty words are used. The first sentence of a response is not counted in order to minimize the effect of dialogue.

Verbal Reflections of Personality

Prior to 1975, attempts to correlate speech and personality were limited to groups of psychologically impaired patients sharing patterns of symptomatic behavior. During that year, a psycholinguistics research team at the University of Michigan challenged me to create personality profiles for two volunteers based entirely upon their ten-minute free speech monologues. The speech samples were prepared by the University of Michigan researchers in the manner previously described, and only verbatim typed transcripts of the electronically recorded monologues were sent. No other information about the speakers was given to me.

After scoring the transcripts, I attempted written personality evaluations of the two speakers and sent them to my University of Michigan colleagues. After comparing my reports with independent assessments of the speakers' personalities, the University of Michigan group concluded that the method had the ability "to accurately tap important personality dimensions" (Binder 1975).

Analyzing the Watergate Transcripts

Encouraged by the University of Michigan pilot study, I decided to take advantage of the publication of the Watergate transcripts to continue my analysis of individual speakers. The Watergate transcripts presented students of verbal behavior with a unique opportunity. To my knowledge, never before in history had spontaneous conversations involving important political leaders been electronically recorded and made available to the public.

Since the Watergate participants could be assumed to have been under considerable stress during most of the published conversations, the transcripts should contain pertinent data relative to the adaptive patterns, as reflected in their styles of speaking, of the four individuals whose remarks make up the bulk of the recorded material. Using the verbal categories, samples of speech attributed to Richard Nixon, H. R. Haldeman, John Ehrlichman, and John Dean were compared with those of a normal control group and of populations of delusional, impulsive, depressive, and compulsive psychiatric patients. The results indicated no abnormal verbal behavior for either Dean or Ehrlichman. President Nixon could not be distinguished from the depressed patients in any of the verbal categories and deviated from the impulsives in only one category. Haldeman's style appeared to be abnormal but unlike any of the patient groups previously studied (Weintraub 1981, 129–35).

Carter and Reagan Compared

In 1986 another verbal analysis of political leaders was published. Using randomly chosen samples of their presidential news conferences, I compared the spontaneous speaking styles of Jimmy Carter and Ronald Reagan. Significant differences between the two presidents' verbal behavior emerged. Carter's use of the verbal categories showed him to be shy, aloof, competitive, and defensive when challenged. In contrast, Reagan was engaging, generous, confident, entertaining, and superficially personal with the White House press. Under pressure, Reagan showed a tendency to deny unpleasant aspects of reality and, in certain instances, to reverse previously made decisions (Weintraub 1986).

Why Analyze Political Leaders?

At this point, readers may wonder what can be learned from the verbal analysis of political leaders that cannot be ascertained by direct observation. Precisely because readers are already familiar with the personality traits of political leaders, verbal analyses can be compared with what is already known about them. Readers can then determine for themselves if the speech patterns generated by the method reflect the public behavior of public leaders. Since grammatical choices are not consciously made, there is always the possibility that information about a political figure's personality not known to the public may be unearthed by verbal behavior analysis.

There is still another reason for studying the speech habits of political leaders. Our method of verbal behavior analysis may be useful to investigators of important individuals who are no longer alive. Historians and biographers studying individuals of past eras often must rely on written documents, such as speeches, memoirs, letters, transcribed conversations, and so forth. These scholars tend to focus primarily on thematic content to the virtual neglect of formal aspects of language. Character analysis based entirely upon anecdotal data tends to be impressionistic and fraught with error. Any method that can compare, in a reasonably systematic way, behavior and styles of speaking may be useful to historians and biographers.

Problems of Method in Psychobiographical Research

Our method differs from those of certain psychobiographers who attempt elaborate psychodynamic formulations and psychogenetic reconstructions on the basis of selected incidents in the lives of historical figures. Attempts to clarify the unconscious conflicts of public figures can never rise above the level of speculative analysis, no matter how intuitive the biographer may be. The surface manifestations of ego and superego functions, on the other hand, are subject to observation and objective recording in a variety of settings. Much greater attention must be paid to the conflict-free areas of ego functioning if we wish to enlarge our understanding of that which distinguishes the makers of history from the rest of humanity. The method used relies entirely upon data available to everyone. It can be learned from published reports and requires no special intuitive powers.

Description of the Verbal Categories

Qualifiers

The category of qualifiers includes expressions of uncertainty ("*I think* I'll go to the ball game today"); modifiers that weaken statements without adding information ("That old house is *kind of* spooky"); and phrases that contribute a sense of vagueness or looseness to a statement ("Then we enjoyed *what you might call* an evening of relaxation").

Qualifiers are almost always uttered before the complete verb is spoken. The message is, therefore, discounted before it is transmitted. When they occur frequently, qualifiers indicate a lack of decisiveness or an avoidance of commitment. The use of qualifiers has also been said to increase with anxiety (Lalljee and Cook 1975). In my study of the speech patterns of post–World War II presidents, Gerald Ford used significantly more qualifiers than the other chief executives, giving his style of speaking a halting, indecisive flavor (Weintraub 1989, 161). A very low frequency of qualifiers conveys a dogmatic flavor to speech.

It is important that speech samples be gathered in the same way when comparing speakers' use of qualifiers. In a study of the use of qualifiers, it has been shown that the use of this category is negatively associated with preparation. Qualifiers serve as fillers, words and phrases that are used when speakers are searching their memories for more informative words (Weintraub and Plaut 1985). A prepared speech will contain many fewer qualifiers than an extemporaneous news conference.

Retractors

Retractors, also referred to as adversative expressions, weaken or reverse previously spoken remarks. They include expressions such as *but,* the most commonly used retractor, *however,* and *nevertheless.* The frequent use of retractors suggests a difficulty in adhering to previously made decisions and imparts a flavor of impulsivity to the speaker's style (Weintraub and Aronson 1964). Compared to other post–World War II presidents, Richard Nixon used significantly more retractors (Weintraub 1981, 130–31). This was particularly true during the anti-Vietnam demonstrations, when Nixon showed marked mercurial behavior.

Impulsivity is not the only personality trait associated with the frequent use of retractors. Many speakers use retractors to achieve "pseudo-consensus," an apparent but not genuine agreement with another speaker's point of view. An example of pseudo-consensus is the following statement: "I agree that your grade deserves to be raised from "B" to "A," *but,* as principal of the school, I must support your teacher."

I and *We*

In political discourse, a speaker's use of *I* and *we* seems to reflect a need to present himself either as his own person (high *I* score, low *we* score) or as a speaker for a party or cause (low *I* score, high *we* score). The use of the imperial *we,* a habit of kings and emperors, is unusual for American politicians. Lyndon Johnson occasionally used this device. Leaders of communist countries effect a certain political humility by using *we* as their preferred personal pronoun. One sign indicating that Gorbachev was a "new" Soviet leader was his relatively frequent use of *I* when interviewed by journalists (Winter et al. 1991a).

Me

The pronoun *me,* the grammatical recipient of action, tends to be used most by passive speakers, such as children, women, elderly people, and certain patient groups (Weintraub 1989, 12). When attacked, Bill Clinton is apt to adopt the role of victim and will use the pronoun *me* quite frequently.

Negatives

The most common examples of the use of the negative category are *not, never,* and *nothing.* Speakers who use many negatives tend to be oppositional and stubborn. They may also be using the coping mechanisms of negation and denial excessively. In my study of the Watergate transcripts, I reported that H. R. Haldeman, known in Washington political circles as the "Abominable No-Man," used negatives significantly more frequently than the other Watergate conspirators (Weintraub 1981, 124).

Explainers

The category of explainers includes words and expressions that suggest causal connections or justification of the speaker's thoughts and actions. The most common explainer is *because.* Other frequently used explainers include *therefore* and *since.* Speakers who use many explainers have a didactic, apologetic, or rationalizing verbal style (Lorenz 1953). Those who use few explainers may be seen as categorical and dogmatic. Part of Hillary Clinton's didactic speaking style is due to her frequent use of explainers.

Expressions of Feeling

All clauses in which the speaker attributes feelings to himself or herself are scored. Examples are "I like to work outdoors" and "Jack's behavior frustrates me." High expressions of feeling scores are often associated in the listener's mind with the expression of emotion (Weintraub 1989, 49–72). (As explained later, expressions of feeling is not the only category associated with emotional speaking). Low expressions of feeling scores reflect an aloof, cool verbal style. Ronald Reagan's cool, unflappable speaking style was due, in part, to his infrequent use of expressions of feeling.

Adverbial Intensifiers

Adverbial intensifiers include all adverbs that increase the force of a statement. Commonly used adverbial intensifiers are *very, really, so,* and *such.* Adverbial intensifiers add color to a speaker's remarks. When used frequently, they produce a dramatic, histrionic effect. Speakers who use very few adverbial intensifiers are perceived by listeners as dull and bland. Among normal speakers, those in the midadolescent age group (fifteen to seventeen) have the highest frequency of occurrence of adverbial intensifiers. Women use this category significantly more frequently than men among both normal and psychiatric patient groups. Depressed patients use this category more than other patient groups (Weintraub 1989, 64–70). Eisenhower was the most dramatic of the post–World War II presidential speakers judging by his use of adverbial intensifiers.

Direct References

Direct references include all explicit references to the interviewer, the interviewing process, or the physical surroundings. Examples are "As I said in answer to your previous question, I do not intend to run for public office in 1996" and "It's a pleasure to meet with you in such a beautiful conference room."

A high direct references score reflects the verbal behavior of an engaging, perhaps manipulative speaker, one who avoids a particular topic by talking about the interviewing process. When the frequency of remarks directed at the interviewer is very high, the speaker may appear to be intrusive and controlling. A very low direct references score may indicate that the speaker is shy or aloof. In my study of post–World War II presidents, I found that the greatest use of direct references was by the friendly and engaging presidents Eisenhower and Reagan. Not surprisingly, the somewhat shy and aloof Jimmy Carter scored lowest in this category (Weintraub 1989, 170). Among psychiatric patients, depressed and impulsive patients make the most direct references because they make demands upon the interviewer for assistance (Weintraub 1981, 31).

Nonpersonal References

Personal references are clauses whose subjects include the speaker and people known to him. "I liked President Kennedy" and "Gerald

Ford was my close personal friend" are personal references. Clauses whose subjects are not known to the speaker are scored as nonpersonal. An almost exclusive use of nonpersonal references suggests detachment to the listener. Infrequent use of nonpersonal references may reflect a concrete preoccupation with oneself and one's immediate surroundings. John F. Kennedy made little use of personal references. This enhanced the impression of a cool, detached leader thoroughly in command of the situation.

Creative or Colorful Expressions

This category includes all occurrences of wit, metaphor, and idiosyncratic use of language. If colorful expressions are of high quality and novel, they may reflect the presence of an original mind. Original or not, colorful expressions are perceived by most listeners as entertaining. Examples of creative expressions would be "a fitfully red sky" and "scenes of riotous dissipation."

Emotional Speech

Previously we identified expressions of feelings as a category that conveys emotion, but it is not the only such category. Listeners associate the following categories as also conveying emotion: (1) the use of *I* rather than *we;* (2) adverbial intensifiers; (3) direct references; and (4) personal rather than nonpersonal references. Most emotional speakers will use several of the feelings categories to convey warmth.

Conversion of Raw Scores to Final Scores

With the exception of nonpersonal references, final scores are occurrences per one thousand words. The final nonpersonal references score is a ratio obtained by multiplying the raw nonpersonal references score by one thousand and dividing the resulting figure by the combined raw nonpersonal and personal references score. Detailed information about computing scores and sample-size issues can be found in Weintraub 1981 (197). Mean verbal scores for the first seven post–World War II presidents can be found in table 6.1.

Deciding Which Personality Traits to Investigate

Once we have decided to study personality traits by analyzing verbal behavior, we must then choose which characteristics we wish to emphasize. In describing the method, I have already discussed certain personality traits, such as impulsivity, decisiveness, and so forth. What traits should be added in order to have a broader base upon which to construct a personality profile? The following list of traits appears to mirror verbal mannerisms that are important in describing human behavior. After listing each personality trait, I indicate which verbal categories appear to be associated with it and, where appropriate, offer examples of how the presence of the trait in question can be detected in samples of free speech.

Some Personality Traits Reflected by Grammatical Choices

1. *Decisiveness.* This trait was previously discussed. Preparation for decision can be measured by the frequency of occurrence of qualifiers. Once the method of data collection has been controlled for, numerous qualifiers suggest indecisiveness. Of the post–World War II presidents, Gerald Ford scored highest in this category.

2. *Reconsideration.* The ability to reconsider a decision after it has been made has also been discussed previously. Reconsideration is best reflected by the moderate use of retractors.

3. *Impulsivity.* This trait has been extensively investigated in a psychiatric patient group (Weintraub and Aronson 1964). A frequent use of retractors and negatives is associated with impulsivity in many cases. During the Watergate crisis, Richard Nixon occa-

TABLE 6.1. MEAN SCORES FOR THE FIRST
SEVEN POST–WORLD WAR II PRESIDENTS

Category	Score
I	35.0
We	20.0
Me	1.5
Negatives	12.0
Qualifiers	11.0
Retractors	6.5
Direct references	2.5
Explainers	5.5
Expressions of feeling	3.5
Adverbial intensifiers	15.0
Nonpersonal references	775.0
Creative expressions	2.5

sionally acted impulsively. This tendency was reflected by greater than average use of retractors and negatives.

4. *Anxious disposition.* An internal rather than an observable state, anxiety as a reflection of grammatical choice has received scant attention in the literature. Most investigators interested in "anxious speech" have stressed vocal dynamics rather than verbal behavior.

What characterizes the typically anxious patient is the excessive use of a number of categories. Self-preoccupation may be reflected by the excessive use of *I* and *me,* defensiveness by the frequency of explainers and negatives, and paralysis of decision by a more than average use of qualifiers. Anxious speakers often have difficulty containing their feelings and may use many expressions of feeling and adverbial intensifiers. Finally, pleas for help from the interviewer may be reflected in the frequent use of direct references. The anxious speaker's frequent use of several categories suggests a need to use all the verbal resources available to him in order to master the interviewing situation. An anxious disposition suggests psychopathology. Few individuals having "verbal anxiety" are likely to be chosen as leaders of their nations.

5. *Moodiness.* We have already identified some of the verbal transmitters of emotion. They are high scores in the following categories: *I/we* ratio, adverbial intensifiers, direct references, expressions of feeling, and personal references. Mercurial speakers are characterized by a tendency to be erratic in their use of emotional categories. Of the post–World War II presidents, Lyndon Johnson and Richard Nixon showed verbal evidence of rapidly shifting moods (Weintraub 1989, 97).

What about evidence of depression in speech? This topic has been extensively researched, and the reader is referred to a previous publication devoted to the speech of depressed patients (Aronson and Weintraub 1967). To summarize our findings, speakers with depressive disorders show a verbal pattern that consists of a paucity of speech, many personal references, and high scores in the following categories: *I, me,* direct references, expressions of feeling, negatives, and adverbial intensifiers. These scores reflect the depressed speaker's uncontrolled affect (high scores in the emotional categories), self-preoccupation (high *I* score), dependent needs (high direct references and *me* scores), and negativity (high negatives score). Richard

Nixon's speech showed evidence of depression during the Watergate scandal.

6. *Angry disposition.* Speakers with angry dispositions frequently become irritable during interviews. Occasionally they explode if challenged by the interviewer. In such cases the use of qualifiers may disappear completely. In the heat of extreme anger, all evidence of indecisiveness vanishes. Another characteristic of angry discourse is extreme negativity. In some samples of angry speech, the use of negatives may be as much as five times that of normal speech. Other findings worthy of mention are the use of rhetorical questions and direct references, indicating an aggressive engagement of the listener. A more complete discussion of the speech pattern associated with anger can be found in Weintraub 1981 (159–60). Angry speech is unusual for world leaders, who generally try to present a calm appearance to their listeners.

7. *Emotionally controlled speakers.* Emotionally controlled individuals tend to have low scores in most or all of the feelings categories. Speakers who are perceived as expressive or warm have high scores in the feelings categories.

8. *Oppositional trait.* The speech of oppositional or stubborn speakers is characterized by the presence of many negatives. In the psychiatric populations we have studied, impulsive speakers have used negatives more frequently than any other patient group (Weintraub and Aronson 1964).

9. *Controlling behavior.* This personality trait is verbally reflected in at least two ways. Controlling speakers are frequently emotionally controlled, that is, they use feelings categories infrequently. To avoid finding themselves in an uncontrolled situation, controlled speakers try to prepare for interviews by limiting journalists' questions to certain topics for which they have carefully studied. Such preparation will be revealed by a low frequency of qualifiers.

10. *Histrionic behavior.* Since this trait suggests the dramatic, the category that lends itself best to the expression of exaggeration—adverbial intensifiers—is frequently used by charismatic leaders to hold the attention of an audience. Eisenhower used more adverbial intensifiers than the other post–World War II presidents.

11. *Passivity.* The most useful verbal reflection of passivity is probably the frequent use of the personal pronoun *me. Me* is almost

always used as the object of a verb and is, therefore, the recipient rather than the initiator of action. Investigations of both normal and deviant speakers have shown that *me* is used significantly more by individuals who are thought of as having passive tendencies, that is, small children, elderly people, women, and depressive and compulsive patients (Weintraub 1981, 103–6).

12. *Domineering behavior.* Verbosity, the use of many connectives (qualifiers, retractors, and explainers), and interruptions best characterize domineering conversational behavior. When domineering behavior becomes intimidating, commands and obscenities may appear in the speaker's verbal behavior. Of the post–World War II presidents, Lyndon Johnson was the most domineering in his verbal behavior.

13. *Creativity.* How can we measure verbal creativity? According to Richard Ohmann (1967), there are three ways in which creativity can be expressed in language. A writer or speaker can create new words; can make new syntactic associations, that is, put words together in novel ways; and can express himself or herself in original metaphors. The most common way most creative speakers use any or all of these devices is through wit.

Does verbal creativity reflect other forms of creativity, or is it simply a characteristic of people with a natural facility for writing or speaking? Although some association between verbal creativity and other forms of originality seems likely, little systematic research on the subject has been carried out.

14. *Familiar behavior.* The verbal manifestations of familiar behavior include the use of first names, a favorite device of Ronald Reagan (Weintraub 1989, 174–75), comments about the interviewer's personal life, and allusions to events or persons conceivably known to the interviewee but not through shared experiences with the interviewer. These verbal mannerisms may be reflected in a high direct references score. Familiar individuals frequently use teasing and clowning in their relationships with others, a tactic many listeners find embarrassing and inappropriate. Lyndon Johnson was the most familiar of the post–World War II presidents (Weintraub 1989, 144).

15. *Resilience.* Resilience is the ability to recover quickly from misfortune. This characteristic can be assessed by measuring the

ability of a speaker to lose and then regain his or her verbal style during the course of an interview or, even better, over the course of several interviews spanning days or weeks. A vulnerable speaker may be so traumatized by a failed verbal performance that his or her ability to respond publicly to questions may be affected for a time. Richard Nixon temporarily lost his usual speaking style during the Watergate scandal. His verbal behavior resembled that of a depressed patient. Following the resolution of the crisis, he regained his customary manner of speaking.

16. *Response to stress.* This trait is best measured when the verbal data have been gathered during stress interviews. The speaker's responses to challenging questions are scored and compared with the individual's other scores when answering more neutral questions. If, for example, a speaker's use of both qualifiers and retractors increases in response to stress questions, we may conclude that the speaker becomes less decisive in crisis situations. If, in response to confrontational questions, a speaker uses the pronoun *I* more and the pronoun *we* less, it is likely that in crisis situations that individual will rely more on his or her own resources and less on help from others. On the other hand, a speaker who cannot accept sole responsibility for crisis situations is apt to react in the opposite way, by using more of the pronoun *we* and less of the pronoun *I.*

7. Measuring the Motives of Political Actors at a Distance

David G. Winter

Political leaders deal in power, but they act out of many different motives. Some seek power for its own sake, of course, but many do not. Recall the farmer Cincinnatus, who in the early years of the Roman Republic was twice given dictatorial powers during an emergency. When the emergency was over, each time he gladly returned to his farm. President Harry Truman found the renunciation of power at the end of his presidential years in the "White Prison" (his term) a welcome experience (Miller 1974). Other leaders may be seeking assurance that they are loved or trying to bolster their self-esteem through accomplishments and public acclaim. Motives supply direction and energy for action. (In contrast, traits reflect style.) Motives influence how leaders construe the leadership role; they sensitize perceptions of opportunity and danger; they affect the accessibility of different styles and skills; and they determine sources of leadership satisfaction, stress, frustration, and vulnerability. Thus assessing a leader's motives is an important part of profiling a leader's personality. Yet it is by no means easy to know a political leader's motives. Motives cannot necessarily be inferred directly from actions or outcomes. They wax and wane (often outside of conscious awareness) in response to external incentives and internal dynamics. Finally, they are subject to distortion, deception (including self-deception), and rationalization. For these reasons, motives are often measured indirectly, through content analysis of people's imaginative verbal behavior. Such an assessment technique readily lends itself to measuring the motives of political leaders at a distance.

This chapter presents the method of measuring three motives—achievement, affiliation, and power—in political leaders, through systematic content analysis of their speeches, interviews, and other verbal material. The broad outlines of the method have already been discussed in chapter 2. In the present chapter, the three motives, and the way in which they are measured through content analysis, are first discussed. Then the major political psychology research studies using this scoring method are reviewed. Finally, the procedures and requirements for motive assessment are discussed, along with issues and problems.

Achievement, Affiliation, and Power as Dimensions of Motivation

As discussed in chapter 2, both theoretical analyses and empirical studies of human motivated behavior consistently suggest that achievement, affiliation, and power are three fundamental dimensions of motivated behavior.[1] This section presents brief scoring definitions for each motive (elaborated in table 7.1) and the results of several decades of research on the associated actions and outcomes (summarized in table 7.2). The following section presents results of political psychology studies, involving at-a-distance assessment of the motives of political leaders.

Achievement Motivation: A Concern for Excellence

Achievement motive imagery is scored in texts or other verbal material when there are references to excellence, doing a "good" or "better" job, or carrying out some unique accomplishment or innovative action. The following are examples of achievement motive imagery in political speeches or interviews.

> "I sense the people are seeking something new and better."
> "The only thing we have that's greater than present wealth is our future potential."
> "We created the least bureaucratic governmental enterprise in modern governmental history."

People who use a lot of achievement motive imagery tend to be successful economically, particularly as entrepreneurs in small, high-tech companies—people who *by their own efforts* organize labor, capital, and technology to produce and market some new product or service. They are more innovative and are quicker and better at using information to modify performance. They are restless and travel around a lot, have high but realistic aspirations, carefully calculate probabilities, and (so long as the chances for success are at least moderate) work with energy and persistence. Thus in such business settings, they usually end up performing well. Achievement motivation is not related to success, however, in academic or scientific settings, in the professions, or in large bureaucratic corporations.

Achievement-motivated people can control themselves and delay gratification, perhaps because they have a sense of time as moving faster and stretching farther into the future. They prefer subdued, even somber styles. On the other hand, they are not always tightly controlled "law and order" types: when they perceive it to be neces-

TABLE 7.1.   BRIEF OUTLINE OF THE SCORING SYSTEMS FOR ACHIEVEMENT, AFFILIATION, AND POWER MOTIVE IMAGERY

Achievement	Someone is concerned about a standard of excellence:
	Directly, by words evaluating the quality of performance, or indirectly, by actions clearly suggesting a concern for excellence or by success in competition.
	By negative emotions or counterstriving in response to failure.
	By carrying out some unique, unprecedented accomplishment.
Affiliation	Someone is concerned about establishing, maintaining, or restoring friendship or friendly relations among persons, groups, etc.:
	By expression of warm, positive, friendly, or intimate feelings toward other people, nations, etc.
	By expression of sadness or other negative feeling about separation or disruption of a friendly relationship or wanting to restore it.
	By affiliative, companionate activities.
	By friendly, nurturant acts.
Power	Someone is concerned about having impact, control, or influence on another person, group, or the world at large:
	By taking strong, forceful actions that inherently have an impact on other people or the world at large.
	By controlling or regulating others.
	By attempting to influence, persuade, convince, make or prove a point, or argue.
	By giving unsolicited help or advice.
	By impressing others or the world at large; prestige or reputation.
	By eliciting a strong emotional reaction in someone else.

Source: Data from Winter 1991, 63. This outline is not adequate for scoring purposes. A complete manual, together with instructions, practice materials, expert scoring, and calibration materials, is available at cost from the author, as noted in the text.

sary, they turn to illegal or even revolutionary tactics. In negotiations, they are rational and cooperative, working toward solutions that maximize the benefits to all parties.

Overall, achievement-motivated people seem to be rational calculators, pursuing their self-interest. Indeed, "rational actor" theories typically assume something like achievement motivation as a universal motive—even the *only* human motive. This would be a mistake, however, for there are other important human social motives that lead to quite different outcomes.

Affiliation Motivation: Concern for Close Relations with Others

Affiliation motive imagery is scored in texts or other verbal material when there are references to warm, close relations among people or nations, concern about disruption of warm relations, or nurturant acts that imply warm relations. The following are examples of affiliation motive imagery from political speeches or interviews.

TABLE 7.2. BEHAVIOR CORRELATES OF THE ACHIEVEMENT, AFFILIATION, AND POWER MOTIVES

Characteristic	Achievement	Affiliation	Power
Associated actions	Moderate risks, using information to modify performance, entrepreneurial success, dishonest means when necessary to reach goal	Cooperative and friendly under "safe" conditions, defensive and even hostile under threat	Leadership and high morale of subordinates, if high in sense of responsibility; profligate impulsivity, if low in sense of responsibility
Negotiating style	Cooperative and "rational"	Cooperative under "safe" conditions, defensive and hostile under threat	Exploitative, aggressive
Seeks help from	Technical experts	Friends and similar others	Political "experts"
Political-psychological manifestations	Frustration	Peacemaking and arms limitation, vulnerability to scandal	Charisma, war and aggression, independent foreign policy, rated greatness
Major reference	Smith 1992, chap. 9	Smith 1992, chaps. 13 and 15	Smith 1992, chaps. 19, 21

Source: Data from Winter 1996, 139.

"Let us together create a new national spirit of unity and
  trust."
"We have given aid out of humanitarian considerations."
"Our government must be compassionate."

People who use a lot of affiliation motive imagery are quite different from achievement-motivated people. They are oriented toward
others: spending time with them, communicating with them, and
cooperating with them. However, their circle of friendly interaction
is limited to those people who are similar to themselves—people
whom they agree with and like. Thus affiliation-motivated people
take advice from friends rather than experts and work harder when
they are working with friends. They are more responsive to the
influence of others they know and trust. If they are surrounded by
friendly, similar people, they are thus able to develop more resources
of social support. As a consequence, they tend to have more enjoyable
marriages, higher subjective well-being, and better adaptation to
life.

When they encounter people they don't know or people they perceive to be "different," however, affiliation-motivated people are
actually *less* friendly and agreeable. When they think they are being
exploited, they can become obstinate, even aggressive. Under threat,
high affiliation motivation can lead to prickly, defensive behavior. In
other words, the behavior of affiliation-motivated people toward others is strongly affected by their perception of the other person and
the relationship. Such perceptions often turn on subtle cues, gestures, and patterns of reciprocation, with the result that the interpersonal behavior of people dominated by the affiliation motive may
appear erratic and unstable. In competitive situations, their performance often deteriorates. Because of their sensitivity to the cues of
friendship, such people are not particularly good at managing, working with, or even getting along with total strangers and people they
do not like.

Power Motivation: Concern for Impact

Power motive imagery is scored in texts or other verbal material
when there are references to one person, group, or nation having
impact on another person, group, or nation (or on the world at large)

or concern about reputation and prestige. The following are examples of power motive imagery in political speeches or interviews.

> "We embraced the ideals that moved nations and shook the world."
> "To make this bargain would be a disgrace from which the good name of our country would never recover."
> "The measures indicated in your statement constitute a serious threat to the security of nations."

The notion of a power motive or "will to power" may stir up images of a Napoleon or Hitler, but power in the sense of affecting the behavior of others is an essential feature—indeed, often a beneficent one—of everyday activity in any kind of organized society. People who use a lot of power motive imagery tend to make themselves visible and well known to others, are active in organizations, and are drawn to certain careers (e.g., business, teaching, therapy, journalism) that give the opportunity (even duty) to directly control and sanction the behavior of other persons. They tend to be successful managers, able to create high morale in their subordinates even if they are not personally liked.[2] They are adept at building alliances with others (especially lower-status others), and in small groups they actively define the situation, encourage people to participate, and influence others.

This is the good side of power motivation, when it is tempered by self-control, a sense of responsibility, altruism, or sheer inhibition. But there is another side to power motivation, a shadow perhaps inherent in power but perhaps especially emergent in the absence of responsibility or self-control. People scoring high in power motive imagery are vulnerable to ingratiation and flattery. They tend to improve only after success, not after failure. In making decisions, they give relatively little attention to moral considerations. They also take extreme risks, are verbally and physically aggressive (even in intimate relationships), and display a variety of impulsive behaviors such as exploitative sex, alcohol use, and drug use. Thus the drive for power (to quote Lord Acton's famous observation) tends to corrupt. Finally, power motivation, especially when combined with stress and the need for control, is associated with excessive sympathetic nervous system activity, lower immune system functioning, and consequent vulnerability to cardiovascular problems and infectious diseases.

Political Psychology Research on Motives

This section reviews several political psychology studies that have assessed the motive imagery of political leaders and groups, often as part of a broader psychological profiling.

Research on Strategic Groups of Political Actors

U.S. Presidents

Extending the original work of Donley (Donley 1968; Donley and Winter 1970), Winter (1987a) published motive scores of the first inaugural addresses of American presidents from Washington through Reagan, subsequently (Winter, in press) adding scores for Bush and Clinton. Table 7.3 presents these scores.

Winter's (1991) review and extension of these studies, illustrated in table 7.4, suggest that presidential motive imagery scores correlate with presidential behaviors and outcomes in predictable ways. These results can be summarized as follows. Power-motivated presidents are rated as "great" by historians. (Along these same lines, House, Spangler, and Woycke [1991] found a relationship between presidential power motivation and objective measures of presidential charisma.) On the other hand, presidential power motivation is also associated with involving the country in war—though, of course, the causal linkage between an individual president's motive imagery and U.S. war entry is complex and tenuous. Affiliation-motivated presidents seek peace but are vulnerable to the influence of self-seeking subordinates and, hence, scandal. Finally, the idealistic restlessness of achievement-motivated presidents often leads them to frustration in the amorphous mire of political intrigue and bargaining.

Since achievement-motivated leaders do well in business as entrepreneurs, it is interesting to consider why this same motive creates problems in politics. American corporate culture is a "command and compliance" culture, in which a chief executive can insist on the "one best solution" to any problem. Once there is a single best solution, further discussion is often preempted. After all (in the words of Jimmy Carter's 1975 presidential campaign autobiography), "Why

TABLE 7.3. MOTIVE IMAGERY SCORES OF THE PRESIDENTS OF THE UNITED STATES, 1789–1993

		Raw Scores (images per 1,000 words)			Standardized Scores (M = 50, SD = 10)		
		Ach	Aff	Pow	Ach	Aff	Pow
Washington	1789	3.85	3.85	4.62	39	52	41
Adams, J.	1797	3.89	3.03	4.76	39	48	41
Jefferson	1801	5.65	3.30	6.59	48	49	51
Madison	1809	6.84	3.42	7.69	54	50	56
Monroe	1817	7.22	2.41	6.62	56	45	51
Adams, J. Q.	1825	5.43	3.40	3.74	47	50	36
Jackson	1829	4.48	2.69	5.38	42	47	44
Van Buren	1837	4.38	2.83	4.38	42	47	40
Harrison, W. H.	1841	2.56	1.52	4.31	32	41	39
Polk	1845	2.65	1.43	6.32	33	41	49
Taylor	1849	6.39	3.65	4.56	52	51	40
Pierce	1853	5.72	2.11	6.33	48	44	49
Buchanan	1857	5.05	2.53	4.69	45	46	41
Lincoln	1861	3.34	2.23	6.97	36	45	52
Grant	1869	7.02	2.63	3.51	55	46	35
Hayes	1877	6.07	2.83	6.07	50	47	48
Garfield	1881	5.09	0.34	6.10	45	36	48
Cleveland	1885	6.52	2.37	8.89	52	45	62
Harrison, B.	1889	3.49	2.18	5.45	37	44	45
McKinley	1897	5.30	1.51	5.55	46	41	45
Roosevelt, T.	1905	8.14	1.02	4.07	61	39	38
Taft	1909	4.79	0.92	7.93	44	39	57
Wilson	1913	8.83	2.94	7.06	64	48	53
Harding	1921	5.41	4.51	4.81	47	55	42
Coolidge	1925	4.69	2.47	5.43	43	46	45
Hoover	1929	9.18	2.16	5.94	66	44	47
Roosevelt, F.	1933	6.37	2.12	8.50	52	44	60
Truman	1949	6.91	5.99	11.98	54	61	77
Eisenhower	1953	4.50	4.50	6.14	42	55	48
Kennedy	1961	5.90	9.59	11.81	49	78	77
Johnson, L.	1965	6.77	4.74	6.09	54	56	48
Nixon	1969	8.94	8.00	7.06	65	70	52
Carter	1977	10.60	4.89	8.16	73	56	58
Reagan	1981	7.78	3.28	9.01	59	49	63
Bush	1989	7.35	10.81	7.35	57	83	54
Clinton	1993	10.23	5.75	9.59	71	60	65
M		6.04	3.44	6.49			
SD		1.97	2.23	2.01			

Source: Data from Winter 1987a, with scores added for Bush and Clinton and all scorers re-standardized. Vice presidents who were not elected (and therefore inaugurated) in their own right are not included.

not the best?" These considerations may suggest that utilitarianism and the idea of meritocracy each have a latent authoritarian "shadow." In democratic politics, however, different constituencies usually have different ideas about what is "best," so that "the best" usually has to be compromised in order to get "the possible." People have to be persuaded, cajoled, and inspired to accept someone else's vision of "the best." In politics, even after compromise programs are passed, they have to be implemented by less-than-the-best officials—officials the president did not appoint, does not fully trust, and cannot remove. To a power-motivated leader like Franklin Roosevelt or John F. Kennedy, these are not obstacles but rather the essence of an interesting and zestful political life. (To achievement-motivated chief executives, however, such problems can bring about a small death each day.) As a result, power-motivated leaders may be tempted to go over the heads of the politicians and take their case directly to "the people" (as did achievement-motivated Woodrow Wilson), to take ethical shortcuts (as did achievement-motivated Richard Nixon), or to exhaust oneself in micromanagement (as did achievement-motivated Jimmy Carter).

Candidates for the Presidency

Motives are also related to campaign performance in presidential elections. In a detailed study of the 1976 campaign, Winter (1982) related candidates' motive imagery scores (from their announcement speeches) to aspects of their campaign strategy and performance. The major results are shown in table 7.5. For example, candidates scoring high in achievement motive imagery maintained a middle-of-the-road ideological position, raised money through large donations,

TABLE 7.4. MOTIVES AND PRESIDENTIAL OUTCOMES

Outcome Variable	Achievement	Affiliation	Power
Historians' consensus rating of "greatness"	.09	.09	.40*
Historians' rating of "idealism"	.51**	.19	.19
Assassination attempt	.09	.17	.40*
War entry	−.03	.16	.52**
Arms limitation treaty	.13	.43	−.05
Scandal	.15	.40*	.01

Source: Data from Winter (1991, table 6), which should be consulted for complete definitions of dependent variables.

*$p < .05$ **$p < .01$.

spent money (rather than time) on the crucial New Hampshire primary, and stayed in the race only as long as their chances of success were moderate. All of these results are consistent with the laboratory studies summarized in table 7.2, which portray achievement-motivated people as efficient entrepreneurs who take moderate risks. In contrast, power-motivated candidates took more extreme ideological positions, concentrated on small donors (perhaps as a means of mobilizing grassroots support), spent considerable time (rather than only money) in New Hampshire before that state's critical primary election, and stayed in the race longer overall.

While these results may be specific to the 1976 campaign and national political environment, Adkins (1994) studied the 1992 presidential candidates and found similar relationships between candidates' achievement and power motives and the level of risk of their campaign strategy.

The relationship between candidates' motive imagery profile and their electoral success is somewhat more complicated. Winter (1987a) found that the greater congruence between a president's motive imagery profile and the profile of American society at that time (measured through content analysis of popular literature), the higher the percentage of popular vote received, the greater the margin of victory, and the more likely the president was to be reelected. In other words, *electoral success*—though not necessarily *rated success* in

TABLE 7.5.   MOTIVE IMAGERY SCORES AND CAMPAIGN BEHAVIOR IN THE 1976 PRESIDENTIAL CAMPAIGN

Campaign Variable	Achievement	Affiliation	Power
Extreme ideological position	−.48	.20	.53+
Fund-raising:			
Via small contributions (≤ $100)	−.70**	−.26	.58*
Via large contributions (≥ $500)	.70**	.38	−.72**
Via own funds	.08	.59*	.22
Time spent in New Hampshire during			
14 months before primary	−.52	−.30	.71+
Persistence at low probability of			
success	−.80**	.08	.49

Source: Data from Winter 1982 (tables 3–5), which should be consulted for complete definitions of dependent variables.

$*p < .05$ $**p < .01$.

historical perspective—is a function of motive "fit" between the political actor and the public.

Supreme Court Justices

Aliotta (1988) studied the motives of fifteen U.S. Supreme Court justices by scoring transcripts of their testimony at confirmation hearings during the period 1925–84. She found that writing majority opinions (a dependent variable reflecting justices' prestige and impact on the Court and society) was, as predicted, positively correlated with power motivation and negatively correlated with achievement and affiliation. Achievement-motivated justices cast relatively fewer concurring or dissenting votes. When they did concur or dissent, however, they were more likely to write a separate opinion. Aliotta interprets this finding as a reflection of their concern with excellence rather than with prestige or visibility. In contrast, affiliation-motivated justices, who are also less likely to concur or dissent, tend *not* to write separate opinions when they do. Presumably this reflects their concern with agreement and being liked.

World Political Leaders

Hermann (1979, 1980a) scored affiliation and power imagery in press conference transcripts of forty-five world leaders and related leaders' scores to their foreign policy orientations. As predicted from laboratory studies, affiliation-motivated leaders pursue a cooperative and interdependent foreign policy, while power-motivated leaders are more independent and confrontational. Leaders' power motivation was also related to the level of hostility (i.e., intense and negative affect) that their nations expressed toward other nations, while their affiliation motivation predicted expressions of friendship.

Soviet Leaders

Hermann (1980b) further illustrated these relationships in a study of the motives of Soviet Politburo members in the late 1970s. Members scoring high in affiliation and low in power were relatively more prodetente than were members with the opposite motive pattern.

Schmitt and Winter (1998) scored the reports given by each of the general secretaries of the Communist party of the Soviet Union (Lenin, Stalin, Khrushchev, Brezhnev, and Gorbachev) to the first party congress after their accession to power and related each leader's score to his leadership style.

African Leaders

Winter (1980) scored interview transcripts from twenty-two political leaders from various southern Africa countries, including heads of state, cabinet ministers, and exiled nationalist guerilla leaders. As expected from laboratory studies, power-motivated leaders were rated by a panel of experts as more likely "to initiate, support, or continue armed conflict" ($R = .71$, $p < .001$). It is interesting to note that these ratings of propensity for violence were unrelated ($R = .14$, $p =$ ns.) to ratings of power motivation made by these same expert judges, although on grounds of shared method variance one might have expected that they would be.

Hermann (1987b) scored interview transcripts from twelve sub-Saharan Africa heads of government and related the results to their foreign policy styles and role orientations, confirming her earlier findings on world leaders (Hermann 1980a).

Studies of Individual Leaders

In recent years, several researchers have used motive imagery scoring of historical materials to make inferences, as part of a systematic psychobiography or personality portrait, about the motives of particular individuals. Some of these studies were based on the scores of one particular president, candidate, or other leader from a group study; others were designed from the beginning as a study of a single leader.

Winter and Carlson (1988) explored how the motive imagery scores of Richard Nixon's 1969 first inaugural address (high achievement and affiliation, average power) could be used to resolve some of the paradoxes of Nixon's personal and political behavior. For example, they suggest that Nixon's twists and changes of political beliefs—from liberal populist in college to postwar "Redhunter" to guest of Mao Zedong in 1972—can be understood as a manifestation of the tendency for achievement-motivated people to modify actions on the basis of results of previous actions. More systematically, they validated Nixon's overall motive imagery profile by gathering accounts of his motive-related behavior from the published memoirs of his principal associates, as well as from Nixon's own autobiographies. They found that Nixon showed almost all of the correlates of achievement and affiliation motivation, as would be expected by his very high scores on those two motives. In contrast, he showed only some correlates (slightly fewer than half) of the power motive, again as would be expected by his average score on that motive.

Hermann used power and affiliation motive imagery scores, along with other personality characteristics measured at a distance, to construct personality portraits of Ronald Reagan (1983) and Syrian leader Hafez al-Assad (1988a). Along these same lines, Snare has constructed portraits of Libyan leader Muammar Qaddafi (1992a) and post-Khomeini Iranian leaders (1990, 1992b).

In another quantitative idiographic study, N. J. G. Winter (1992) scored selected speeches of Mussolini and found a significant increase in power motivation and decrease in affiliation after his September 1937 meeting with Hitler that marked the beginning of their close relationship. Such changes may help to explain the marked decrease in the wisdom and success of Mussolini's policies from that same time onward.

Other leaders who have been studied through the use of motive imagery scores include U.S. president George H. W. Bush and former Soviet president Mikhail Gorbachev (Winter et al. 1991b, 1991a); Bill Clinton (Winter 1998b); Woodrow Wilson (Watson and Winter 1997); and (more briefly) John F. Kennedy (Winter 1991, in press).

Studies of Political and Social Processes

Conflict Escalation and War

The motive-scoring technique has also been applied to scoring cultural documents in order to explain motivational contributions to important social processes such as war and peace. Extrapolating from laboratory studies of individuals and prior archival work, Winter (1993b) hypothesized that war and the aggressive resolution of crises would be associated with high levels of power motivation and low levels of affiliation, while peacefully resolved crises would show the reverse pattern. He tested this hypothesis by scoring three sets of historical materials: (1) the Speech from the Throne (or "Queen's Speech") that British sovereigns give at the opening of each session of Parliament, (2) the direct government-to-government communications between Great Britain and Germany in the July 1914 weeks of crisis immediately before the outbreak of World War I, and (3) the statements and letters exchanged by President Kennedy and Premier Khrushchev during the Cuban Missile Crisis of 1962. He found that power motivation increased and affiliation decreased in the years just before Britain entered a war, as compared to the years during which Britain stayed at peace. The same trends occurred during July 1914, as the World War I crisis escalated to war; in the peacefully resolved Cuban Missile Crisis, however, the opposite trends occurred, as power went down while affiliation went up.

Entrepreneurship and Economic Development

In his classic study, *The Achieving Society,* McClelland (1961) demonstrated numerous links between high achievement motivation and economic development, especially entrepreneurial behavior and innovation. At the individual and corporate level, these links have been established through laboratory and longitudinal studies of individuals, as well as archival studies of corporate documents. For example, Diaz (1982) scored motive imagery in the annual letters to stockholders of two American automobile manufacturers and one Japanese automobile manufacture from 1952 to 1980. He found that a company's achievement motive imagery scores from one year predicted that company's relative market share in subsequent years. Wormley (1976) studied mutual fund managers and found that the portfolios of managers with high achievement motivation increased more rapidly over a five-year period, while portfolios of managers with high power motivation showed more volatility (swinging both higher and lower than the market trends).

At the national or cultural level, McClelland (1961) established the connection between achievement motivation and economic development by correlating achievement motive imagery scores from children's school readers (and other cultural documents) with subsequent national economic growth. Among preindustrial cultures, achievement motive imagery in folktales was associated with the prominence of full-time entrepreneurs and more advanced methods of producing food (hunting or agriculture rather than gathering).

Procedures and Materials for Scoring Motives at a Distance

Selecting Political Actor(s) or Group(s)

The first step in any at-a-distance research is to select the persons or groups to be studied. Obviously this depends on the questions and interests of the researcher, but some aspects of this decision have important implications for the overall design of the research.

Election Appropriate Comparison Material

The results of motive imagery scoring are raw motive imagery scores, typically expressed in images per one thousand words. By themselves, these scores are difficult to interpret, since they are undoubtedly affected by many factors besides the actual motives of the political actor: the *type of discourse* (prepared speech, informal remarks, answers to interview questions, written letters, reports, telegrams, diaries, etc.), the *intended audience* (an individual leader, a friend, a public audience, the mass media), the *occasion* (an electoral campaign, an inauguration, a crisis speech, a relaxed interview), the political atmosphere (what issues are salient), and the *compositional mode* (reflective prose, spontaneous remarks, off-the-cuff utterances).

With so many other potentially obscuring factors, researchers may wonder how it is ever possible to detect the effects of individual motives. The answer lies in establishing a comparison sample against which to evaluate these raw scores. Such comparisons are a way to hold constant (or at least to make an effort to hold constant) these other, extraneous factors.

Once a comparison group is identified, the raw motive imagery scores of all persons (those being studied and the comparisons) can be pooled and converted to standardized form. (A standard score is the raw score minus the mean of the entire pooled group, all divided by the standard deviation of the pooled group. It describes a person's raw score in comparison to those of the rest of the standardization group. Scores from the Scholastic Aptitude Test or Graduate Record Examination, for example, are expressed in standardized form, with an overall mean of 500 and a standard deviation of 100.) Once raw scores have been standardized on the basis of the scores of the comparison sample, they can then be compared to any other scores from any other source, based on any other kind of material.[3] The decision of which comparison group to use is critical in two respects. First, it establishes the normative population against which the particular person being studied will be compared. Second, the standardization group decision also affects the selection of actual documents to be scored, since the scores of all persons in the standardization group should be based on the same kinds of documents. The process of identifying comparison groups is subsequently illustrated with some examples.

Identifying Comparison Groups

Often the appropriate comparison group will be obvious. Thus the motive imagery scores of any particular president's first inaugural address can be compared to the scores of all other first inaugural addresses, as shown in table 7.3. Or the scores of one presidential candidate's announcement speech can be compared to the speeches of all other candidates for that year (as in Winter 1982). Hermann (1979, 1980a, 1988b) has used her accumulated sample of world leaders as a comparison group for present and future scorings of additional individual leaders.

Sometimes comparisons can be drawn among different subgroups of a single larger group: for example, in his study of twenty-two southern Africa leaders, Winter (1980) compared the motive imagery scores of white leaders, "front line" heads of state, Zimbabwean nationalist leaders, South African nationalist leaders, and South African "homeland" leaders.

Sometimes a single leader can be studied over time, using similar kinds of verbal material. For example, Winter (1998b) studied changes in the motive imagery levels of Bill Clinton's State of the Union speeches from 1993 through 1996, in effect using Clinton as his own comparison group.

The Case of Ross Perot as an Illustration of Problems in Identifying Comparison Groups

Sometimes the appropriate comparison group is not obvious or is difficult to construct. Such constraints may then affect the kinds of questions that can be asked and limit the hypotheses that can be formulated. The case of Ross Perot's 1992 candidacy for president can be used as an interesting example—for methodological purposes, at least, if not for the enduring substantive importance of Perot as a political leader. Winter (1995) wanted to assess Ross Perot's motive profile as a part of his study of the 1992 U.S. presidential candidates and campaign, since the unusual rise-and-fall cycle of Perot's candidacy had generated considerable popular and journalistic interest. At the time of the initial research (March 1992), the precise nature and status of Perot's campaign were not clear, since he had not made any formal announcement of candidacy. To get some estimate of his motive imagery profile, therefore, Winter scored transcripts of four published interviews in national magazines, comparing the resulting raw scores to other interview-based raw scores (from a sample of interviews with world leaders) rather than to the other presidential candidacy announcement speeches. Then, since Perot formally withdrew from the campaign in July 1992 but reentered it on October 1, his statement of candidacy on that latter occasion could be compared with the other 1992 announcement speeches of the other 1992 candidates.

It is interesting to note that the two estimates of Perot's motive profile were, in standardized terms, quite different; discussion of the differences illustrates how selection of material and identification of comparison groups affect the kinds of interpretations that can be made. In the interviews (standardized on the group of world leaders' interviews), Perot scored very high in achievement, low in affiliation, and a little below average in power. Such a profile is consistent with Perot's previous success as an entrepreneur. The later announcement statement, however, had much lower levels of achievement motivation—below the average for the other 1992 candidates and not much higher than affiliation or power.

Why the difference? Which was Perot's "true" level of achievement motivation? Actually, the *raw* achievement scores for the interviews and announcement were about the same; using different standardization samples for the two kinds of material (a reasonable procedure, given the methodological considerations noted at the beginning of this section) caused the apparent difference in the two achievement motive imagery scores. In other words, in comparison to world leaders responding to interview questions, Perot scored high in achievement motivation; in comparison to other candidates making an announcement speech, he did not. Was this an artifactual or real difference?

Such a question could have several answers, each involving different assumptions about the comparison and standardization processes. (1) The apparent difference in Perot's scores could simply be an artifact of the different comparison samples used; hence Perot's "true" achievement motive imagery score would be either high (on the basis of the interview comparison group) or low (on the basis of the announcement statement comparison group). (2) The world leaders are a political sample and therefore not a good comparison group for Perot's interview-based scores. A sample of business leaders would have been better; in comparison with such a sample, Perot's raw achievement motive score might have been much lower. (3) The apparent difference may be due to the fact that Perot's announcement of candidacy was made as an opening statement in a news conference rather than as a set speech, as were the other candidates' announcements to which it was compared. (4) The difference may be real, but it is the result of Perot's not adjusting his achievement imagery upward to the baseline typical of political announcement speeches, which was a new genre for him. In other words, his announcement was poorly matched to the demands of the occasion and did not reflect his true high level of achievement motivation.

These four answers are essentially methodological hypotheses. More interesting is another answer that involves a substantive explanation: (5) the difference is real and reflects an actual *decline* or disengagement of Perot's achievement motivation during the course of the presidential campaign. Perhaps he did not "have his heart" in the later, October campaign and was just going through the motions of the announcement during the television debates. After all, his probability of success had dropped precipitously by then, and under such circumstances achievement-motivated candidates tend to get out of the race (Winter 1982). Perhaps he only reentered the presidential race to avoid alienating his supporters and so preserve his base of support for future strategic purposes. Hence his announcement statement had lower levels of achievement motivation than it would have had if it had been composed and delivered several months earlier.

Selection of Specific Documents

Once the political actor(s) of interest and appropriate comparison groups have been identified, the next step is to select specific documents. (*Document* as used here means any verbal material that is scored for motive imagery.) The use of comparable documents is just as important as the use of comparable people and for the same reason: any motive imagery scores or differences are always vulnerable to an alternative interpretation or explanation that they are the result of the nature of (i.e., differences in) the material scored rather than true differences between persons.

The need for having similar documents can put constraints on research. For example, suppose a researcher wanted to compare U.S. presidents Jefferson, Lincoln, and Kennedy. American presidents have only given live press conferences since Hoover; only since Kennedy have these been broadcast live. Thus we cannot compare the press conference transcripts of these three presidents. American presidents have only delivered their annual State of the Union message to Congress in person since Wilson; before that time, the message was transmitted in writing. Thus State of the Union messages are not comparable. While inaugural addresses do go back to George Washington, they have certainly changed over two centuries: in literary style, in the nature and size of the audience, and—most important—in the mass media. (Harding's inaugural, for example, was the first to be broadcast on the radio.) And over the years, other modes of presidential communication have changed radically. Letter writing (often done by Jefferson and Lincoln) has given way to telegrams, telephone calls (common in the Kennedy era), and now email. For a Jefferson-Lincoln-Kennedy comparison, then, inaugural addresses may be one of the few even partly comparable sources of data, despite their obvious situational, political, and rhetorical differences.

In international relations research, diplomatic messages, speeches, interviews, diaries, and memoirs may not be comparable with each other on formal or structural grounds or even with themselves across different eras. Again, careful comparisons and selections must be made and advantages and disadvantages balanced.

The Paired Comparisons Method

Winter's study of international crises (1997) illustrates another way of handling the problem of comparability of material. He intended to compare motive imagery in paired crises, one of which escalated to war and the other of which was peacefully resolved. To ensure generality of the results, he drew from a broad range of crises (e.g., the Mexican War verus the Oregon boundary settlement; the 1909 Bosnian crisis versus World War I; Soviet 1956 intervention in Hungary versus nonintervention in Poland; U.S. nonintervention in Indochina in 1954 versus intervention in 1964–65; and Iraq's threatened annexation of Kuwait in 1961 versus its actual invasion in 1990). No single kind of comparable documents exists for all these crises. However, *within* each pair there were one or more kinds of comparable documents, so that it is possible to construct a series of within-pair comparisons.

For example, both the Mexican War and the Oregon boundary settlement are extensively mentioned in President Polk's published diary and his annual messages to Congress, and the diplomatic exchanges with Mexico and Great Britain are also published. For both Indochina in 1954 and Vietnam in 1964–65, there are presidential press conferences and speeches by other American officials, from which material relevant to the topic at hand (i.e., the crisis) can be selected for scoring.[4] For the Jefferson-Lincoln-Kennedy comparison discussed previously, the inaugurals of each president could be compared to those of the presidents serving immediately before and immediately after them, as a way of ruling out extraneous influences and further tightening the comparisons.

Texts

Scoring should be done on verbatim texts. For U.S. research, the *Public Papers of the Presidents* series (and its more quickly available serial form, *Weekly Compilation of Presidential Documents*) provides a verbatim record of every word that the president speaks "on the record." This series goes back as far as Herbert Hoover; before that time, the series *A Compilation of the Messages and Papers of the Presidents* includes major presidential speeches and papers. For the U.S. Congress there is the *Congressional Record* and its predecessor, the *Congressional Globe*.

(Since these two sources have permitted members to revise and extend their remarks before publication, and even to add additional material, they are an imperfect record of what members actually *said* on the floors of Congress, although they are a good record of the verbal material that members *wanted to disseminate.*) The equivalent for Great Britain, from the seventeenth century to the present, is *Hansard's Parliamentary Debates.* For non-U.S. leaders, many verbatim texts of speeches and interviews are included in the *Foreign Broadcast Information Service Daily Report.* This publication has gone through several changes from its beginning in 1947 to the present: from microfilm of mimeographed hard copy to microfiche of printed hard copy; most recently (if not as comprehensively), on-line texts have been available on the Internet. Other on-line sources, such as Lexis-Nexis, are proliferating rapidly. Archival materials that include verbatim texts from political leaders are also published (and nowadays made available on-line) by many governments.

Preparation of Documents

Several steps can be taken to improve the objectivity of scoring. To the maximum extent possible, scorers should be blind to the research hypothesis and to the differences among the different documents (sources, comparisons to be made, etc.). In some cases it may even be appropriate to mask information that could identify the source or in some other way bias the scoring, such as names of persons or countries, dates, and so forth. The entire set of material to be scored (for example, the speeches of all candidates or the documents from both war and nonwar crises) should be randomly mixed together to reduce effects of serial position, scorer fatigue, and similar factors. (True randomization can easily be carried out by assigning four- or five-digit serial numbers from a table of random numbers and then sorting the documents by serial number.)

Scoring

The complete manual "Integrated System for Scoring Motives in Running Text," together with instructions for learning, several different kinds of practice materials, expert scoring, and documentation, can be obtained at cost from the author.[5] The original versions of the three motive scoring systems, together with a wealth of other information, are available in *Motivation and Personality: Handbook of Thematic Content Analysis* (Smith 1992).

Before scoring for research purposes, scorers should have attained a high degree of agreement with expert scoring on the practice materials. The running text manual provides step-by-step instructions for doing this (see also Smith 1992, 526–632). The usual standard of interscorer reliability for research purposes is category agreement (see Smith 1992, 529) and r both greater than .85.

Psychometric and Interpretation Issues

Motives of Leaders or Speech Writers?

When the speeches and other verbal material of political leaders are scored for motive imagery, do the resulting scores reflect the motives of the leaders themselves or the motives of their speech writers? And if speech writers are trying to emphasize salient cultural values in order to create the broadest popular appeal, do the scores really reflect *anybody's* personality? On the other hand, candidates do select their speech writers. Speech writers, in turn, know how to craft words, phrases, and images to fit the style and personalities of their clients. (See Crown 1968, 34–38, on Kennedy and Sorenson; Safire 1975 on writing for Nixon versus writing for Agnew; Noonan 1990 on Reagan; Scott 1993 on Clinton; and Gelderman 1997 on presidential speech writers generally.) Finally, for any important speech such as an announcement of candidacy or an inaugural, the candidate and other close associates review and rework successive drafts until they feel appropriate and comfortable. In 1960, for example, Kennedy personally wrote out a late draft of his inaugural and inserted some scorable motive images into Theodore Sorenson's penultimate typed draft.

Using more spontaneous interview material may reduce (though it does not fully eliminate) this problem, since many "spontaneous" interviews are carefully prepared, even scripted. Yet in a larger sense, concerns about the effect of the speech writer may not matter. Whatever their status, prepared texts do exist as the leader's words; they are taken as the leader's words; and they have effects as the leader's words. We can assume that scores based on these words are a reasonable guide to the leader's personality, *if* they are useful in predicting or interpreting the author's behavior. However, that very same conditional also applies to any other method of making inferences about the personality of a leader or, indeed, any other person.

Factors such as audience, campaign issues, popular mood, cultural values, and political stereotypes do affect speech content, but there is evidence that by themselves they do not wholly determine motive imagery scores (see Hermann 1980a, 344; Winter and Stewart 1977a, 51). Thus it is possible for a political leader to talk about topics such as the economy, national heritage, and even war and peace from almost any manifest policy perspective and either use or not use achievement, affiliation, or power images. In other words, the motive imagery scoring systems seem to pick up the subtle shades of image or emphasis that reflect personal factors rather than merely reflecting the common currency of cultural symbols or ideological stances.

Reliability

Since the motive imagery content analysis system was derived from TAT scoring systems, which have a reputation for low test-retest reliability (see Entwisle 1972), many readers may wonder whether this at-a-distance technique is reliable. Actually, several researchers have shown that the common impression of low TAT reliability is not, in fact, accurate (Smith 1992, 126–39; Winter and Stewart 1977b). Moreover, Winter (1991, 70–71) has shown that the at-a-distance adaptation of these scoring systems gives split-half over-time reliability coefficients in the range of .62 to .77, which suggests considerable temporal stability.

Translation

The research that has been done on the effects of translation on motive imagery scores (Hermann 1980b, 352 n. 2; Winter 1973, 92–93) suggests that translated documents yield about the same scores as originals, so long as the translation was a careful one.

Final Cautions

While the motive imagery scoring procedure has furnished useful insights in case studies and useful generalizations in research on groups, some final cautions about the technique are in order. We must remember that any kind of content analysis depends on the written record. But not all records are accessible, or even known, to researchers. For example, the existence of tape recordings of the deliberations of President Kennedy and his advisers during the Cuban Missile Crisis was not publicly disclosed until twenty-five years afterward. Only recently have some of the taped discussions and conversations of Presidents Johnson and Nixon become available to scholars.

Many important "messages," furthermore, are not to be communicated in such a way that they end up in the public archive. For example, shortly after the outbreak of the first Balkan War (October 14, 1912), Sir William Tyrrell (private secretary to British foreign secretary Grey) dined with German chargé d'affaires Richard von Kühlmann (Nicolson 1930, 279–80). At that dinner, according to Kühlmann's later telegram to German chancellor Bethmann-Hollweg, Tyrell transmitted Grey's "serious and decisive proposal" for "heartfelt and durable conciliation," whereby Germany and Britain would walk "hand in hand" in resolving not only the Balkan crisis but also all other areas of potential conflict. In reply, however, the German foreign secretary doubted whether Grey would communicate such a significant proposal in a "dinner table conversation." In fact, there is no record of these events in any official British archive and no written record of the ultimate result of the conversation in German or British archives. Precisely what transpired during that dinner, then, is not available for content analysis

Similarly, many of the most important aspects of the Cuban Missile Crisis, especially from the Soviet side, do not exist, are not available in official documentation, or have not yet been declassified. For example, several important conversations between American news reporters and Soviet officials, at the height of the crisis, were remembered differently by different people (Fursenko and Naftali 1997, 258, 260–61, 270, and esp. 264–65). Our knowledge of the conversations between Robert Kennedy and Soviet ambassador Dobrynin is similarly based only on reports and memoirs (Fursenko and Naftali 1997, 252–53, 281–82). In short, recollected texts, being subject to distortion (see Winter 1987b), are not verbatim texts.

Even verbatim texts rarely capture many nuances of human speech and communication such as irony, emphasis, hesitation, and doubt.

Such nuances may be crucial to meaning and action, but they are not likely to be picked up by the motive imagery scoring systems. Finally, some things do not even have to be said in so many words; they operate, in Joll's (1968) term, as "unspoken assumptions." For all these reasons, the content of the available written record may not always be isomorphic with the psychological states of political leaders, groups, and peoples, and so we are obliged to use content analysis of that record with caution and humility.

Notes

1. Much of the material in this section is based on Winter 1996 (chap. 5), which contains an extensive list of further references.

2. The difference between the achievement and power motives can be phrased in terms of the old proverb "Build a better mousetrap and the world will beat a path to your door." People high in achievement motivation might indeed build the better mousetrap, but power-motivated people would try to get the world coming to their door without having to build the better mousetrap first— perhaps by buying, renting, or appropriating someone else's mousetrap.

3. Standardization does have the effect of setting the overall standardized means and standard deviations of each group that has been standardized equal to each other. Thus, while it would be possible to compare the standardized motive imagery scores of any two or more presidents with each other, or any president with any candidate from a candidate standardization group, the presidents as a whole, and the candidates as a whole, will have the same mean and standard deviation. Thus we cannot determine motive imagery differences between two different standardization groups as wholes.

4. The assumption that only passages relevant to the crisis should be selected can, of course, be debated.

5. Requests for this material can be sent to the following address: David G. Winter, Department of Psychology, University of Michigan, 525 E. University Avenue, Ann Arbor, MI 48109–1109, U.S.A.

8. Assessing Leadership Style: Trait Analysis

Margaret G. Hermann

More often than not when conversation turns to politics and politicians, discussion focuses on personalities. There is a certain fascination with analyzing political leaders. As a result, biographies on current political figures become best-sellers and the triumphs as well as the tragedies of political leaders become newspaper headlines. A major reason for our curiosity about the personal characteristics of such leaders is the realization that their preferences, the things they believe in and work for, and the ways they go about making decisions can influence our lives.

But how can we learn about the personalities and, in particular, the leadership styles of political leaders in more than a cursory fashion? It is hard to conceive of giving people like Tony Blair, Saddam Hussein, or Boris Yeltsin a battery of psychological tests or having them submit to a series of clinical interviews. Not only would they not have time for, or tolerate, such procedures, they would be wary that the results, if made public, might prove politically damaging to them.

One way of learning more about political leaders that does not require their cooperation is by examining what they say. Only movie stars, hit rock groups, and athletes probably leave more traces of their behavior in the public arena than politicians. U.S. presidents' movements and statements, for example, are generally recorded by the mass media; little of what a U.S. president does escapes notice. Such materials provide a basis for assessment.

By analyzing the content of what political leaders say, we can begin to learn something about the images they display in public, even when such individuals are unavailable for the more usual assessment techniques. To illustrate how political leaders' statements can be studied to learn more about them, the rest of this chapter will present a technique for using such material to assess leadership style.

Focusing on Spontaneous Material

Two major types of statements are readily available for most political leaders in the latter part of the twentieth century—speeches and interviews with the media. Some caution must be exercised in examining speeches to assess what a leader is like since such materials are generally written for him or her by speech writers or staff members. But care and thought have generally gone into what is said and how it is said. Interviews with the media, however, are a more spontaneous type of material. During the give-and-take of a question-and-answer period, leaders must respond quickly without props or aid. What they are like can influence the nature of the response and how it is worded. Although there is often some preparation of a political leader prior to an interview with the press (for example, consideration of what questions might be asked and, if asked, how they should be answered), during the interview leaders are on their own; their responses are relatively spontaneous.

Because of the interest here in assessing the personality characteristics of the political leader and, in turn, his or her leadership style, interviews are the material of preference. In the interview, political leaders are less in control of what they say and, even though still in a public setting, more likely to evidence what they, themselves, are like than is often possible when giving a speech. (For research exploring the differences between speeches and interviews in the assessment of personality at a distance, see, e.g., Hermann 1977, 1980a, 1986b; Winter et al. 1991a; Schafer, forthcoming). The trait analysis described in what follows uses as its unit of analysis the interview response. Interviews are decomposed into individual responses and the question that elicited the response.

Leaders' interviews with the media are available in a wide variety of sources. Interviews with political figures located in governments outside the United States are collected in the *Foreign Broadcast Information Service Daily Report,* which is distributed through World

News Connection, and are reported by other governments' information agencies on their Web sites. Interviews with political elites who reside within the United States are often found in such newspapers as the *New York Times* and *Washington Post,* as well as in weekly news magazines and as recorded from weekly television news programs. Presidential press conferences and other interviews with the presidents can be found in each one's *Presidential Papers.*

It is particularly important in collecting interview materials that one locate verbatim responses—that, indeed, the full text as spoken by the leader is available. At times, newspapers and magazines will survey or edit interviews with leaders, making it difficult to know how representative the reported material is of what was said. We are not interested in what the particular media outlet believes will sell newspapers or magazines but in how the leaders presented themselves in that setting.

In the course of my completing profiles of the leadership styles of some 122 political leaders, it has become evident that the analyst can develop an adequate assessment of leadership style based on fifty interview responses of one hundred words or more in length. Confidence in one's profile, of course, increases the number of interview responses the analyst can assess, but any profile will suffer if it is determined on fewer than fifty responses. To ensure that the description of leadership style is not context-specific, the fifty interview responses that are analyzed should span the leader's tenure in office, as well as have occurred in different types of interview settings, and should focus on a variety of topics. Collecting and categorizing interview responses by time, audience, and topic provide a means for assessing how stable the traits composing leadership style are. Such data indicate how relatively sensitive or insensitive to the context a particular leader is.

It is also possible to classify interviews on their degree of spontaneity, facilitating the analyst's gaining some insight into the differences between a leader's public and private selves. The least spontaneous interviews are those where the political figure calls interviewers into his or her office to present a plan or to report on what is happening or where the political leader asks reporters to submit questions ahead of time and preselects those to answer, planning the responses. The most spontaneous interviews are those where the leader is caught by the press in an unplanned encounter, for example, leaving a meeting, getting on or off a plane, in the corridors of a building, or where there is a recording of a meeting between the leader and advisers. By differentiating the interview responses on degree of spontaneity as well as context, one can gain information not only about the stability of a leader's profile but also about what he or she is particularly sensitive to if there is a lack of stability.

Leadership Style

As the world grows more complex and an increasing number of agencies, organizations, and people participate in policy-making, both at the domestic and international levels, political leaders face several dilemmas in affecting policy, such as how to maintain control over policy while still delegating authority (or having it delegated for them) to other actors in the government and how to shape the policy agenda when situations are being defined and problems as well as opportunities are being perceived and structured by others in the political system. The particular leadership style that leaders adopt can affect the manner in which they deal with these dilemmas and, in turn, the nature of the decision-making process. Barber (1977) has argued that leadership style often results from those behaviors that were useful in securing the leader's first political success; these actions become reinforced across time as the leader relies on them to achieve the second, third, and so forth successes. The term *leadership style* means the ways in which leaders relate to those around them—whether constituents, advisers, or other leaders—and how they structure interactions and the norms, rules, and principles they use to guide such interactions.

In assessing the individual differences of 122 national leaders across the past two decades (e.g., Hermann 1980a, 1980b, 1984a, 1987b, 1988b, 1993; Hermann and Hermann 1989; Kaarbo and Hermann 1998), I have uncovered a set of leadership styles that appears to guide how presidents, prime ministers, kings, and dictators interact with those they lead or with whom they share power. These leadership styles are built around the answers to three questions: (1) How do leaders react to political constraints in their environment—do they respect or challenge such constraints? (2) How open are leaders to incoming information—do they selectively use information or are they open to information directing their response? (3) What are the leaders' reasons for seeking their positions—are they driven by an internal focus of attention within themselves or by the relationships that can be formed with salient constituents? The answers to these three queries suggest whether the leader is going to be generally sensitive or insensitive to the political context and the degree to which he or she will want to control what happens or be an agent for the viewpoints of others. These answers combine to suggest a particular leadership style. Let us examine each of the questions in more detail and then discuss their combination.

In considering leaders' responsiveness to political constraints, we are interested in how important it is for them to exert control and influence over the environment in which they find themselves, and the constraints that environment poses, as opposed to being adaptable to the situation and remaining open to responding to the demands of domestic and international constituencies and circumstances. Research has shown that leaders who are predisposed to challenge constraints are more intent on meeting a situation head-on, achieving quick resolution to an issue, being decisive, and dealing forcefully with the problem of the moment (e.g., Driver 1977; Hermann 1984a; Tetlock 1991; Suedfeld 1992a). Their personal characteristics are highly predictive of their responses to events (e.g., Suedfeld and Rank 1976; Driver 1977; Hermann 1984a) because constraints are viewed as obstacles but not insurmountable ones. To facilitate maintaining direction over events, such leaders work to bring policy-making under their control (e.g., Hermann and Preston 1994; Hermann and Kegley 1995; Kowert and Hermann 1997). Leaders who are more responsive to the context have been found to be more empathetic to their surroundings; interested in how relevant constituents are viewing events and in seeking their support; more open to bargaining, trade-offs, and compromise; and more likely to focus on events on a case-by-case basis (e.g., Driver 1977; Ziller et al. 1977; Hermann 1984a, 1987b; Tetlock 1991; Suedfeld 1992; Kaarbo and Hermann 1998). Because constraints set the parameters for action for such leaders, their personal characteristics suggest the degree of support and closure they will need from the environment before making a decision and where that support will be sought (e.g., Driver 1977; Hermann 1984a; Winter et al. 1991a). Flexibility, political timing, and consensus building are viewed as important leadership tools (e.g., Stoessinger 1979; Snyder 1987; Hermann 1995).

In examining the decision making of American presidents, George (1980) observed that the kinds of information they wanted in making a decision was shaped by whether they came with a well-formulated vision or agenda that framed how data were perceived and interpreted or were interested in studying the situation before choosing a response. Presidents with an agenda sought information that reinforced a particular point of view and sought people around them who were supportive of these predispositions. Presidents more focused on what was happening politically in the current context wanted to know what was doable and feasible at this point in time and were interested in expert opinion or advice from those highly attuned to important constituencies. Leaders who are less open to information have been found to act as advocates, intent on finding information that supports their definition of the situation and over-looking evidence that is disconfirmatory; their attention is focused on persuading others of their position (see, e.g., Axelrod 1976; Jonsson 1982; Fazio 1986; Lau and Sears 1986; Stewart, Hermann, and Hermann 1989; Kaarbo and Hermann 1998). Leaders who are more open to information are reported to be cue takers, both defining the problem and identifying a position by checking what important others are advocating and doing. Such leaders are interested in information that is both discrepant and supportive of the options on the table at the moment, seeking political insights into who is supporting what and with what degree of intensity (e.g., Axelrod 1976; Stewart, Hermann, and Hermann 1989; Kaarbo and Hermann 1998).

Leaders' motivations define the manner in which they "orient [themselves] toward life—not for the moment, but enduringly" (Barber 1977, 8). Motives shape their character—what is important in their lives and what drives them to act. A survey of the literature exploring motivation in political leaders suggests that a variety of needs and incentives push persons into assuming leadership positions in politics (see, e.g., Barber 1965; Woshinsky 1973; McClelland 1975; Winter and Stewart 1977a; Walker 1983; Payne et al. 1984; Snare 1992a; Winter 1992b). Examination of the list that results, however, indicates that political leaders are driven, in general, either by an internal focus—a particular problem or cause, an ideology, a specific set of interests—or by the desire for a certain kind of feedback from those in their environment—acceptance, approval, power, support, status, acclaim. In one case, they are driven internally and pushed to act by ideas and images they believe and advocate. In the other instance, leaders are motivated by a desired relationship with important others and, thus, pulled by forces outside themselves into action. For those for whom solving problems and achieving causes is highly salient, mobilization and effectiveness feature prominently in movement toward their goal; for those motivated by their relationships with others, persuasion and marketing are central to achieving their goal.

Knowledge about how leaders react to constraints, process information, and are motivated to deal with their political environment provides us with data on their leadership style. Table 8.1 indicates the leadership styles that result when these three dimensions are interrelated. A more detailed description of these various leadership styles and the ways that the three factors interrelate can be found in Hermann, Preston, and Young 1996. The empirical relationships between these particular leadership styles and political behavior have been explored by Hermann (1980a, 1984a, 1995); Hermann and Hermann (1989); Stewart, Hermann, and Hermann (1989); Hermann and Preston (1994); and Kaarbo and Hermann (1998).

Using Trait Analysis to Assess Leadership Style

Seven traits have been found to be particularly useful in assessing leadership style: (1) the belief that one can influence or control what happens, (2) the need for power and influence, (3) conceptual complexity (the ability to differentiate things and people in one's environment), (4) self-confidence, (5) the tendency to focus on problem solving and accomplishing something versus maintenance of the group and dealing with others' ideas and sensitivities, (6) general distrust or suspiciousness of others, and (7) the intensity with which a person holds an in-group bias. Based on previous research linking leaders' personal characteristics to their political behavior (e.g., Druckman 1968; Byars 1973; McClelland 1975; Lefcourt 1976; Driver 1977; Hermann and Kogan 1977; Ziller et al. 1977; Her-

TABLE 8.1. LEADERSHIP STYLE AS A FUNCTION OF RESPONSIVENESS TO CONSTRAINTS, OPENNESS TO INFORMATION, AND MOTIVATION

Responsiveness to Constraints	Openness to Information	Motivation	
		Problem Focus	Relationship Focus
Challenges constraints	Closed to information	*Expansionistic* (Focus of attention is on expanding leader's, government's, and state's span of control)	*Evangelistic* (Focus of attention is on persuading others to join in one's mission, in mobilizing others around one's message)
Challenges constraints	Open to information	*Actively Independent* (Focus of attention is on maintaining one's own and the government's maneuverability and independence in a world that is perceived to continually try to limit both)	*Directive* (Focus of attention is on maintaining one's own and the government's status and acceptance by others by engaging in actions on the world stage that enhance the state's reputation)
Respects constraints	Closed to information	*Incremental* (Focus of attention is on improving state's economy and/or security in incremental steps while avoiding the obstacles that will inevitably arise along the way)	*Influential* (Focus of attention is on building cooperative relationships with other governments and states in order to play a leadership role; by working with others, one can gain more than is possible on one's own)
Respects constraints	Open to information	*Opportunistic* (Focus of attention is on assessing what is possible in the current situation and context given what one wants to achieve and considering what important constituencies will allow)	*Collegial* (Focus of attention is on reconciling differences and building consensus— on gaining prestige and status through empowering others and sharing accountability)

mann 1980b, 1984a, 1987b; Bass 1981; Walker 1983; Snyder 1987; Hermann and Hermann 1989; Stewart, Hermann, and Hermann 1989; Winter et al. 1991; Suedfeld 1992; Winter 1992; Kaarbo and Hermann 1998), these seven traits provide information that is relevant to assessing how political leaders respond to the constraints in their environment, how they process information, and what motivates them to action. Knowledge about the degree to which leaders believe that they can influence what happens and their need for power suggests whether they will challenge or respect the constraints that they perceive in any setting in which they find themselves. Assessing leaders' conceptual complexity and self-confidence helps us determine how open they will be to information. And measuring the extent of their in-group bias, general distrust of others, and tendency to prefer problem-solving functions to those involving group maintenance assists us in learning what motivates leaders. In what follows, we will describe how each trait can be determined through content analysis of leaders' interview responses, as well as indicate what scores on the various traits mean for leadership style, both singly and in combination.

In this trait analysis, an assumption is made that the more frequently leaders use certain words and phrases in their interview responses, the more salient such content is to them. In effect, the trait analysis is quantitative in nature and employs frequency counts. At issue is what percentage of the time in responding to interviewers' questions when leaders could exhibit particular words and phrases are they, indeed, used. The percentages that result for one leader can currently be compared to those for 87 heads of state from around the world or to those for 122 political leaders filling a range of positions in governments in countries in the Middle East, Africa, the former Soviet Union, and Western industrialized democracies. Through such comparisons, the researcher or analyst can determine whether the particular leader is high or low on a trait. This procedure will become clearer after we describe how to code for the seven traits. Currently a computer program is being developed that will automatically code for the traits discussed here. Entitled "Profiler" (Young, forthcoming), the program will provide a researcher or analyst with the trait scores for a specific leader based on either speeches or interviews. (A more detailed description of the steps involved in doing a manual content analysis of the traits can be found in Hermann 1987c).

Let us now turn to specifying how the traits relate to the questions asked earlier concerning leadership style and how each trait can be coded.

Does the Leader Respect or Challenge Constraints?

Political leaders who are high in their belief that they can control what happens and in the need for power have been found to challenge the constraints in their environments, to push the limits of what is possible (see, e.g., McClelland 1975; Winter and Stewart 1977; Hermann 1980b; Walker 1983; Hermann and Preston 1994; Kowert and Hermann 1997; Kaarbo and Hermann 1998). These leaders are in charge, and they know what should happen. Moreover, they are skillful both directly and indirectly in getting what they want. Those leaders, however, who are low in these two traits appear to respect, or at least accede to, the constraints they perceive in their environments and to work within such parameters toward their goals. Building consensus and achieving compromise are important skills in their minds for a politician to have and to exercise. Leaders who are moderate on both these traits have the ability of moving either toward challenging or toward respecting constraints, depending on the nature of the situation; they will be driven by their other characteristics and what they believe is called for by the context.

But what if a leader is high on one trait but low to moderate on the other? Leaders who are high in the belief that they can control events but low in the need for power will take charge of what happens and challenge constraints, but they will not do as well in reading how to manipulate the people and in working behind the scenes to have the desired influence. Such leaders will not be as successful in having an impact as those high in both traits. They will be too direct and open in their use of power, signaling others on how to react without really meaning to. And what about the leaders who are low in the belief that they can control events but high in the need for power? These individuals will also challenge constraints, but they will be more comfortable doing so behind the scenes, in an indirect fashion, rather than out in the open. Such leaders are especially good in settings where they are the "power behind the throne," where they can pull the strings but are less accountable for the result.

Table 8.2 summarizes this discussion. In previous research (e.g., Hermann 1980a, 1980b, 1984a, 1987b; Hermann and Hermann 1989; Hermann and Preston 1994; Kaarbo and Hermann 1998), as noted earlier, I have collected data on the personality traits described here of 122 political leaders, some 87 of them being heads of government. The leaders in that sample span the years 1945–99 and represent all regions of the world. For this group of leaders, scores on the belief in one's own ability to control events are correlated with those on the need for power—0.17 in the sample of 87 heads of state and 0.21 for the 122 political leaders. These correlations indicate that the two characteristics are distinctive and that there will be instances where the individual being studied is high on one trait and low on the other. To put this discussion into context, let us now define the two traits in more detail.

Belief in One's Own Ability to Control Events

The belief in one's own ability to control events is a view of the world in which leaders perceive some degree of control over the situations

TABLE 8.2.   LEADERS' REACTIONS TO CONSTRAINTS

Need for Power	Belief Can Control Events	
	Low	High
Low	**Respect** constraints; work within such parameters toward goals; compromise and consensus building important.	**Challenge** constraints but less successful in doing so because too direct and open in use of power; less able to read how to manipulate people and setting behind the scenes to have desired influence.
High	**Challenge** constraints but more comfortable doing so in an indirect fashion—behind the scenes; good at being "power behind the throne" where they can pull strings but are less accountable for result.	**Challenge** constraints; are skillful in both direct and indirect influence; know what they want and take charge to see it happens.

in which they find themselves; there is a perception that individuals and governments can influence what happens. In coding for belief in control over events, the focus is on verbs or action words. We assume that, when leaders take responsibility for planning or initiating an action, they believe that they have some control over what happens. The focus here is on actions proposed or taken by the leader or by a group with whom he or she identifies. A score on this trait is determined by calculating the percentage of times the verbs in an interview response indicate that the speaker or a group with whom the speaker identifies has taken responsibility for planning or initiating an action. The overall score for any leader is the average of this percentage across the total number of interview responses being examined.

Leaders who believe that they can influence what happens in the world are generally more interested and active in the policy-making process. Those who are high in this trait will want to maintain control over decision making and implementation to ensure that things, indeed, do happen. After all, if they are not involved, something may go awry. Thus, such leaders are likely to call subordinates to check on what they are doing, to make surprise visits to places where policy is being implemented, and to be interested in meeting face-to-face with other leaders to see how far they are willing to go. Leaders high in this belief are less likely to delegate authority for tasks and are likely to initiate activities and policies rather than wait for others to make suggestions. They are often "running ideas up the flagpole to see who salutes them." In some sense this trait has aspects of a self-fulfilling prophecy. Leaders who believe that they can affect what happens are more likely to initiate and oversee activities to ensure that policies are enacted; they are more likely to take charge because they perceive they can influence events. Moreover, because such leaders are so sure they can have an impact on the world, they are less prone to compromise or to work out a deal with others. Once they decide, they exude confidence in their decision—they know what should be done.

Leaders who are low in the belief that they can control what happens tend to be more reactive to situations, waiting to see how the situation is likely to play out before acting. They are less likely to take initiatives, preferring instead to let others take the responsibility for anything too daring and out of the ordinary. Such leaders want to participate and lead in contexts where there is at least a 50 percent chance of success. They are willing to delegate authority, hoping others may have more luck than they seem to have in influencing outcomes. As a result, such leaders are also able to shift the blame when something goes wrong. Unlike their counterparts who think they can affect their external environments, these leaders do not shoulder responsibility and move on but, rather, are quick to accuse others of making it difficult for them to act. For political leaders who do not believe they can control what happens, fear of failure may supersede and crowd out sense of timing.

Need for Power and Influence

The need for power indicates a concern for establishing, maintaining, or restoring one's power; in other words, it is the desire to control, influence, or have an impact on other persons or groups (see Winter 1973). As with coding of the previous trait, coding of the need for power focuses on verbs. Is the speaker with this proposed action attempting to establish, maintain, or restore his or her power? Some of the conditions where the need for power would be scored are when the speaker (1) proposes or engages in a strong, forceful action, such as an assault or attack, a verbal threat, an accusation, or a reprimand; (2) gives advice or assistance when it is not solicited; (3) attempts to regulate the behavior of another person or group; (4) tries to persuade, bribe, or argue with someone else so long as the concern is not to reach agreement or avoid disagreement; (5) endeavors to impress or gain fame with an action; and (6) is concerned with his or her reputation or position. Once again the focus is on actions proposed or taken by the leader or a group with whom he or she identifies. A score on the need for power is determined by calculating the percentage of times the verbs in an interview response indicate that the speaker or a group with whom the speaker identifies has engaged in one of these behaviors. The overall score for any leader is the average of this percentage across the total number of interview responses examined.

When the need for power is high, leaders work to manipulate the environment to have control and influence and to appear as a winner.

They are good at sizing up situations and sensing what tactics will work to achieve their goals. Indeed, they are highly Machiavellian, often working behind the scenes to ensure that their positions prevail. Leaders high in the need for power are generally daring and charming—the dashing hero. But they have little real regard for those around them or for people in general. In effect, other people and groups are viewed as instruments for the leader's ends; guile and deceit are perceived as part of the game of politics. Such leaders set up rules to ensure conformity to their ideas—rules that can change abruptly if the leader's goals or interests change. At first followers are beguiled by leaders who are high in this motive since they are able to produce results and are charismatic, but the "bloom often leaves the rose" over time as such leaders exploit their followers and as their goals diverge from what the people want or feel they need.

Leaders high in the need for power will test the limits before adhering to a course of action, bartering and bargaining up until the last moment in order to see what is possible and what the consequences will be of pushing further toward their goals. These leaders are more skillful in such negotiations when they can interact directly with those involved; without face-to-face interaction, such leaders can misjudge the assumptions the other party is making and how far they are willing to go.

When the need for power is low, leaders have less need to be in charge; they can be one among several who have influence. It is perfectly OK with them that others receive credit for what happens. Indeed, empowering others is important for such a leader. They are willing to sacrifice their own interests for those of the group, since in their view what is good for the group is, in truth, good for them. Leaders low in the need for power enable their followers to feel strong and responsible by empowering them to act as emissaries and expand the group or the group's assets. Through this process these leaders engender high morale in their followers and a sense of team spirit and goal clarity. Such leaders also have a sense of justice. They deal with people evenhandedly based on the norms of the group; they play no favorites so people know where they stand and what will happen if they violate the norms. Their intent is to build a relationship of trust with their followers and a sense of shared responsibility and accountability for what happens. In effect, these leaders become the agent for the group, representing their needs and interests in policy-making.

Is the Leader Open or Closed to Contextual Information?

Political leaders tend to differ on their degree of openness to contextual information based on their levels of self-confidence and conceptual complexity (see, e.g., Driver 1977; Ziller et al. 1977; Stuart and Starr 1981–82; Jonsson 1982; Hermann 1984a; Snyder 1987; Stewart, Hermann, and Hermann 1989; Tetlock 1991; Suedfeld 1992; Kaarbo and Hermann 1998). Ziller and his colleagues (1977) observed that these two traits interrelate to form a leader's self-other orientation. The self-other orientation indicates how open the leader will be to input from others in the decision-making process and from the political environment in general. Those whose scores on conceptual complexity are higher than their self-confidence scores are open and generally more pragmatic and responsive to the interests, needs, ideas, and demands of others. Such leaders are generally those who get elected in local and state elections in America. They are sensitive to situational cues and act based on what they sense is acceptable under current conditions. They appear to others to be open and to listen. These leaders are able to get others to do things because the leaders seem interested in what happens to these others and concerned about helping them. Such leaders are more likely to organize collegial decision structures that allow for a free give-and-take and, thus, to maximize the contextual information they can have about the opinions and needs of those around them. These leaders deal with problems and events on a case-by-case basis.

Leaders whose self-confidence scores are higher than their scores on conceptual complexity tend to be closed; they are ideologues, principled and driven by causes. These leaders know what is right and what should happen and set about to persuade others of the appropriateness of their course of action. Such leaders are fairly unresponsive or insensitive to cues from the environment. Instead they reinterpret the environment to fit their view of the world. Moreover, they are not above using coercive or devious tactics to ensure that their views are adopted by a group. Indeed, they are highly active on behalf of their cause, eagerly pursuing options they believe will succeed. These leaders are more likely to organize the decision-making process in a hierarchical manner to maintain control over the nature of the decision. They generally do not win any "most popular leader" contests but are usually admired for what they can do.

When the scores on these two traits are relatively equal, leaders' behavior will depend on whether the scores are high or low when compared to other leaders (for example, either the sample of 87 or 122 on which I have collected data or regional subsamples of these two groups). If both are high, leaders will be open and more strategic, focusing their attention on what is possible and feasible at any point in time. Their high self-confidence facilitates having patience in the situation and taking their time to see what will succeed. These leaders will combine the best qualities of both these characteristics—a sense of what they want to do but the capability to check the environment to see what will work. It is interesting to note that this type of leader is less likely to be elected in democratic systems (Ziller et al. 1977), perhaps because their behavior seems to the outside observer and interested constituent to be erratic and opportunistic. If one knows the goals and political contexts of such leaders, their decisions and actions become more logical. Without this knowledge, however, they may seem indecisive and chameleonlike in their behavior.

If the scores on both traits are low in comparison to other leaders, the individual is likely to be closed, reflecting the views of those around him or her, and inclined to rather easily lock onto a position that will seem likely to be successful. These are the leaders that Lasswell (1930; see also Barber 1965) observed entered into politics to compensate for their low self-esteem. They are easy targets for groups that seek someone who will tenaciously advocate for a particular position in exchange for influence and authority, however tenuous and fleeting the assignation may be. These leaders may evidence some of the signs of narcissism, relishing the spotlight, pushing for even more extreme moves than the group may perceive are necessary, and being preoccupied with fantasies of unlimited success.

Table 8.3 summarizes this discussion, suggesting some rules to follow in determining how open a leader will be to information based on his or her scores on conceptual complexity and self-confidence. Self-confidence and conceptual complexity scores are correlated 0.10 for the 87 heads of state in my sample of leaders and 0.33 for the broader set of 122 political leaders. Both correlations suggest that we will find all combinations of the trait scores among world leaders. These two traits are assessed in the following way.

Self-Confidence

Self-confidence indicates one's sense of self-importance, an individual's image of his or her ability to cope adequately with objects and persons in the environment. Indeed, self-confidence "is that component of the self system which is involved in regulating the extent to which the self system is maintained under conditions of strain such as occur during the processing of new information relative to the self" (Ziller et al. 1977, 177; see also Ziller 1973). Stimuli from the environment are mediated by a person's sense of self. Since people tend to develop their self-confidence as a result of evaluating themselves in comparison with others and their experiences, this trait often becomes the frame of reference for positioning one's self in a particular context.

In coding for self-confidence, the focus is on the pronouns *my, myself, I, me,* and *mine.* When speakers interject these pronouns into their speech, how important do they see themselves compared to what is happening? Does the use of the pronoun reflect that the leader is instigating an activity (e.g., "I am going to . . ." or "That is my plan of action"), should be viewed as an authority figure on this issue (e.g., "If it were up to me . . ." or "Let me explain what we mean"), or is the recipient of a positive response from another person or group (e.g., "You flatter me with your praise" or "My position was accepted")? In each of these instances, there is an enhanced sense of

TABLE 8.3.   RULES FOR DETERMINING OPENNESS TO INFORMATION

Scores on Conceptual Complexity and Self-Confidence	Openness to Contextual Information
Conceptual Complexity > Self-Confidence	Open
Self-Confidence > Conceptual Complexity	Closed
Conceptual Complexity and Self-Confidence Both High	Open
Conceptual Complexity and Self-Confidence Both Low	Closed

self-worth and a show of self-confidence. A score on this trait is determined by calculating the percentage of times these personal pronouns are used in an interview response that meet the three criteria. The overall score for any leader is his or her average percentage across the total number of interview responses collected for that particular person.

Leaders whose self-confidence is high are more immune to incoming information from the environment than are those with low self-confidence. They are more generally satisfied with who they are and are not searching for more material on which to evaluate themselves and their behavior. "New information relative to the self is . . . ignored or transformed in such a way as to maintain consistency in behavior" (Ziller et al. 1977, 177). Such leaders are not subject to the whims of contextual contingencies. They are neither the victims of events nor are they compelled to adapt to the nature of the situation—consistency in behavior is too important. Information is filtered and reinterpreted based on their high sense of self-worth.

Political leaders, however, who are low in self-confidence are easily buffeted by the "contextual winds." Without a well-developed sense of who they are, such leaders tend to continually seek out information from the environment in order to know what to do and how to conform to the demands of the circumstances in which they find themselves. Input from others about what they are thinking and feeling is critical to knowing how to act in any situation. Thus, the behavior of these individuals often appears highly inconsistent, matched as it is to the nature of the setting, not to the needs and desires of the individual. To compensate for feelings of inadequacy, these leaders seek to become the agents, representatives, or delegates of political groups that can help to enhance their self-confidence.

Conceptual Complexity

Conceptual complexity is the degree of differentiation that an individual shows in describing or discussing other people, places, policies, ideas, or things. The conceptually complex individual can see varying reasons for a particular position, is willing to entertain the possibility that there is ambiguity in the environment, and is flexible in reacting to objects or ideas. In the opposite manner, the conceptually simple individual tends to classify objects and ideas into good-bad, black-white, either-or dimensions; has difficulty in perceiving ambiguity in the environment; and reacts rather inflexibly to stimuli.

In coding for conceptual complexity, the focus is on particular words—words that suggest the speaker can see different dimensions in the environment as opposed to words that indicate the speaker sees only a few categories along which to classify objects and ideas. Words that are suggestive of high conceptual complexity are *approximately, possibility, trend,* and *for example;* words indicative of low conceptual complexity include *absolutely, without a doubt, certainly,* and *irreversible.* As with the other traits previously discussed, the score for conceptual complexity is the percentage of high and low complexity words in any interview response that suggest high complexity. The overall score for any leader is his or her average score across interview responses.

Political leaders who are high in conceptual complexity attend to a wider array of stimuli from their environment than do those who are low. Indeed, they have a sense that issues are more gray than black or white and seek a variety of perspectives through which to organize the situation in which they find themselves. These leaders remain highly attuned to contextual information since they do not necessarily trust their first response to an event. In the view of the conceptually complex leader, to understand a situation and plan what to do, one must gather a large array of information and seek out others' opinions on what should be done—there is always room for one more piece of data or perspective. Such leaders often take their time in making decisions and involve a large array of actors in the decision-making process. Flexibility is seen as the key to behavior.

Leaders who are low in conceptual complexity trust their intuition and often are willing to go with the option that presents itself first. Action is preferable to thinking, planning, or searching for more information. Contextual information is generally classified according to a set of stereotypes; because there is often a good fit between this categorization system and the conceptually more simple individual's orientation to politics, the world is highly ordered and structured. It is relatively easy to decide what to do since the individual's closed conceptual system evaluates and transforms information from any situation into the specified categories. Interpretation and consistency are the keys to behavior.

Is the Leader Motivated by Problems or Relationships?

In politics, the literature (e.g., Wriggins 1969; Burns 1978; Nixon 1982; Hermann 1986a; Hargrove 1989; Heifetz 1994; Bennis and Nanus 1997; Hermann and Hagan 1998) suggests that leaders have certain reasons for assuming their positions of authority that have to do with them and with the relevance of the groups (e.g., parties, juntas, ethnic groups, unions, administrations, cabinets, and governments) with whom they identify. As noted earlier, leaders are driven, in general, either by an internal focus (a problem)—a particular cause, an ideology, a specific set of interests—or by the desire for a certain kind of feedback from those in their environment (a relationship)—acceptance, power, support, acclaim. They also appear to become activated by needs to protect their own kind. Whereas leaders who are more closely identified with particular groups work to ensure such entities' survival and often perceive the political world as full of potential threats to their groups, those who are less strongly tied to a specific group view the world as posing potential opportunities for working with others for mutual or their own benefit. Thus, in assessing motivation, we are interested in both why the leader sought office *and* their need to preserve and secure the group they are leading (and, in turn, their position).

Three traits are used to measure these two types of motivation: task focus, in-group bias, and distrust of others. Task versus interpersonal focus provides information about the leaders' reasons for seeking office; in-group bias and distrust of others assist in assessing identification with the group. Let us consider each of these traits in more detail.

Motivation for Seeking Office (task focus)

Leaders have been recognized as performing two distinct functions in groups, that of moving the group toward completion of a task (solving problems) and that of maintaining group spirit and morale (building relationships). These two functions can be represented by a continuum, with one extreme representing an emphasis on getting

the task done and the other extreme an emphasis on group maintenance. Task focus suggests the relative emphasis a leader places in
interactions with others on dealing with the problems that face the
government as opposed to focusing on the feelings and needs of relevant and important constituents. For leaders who emphasize the
problem, moving the group (nation, government, ethnic group, religious group, union, etc.) forward toward a goal is their principal
purpose for assuming leadership. For those who emphasize group
maintenance and establishing relationships, keeping the loyalty of
constituents and morale high are the central functions of leadership.
Research (e.g., Byars 1972, 1973; Hermann and Kogan 1977; Bass
1981) has suggested that charismatic leaders are those who fall in the
middle of this continuum, focusing on the problem when that is
appropriate to the situation at hand and on building relationships
when that seems more relevant. The charismatic leader senses when
the context calls for each of these functions and focuses on it at that
point in time. Table 8.4 summarizes this discussion.

In coding for task focus, just like in coding for conceptual complexity, attention is directed toward counting specific words, in this
case words that indicate work on a task or instrumental activity, as
well as words that center around concern for another's feelings,
desires, and satisfaction. Examples of the task-oriented words are
accomplishment, achieve(ment), plan, position, proposal, recommendation,
and *tactic.* Illustrative of the group-maintenance types of words are
appreciation, amnesty, collaboration, disappoint(ment), forgive(ness), harm,
liberation, and *suffering.* The score for task focus is determined by calculating the percentage of task-oriented words relative to the total
number of task-oriented and group-maintenance words in a particular interview response. The overall score is the average percentage
across the interview responses examined.

TABLE 8.4.   RULES FOR ASSESSING MOTIVATION FOR
SEEKING OFFICE

Score on Task Focus	Motivation for Seeking Office
High	Problem
Moderate	Both problem and relationship depending on the context
Low	Relationship

Leaders with a task focus are often taskmasters, always pushing a group to work on solving the particular problem of the moment. They tend to see the world in terms of problems and the role of the group as providing solutions to these problems. These leaders view people less as individuals than as instruments. Such leaders are constantly asking for movement on a project, about what is happening in the implementation of a solution to a problem, and for options to deal with a problem. The substance, not the people involved, is the focus of attention. Leaders with a task emphasis are willing to sacrifice a high level of morale in the group for accomplishing the task. As these leaders note: "You can't keep all the people happy; leaders have to make hard decisions for the good of the group, and the people will just have to understand." These leaders seek followers who share their interest in solving problems and who will work hard to implement any decisions that are made.

Leaders with a group-maintenance or relationship focus want to keep the morale and spirit of their groups high. These leaders are generally sensitive to what the people want and need and try to provide it. They will only move the group toward its goals as fast as the members are willing to move. Camaraderie, loyalty, and commitment to the group are critical for leaders with this emphasis. The people in the group, not what needs to be done, are the focus of attention. These leaders work to foster a sense of collegiality and of participation in their groups. Members have the feeling that they are a part of what happens and that their views are sought and listened to. For these leaders, mobilizing and empowering members are what leadership is all about. As a result, they are likely to build teams and to share leadership, often seeking out opinions about what is feasible among relevant constituencies at any point in time.

Motivation toward World (in-group bias and distrust of others)

Table 8.5 suggests how information about a leader's scores on in-group bias and distrust of others provides us with evidence concerning whether the leader is driven by the threats or problems he or she perceives in the world or by the opportunities to form cooperative relationships. There is a growing literature indicating that leaders' ways of approaching the world can affect how confrontational their country is likely to be, how likely they are to take initiatives, and when they are likely to engage in economic sanctions and military interventions (see, e.g., Levine and Campbell 1972; Driver 1977; Kelman 1983; Vasquez 1993; Snyder 1991; Hagan 1994, 1995; Hermann and Kegley 1995). Indeed, this writing has been referred to as the "statist approach" to foreign policy decision making since it focuses on how leaders' needs to protect their own kind, when shared by an administration, can shape how conflictual or cooperative a government and country will be in the international arena (see Hagan 1994). The research suggests that the more focused leaders are on protecting their own kind, the more threats they are likely to per-

TABLE 8.5. MOTIVATION TOWARD WORLD

In-group Bias	Distrust of Others	
	Low	High
Low	World is not a threatening place; conflicts are perceived as context-specific and are reacted to on a case-by-case basis; leaders recognize that their country, like many others, has to deal with certain constraints that limit what one can do and call for flexibility of response; moreover, there are certain international arenas where cooperation with others is both possible and feasible. *(Focus is on taking advantage of opportunities and relationships)*	World is perceived as conflict-prone, but because other countries are viewed as having constraints on what they can do, some flexibility in response is possible; leaders, however, must vigilantly monitor developments in the international arena and prudently prepare to contain an adversary's actions while still pursuing their countries' interests. *(Focus is on taking advantage of opportunities and building relationships while remaining vigilant)*
High	While the international system is essentially a zero-sum game, leaders view that it is bounded by a specified set of international norms; even so, adversaries are perceived as inherently threatening and confrontation is viewed to be ongoing as leaders work to limit the threat and enhance their countries' capabilities and relative status. *(Focus is on dealing with threats and solving problems even though some situations may appear to offer opportunities)*	International politics is centered around a set of adversaries that are viewed as "evil" and intent on spreading their ideology or extending their power at the expense of others; leaders perceive that they have a moral imperative to confront these adversaries; as a result, they are likely to take risks and to engage in highly aggressive and assertive behavior. *(Focus is on eliminating potential threats and problems)*

ceive in the environment and the more focused they will be on confronting those responsible. Leaders who are not so intense in this desire are capable of seeing the possibilities for win-win agreements and for building relationships in international politics since the world is viewed as containing opportunities as well as threats.

The two traits, in-group bias and distrust of others, are correlated 0.62 in my sample of 87 heads of state and 0.29 in the broader sample of 122 leaders. In the head of state sample, the rather high correlation indicates that, when such leaders are highly identified with their country, they are also probably highly distrustful and vice versa. In other words, just as in common parlance, heads of state tend to be hawks or doves, hardliners or accommodationists—more threat and problem oriented or more opportunity and relationship oriented.

In-group bias is a view of the world in which one's own group (social, political, ethnic, etc.) holds center stage. There are strong emotional attachments to this in-group, and it is perceived as the best. Moreover, there is an emphasis on the importance of maintaining in-group culture and status. Any decisions that are made favor the in-group. In coding for in-group bias, the unit of analysis is a word or phrase referring to the particular leader's own group. Of interest is ascertaining the following information when the leader makes a reference to his or her own group: are the modifiers used favorable (e.g., *great, peace-loving, progressive, successful, prosperous*); do they suggest strength (e.g., *powerful, capable, made great advances, has boundless resources*); or do they indicate the need to maintain group honor and identity (e.g., "need to defend firmly our borders," "must maintain our own interpretation," "decide our own policies")? If any of these modifiers are present, the phrase indicates in-group bias. The score for in-group bias is the percentage of times in an interview response that a leader refers to in-groups that meet the criteria just outlined. The leader's overall score is the average of these percentages across all the interview responses under examination.

Political leaders high in in-group bias are interested in maintaining the separate identity of their groups at all costs. They become quite concerned when other groups, organizations, governments, or countries try to meddle in what they perceive are the internal affairs of their group. The higher the score, the more isomorphic the leader and group become—the leader is the group; if anything happens to the group it happens to the leader and vice versa. Leaders with high scores for in-group bias tend to see the world in *we* and *them* (friends and enemies) terms and to be quick to view others as challenging the status of their group. They are prone to perceive only the good aspects of their group and to deny or rationalize away any weaknesses. Thus, such leaders are often relatively late in becoming aware of problems that may undermine their authority.

Leaders high in in-group bias are likely to use external scapegoats—their perceived enemies—as the cause for all of the group's (government's, country's) problems and to mobilize the support of their own population through this external threat. In the extreme, such leaders may keep their group mobilized militarily indefinitely to deal with *the perceived* external enemy. Leaders with high scores are likely to view politics as a zero-sum game where one group's gain is another's loss. Therefore, they must always be vigilant to make sure that it is their group that wins, not loses. Such leaders will want people around them who are also highly identified with the group and loyal—selecting advisers on the basis of their sense of commitment to the group and its goals and interests.

It is important to note here that leaders who are low in in-group bias are still patriots interested in the maintenance of their groups as a separate entity. They are, however, less prone to view the world in black-and-white terms and more willing to categorize people as *we* or *them* based on the nature of the situation or problem at hand so that such categories remain fluid and ever changing depending on what is happening in the world at the moment. These leaders are less likely to use scapegoats as a means of dealing with domestic opposition; instead they may use interactions such as summit conferences and positive diplomatic gestures as strategies for tempering domestic discontent.

Distrust of others involves a general feeling of doubt, uneasiness, misgiving, and wariness about others—an inclination to suspect the motives and actions of others. In coding for distrust of others, the focus is on noun and noun phrases referring to persons other than the leader and to groups other than those with whom the leader identifies. Does the leader distrust, doubt, have misgivings about, feel uneasy about, or feel wary about what these persons or groups are doing? Does the leader show concern about what these persons or groups are doing and perceive such actions to be harmful, wrong, or detrimental to himself or herself, an ally, a friend, or a cause important to the leader? If either of these conditions is present, the noun or noun phrase is coded as indicating distrust. A leader's score on this trait is the percentage of times in an interview response that he or she exhibits distrust toward other groups or persons; the overall score is the average of these percentages across the interview responses being studied.

Leaders who are high in distrust of others are given to being suspicious about the motives and actions of others, particularly those others who are viewed as competitors for their positions or against their cause or ideology. These others can do nothing right; whatever they do is easily perceived as for ulterior motives and designs. In its extreme, distrust of others becomes paranoia in which there is a well-developed rationale for being suspicious of certain individuals, groups, or countries. Distrust of others often makes leaders not rely on others but do things on their own to prevent any sabotage of what they want done. Loyalty becomes a sine qua non of working with the leader and participating in policy-making. And such leaders often shuffle their advisers around, making sure that none of them is acquiring a large enough power base to challenge the leader's authority. To some extent distrust of others may grow out of a zero-sum view of the world—when someone wins, someone else loses. The desire not to lose makes the leader question and assess others' motives. Leaders who distrust others tend to be hypersensitive to criticism—often seeing criticism where others would not—and they are vigilant, always on the lookout for a challenge to their authority or self.

Some wariness of others' motives may be an occupational hazard of political leaders. But leaders low in distrust of others tend to put it into perspective. Trust and distrust are more likely to be based on past experience with the people involved and on the nature of the current situation. A person is distrusted based on more realistic cues and not in a blanket fashion.

Constructing a Profile

Once a leader's interview responses have been coded and overall scores have been calculated for each of the seven traits described here, it is time to put the scores into perspective by determining how they compare with those of other leaders. Without doing such a comparison, there is little basis on which to judge whether the particular leader's traits are unusually high or low or about average. The issue is deciding what group of leaders to use as the comparison—or norming—group. Table 8.6 presents scores on all seven traits for the 87 heads of state and the 122 more general political leaders mentioned earlier. The table presents the mean or average score on a particular trait for the two samples of leaders, as well as the scores that are one standard deviation above and below that mean. If the leader under study has a score that exceeds that listed as one standard deviation above the mean for the sample of leaders, he or she is high on the trait; if the leader's score is more than one standard deviation below the mean for the sample of leaders, he or she is low on the trait. If the leader's score falls around the mean for the sample (neither one standard deviation above nor below the mean), he or she is moderate in the trait and is like the average leader in that comparison group. The 87 heads of state represent some forty-six countries

TABLE 8.6.   POTENTIAL COMPARISON GROUPS

Personality Trait	87 Heads of State	122 Political Leaders
Belief can control events	Mean = .44	Mean = .45
	Low < .30	Low < .33
	High > .58	High > .57
Need for power	Mean = .50	Mean = .50
	Low < .37	Low < .38
	High > .62	High > .62
Self-confidence	Mean = .62	Mean = .57
	Low < .44	Low < .34
	High > .81	High > .80
Conceptual complexity	Mean = .44	Mean = .45
	Low < .32	Low < .32
	High > .56	High > .58
Task focus	Mean = .59	Mean = .62
	Low < .46	Low < .48
	High > .71	High > .76
In-group bias	Mean = .42	Mean = .43
	Low < .32	Low < .34
	High > .53	High > .53
Distrust of others	Mean = .41	Mean = .38
	Low < .25	Low < .20
	High > .56	High > .56

from all parts of the globe; the 122 leaders are drawn from forty-eight countries and include, in addition to the 87 heads of state, members of cabinets, revolutionary leaders, legislative leaders, leaders of opposition parties, and terrorist leaders. The sample includes leaders who held positions of authority from 1945 to the present. Scores for particular regional, country, or cultural groups embedded in these 122 leaders are available from the author.

Once the analyst has determined how a leader's scores compare to those of other leaders, it is feasible to use the tables and discussion presented earlier on the traits and leadership styles to develop a profile of the leader. How is the leader likely to respond to constraints (scores on the belief he or she can control events and the need for power)? How open is he or she likely to be to information (scores on self-confidence and conceptual complexity)? What is the nature of the leader's motivation for seeking authority and influence (score on task focus as well as on in-group bias and distrust of others)? By noting whether a leader is more likely to respect or challenge constraints, to be more or less open to information, and to be more internally or externally driven, the analyst can ascertain the particular leadership style (see table 8.1) that leader is likely to exhibit.

Thus, for example, suppose we were developing a profile of Hafez al-Assad, current head of state of Syria. And suppose his scores when compared to the other eighty-seven heads of state show that he (1) is high in the belief he can control events and in the need for power, indicating he is likely to challenge constraints (see table 8.2); (2) has a conceptual complexity score that is higher than his score for self-confidence, suggesting he is open to incoming information (see table 8.3); (3) is high in task focus, denoting that his attention is more centered around the problem rather than relationships; and (4) has an in-group bias though he is relatively low in distrust of others, leading to a focus on being strategic in the way he deals with problems (see table 8.5). According to table 8.1, Assad will evidence an actively independent leadership style. He will be highly interested in maintaining his own and Syria's maneuverability and independence in a world that he perceives continually tries to limit both. Although Assad perceives that the world is conflict prone, he also views all countries as being somewhat constrained by international norms, affording him some flexibility in what he can do. However, he must vigilantly monitor developments in the international arena and prudently prepare to contain an adversary while still pursuing Syria's interests (see Hermann 1988a for more detail on Assad's profile). By using the trait scores, we can begin to build a profile or image of the leader in comparison to other political leaders.

Contextualizing the Profile

Much of the research on personality suggests that some people use contextual cues to determine what they do and, thus, may evidence changes in their trait scores depending on the nature of the situation. Other people's personalities are fairly stable across situations. By examining diverse material on a political leader, it is possible to determine how stable his or her leadership traits are. By analyzing material that cuts across a period of time, across different substantive topics, across different audiences, and is inside or outside of the leadership group (or political unit), we can determine the stability of the leadership traits. Moreover, by examining different aspects of the context such as the topic, audience, and whether the focus of attention is on the domestic or international domains, we can learn if leaders are sensitive to certain cues in their environment but not to others. If there is variability in the scores, then, we can determine if the differences give us insights into how the leader's public images differ—the various ways political leaders adapt to the situations in which they find themselves. We gain cues about how they are likely to change their behavior and what contextual features generate such change.

Nature of Topics Covered

To examine whether and how a leader's traits may differ by substantive topic, it is necessary to ascertain what topics are covered in the material under analysis. At issue is determining what the leader is talking about in each interview response that is being coded. What topics are under discussion? After noting the topics that are covered in the interview responses being studied, it is generally possible to arrive at a set of categories by checking where the topics are similar and which topics are discussed the most. In effect, some topics can be combined into a more generic topic (e.g., technological development and trade/aid topics might be collapsed into a category called *eco-*

nomic issues). Generic topics that are often discussed by heads of state are military issues, economic issues, relations with another country, relations with an enemy, domestic political stability, and regional politics. Topics that are covered only sporadically in the material are good candidates for combining into more generic categories.

Nature of Audience

Interviews with political leaders are done in a variety of settings and, thus, are often targeted toward different audiences. To examine the effects of audience on a leader's scores, it becomes important to note who is doing the interview and in what setting. For example, in profiling a head of state, an analyst will want to record if the interview involves the domestic or international press. If it is the domestic press, is the interviewer closely affiliated with the particular leader, more affiliated with that leader's opposition, or neutral in orientation? If it is the international press, to whom is the interview likely to be reported—people in an adversary's country, an ally's country, a country whose government the leader would like to influence, or a fairly neutral source? Of interest is whether the leader's trait scores show a pattern of change across these various types of audiences.

Effects of Events and Tenure in Office

Consider whether there have been any events (e.g., negotiations, crises, scandals, international agreements) that have occurred during the tenure of the leader under examination. By noting when these events happened and by choosing interview responses that span these points in time, it is possible to explore whether the leader's scores are affected by specific types of situations. In democratic societies, such an analysis might be conducted for periods before and after elections. For leaders with a long tenure in office, one might consider whether there are any changes that have occurred across time or whether the leader remains very much the same as when he or she began.

Determining whether Changes Are Significant

If the analyst wants to assess mathematically whether the changes in scores across time, topic, or audience on any of the personal characteristics for a leader are statistically significant, an analysis of variance will provide such data. Most statistical packages for personal computers have a one-way analysis of variance procedure that can easily be applied to exploring this question. If the one-way analyses of variance "F-tests"are significant (have a probability value of .05 or less), then the leader's scores differ on that trait for that context factor (time, topic, audience); in effect, the leader is being adaptive in that type of situation. By noting where a leader's scores change, the analyst can put the leadership profile into context. One can note if the leader puts on a different face when dealing with foreign diplomats than when interacting inside his or her own country; if the leader has different strategies for dealing with different types of problems; if he or she adapts to being a political leader in a different way with experience and a longer tenure in the position. This contextual analysis adds depth and nuance to the more general profile constructed

Problems Often Faced in Constructing a Profile

What if leaders' scores change dramatically across topics, audiences, and time? Dramatic changes or differences in scores across contextual categories usually suggest that a leader is highly sensitive to the situation. Such leaders tend to judge what their options are based on what is happening at the moment by assessing who is supporting what and the nature of the problem. Action is only taken after such leaders have a chance to survey the scene and to define what important others are likely to do. For these leaders, analysts are going to need to know a lot more about the situations the leaders are facing in order to know what they will do. Examining just where the changes occurred can provide information about what part of the context is important for that leader. If the changes are found for audience, chances are that these leaders are influenced by the people, groups, and organizations with whom they are interacting. If, however, the changes occur by topic, then the leaders are probably attending to solving the problem at hand and tailoring their behavior to deal with what is happening.

What if leaders' scores are very different when they are talking to a domestic audience rather than to an international one? This question is an important one because leaders of third world countries often show such differences. They are much less directive, more charming, and more diplomatic in dealing with the governments of larger, more developed states from whom they may want something than when they focus on their own countries. Toward the domestic scene, they can be highly authoritarian and autocratic, knowing exactly what needs to be done and when. It is important to highlight these differences in any profile since they have implications for what leaders are likely to do where and can lead to misinterpretations of the leadership styles of these leaders.

Do leaders' scores differ in a crisis as opposed to a noncrisis situation? If you have scores for your leader by topic, you may be able to judge whether there is a difference between his or her public images for crisis and noncrisis situations, because some of the topics are more crisislike in tone than others. Therefore, if the topics include "aggression from another country" or "threats to ethnic group," the scores probably reflect crisis behavior—at least more so than when the leader is focusing on the economy or education (unless, of course, there are problems in these domains). Differentiating crises from noncrises becomes important because leaders often experience stress during crises and tend to accentuate the traits in which they are high. They tend to become more extreme in their profile. For example, if they believe they can control what happens more generally, they have even more faith in this belief during a crisis; if they usually have a high need for power, it will be accentuated in a crisis. This accentuation is most visible in leaders whose scores are fairly stable across time, topic, and audience—those who are relatively insensitive to the environment. Leaders who scores show marked variability by these context factors appear to become more vigilant in crises and more indecisive, reacting to rather than initiating activity and relying on others' help and support more than usual.

Reliability of the Profiles

There are two types of reliability that are often calculated in building profiles. The first assesses how easy it is for those unfamiliar with the content analysis coding system to learn and apply it to leaders' interview responses with the same skill as its author. In other words, is it possible for others to be trained to use the coding system and to achieve a high degree of agreement with the person who developed the profiling technique? The second reliability examines the stability of the leader's scores, trying to ascertain how sensitive the leader is to the political context. Both kinds of reliability have been determined for the coding system described here.

Across a number of studies (e.g., Hermann 1980a, 1980b, 1984a, 1987b; Hermann and Hermann 1989), the intercoder agreement for the seven traits described in this chapter has ranged from .78 to 1.00 between a set of coders and the author. Where there were disagreements, the discussions that followed between coders permitted refinements of the coding system. Generally, a coder currently is not permitted to content analyze a leader's interview responses to be included in the larger data set until he or she achieves intercoder reliabilities with the author on all traits that are .90 or higher. As the automated coding system is being developed, similar types of reliability coefficients are being calculated to determine how accurately that coding system is in reflecting the original intent of the author.

Information about the leader can be gained by assessing trait reliabilities for that particular person. By correlating a leader's odd- and even-numbered interview responses, the analyst can ascertain how stable the traits are across time and issues. This index provides another way of determining how open and closed the leader is likely to be to contextual information (see, e.g., Hermann 1980a, 1984a).

One of the questions often raised about content analysis coding systems that use translated material, which we are often forced to do, regards the effect of the translation on the resulting scores. To ascertain whether there were any effects and the nature of such effects, in several instances intercoder agreement has been calculated between a native speaker coding text in the original language and the author focusing on the translated text. The languages were Russian and French. In both cases, agreement averaged .92 across the seven traits (Hermann 1980b, 1987a, 1987b).

Validity of This Profiling Technique

How valid is this particular way of determining leadership style? That is, how accurate is it in capturing the leadership styles that heads of state and others in leading party and bureaucratic positions actually exhibit? Although I have received numerous suggestions about how to determine the validity of this technique, ranging from running experiments with college students to participant observation in city councils, it seemed important to find some means of comparing the results from this coding system with the experiences of those who had interacted with heads of state. In a series of studies, I (Hermann 1984b, 1985, 1986b, 1988b) developed profiles on twenty-one leaders following the procedure described here and, based on these profiles, indicated on a series of rating scales the nature of the leadership behaviors a particular head of state should exhibit given a particular leadership style. These ratings were compared with those made by journalists and former government personnel who had had the opportunity to observe or interact with the particular leaders. The correlations between the two sets of ratings averaged .84 across the set of leaders, suggesting that the profiles derived from this at-a-distance technique furnished me with similar types of information on which to judge behavior, as had the other raters' experiences with the actual figures.

Conclusion

By doing a trait analysis of seven dimensions of personality, I have proposed that it is possible for a researcher or analyst to develop a profile of the leadership style a particular political leader is likely to exhibit. The seven personal characteristics provide information about whether the leader will respect or challenge constraints, will be open or closed to information from the environment, will focus more on solving problems or building community, and will be more hardline or more accommodationist. The traits also interrelate to suggest which leadership style from a rather wide range is likely to be dominant in any leader. Constructing such a profile has become more feasible with the design of computer software that can analyze leaders' interview responses and with the collection of trait data on 122 political leaders from around the world that comprise a norming group with which to compare any one leader's scores.

Not only is it feasible now to construct a general profile of a particular leader, but it is also possible to place such a profile into perspective by examining a number of contextual factors that indicate how stable the characteristics are with certain kinds of changes in the situation. We can ascertain what the leader is like in general and, then, what kinds of information he or she is likely to be responsive to in the political environment. Thus, the general profile indicates where a specific leader fits in a broader discussion of leadership style; the contextualized profile suggests how that leader has individualized his or her responses to manifest more unique characteristics. With knowledge about both the general and the more individualized profiles, the researcher and analyst gain a more complete portrait of the leader. Not only does the person become representative of a particular type of leader, but we know when and to what degree he or she has modulated his or her behavior to take the context into account.

Note

I would like to thank Social Science Automation, Inc., for a grant that supported the writing of this chapter. I am also grateful to Kent Kille, Thomas Preston, Charles Snare, and Michael Young for comments on earlier drafts of this chapter and for their help in refining the coding system and the theoretical underpinnings of this assessment-at-a-distance technique.

C. Cognitive Analyses

9. Profiling the Operational Codes of Political Leaders

Stephen G. Walker, Mark Schafer,

and Michael D. Young

Operational code analysis emerged as a leadership assessment tool after World War II in response to the puzzle of Soviet negotiating behavior and the escalation of U.S.-Soviet relations into a cold war. The prototypical studies by Leites (1951, 1953) at the RAND Corporation identified the operational code of the Soviet Politburo as the beliefs about the exercise of political power in the Bolshevik ideology, which reflected motivational biases in Lenin's character and Russian political culture. He argued that these beliefs accounted for Soviet negotiating strategy and tactics in dealing with the West at the end of World War II over such issues as German reunification; economic recovery in Europe; and a general peace settlement with Germany, Italy, and Japan.

This chapter contains systematic procedures developed since the RAND project for identifying a leader's operational code and inferring likely patterns of leadership behavior. To employ operational code analysis as a method of assessing leadership behavior, it is desirable to know something about its evolution and previous applications. It is also important to be aware of how the techniques for identifying beliefs and drawing inferences about behavior have developed. These topics are discussed briefly before turning to the task of forecasting behavior from operational code beliefs. First, there is a summary of the evolution of operational code analysis and the development of the Verbs in Context System (VICS) of content analysis for retrieving and analyzing a leader's operational code beliefs. Second, there is a set of examples that illustrate how to analyze a leader's operational code and estimate likely behavior at different levels of decision.

What Is Operational Code Analysis?

Operational code analysis is an approach to the study of political leaders that may focus narrowly on a set of political beliefs or more broadly on a set of beliefs embedded in the personality of a leader or originating from the cultural matrix of a society. Leites (1953) employed the broader view of operational code analysis that incorporated cognition, character, and culture, but his approach was modified in later applications. George (1969) argued that a leader's operational code should be identified simply as a political belief system in which some elements (philosophical beliefs) guide the leader's diagnosis of the context for action and others (instrumental beliefs) prescribe the most effective strategy and tactics in achieving goals.

While George recommended that political scientists limit their efforts to the study of beliefs, which "can be inferred or postulated by the investigator on the basis of the kinds of data, observational opportunities, and methods generally available to political scientists," he clearly anticipated studies that would link cognition and character.

> [I]t is one of the attractive features of the operational code construct for behaviorally-inclined political scientists that it can serve as a useful "bridge" or "link" to psychodynamic interpretations of unconscious dimensions of belief systems and their role in behavior under different conditions. . . . Thus, once an actor's approach to political calculation has been formulated by the researcher, he can proceed—if he so wishes and is able to do so—to relate some of the beliefs in question to other motivational variables of a psychodynamic character. (George 1969, 195–96)

How Has Operational Code Analysis Evolved as a Leadership Assessment Tool?

The subsequent evolution of operational code analysis has followed the course anticipated by George, focusing initially on beliefs and then on motivational variables. In the 1970s, operational code studies focused on the *philosophical* and *instrumental* beliefs of leaders, identified as the "answers" to the ten questions posed by George (1969), which appear in figure 9.1. Philosophical beliefs are those held by the leader to assess the nature of the political universe and other actors. Instrumental beliefs are those that inform the leader's own preferences for political actions in terms of strategies and tactics. Holsti (1977) answered these questions with the development of a typology of belief systems, which he suggested were ideal types of operational codes. Both George and Holsti were guided in their thinking by cognitive consistency theory, which assumed that a leader's operational code beliefs were internally consistent with one another and that a leader's decisions were consistent with these beliefs. Specifically, they argued that a leader's philosophical beliefs about the nature of the political universe acted as a "master belief," which influenced the contents of the remaining philosophical and instrumental beliefs.

Holsti (1977) employed this assumption of a master belief in the construction of his operational code typology. He speculated that the leader's beliefs about the nature and source of conflict in the political universe were the basis for other philosophical beliefs about the prospects for realizing fundamental goals, the predictability of the political future, the leader's control over historical development, and the role of chance. In turn, these philosophical beliefs influenced the instrumental beliefs of the leader regarding the most effective strategy and tactics, the optimum approach to the calculation and management of risks, and the utility and timing of employing different means to protect or achieve political objectives.

For example, a leader who believes that political conflict is a permanent feature of the political universe is likely to be relatively pessimistic about the prospects for achieving fundamental political values, to view the political future as less predictable, to believe that control over historical development is relatively low, and to assign a higher role to chance in political affairs. On the other hand, a leader who views conflict as temporary is likely to be more optimistic about realizing goals, to be more confident in the predictability of the future, to believe in greater control over historical development, and to assign less importance to chance.

The Philosophical Beliefs in an Operational Code

P-1.   What is the "essential" nature of political life? Is the political universe essentially one of harmony or conflict? What is the fundamental character of one's political opponents?

P-2.   What are the prospects for the eventual realization of one's fundamental values and aspirations? Can one be optimistic, or must one be pessimistic on this score; and in what respects the one and/or the other?

P-3.   Is the political future predictable? In what sense and to what extent?

P-4.   How much "control" or "mastery" can one have over historical development? What is one's role in "moving" and "shaping" history in the desired direction?

P-5.   What is the role of "chance" in human affairs and in historical development?

The Instrumental Beliefs in an Operational Code

I-1.   What is the best approach for selecting goals or objectives for political action?

I-2.   How are the goals of action pursued most effectively?

I-3.   How are the risks of political action calculated, controlled, and accepted?

I-4.   What is the best "timing" of action to advance one's interests?

I-5.   What are the utility and role of different means for advancing one's interests?

Fig. 9.1.   George's ten questions about operational code beliefs

According to the logic of cognitive consistency theory, these differences in the diagnosis of the political universe should lead to different prescriptions for political action. The first leader's pessimism is likely to be accompanied by beliefs that strategy should be limited in its goals, tactics should be flexible, the calculation and control of risks should be cautious and conservative, and force should be a last resort as a means to achieve political ends. The second leader's optimism is more likely to generate beliefs in grand strategic goals, relatively inflexible tactics, long-shot calculations in the assessment of risks, and the utility of force as a tool of statecraft.

The six types of operational code belief systems in figure 9.2 represent this kind of reasoning, with the pessimists lumped together in the lower left-hand quadrant as types D, E, and F. While the pessimists differ over the sources of conflict—individual (D), society (E), international system (F)—they share common beliefs about its permanence and the corresponding implications for the remaining philosophical and instrumental beliefs (Walker 1983). The remaining types of belief systems (A, B, and C) share the optimism derived from the master belief that conflict is temporary. However, they disagree over the source of conflict: individual misperceptions (A), pathological societal institutions (B), or the anarchical organization of the international system (C). These latter differences dispose them toward some disagreement over the remaining philosophical and instrumental beliefs.

Holsti theorized that these internally consistent belief systems remain relatively stable over time and across policy domains for the leaders who hold them. However, both George and Holsti realized that the Bolshevik belief system and the Holsti typology did not exhaust the rich variety and cognitive complexity of political leaders. They may have master beliefs that differ in degree as well as in kind regarding the stability and source of conflict in the political universe. Moreover, not all leaders have a single, well-defined set of operational code beliefs, and leaders may change their beliefs over time (George 1969; Holsti 1977).

Research into the operational codes of several leaders in the 1980s and 1990s has validated this forecast. The results from several studies indicate that a leader's operational code beliefs are likely to contain elements from more than one of Holsti's types and vary at least

High
nAff
(Essential Alikeness)

<table>
<tr>
<td>

TYPE A

Conflict is temporary, caused by human misunderstanding and miscommunication. A "conflict spiral," based upon misperception and impulsive responses, is the major danger of war. Opponents are often influenced by nonrational conditions but tend to respond in kind to conciliation and firmness. Optimism is warranted, based upon a leader's ability and willingness to shape historical development. The future is relatively predictable, and control over it is possible. Establish goals within a framework that emphasizes shared interests. Pursue broadly interational goals incrementally with flexible strategies that control risks by avoiding escalation and acting quickly when conciliation opportunities arise. Emphasize resources that establish a climate for negotiation and compromise, and avoid the early use of force.

</td>
<td>

TYPE C

Conflict is temporary; it is possible to restructure the state system to reflect the latent harmony of interests. The source of conflict is the anarchical state system, which permits a variety of causes to produce war. Opponents vary in nature, goals, and responses to conciliation and firmness. One should be pessimistic about goals unless the state system is changed, because predictability and control over historical development is low under anarchy. Establish optimal goals vigorously within a comprehensive framework. Pursue shared goals, but control risks by limiting means rather than ends. Act quickly when conciliation opportunities arise, and delay escalatory actions whenever possible; resources other than military capabilities are useful.

</td>
</tr>
</table>

Nuclear

Self

High
nAch

(Ideals)

<table>
<tr>
<td>

Conflict is permanent, caused by human nature (D); nationalism (E), or international anarchy (F). Power disequilibria are major dangers of war. Opponents may vary, and responses to conciliation or firmness are uncertain. Optimism declines over the long run and in the short run depends upon the quality of leadership and a power equilibrium. Predictability is limited, as is control over historical development. Seek limited goals flexibly with moderate means. Use military force if the opponent and circumstances require it, but only as a final resource.

</td>
<td>

Conflict is temporary, caused by warlike states; miscalculation and appeasement are the major causes of war. Opponents are rational and deterrable. Optimism is warranted regarding realization of goals. The political future is relatively predictable, and control over historical development is possible. One should seek optimal goals vigorously within a comprehensive framework. Control risks by limiting means rather than ends. Any tactic and resource may be appropriate, including the use of force when it offers prospects for large gains with limited risk.

</td>
</tr>
</table>

TYPE DEF

(Ambition)
High
nPow

TYPE B

Fig. 9.2. Contents of the revised Holsti operational code typology

in degree over time and for different issue areas in the political universe (Walker and Falkowski 1984b; Walker, Schafer, and Young 1998, 1999; Schafer, Young, and Walker 1995; Crichlow 1998; Walker and Schafer 2000; Schafer and Crichlow 2000; Marfleet 2000; Dille 2000). As representations of reality, philosophical beliefs are more prone to fluctuation by domain and over time in response to changes in context (Walker, Schafer, and Young 1998; Schafer and Crichlow 2000). A leader's instrumental beliefs are less volatile, making the internal consistency between philosophical and instrumental beliefs difficult to maintain (Walker, Schafer, and Young 1998, 1999).

What Is the Link between Beliefs and Motivations?

One explanation for the relative stability of instrumental beliefs is that they are partly expressions of the leader's identity in the form of motivational biases rather than simply the products of lessons learned from changing experiences in the political universe. This explanation is consistent with the broader formulation of operational code analysis associated with Leites (1951, 1953). George recognized this link explicitly in his discussion of the relationship between beliefs and character in the Bolshevik operational code.

> The maxims of political strategy that comprise the "operational code" take on the character of *rules of conduct* held out for good Bolsheviks and *norms of behavior* that, ideally, are internalized by the individual who thereby acquires a new and different character structure—that of the reliable, "hard-core" Bolshevik. In the terminology of modern ego psychology, the individual who succeeds in internalizing this preferred character structure thereby accomplishes an "identity transformation." (George 1969, 194, original emphasis)

This link between beliefs and character was also recognized by Holsti (1977), who was agnostic about whether individuals acquired their operational code beliefs by virtue of socialization into a particular political role or were drawn to a role by a subtle process of self-selection based on the compatibility of the individual's personality traits and the operational code beliefs associated with the role.

In a reanalysis of the Holsti typology, Walker (1983) found that the four types in figure 9.2 differed in the motivational imagery associated with them. Type A's beliefs contained images of affiliation, while the beliefs for type DEF expressed images of power. The other two types shared an image of achievement while differing in their images of power (type B) and affiliation (type C). The four quadrants in figure 9.2 represent not only the ideal types of belief systems in the Holsti typology but also a two-dimensional simplification of what is really a three-dimensional personality structure in which the beliefs are embedded in a motivational foundation established by the needs for power, affiliation, and achievement emanating from the nuclear self (Winter and Stewart 1977a; Walker 1983, 2002; Kohut 1971, 1977, 1984; Walker).

In the application of these belief systems to real leaders, Walker and Falkowski (1984a, 1984b) found that the operational code beliefs of U.S. presidents and secretaries of state contained the motivational imagery regarding the needs for power, affiliation, and achievement attributed to them by other analysts. Their belief systems were hybrids containing beliefs that were not internally consistent with any one of the ideal types in Holsti's typology of operational codes. The relative frequency of beliefs from each type of belief system tended to correlate with independent measures of their motivational imagery. The findings support the interpretation that leaders are "structured individuals" whose needs for power, affiliation, and achievement are related to their belief systems in theoretically and empirically consistent patterns (Walker and Falkowski 1984a, 1984b; see also Walker, Schafer, Young 1999).

These results reenforced the Leites (1953) hypothesis, noted later by George (1969), that character and cognition were linked. The cognitive scripts for political action in the leader's operational code beliefs may also be character prescriptions that express the identity of the leader as an actor in the political universe. If so, then the operational code beliefs of political leaders are not merely diagnostic aids for processing information from the social environment. They also include internalized prescriptions that act as causal mechanisms of political action by virtue of their normative power to express such motivations as the needs for power, affiliation, and achievement (Walker 1983).

How Do Beliefs and Motivations Form a Coherent Personality?

Seen in this dual perspective and without the assumption of internal cognitive consistency, the cognitive and motivational elements of a leader's operational code nonetheless form a coherent personality. As George and Holsti speculated and as the studies cited previously have confirmed, however, this personality may be rather complex and may engage different "states of mind" in different domains of the political universe. Thus, the typology of operational codes in figure 9.2 may coexist in the same leader and become aroused differentially, depending on the domain in which he or she is engaged and the cues from that environment (Walker 1995; Walker, Schafer, and Young 1998, 1999).

This perspective suggests that the empirical task of mapping a leader's operational code beliefs should proceed from the bottom up, by aggregating targeted beliefs about particular issues in different domains of political action, rather than from the top down, as deductions from an idealized typology of operational code belief systems. Any generalizations about a leader's general operational code will depend on whether and to what extent his or her beliefs regarding self and others are consistent across domains and over time. In turn, predicting a leader's behavior from operational code beliefs will require careful attention to scope conditions that specify the level of generalization on which the prediction is based. The VICS method of content analysis was developed as part of a bottom-up strategy to identify a leader's operational code beliefs and to make contingent forecasts of his or her likely strategies, tactics, and moves.

The Verbs in Context System

The VICS method draws inferences about a leader's operational code from public sources—speeches, interviews, or other public statements by the individual. The most relevant source for the systematic prediction of the state's behavior is probably the public speech. It is a theoretical assumption of operational code analysis that a leader's public behavior is constrained by his public image and that, over time, his public actions will consistently match his public beliefs. This assumption seems counterintuitive, because it appears not to allow for the possibilities of impression management and deception strategies by the leader in public utterances. While it is possible for a leader's beliefs and behavior to be at odds for short (and perhaps crucial) periods, the opposite is the norm. This principle of cognitive consistency theory is based on the general bounded rationality axiom that individuals act rationally (make behavioral choices) based on what they believe (Tetlock 1998; Simon 1957) and the corollary that others in a social situation expect them to do so.

What Is the VICS Method?

The VICS method of content analysis is a set of techniques for retrieving belief patterns from a leader's public statements and drawing inferences about public behavior that are compatible with these beliefs (Walker, Schafer, and Young 1998, 1999). To the extent that a particular leader is in control of the state's behavior or to the extent that a leader's beliefs are shared by those individuals with the power to act on behalf of the state, these inferences become predictions about a state's behavior. While the retrieval unit is the public statement, the recording unit is the "utterance," which is each verb in the statement and the corresponding parts of speech associated with each verb—the subject and object (if it is a transitive verb) or the subject and predicate nominative or adjective (if it is an intransitive verb). As figure 9.3 illustrates, the VICS method extracts values for six attributes for each recording unit (verb) and its surrounding context: *subject, verb category, domain of politics, tense of the verb, intended target,* and *context.*

Self or Other designates whether the speaker or some other actor is the subject of the verb. The verb is categorized in its tense as either a positive (+) or negative (−) intransitive verb or a positive (+) or negative (−) transitive verb. If it is a transitive verb, it is categorized further as representing either a cooperative (+) or conflictual (−) behavior that takes the form of a word or a deed. Positive transitive deeds are coded as Rewards (+3) while negative transitive deeds are coded as Punishments (−3). Positive transitive words are coded as either Promises (+2) or Appeal/Support (+1), while negative transitive words are coded as either Threats (−2) or Oppose/Resist (−1).

Verbs that do not fit into one of these categories or that do not have a political context (i.e., do not deal with a policy domain or are not directed toward a political target) are coded as Neutral (0) and

STEPS IN THE VERBS IN CONTEXT SYSTEM

1. IDENTIFY THE SUBJECT AS

SELF   OR   OTHER

2. IDENTIFY THE TENSE OF THE TRANSITIVE VERB AS

PAST   PRESENT   FUTURE

AND IDENTIFY THE CATEGORY OF THE VERB AS

POSITIVE (+) OR   NEGATIVE (–)

	APPEAL, SUPPORT (+1)	OPPOSE, RESIST (–1)
WORDS	OR	OR
	PROMISE BENEFITS (+2)	THREATEN COSTS (–2)

DEEDS	REWARDS (+3)	PUNISHMENTS (–3)

3. IDENTIFY THE DOMAIN AS

DOMESTIC   OR   FOREIGN

4. IDENTIFY TARGET AND PLACE IN CONTEXT

AN EXAMPLE

A quote taken from President Carter's address to the nation on January 4, 1980: "Massive Soviet military forces have invaded the small, non-aligned, sovereign nation of Afghanistan."

1. **Subject**. The subject is "Massive Soviet military forces," which is coded as other; that is, the speaker is not referring to his or to her self or his or her state.

2. **Tense and category** . The verb phrase "have invaded" is in the past tense and is a negative deed coded, therefore, as punish.

3. **Domain**. The action involves an actor (Soviet military forces) external to the speaker's state (the United States); therefore, the domain is foreign.

4. **Target and context** . The action is directed toward Afghanistan; therefore, the target is coded as Afghanistan. In addition, we designate a context: Soviet-Afghanistan-conflict-1979-88.

The **complete data line** for this statement is other –3 foreign past afghanistan soviet-afghanistan-conflict-1979-88.

Fig. 9.3.   Steps in the Verbs in Context System for coding verbs

discarded. The remainder describes the leader's beliefs about the intended or imagined exercise of power by self and others regarding the political issues raised in the public statement. They are also the basis for drawing inferences about subsequent behavior by the leader's government. Predictions based on these inferences can be very general or rather specific, depending on the variety of policy domains and issue areas and the volume of attributes available to be coded from the universe of public statements.

How Are VICS Indices Calculated and Interpreted?

These assessments are inferred from four kinds of indices constructed from the balance, central tendency, proportion, and dispersion of verb attributions in these sources. For example, the *balance* between the frequencies of positive (+) and negative (−) verbs attributed to others in public statements indicates the leader's beliefs about the friendly or hostile nature of politics and image of others in the political universe. The same calculation for verbs attributed to self indicates the strategic orientation (cooperation or conflict) of the speaker toward others in the political universe.

Assigning weights to the same verb categories and multiplying them by their frequencies measures the intensity of positive and negative attributions by self and others. The *central tendencies* of these weighted self and other attributions, respectively, are indicators of the leader's beliefs about effective tactics and the prospects for realizing political values. These four indices summarize at the most general level of aggregation the leader's diagnostic propensities regarding the nature of the political universe and the prospects for success, plus the leader's choice propensities for effective strategies and tactics. The calculation and interpretation of these indices are fairly straightforward and are summarized as follows.

The balance indices for the nature of the political universe (P-1) and strategic direction (I-1) vary between −1.0 (e.g., Extremely Hostile for P-1) and +1.0 (e.g., Extremely Friendly for P-1), calculated by subtracting the number of negative verbs from the number of positive verbs and dividing the result by the total number of negative and positive verbs. The scale illustrates the range of values associated with each index and the remaining descriptors used to anchor and interpret the scores. A particular score is anchored to an inter-

P-1. Nature of the Political Universe (hostile/friendly)

HOSTILE   FRIENDLY

Extremely	Very	Definitely	Somewhat	Mixed	Somewhat	Definitely	Very	Extremely
-1.0	$-.75$	$-.50$	$-.25$	0.0	$+.25$	$+.50$	$+.75$	$+1.0$

I-1. Direction of Strategy (conflict/cooperation)

CONFLICT   COOPERATION

Extremely	Very	Definitely	Somewhat	Mixed	Somewhat	Definitely	Very	Extremely
-1.0	$-.75$	$-.50$	$-.25$	0.0	$+.25$	$+.50$	$+.75$	$+1.0$

pretation based on the distance between the score and the nearest descriptor.

For example, a score of $-.21$ is anchored to the descriptor "Somewhat Hostile" on the nature of the political universe scale for P-1, because it is closest to $-.25$ on the continuum of possible balance scores. A score of $+.41$ is anchored to the descriptor "Definitely Cooperative" on the direction of strategy scale for I-1, because it is closest to $+.50$ on the continuum of possible scores. The interpretation of these two scores for a leader takes the following form: *"He or she believes that the political universe is somewhat hostile, and he or she also believes that a definitely cooperation-oriented direction is the best strategy in this universe."*

The central tendency indices for the leader's beliefs about the prospects for realizing political values (P-2) and his or her beliefs about the intensity of tactics (I-2) also vary between -1.0 (e.g., Extremely Pessimistic) and $+1.0$ (e.g., Extremely Optimistic). The indices are calculated by multiplying each verb by the scale values

P-2. Realization of Political Values (pessimism/optimism)

PESSIMISTIC   OPTIMISTIC

Extremely	Very	Definitely	Somewhat	Mixed	Somewhat	Definitely	Very	Extremely
-1.0	$-.75$	$-.50$	$-.25$	0.0	$+.25$	$+.50$	$+.75$	$+1.0$

I-2. Intensity of Tactics (conflict/cooperation)

CONFLICT   COOPERATION

Extremely	Very	Definitely	Somewhat	Mixed	Somewhat	Definitely	Very	Extremely
-1.0	$-.75$	$-.50$	$-.25$	0.0	$+.25$	$+.50$	$+.75$	$+1.0$

associated with its coding category, summing the results, then calculating the average (mean) score and dividing it by three. The following scale shows the range of values and descriptors for these two indices, which anchor the scores with an interpretation. The interpretation rule for the (P-2) and (I-2) indices is the same as for the (P-1) and (I-1) indices: assign the descriptor that is closest to the score.

For example, if a leader's P-2 score is −.31, then he or she is "Somewhat Pessimistic" about the prospects for realizing fundamental political goals. An I-2 score of +.27 would indicate that he or she believes in "Somewhat Cooperative" tactics. The interpretation of these two scores for a leader takes the following form: *"He or she believes that the prospects for realizing fundamental political goals are somewhat pessimistic, and he or she also believes that somewhat cooperative tactics are best under this condition."*

A series of *proportion* indices measure the leader's beliefs regarding control over historical development and the relative utility of different ways of exercising political power. The number of self or other attributions as a percentage of the total number of self and other attributions varies between 0.0 (Very Low) and 1.0 (Very High). This index measures the locus of control attributed to self (P-4a) over historical development while the number of other attributions as a percentage of the total number of self and other attributions (or 1 minus 4a) is the locus of control (P-4b) attributed to others. As in the case of the balance and central tendency indices, the actual scores for a leader are anchored with a descriptor that is closest to its value. *So a leader with a P-4a score of .53 believes that he or she has a medium degree of control over historical development while also attributing a medium level of control (P-4b = .47) to others in the political universe.*

The same basic logic applies for calculating and interpreting the utility of means indices. With six categories for the exercise of political power rather than two categories for the locus of historical control, however, the medium proportion of equal utility for each one is .16 (1.0/6) instead of .50 (1.0/2). Proportions that exceed or fail to

P-4. Control over Historical Development (very low/very high)

CONTROL				CONTROL
Very Low	Low	Medium	High	Very High
0.0	.25	.50	.75	1.0

reach that level are assigned higher or lower descriptors of utility. Although this index can vary between 0.0 and 1.0, it is relatively unlikely with six categories that the upper boundary will be reached, and so .32 is defined as the descriptor in the following scale for a Very High proportion—twice the expected proportion when each category is equally useful. The interpretation of the utility of means scores can take two forms. They can be analyzed proportionately or simply by their descriptors.

So, for example, a leader with percentage scores of Reward (.20) + Promise (.17) + Appeal/Support (.34) + Oppose/Resist (.16) + Threat (.06) + Punish (.07) = 1.0 believes the following about the utility of means in his or her political universe. *Appeals and expressions of support (.34) are about twice as useful as statements of opposition/resistance (.16) or promises (.17), which are over twice as useful as threats (.06) or punishments (.07), and, finally, rewards (.20) are approximately three times as useful as threats (.06) or punishments (.07).* It is also possible to make inferences from the descriptors rather than from the scores. *A leader with these scores believes that the comparative utility of appeal/support statements is very high, the comparative utility of rewards is high, the comparative utility of promises and expressions of opposition/resistance is medium, and the comparative utility of threats and punishments is low.*

There are four indices that take into account the *dispersion* of verbs across the six categories for the exercise of political power. Two are the predictability of the political future and risk orientation. Both of them employ a measure of dispersion, the Index of Qualitative Variation (IQV), which assesses the variation in the distribution of obser-

I-5. Utility of Means (very low/very high)

A. Cooperative Means Appeal/Support, Promise, Reward

UTILITY				UTILITY
Very Low	Low	Medium	High	Very High
0.0	.08	.16	.24	.32

B. Conflict Means Oppose/Resist, Threaten, Punish

UTILITY				UTILITY
Very Low	Low	Medium	High	Very High
0.0	.08	.16	.24	.32

vations among the six categories for self and others. Calculated separately for self and other attributions, the IQV score is subtracted from 1.0 to estimate the predictability of the political future (predictability of others' behavior) and one's own risk orientation (the predictability of one's own behavior). The higher the estimates from these calculations, respectively, the more predictable are the political future and one's own risk orientation. *For example, a leader's beliefs with scores of .08 for P-3 and .03 for I-3 attribute very low predictability to others and to self.*

P-3. Predictability of Political Future (very low/very high)

PREDICTABILITY				PREDICTABILITY
Very Low	Low	Medium	High	Very High
0.0	.25	.50	.75	1.0

I-3. Risk Orientation (very low/very high)

RISK AVERSE				RISK ACCEPTANT
Very Low	Low	Medium	High	Very High
0.0	.25	.50	.75	1.0

Interpretation of these scores is enhanced by the indices for two related indices of the importance of timing: flexibility in shifting between different kinds of tactics as a risk management technique. These indices are calculated by subtracting the absolute value of the balance index for cooperation/conflict and words/deeds from one. *For example, a leader's beliefs with scores of .57 and .53 for shifts between cooperation/conflict and words/deeds, respectively, manage the very low predictability of the political future by attributing a risk orientation of medium flexibility in both cooperation/conflict and words/deeds to himself or herself.*

Finally, there is an index for the role of chance, which takes into account the predictability of the political future and the degree of control over historical development. It is calculated by multiplying the leader's scores for the latter two beliefs and subtracting the product from one. The logic of the index is that the higher the predictability of the political future and the greater the leader's belief in his or her ability to control historical development, the less the role of chance. It is interpreted the same way as the other indices that

I-4. Flexibility of Tactics (very low/very high)

A. Between Cooperation and Conflict

FLEXIBILITY				FLEXIBILITY
Very Low	Low	Medium	High	Very High
0.0	.25	.50	.75	1.0

B. Between Words and Deeds

FLEXIBILITY				FLEXIBILITY
Very Low	Low	Medium	High	Very High
0.0	.25	.50	.75	1.0

incorporate measures of dispersion into their formulae. *For example, a leader with an index of .96 attributes a very high role to chance.*

P-4. Role of Chance (very low/very high)

CHANCE				CHANCE
Very Low	Low	Medium	High	Very High
0.0	.25	.50	.75	1.0

Collectively, the VICS indices provide information about a leader's diagnostic, choice, and shift propensities regarding the exercise of power in different political contexts. Operational code analysis defines politics as the exercise of power between actors, in which the beliefs of each actor about the nature of the political universe and the most effective strategies and tactics in this universe influence the choices of means, tactics, and strategies and the ensuing outcomes of interaction episodes between them.

Assessing Leaders' Beliefs: Steering and Learning Effects

The belief template for mapping the interface among beliefs, behavior, and interaction is an expanded version of the Holsti typology of belief systems in figure 9.2. Where Holsti assumed consistency between philosophical and instrumental beliefs, the present analysis allows for instrumental beliefs to be independent from philosophical beliefs. Taking each set of instrumental beliefs (I) and pairing them not only with the corresponding philosophical beliefs (P) in the Holsti typology but with the others as well, there are a total of sixteen types of belief systems possible in figure 9.2.

Holsti's four pairs are as follows: A(I) with A(P), B(I) with B(P), C(I) with C(P), and DEF(I) with DEF(P). The twelve additional hybrids are A(I) with DEF(P), A(I) with B(P), A(I) with C(P), DEF(I) with B(P), DEF(I) with C(P), DEF (I) with A(P), B(I) with C(P), B(I) with A(P), B(I) with DEF(P), C(I) with A(P), C(I) with DEF(P), and C(I) with B(P). Collectively, these combinations of beliefs map different definitions of the "self-in-situation" in which different levels of decision are made.

Key VICS indices locate the "self-in-situation" coordinates of a leader's operational code within the template in figure 9.4. Two indices are used to place Self in one of the four quadrants associated with Holsti's four types of belief systems. They are the strategic (I-1) index plus Self's locus of historical control (P-4a) index. They are mapped in figure 9.4 to parallel the axes formed by the power, affiliation, and achievement axes in the Holsti typology of belief systems in figure 9.2. The VICS strategic index (I-1) scores are plotted on the vertical axis, and the VICS scores for the locus of control (P-4a) index are plotted along the horizontal axis.

The association of nPow with conflict (–), nAff with cooperation (+), and nAch with greater control over outcomes is consistent with previous research on the cognitive and behavioral correlates of these motivations (Winter and Stewart 1977a). The intersection of the locus of control index for Self (P-4a) with the strategic (I-1) index determines the leader's location in one of the four quadrants in figure 9.4. The verbal interpretation of the leader's scores should resemble more closely the instrumental beliefs for the Holsti ideal type located in this quadrant than the instrumental beliefs for the other types.

The indices for the philosophical beliefs of this leader may or may not be located in the same quadrant as the indices for his or her instrumental beliefs. The indices for the nature of the political universe (P-1) are plotted on the vertical axis, and Other's locus of control (P-4b) index is plotted on the horizontal axis. They locate Other in the political universe.

Once a leader's self-image is located in one of the four quadrants

	TYPE A QUADRANT		TYPE C QUADRANT	
P-1/I-1 **Axis**				
	Appease DED	Reward DDD	Reward DDD	Exploit DDE
	FOLLOW/COOPERATE STRATEGIES		COOPERATE/LEAD STRATEGIES	
	Bluff EED	Deter DEE	Punish EEE	Compel EDD
±0.00				**P-4** **Axis**
	Bluff EED	Deter DEE	Punish EEE	Exploit DDE
	SUBMIT/CONFLICT STRATEGIES		CONFLICT/DOMINATE STRATEGIES	
	Bully EDE	Punish EEE	Compel EDD	Bully EDE
P-1/I-1 **Axis**				
	TYPE DEF QUADRANT		**TYPE B QUADRANT**	

Note: Key indices of beliefs in the operational code typology are scaled along the vertical and horizonatal axes to locate a leader's generalized images of self and other in a quadrant. Reward, Deter, Punish, and Compel tactics are variants of a general strategy of reciprocity in which Self initiates either an escalatory (E) move or de-escalatory (D) move and then responds in kind to whether Other escalates (E) or de-escalates (D) in response to Self's initial move. Appease, Bluff, Exploit, and Bully tactics are variants of a general strategy of cooperation or conflict in which Self initiates either an escalatory (E) move or de-escalatory (D) move and then violates the norm of reciprocity after Other escalates (E) or de-escalates (D) in response to Self's initial move.

Fig. 9.4.   Prediction template for key VICS indices. (Data from Walker, Schafer, and Marfleet 2001.)

with these scores, it is possible to make some behavioral predictions with different degrees of confidence about tactics and strategies shared with other leaders whose self-images fall into the same quadrant. The following predictions are based on their shared preferences for cooperation or conflict as the dominant strategy and a shared sense of the degree of control over historical development.

Leaders in the type A quadrant with a relatively cooperative strategic orientation and a relatively low sense of historical control are more likely to exhibit choice and shift propensities that favor the tactics of Appease and Bluff within a general strategy of cooperation. The more cooperative the tactical intensity index and the lower the locus of historical control index, the higher the confidence level for this prediction as a deviation from the norm of reciprocity.

Leaders in the type C quadrant with a relatively cooperative strategic orientation and a relatively high sense of historical control are likely to exhibit choice and shift propensities that favor the tactics of Exploit and Compel within a general strategy of cooperation. The more intense the tactical cooperation index and the higher the locus of historical control index, the higher the confidence level for this prediction as a deviation from the reciprocity norm.

Leaders in the type DEF quadrant with a relatively conflictual strategic orientation and a relatively low sense of historical control are likely to exhibit choice and shift propensities that favor the tactics of Bluff and Bully within a general strategy of conflict. The more intense the tactical conflict index and the lower the locus of historical control index, the higher the confidence level for this prediction as a deviation from the reciprocity norm.

Leaders in the type B quadrant with a relatively conflictual strategic orientation and a relatively high sense of historical control are likely to exhibit choice and shift propensities that favor the tactics of Exploit and Bully within a general strategy of conflict. The more intense the tactical conflict index and the higher the locus of control index, the higher the confidence level for this prediction as a deviation from the norm of reciprocity.

These predictions are forecasts of likely deviations from the norm of reciprocity expected as a response to a stimulus, based on an assessment of the leader's operational code (Leng 1993, 2000). It refers to the mix of other behavior that accompanies the elements of the response that match the stimulus and represents movement along a continuum of escalation and deescalation anchored by an actor's own previous move. Leaders with a locus of historical control index that attributes roughly equal control to Self (P-4a) and Other (P-4b) are most likely to follow a general strategy of reciprocity norm represented by the Reward, Deter, Punish, and Compel tactics in figure 9.4.

The following example is based on the earlier illustrations for the calculation and interpretation of VICS indices in the previous section of this chapter. Those scores are from a speech by U.S. secretary of state Dean Rusk and are reproduced along with their interpretations in table 9.1. According to the data in table 9.1, the leader's instrumental

TABLE 9.1.   A SAMPLE OPERATIONAL CODE PROFILE FOR SECRETARY OF STATE DEAN RUSK

		Score	Interpretation
Diagnostic Propensities			
P-1.	Nature of the political universe	−.21	Somewhat hostile
P-2.	Realization of political values	−.31	Somewhat pessimistic
P-3.	Predictability of political future	.08	Very low predictability
P-4.	Control over historical development		
	a. Self's control	.53	Medium control
	b. Other's control	.47	Medium control
P-5.	Role of chance	.96	Very high role
Choice and Shift Propensities			
I-1.	Strategic approach to goals	+.41	Definitely cooperative
I-2.	Tactical pursuit of goals	+.27	Somewhat cooperative
I-3.	Risk orientation	.03	Very low predictability
I-4.	Timing of action		
	a. Cooperation/conflict	.57	Medium flexibility
	b. Words/deeds	.53	Medium flexibility
I-5.	Utility of means		
	a. Reward	.20	High utility
	b. Promise	.17	Medium utility
	c. Appeal/support	.34	Very high utility
	d. Oppose/resist	.16	Medium utility
	e. Threaten	.06	Low utility
	f. Punish	.07	Low utility

Source: Speech at the Annual Meeting of the American Historical Association, Washington, D.C., Dec. 30, 1961.

beliefs indicate the following choice and shift propensities. Rusk believes in a definitely friendly strategy in his approach to political goals and believes in somewhat cooperative tactics to pursue them. He has an approach to the calculation and control of risk characterized overall by a very low score. This risk-averse orientation is marked by a propensity at a medium level to shift flexibly *both* between conflict and cooperation *and* between words and deeds. When this leader's score for I-1 is plotted against the score for Self's control over historical development (P-4a), the coordinates indicate that Rusk locates Self in the type C quadrant of the template in figure 9.4.

The secretary of state's scores for philosophical beliefs show a leader with the following diagnostic propensities: the political universe is somewhat hostile, and he is somewhat pessimistic about the prospects for realizing fundamental political values. He views the political future as very low in predictability, believes that he has a medium level of control over historical development, and attributes a very high role to chance. When this leader's scores for the nature of the political universe (P-1) is plotted against the score for Other's locus of control (P-4b), the coordinates indicate that Rusk's view of Other falls close to the center of the template in the type DEF quadrant of figure 9.4.

Depending on the amount of information available from public statements, it is possible to refine these predictions and raise further the confidence level for a particular leader in two ways.

First, it is desirable to use the additional information about risk orientation and shift propensities from Rusk's profile to qualify or strengthen the confidence level of the predictions. In the example from table 9.1, the predictions for a leader in the type C quadrant are choice propensities to use Reward and Deter tactics as part of a general cooperative strategy. However, the leader's medium (.53) level of control over historical development, very low (.03) orientation toward taking risks, and medium (.57 and .53) propensities to shift tactics make it relatively likely that he or she will use other tactics, too.

Second, if there is sufficient available information, these refinements are subject to further qualifications. It is possible to partition the observations by time, domain, issue area, and target and then recalculate the VICS indices. The effects of disaggregating beliefs are (a) to narrow the scope of their steering effects to apply only for a particular issue toward a specific target and (b) to detect learning effects on the leader's beliefs over time. As the following example reveals, this effort may or may not significantly refine the predictions.

In a study of President Jimmy Carter's operational code (Walker, Schafer, and Young 1998), the results indicate that the elements of Carter's belief system remained relatively stable over time for much of his administration. No statistically significant changes in the VICS indices occurred for his general operational code until after the Soviet invasion of Afghanistan (see table 9.2). Even then, the key VICS indices that locate Carter in the type C quadrant (I-1 and I-2) did not change enough to move him unequivocably to a different quadrant; however, the key indices that summarize the nature of the political universe (P-1 and P-2) did clearly move from type A in the direction of the type DEF quadrant.

The effect of the Soviet invasion of Afghanistan on Carter's operational code toward the Soviet Union was more dramatic, shifting Carter's beliefs about Soviet-American relations into different quadrants of the operational code template. Shifts in the key VICS indices for Carter's diagnostic propensities from cooperation to conflict plus a change in the balance of control over historical development relocated Soviet-American relations. The data in table 9.3 show that Carter's view of the Soviet Union shifted from an extremely friendly orientation to a somewhat hostile orientation. This shift was accompanied by a decrease in the cooperation of his strategic and tactical choice propensities toward the USSR and a strong increase in his propensities to shift between conflict and cooperation and between words and deeds.

How Do You Predict Behavioral Differences between Leaders?

A comparison of the VICS indices for two different leaders can reveal points of agreement and disagreement about the nature of the political universe and the most effective moves, tactics, and strategies for realizing political goals. Such comparisons can reveal what the possible effects of a change in leaders within or between states might be. To illustrate these possibilities, let us consider the results of a comparative study of two Israeli leaders, Yitzhak Rabin and Shimon Peres, during two different decades, 1974–77 and 1992–95

TABLE 9.2.   PRESIDENT JIMMY CARTER'S GENERAL OPERATIONAL CODE, 1977–79 VS. 1980

		1977–79	1980	$p**$
	Diagnostic Propensities			
P-1.	Nature of the political universe	+.68 (very friendly)	+.06 (mixed)	.00
P-2.	Realization of political values	+.51 (definitely optimistic)	+.05 (mixed)	.01
P-3.	Predictability of political future	.37 (low)	.34 (low)	.38
P-4.	Control over historical development			
	a. Self's control	.65 (high)	.75 (high)	.18
	b. Other's control	.35 (low)	.25 (low)	.18
P-5.	Role of chance	.75 (high)	.74 (high)	.41
	Choice and Shift Propensities			
I-1.	Strategic approach to goals	+.86 (extremely friendly)	+.73 (very friendly)	.03
I-2.	Tactical pursuit of goals	+.59 (Definitely cooperative)	+.57	.37
I-3.	Risk orientation	.36 (low)	.30 (low)	.26
I-4.	Timing of action			
	a. Cooperation/conflict	.14 (low)	.27 (low)	.03
	b. Words/deeds	.57 (medium)	.79 (high)	.02
I-5.	Utility of means			
	a. Reward	.33 (v. high)	.40 (v. high)	.25
	b. Promise	.45 (v. high)	.45 (v. high)	.45
	c. Appeal/support	.14 (medium)	.02 (v. low)	.01
	d. Oppose/resist	.00 (v. low)	.01 (v. low)	.08
	e. Threaten	.01 (v. low)	.00 (v. low)	.17
	f. Punish	.06 (low)	.11 (low)	.07

Source: Data from Walker, Schafer, and Young 1998.

$**p$ = one-tailed F-test for difference of means.

TABLE 9.3. KEY VICS INDICES OF CARTER'S USSR OPERATIONAL CODE, 1977–79 VS. 1980

		1977–79[a]	1980[b]
	Diagnostic Propensities		
P-1.	Nature of the political universe	+.94 (extremely friendly)	−.19 (somewhat hostile)
P-2.	Realization of political values	+.86 (very optimistic)	−.17 (somewhat pessimistic)
P-4.	Control over historical development		
	a. Self's control	.59 (medium)	.37 (low)
	b. Other's control	.41 (medium)	.63 (high)
Other's Predicted Quadrant Type		A	B
	Choice and Shift Propensities		
I-1.	Strategic approach to goals	+1.0 (extremely coop)	+.64 (very coop)
I-2.	Tactical pursuit of goals	+.77 (very coop)	+.55 (definitely coop)
I-4.	Flexibility in timing of action		
	a. Conflict/cooperation	.00 (very low)	.64 (high)
	b. Words/deeds	.37 (low)	.62 (medium)
Self's predicted quadrant type		C	A

Source: Data from Walker, Schafer, and Young 1998 and the data set for this source.

[a]VICS index calculated across speeches for pre-Soviet invasion period.

[b]VICS index calculated across speeches for post-Soviet invasion period.

(Crichlow 1998). The two leaders of the Labor party in Israel exhibited different operational codes in the earlier decade and moved toward convergence in the later decade.

In the early 1970s Rabin and Peres viewed the political universe as definitely hostile but with different degrees of pessimism. While Peres was not significantly more pessimistic than Rabin, he was significantly less confident about the ability to control historical development (Crichlow 1998). This difference in diagnostic propensities located the two leaders in different quadrants of the political universe for this time period. Moreover, a statistically significant *self* difference in strategic choice propensities in the earlier decade (Crichlow 1998) bolsters the different predictions for moves, tactics, and strategies by the two leaders during the 1970s. These differences are summarized in table 9.4.

In contrast, the remaining data in table 9.4 indicate that the diagnostic propensities of the two leaders converged during the early 1990s. They agreed that the nature of the political universe was a mixture of friendly and hostile forces, shared a mixture of optimism and pessimism about the realization of political goals, and were highly confident in their ability to control historical development. Their strategic and tactical choice propensities also converged in a definitely cooperative orientation. While both leaders shifted their views of the political universe, Peres shifted his strategic and tactical orientations toward agreement with Rabin, who exhibited relatively little change across the decades (Crichlow 1998).

How Do You Apply These Assessments to Interpreting Behavior?

The application of assessments from an operational code profile is at once a relatively simple and a relatively complex task. No matter which of the following levels of complexity is adopted in applying assessments, it is necessary for the leadership analyst to supply the subsequent observations of behavior and make the judgment about whether the observed behavior matches the behavior that was forecast in the assessment. While the following applications focus on foreign policy behavior *by* leaders, it is also possible to analyze international interactions *between* leaders at different levels of decision (Leng and Walker 1982; Brams 1994). However, this shift in focus changes the objective of operational code analysis from assessing a

TABLE 9.4. KEY VICS INDICES FOR ISRAELI LEADERS RABIN AND PERES, 1970S VS. 1990S

		1970s[a]		1990s[a]	
		Rabin	Peres	Rabin	Peres
	Diagnostic Propensities				
P-1.	Nature of the political universe	−.48	−.60	+.04	−.06
		(definite)		(mixed)	
P-2.	Realization of political values	−.36	−.47	−.05	−.03
		(somewhat)	(definite)	(mixed)	
P-4.	Control over historical development				
	a. Self's control	.69	.39	.72	.66
		(high)	(medium)	(high)	
	b. Other's control	.31	.61	.28	.34
		(low)	(medium)	(low)	
Other's Predicted Quadrant Type		DEF	B	A or DEF	
	Choice and Shift Propensities				
I-1.	Strategic approach to goals	+.71	+.34	+.53	+.68
		(very)	(somewhat)	(definite)	(very)
I-2.	Tactical pursuit of goals	+.47	+.11	+.40	+.40
		(definite)	(mixed)	(definite)	
I-4.	Flexibility in timing of action				
	a. Conflict/cooperation	.28	.79	.44	.34
		(low)	(very)	(medium)	(low)
	b. Words/Deeds	.74	.93	.82	.70
		(high)	(very high)	(high)	
Self's predicted quadrant type		C	A	C	C

Source: Data from Crichlow 1998.
[a]VICS indices are mean scores.

state's leaders and decisions to explaining the outcomes of interactions between states, which is not the focus of the present volume.

Level 1. Simple Assessments of Single Cases

It is possible simply to calculate the VICS indices for a particular leader, for example, Secretary of State Dean Rusk, and extrapolate a narrative profile of his operational code in the future tense that translates his VICS indices into a forecast of his general diagnostic, choice, and shift propensities. The following text illustrates this kind of forecast, organized as "answers" in the future tense to George's (1969) ten questions in figure 9.1 and based on the VICS indices in table 9.1 for Rusk's 1961 speech before the American Historical Association.

Based on his philosophical beliefs, Dean Rusk will have a propensity to diagnose the political universe as somewhat hostile, be somewhat pessimistic regarding the realization of political values, view the predictability of the political future as very low, believe that he has a medium level of control over historical development, and attribute a very high role to chance.

Based on his instrumental beliefs, Dean Rusk will have a propensity to choose a definitely cooperative strategy in the political universe and implement it with somewhat cooperative tactics. He will be very low in his orientation toward accepting risk and will manage risk by being moderately flexible in his propensity to shift between conflict and cooperation and between words and deeds in executing his strategy and tactics. He has a very high propensity to choose appeals and support statements, a high propensity to choose rewards, a medium propensity to choose promises or expressions of opposition or resistance, and a low propensity to choose threats and punishments.

Level 2. Complex Assessments of Comparative Cases

It is possible to compare the operational codes of one or more leaders over time and to predict corresponding similarities or differences in behavior. We have demonstrated these possibilities first with the comparative analysis of President Jimmy Carter's general operational code profile in table 9.2. Scanning this table, it is easy to identify statistically significant changes in the philosophical and instrumental elements of his operational code that forecast changes in his diagnostic, choice, and shift propensities. These changes can then be formulated as a narrative text in the future tense, as illustrated previously in the case of Dean Rusk, to make forecasts about changes in his behavior. Or they may take the format of statistical comparisons, as in table 9.2 for Carter. The same logic can be applied to two leaders in the same time period and also for each one over time.

Level 3. General Typological Comparisons

It is possible to use the VICS scores for the summary indices of a leader's philosophical and instrumental beliefs and make assessments based on the leader's attributions of strategic and locus of control beliefs to Self and Other. Collectively, the key VICS indices take into account both the dispositions of the leader (I-1, P-4a) and important features of the context for decision (P-1, P-4b) to reach a definition of the "self-in-situation." This definition of the situation reflects the choice and shift propensities attributed to Self and expected of Other, as described in the general types of instrumental beliefs associated with the locations of Self and Other in the quadrants of the Holsti typology.

The changing locations for the generalized *self* and *other* images of Carter, Rabin, and Peres across the quadrants of the template in figures 9.3 and 9.4 lead to different diagnoses regarding the expected behavior of others and their own likely choice and shift propensities for different kinds of strategies and tactics. They are based on the antecedent conditions specified by the VICS indices that locate both Self and Other in their respective quadrants of the prediction template in figure 9.4. The results in table 9.3 for Carter and in table 9.4 for the Israeli leaders Rabin and Peres are examples of this type of analysis.

Finally, over the past two years the generation of several leader profiles with an automated version of the VICS content analysis procedures has led to the transformation of raw VICS scores for leaders into normed scores calculated as the number of standard deviations from the mean score for each element of the operational code construct (see Young 2001; Schafer and Walker 2001; Walker, Schafer, and Marfleet 2001). The anchor descriptors on the continua for the raw scores (Somewhat, Definitely, Very, and Extremely) are now applied to these standardized scores at intervals of one-half standard deviation above and below their respective means for a group of twenty world leaders from a variety of geographical regions and historical eras.

The standardized scores express a leader's score for each index compared to the average for the reference group. The operational code profiles of William Jefferson Clinton and Saddam Hussein in this volume will employ standardized scores to interpret each leader's diagnostic, choice, and shift propensities in the context of this sample of world leaders. They will allow us to determine if their scores are typical or whether and how they deviate from the average scores for the reference group.

Conclusion

No matter what assessment strategy is employed, it is important to keep some cautions in mind about the validity of the results. These injunctions take the form of several comparisons that are desirable to make when it is feasible to do so. Some of them are possible within the framework of operational code analysis while others require additional resources.

1. Compare the VICS indices for a leader based on public statements with VICS indices from private sources and with assessments of the leader from other sources, for example, forecasts from other personality profiling methods or qualitative interpretations based on biographical analysis.

2. Compare the VICS indices for the leader with the same indices for advisers and others in the government to see if there is a consensus. This step is particularly important if there is doubt about whether the sources for the original analysis represent the views of a single leader or the prevailing view within a government.

3. Compare the VICS indices from public and private sources for different policy domains, issue areas, and targets in order to refine the assessments. Use tests of statistical significance as criteria for determining how likely differences in VICS indices could have occurred by chance.

4. Compare the assessments from an operational code analysis against rival predictive models, for example, models of foreign policy decision making that emphasize other domestic or external variables than the ones captured by the VICS indices. They could be forecasts from geographic area experts or from other schools of international relations theory.

All of these comparisons are potentially useful in deciding whether operational code assessments are consistent with other evidence and reside within the mainstream of conventional wisdom. When the forecasts are outside an existing consensus, or when there is no consensus from the application of different kinds of forecasting tools, then the operational code predictions should be treated with caution. However, it is under precisely these conditions that operational code forecasts may also turn out to be most useful in avoiding unpleasant surprises and in taking advantage of unexpected opportunities created by the otherwise unanticipated behavior of the leader or state under study.

10. Assessing Integrative Complexity at a Distance: Archival Analyses of Thinking and Decision Making

Peter Suedfeld, Karen Guttieri,

and Philip E. Tetlock

Some psychologists hold the view that cognitive functioning cannot be rigorously studied because it is internal and therefore not amenable to direct observation (see Dominowski and Bourne 1994). Nonetheless, research has established the value of indirect measures through both experimental and observational (including archival) techniques. It is obvious that thought processes underlie spoken or written communication; we can perhaps see this most clearly when people engage in problem solving, decision making, information dissemination, or persuasion. We may reasonably infer, as in the case of motives and other intrapsychic processes, that the process and the product are related and that the product reflects some important aspects of the process. This is the inference on which most research on integrative complexity is based, and a large number and wide variety of research projects have supported its validity.

Integrative complexity is one of a number of "cognitive style" variables—including authoritarianism, dogmatism, field independence, personal constructs, explanatory style, and many others (see, e.g., Goldstein and Blackman 1978; Mancuso 1970; Schroder and Suedfeld 1971)—to have been used in the study of information processing. It differs from the others in two major ways. Unlike related theories that emphasize stable individual differences in cognitive processes, integrative complexity theory and research are primarily focused on the internal and external factors that govern the level of complexity at which a person is functioning at a specific time and in a specific situation. Although, as is explained in more detail later, it is recognized that the level of complexity has both trait ("conceptual complexity") and state ("integrative complexity") characteristics, the research emphasis is on the latter—partly to counterbalance the more common orientation toward the former.

Scores on integrative or conceptual complexity assess the differentiation and integration of information processing (Schroder, Driver, and Streufert 1967; Suedfeld, Tetlock, and Streufert 1992). Unlike most approaches in this area, the procedure for scoring these two components has been adapted for use with almost any connected verbal material, such as speeches and interviews. This is what makes the system applicable to "measuring personality at a distance." Differentiation refers to an individual's or group's recognition of different perspectives, characteristics, or dimensions of stimuli (which may be people, events, theories, policies, etc.); integration is the perception of connections among those differentiated perspectives, characteristics, or dimensions. Differentiation is indicated when a passage makes references to alternative characteristics or viewpoints, at least two of which are viewed as legitimate. Integration is indicated when the passage makes references to trade-offs between alternatives, constructs a synthesis that combines them, or situates them in an overarching contextual structure. Both of these variables can be assessed from most kinds of connected verbal material.

History and Status of the Construct

The idea of conceptual complexity as a stable personality variable (Schroder, Driver, and Streufert 1967) grew out of personal construct theory (Kelly 1955) and conceptual systems theory (Harvey, Hunt, and Schroder 1961). Subsequent variants have included cognitive complexity (Goldstein and Blackman 1978; Schroder and Suedfeld 1971; Scott, Osgood, and Peterson 1979), interactive complexity (Streufert and Streufert 1978; Streufert and Swezey 1986), and integrative complexity (e.g., Suedfeld and Tetlock 1991). All of these are explicitly structure oriented, and the more recent versions have emphasized either situation- and context-related changes in complexity or the interplay between such influences.

Structure versus Content

One basic difference between cognitive style variables and many personality variables with cognitive aspects is the emphasis of most of the former group on structure rather than content: *how* a person thinks as opposed to *what* a person thinks (Schroder, Driver, and Streufert 1967, 5, emphasis added). Several (although not all) cognitive style theories emphasize structure, looking at such factors as the rigidity with which plans are pursued (regardless of what those plans are) and openness to new information (regardless of what the information is). A key feature of the conceptual/integrative complexity construct is its concern with structure as opposed to content, structure referring to the conceptual rules (i.e., differentiation and integration) utilized in thinking, deciding, and interrelating. By contrast, personality constructs that incorporate ideas about information processing tend to emphasize content variables, such as the focus of authoritarianism theory on moralistic punitiveness and hostility toward minority groups.

Because it is not based on content analysis, integrative complexity scoring cannot depend upon the appearance or frequency of specific words or phrases. However, at least at lower complexity levels, such appearances can be used as signals to alert the scorer to possible structural characteristics. For example, the scoring manual (Baker-Brown et al. 1992) indicates that such words and phrases as *absolutely* and *everyone agrees* are "content flags" that indicate the possibility of an undifferentiated (and therefore, by definition, unintegrated) thought structure, which would call for a score of 1 for the passage; such phrases or words as *on the other hand* and *nevertheless* may be content flags for a differentiation score (3). However, the manual also emphasizes that such flags are neither necessary nor sufficient justification for assigning a particular score, and they may appear in passages that are actually higher or lower than the flag would imply.

Trait versus State Characteristics

Current complexity theories (reviewed in Suedfeld, Tetlock, and Streufert 1992) recognize that the variable has both a trait component, the chronic or customary level at which the person operates (now usually referred to as conceptual complexity), and a state component specific to a given situation (integrative complexity). Whereas conceptual complexity theory traces consistent levels of complexity that characterize a given individual's functioning, integrative complexity theory emphasizes that differentiation and integration vary from situation to situation for each individual. For example, Saddam Hussein's complexity increased and decreased as his invasion of Kuwait first succeeded, then was threatened by Desert Shield, and was eventually reversed by Desert Storm (Suedfeld, Wallace, and Thachuk 1993). The degree to which a personality predisposition is determinative and what role situational factors play are the fundamental questions in the state-trait debate.

Trait Complexity

A longitudinal examination of Robert E. Lee's integrative complexity (Suedfeld, Corteen, and McCormick 1986) effectively confirms the dual trait and state nature of information processing complexity. Lee's complexity was generally high throughout most of his adult life but declined as the adversities of prolonged war against an enemy of superior strength became more and more severe. With the end of the Civil War, it recovered its previous high level.

Suedfeld suggests that the trait component of complexity predisposes people to react to environmental factors with different levels of state complexity. The subsequent level of state complexity is jointly determined by trait complexity and the characteristics of the problem situation. This, the *cognitive manager* model (Suedfeld 1992a), argues that complexity is adjusted on the basis of the importance and urgency of the problem, other problems having to be solved in the same time frame, the individual's intellectual and other relevant resources, and the environmental and social factors discussed later in this chapter.

An alternative explanation is that state complexity affects the relationship between trait complexity and behavior—that is, as a moderator variable (Tellegen, Kamp, and Watson 1982). Clearly, research on how these components interact in a variety of contexts, both replicating and expanding the findings concerning General Lee's pattern, would be desirable.

In formulations of conceptual complexity, differentiation and integration are stable personality traits of information processing style that vary among individuals (Harvey, Hunt, and Schroder

1961; Schroder, Driver, and Streufert 1967). Measurement relies upon responses to general questions within fundamental contexts such as relationship with authority and reactions to uncertainty, and these predetermined questions are administered in a classroom or laboratory setting devoid of emotional significance or conflict (Schroder, Driver, and Streufert 1967). Early attempts to find associations between trait complexity and other personality variables have found modest relationships with content-laden cognitive styles such as authoritarianism (Adorno et al. 1950), dogmatism (Rokeach 1960), and field independence (Witkin et al. 1962). Intelligence and complexity are correlated at a moderate level, which varies with the sample and the IQ test used (Schroder, Driver, and Streufert 1967). Conceptual complexity has been found to have only a modest correlation with mental abilities, including verbal ability, crystallized intelligence, fluid intelligence, and divergent thinking, at least in restricted-range university student populations (Schroder, Driver, and Streufert 1967; Suedfeld and Coren 1992).

Moderate correlations have also been found between trait (conceptual) complexity and a long list of general personality characteristics: openness and creativity, low social compliance and conscientiousness, narcissism and antagonism, high initiative, power motivation and self-objectivity (Schroder, Driver, and Streufert 1967; Tetlock, Peterson, and Berry 1993; Tetlock, Skitka, and Boettger 1989), social adeptness, gregariousness, extroversion, warmth and nurturance, and nonconformity (Coren and Suedfeld 1995). Conceptual complexity may in fact be associated with some unattractive personality traits, which lead others to perceive one as being easily bored, self-centered, and narcissistic (Tetlock, Peterson, and Berry 1993); but those judgments may have reflected the reactance of more complex participants against the grueling weekend of intense assessment during which the measures were taken.

Trait complexity may be a factor in leadership success. For example, leaders notable for their length of tenure in high office (such as Andrei A. Gromyko in the twentieth century and the Duke of Wellington in the nineteenth century) maintained relatively high levels of complexity even during crises where their colleagues and counterparts showed disruptive stress leading to reduced complexity (Wallace and Suedfeld 1988). General Lee consistently functioned at highly complex levels during his military career. When drastically less complex Union commanders faced Lee (McClellan, Burnside, and Hooker at Antietam, Fredericksburg, and Chancellorsville, respectively), they were unable to gain decisive victory against him, despite superior numbers of Union troops. Lee's complexity level decreased as the Confederacy weakened and his troops shrank in numbers, energy, and supplies (from 4.60 at the first battle studied, Antietam, to 1.50 at Spotsylvania). He eventually encountered opponents who were functioning at complexity levels almost as high as his (Meade at Gettysburg) or higher (Grant in the Wilderness and at Spotsylvania), against whom he was not nearly as successful (Suedfeld, Corteen, and McCormick 1986). One interesting point is that after Lee decided to surrender at Appomattox his complexity level immediately reached new heights and remained there during the rest of his life.

Although these data may reflect the existence of a stable level of complexity whose expression may be modified under some circumstances, there is another possibility. Conceptual complexity may be an interaction trait rather than a main effect trait. The most important stable factor here may be the ability to recognize and adapt to environments that demand different levels of complexity (Suedfeld 1992a). This hypothesis has not yet been tested on archival materials, although it has been supported by the results of an extensive series of simulation studies of decision making among business executives (Streufert and Swezey 1986).

State Complexity

Researchers have explored a range of possible influences on the level of complexity exhibited in any specific situation. These include intrapsychic factors as well as several categories of situational factors: the environment, social or political considerations, and the nature of the task.

Intrapsychic Factors

A number of intrapsychic factors can be viewed as intervening between stable and pervasive trait complexity and the more dynamic and responsive dimension of state complexity. Although content and structure are generally independent, such internal characteristics may also act to increase the correlation between them.

Most of the research on intrapsychic factors has focused on the need to resolve a conflict or contradiction among goals, beliefs, or values. For example, Tetlock and his colleagues have found that political liberals (i.e., those moderately left of center) tend to produce policy statements that are higher in complexity than more extreme adherents of either the left or the right wing. Tetlock (1981a, 1984) has reported consistent data from both American and British politicians showing the same pattern, which was replicated in a sample of Canadian members of Parliament (MPs) (Suedfeld et al. 1990). Although a number of alternative explanations have been proposed, Tetlock argues that liberalism or liberals are not somehow intrinsically complex. Rather, it is at this portion of the left-right political spectrum that *value conflict* or *value pluralism* reaches its highest level (Tetlock 1981a, 1983a, 1984). Value conflict occurs when two important values cannot both be maximized; in politics, it is experienced by liberals as the urge to foster both equality and individual freedom. When the two conflict, as they often do when policy strategies are being chosen in Western democratic states, conservatives tend to find freedom more important, whereas socialists opt for equality. Both of these groups therefore experience less conflict, and have less need for highly complex solutions, than do liberals (although tactics to resolve value conflict without increasing differentiation and integration have been identified, e.g., Bar-Siman-Tov 1995; Tetlock 1998; Tetlock and Boettger 1994; Tetlock, Peterson, and Lerner 1996). The curvilinear relationship between complexity and ideological position on the left-right dimension has been supported by experimental studies as well (Suedfeld and Epstein 1973; Suedfeld et al. 1994; Tetlock 1986).

Research has also explored the power of value conflict to motivate integrative complexity at different points of the ideological spectrum. For instance, in a laboratory study, Tetlock (1986) found that moderate liberals, who ranked both equality and their own economic prosperity highly on the Rokeach Value Survey, reached their maximal complexity in response to the question of whether they were willing to pay higher taxes to help the poor. By contrast, moderate conservatives, who ranked both national defense and their own prosperity highly, reached their highest complexity level when responding to the question of whether they were willing to pay higher taxes for the purpose of enhancing national defense. One key lesson of the value pluralism model is, therefore, not to expect reliable main effects of ideology. Rather, the model predicts ideology by issue interactions in which the point of maximal complexity of reasoning shifts as a function of both the value priorities of the respondents and the perceived relevance of "issue framing" to highly ranked values.

The left-right spectrum is not the only foundation for differential value conflict. For example, pre–Civil War moderates who were opposed to slavery but also wanted to preserve the Union were obviously in more conflict and, as predicted, showed higher integrative complexity than either radical abolitionists or supporters of slavery (Tetlock, Armor, and Peterson 1994). In another archival study, the provincial government of British Columbia and a panel of scientists that it had appointed to develop forest management policy in a sensitive old-growth area were caught in the midst of a controversy between groups wanting to maintain the economic benefits of logging and those wanting to ensure the protection of forested wilderness (Lavallee and Suedfeld 1997). As Tetlock's model predicted, the government and its scientists showed higher complexity than did environmental activists and representatives of timber companies. In an experimental setting, students also write significantly more complex essays discussing the relation between two values that they rated as highly conflicting (e.g., preserving the environment vs. a growing economy) than in discussing two not very conflicting values (e.g., a growing economy and the preservation of human life) (Suedfeld and Wallbaum 1992).

Value pluralism, then, will lead to higher levels of complexity when there are two or more values that are fairly well balanced in importance, so that any resolution must accept the legitimacy of both. The situation must be such that maximization of either would lead to infringement of the other; the only way out is to try to see how they can be related and what kind of trade-off or compromise could obtain at least some reasonably satisfactory level of both. This is, of course, the very definition of a complex solution to a problem. By contrast, those who must advance only one important value do not need to develop such compromise positions.

Lavallee and Suedfeld (1997) have suggested that a similar mechanism affects complexity levels in situations that evoke *motive plural-*

ism. This occurs when individuals or organizations may simultaneously experience at least somewhat incompatible motives, such as the desire to exert power over another person or group (need for power) and at the same time be liked by the target of the influence attempt (need for affiliation).

Situational Characteristics

Situational characteristics whose impact on complexity has been investigated include the severity of environmental stressors, social factors, and the nature of the task. The measure of integrative complexity captures environmental influences such as domain and task complexity. Building on this research, cognitive management and metacomplexity theorists need further to examine the ways in which individuals are able (or choose) to bring psychological propensities such as compartmentalization and attribution to bear on particular problem situations.

The Task Environment

The theory of integrative complexity calls for the study of how environmental factors influence the level of complexity at which an individual processes information and behavioral consequences as the individual's complexity level in turn affects the response to particular environmental conditions. Information load (Schroder, Driver, and Streufert 1967), time pressure, perception of threat, perception of high consequences, fatigue, uncertainty, in-group conflict, and challenge to or loss of control are examples of environmental factors that affect integrative complexity (Streufert and Swezey 1986).

When time is limited, information load is nonoptimal, and/or outcomes are negative, planning and decision making in simulation experiments become less integrated (Schroder, Driver, and Streufert 1967). Participants writing a paragraph based upon a set theme achieve lower complexity scores, omitting qualifications and consideration of alternatives in preference for responses that are dominant in the respondent's hierarchy (Suedfeld and Coren 1990).

Severe and prolonged ("disruptive") stress is hypothesized to account for an inverse correlation between the onset of violent conflict and the level of complexity, as in studies of executive decision makers in foreign policy crises (e.g., Suedfeld and Tetlock 1977). In crisis situations, especially those in which violent conflict is a probable outcome, outside observers typically judge that the situation calls for high complexity among national decision makers. Decision makers confront threats to vital national interest, characterized by a risk of war (possibly nuclear war); uncertainty about the intentions of adversaries, allies, and neutrals; a stream of possibly confusing intelligence data; and the need to maintain effective control over one's own bureaucratic and military machinery and political base and to engage in lengthy and fatiguing deliberations (Bracken 1983; George 1980; Gottfried and Blair 1988; Wallace 1991).

The impact of environmental factors on complexity has been a subject of repeated scrutiny in relation to leadership decision making during international crises. International crises are stressful almost by definition, and many researchers have looked at the relationship between crisis outcome and complexity. A case study of Neville Chamberlain during the sequence of events comprising the Anglo-German crises of 1938–39 (Walker and Watson 1994) shows fluctuations in complexity as the leader shifted between cooperative and competitive strategies. In crises that lead to war, the complexity levels of leaders show reliable reductions prior to the breakdown of diplomatic efforts. Suedfeld and Tetlock (1977) found that leader complexity dropped between the preliminary and climax phases in two crises culminating in war (World War I, Korean War) and that Israeli and Arab speeches in the UN General Assembly showed marked drops within the few months prior to the outbreak of major Middle East wars (Suedfeld, Tetlock, and Ramirez 1977).

On the other hand, continuing high complexity is often associated with negotiated, nonviolent resolutions. In the Suedfeld and Tetlock study (1977), complexity remained stable or rose across the two phases in other crises that involved the same nations and some of the same leaders but were resolved without war (the Agadir Incident of 1911, the Berlin Blockade of 1948, and the Cuban Missile Crisis). It is especially noteworthy that, while conflict spirals (as the outbreak of World War I, for example, is frequently described) induce lowered complexity among the leaders of all nations involved, surprise strategic attacks are consistently presaged by a drop in the complexity of the eventual attacker but not in the complexity of the victim (Suedfeld and Bluck 1988).

War is not the only crisis event relevant to complexity. A decrease in complexity may indicate the onset of a confrontation, which may be terminated peacefully when complexity is regained: the complexity of American and Soviet leaders dropped in the months immediately preceding the onset of the two major Berlin crises but rose over the course of the crises (Raphael 1982). Nor is disruptive stress necessarily associated with armed conflict, but sometimes only with the abandonment of a balanced, compromise- or consensus-oriented policy. A study of Canadian prime ministers has shown that decisive, unidimensional solutions to critical domestic political controversies are also accompanied by a decrease in complexity (Ballard 1983). Such findings point to one potential application of the integrative complexity approach: real-time monitoring of the complexity of utterances may warn observers of imminent changes in the strategy of a protagonist.

Another perspective on the relationship between crises and decision-maker complexity has been provided by Satterfield (1997), who analyzed verbal materials produced by Churchill, Hitler, Stalin, and Roosevelt before and after personal and political crises. Assessing the individual's psychological functioning (resilience) using change scores on the Global Assessment of Functioning Scale (APA 1994), Satterfield found that leaders who exhibited higher integrative complexity prior to a crisis showed higher resilience—that is, fewer negative effects of stress—afterward. In another recent study, Kowert (1996) found that U.S. presidents who were rated as "open" (i.e., who consulted more advisers, considered more options, etc.) showed less decrease in integrative complexity during crises.

This may be a good place to emphasize that complexity, as a structural variable, is normatively neutral. It is unrelated either to morality or to the appropriateness or correctness of the final behavior (Suedfeld and Tetlock 1991). Not only is there no theoretical or historical reason to equate complex decisions with good decisions, even a recently developed computer-based decision support system failed to find such a relationship (Wilkenfeld et al. 1996). Because complex strategies cost more in time, effort, and resources for handling other problems (Suedfeld 1992a), and may divert attention from crucial to trivial information (Tetlock and Boettger 1989, 1994), optimal decision making may involve managing available resources according to a (possibly implicit) cost-benefit analysis (Suedfeld 1992a). Both theory and data indicate that a stubborn, hostile, or simple-minded adversary may be best met with an unequivocal response that would be delayed, obscured, or diluted by complex information processing (Suedfeld 1992a; Suedfeld and Tetlock 1991; Tetlock and Tyler 1996). Thus—although the ability to maintain complexity in the face of crisis may be correlated with personal career success among statesmen (Wallace and Suedfeld 1988)—either low or high levels of complexity may lead to successful resolution of problems or conflicts, depending on the situation and the opponent. The verdict of history is that Chamberlain, comparatively complex during the Munich Conference, was outmaneuvered by Hitler in spite of the latter's low level of complexity. We would also reject the conclusion of many colleagues that a declaration of war ipso facto denotes a failure of decision making: under certain circumstances, abandoning negotiations and embarking upon armed conflict may be the morally superior, or pragmatically successful, move—or both moral *and* successful.

The moral irrelevance of complexity has often been ignored by scholars who firmly believe that complex (negotiated, compromise) outcomes occupy the high ground (see Suedfeld 1992a; Suedfeld and Tetlock 1991). But, as so often happens, the abstract value breaks down when we look at specifics. Three historical examples illustrate the complex relationship among complexity, morality, and success.

1. Many academic and media commentators disapprove of Ronald Reagan's integratively simple characterization of the Soviet Union as an evil empire. Nevertheless, President Reagan's description had both moral and pragmatic justification, given the history of Soviet oppression and the chronological—and arguably causal—association between American strategies based on Reagan's viewpoint and the demise of Communist hegemony in Eastern Europe.

2. On the other hand, most observers today applaud the integratively simple abolitionists of the 1850s, who

demanded the end of slavery even if the cost would be the massive bloodletting of a civil war and/or the dissolution of the Union—as integratively complex moderates in both the Democratic and Republican parties accurately predicted at the time.

3. Most (although not all) present-day experts also extol the integratively simple approach of Winston Churchill, who in the 1930s denounced Nazi Germany as a gangster state that understood only the language of force and deterrence. Churchill accordingly demanded an end to Chamberlain's integratively complex policy, which had been predicated on balancing deterrence with reassurances that the British understood legitimate German security concerns.

Social Factors

A variety of social factors are relevant to complexity, including the desire to project a certain image, the nature and perceived opinions of the audience in a persuasion situation, the source's position, which also determines accountability, and intragroup cohesiveness and diversity.

Impression Management

Most of the integrative complexity research reviewed in this chapter assumes that complexity reveals *intrapsychic* processes: that people who speak or write in integratively simple or complex ways are thinking about the issue in roughly equivalent simple or complex ways. By contrast, an *impression management* explanation asserts that the way people speak and write is a function of the political goals they have in the interpersonal or institutional world they inhabit. In this view, an issue may be discussed not at the level of complexity at which the source actually thinks about it but rather at the level that the source believes will create the desired impression on the target audience. For example, Tetlock (1985a, 1985b) has argued that deliberate simplification of statements can be used to signal firmness to an opponent, while more complex formulations could be used to project a misleading image of reasonableness and willingness to listen to the other side. One may also want to allay or avoid criticism by appearing to have considered all points of view before choosing a policy and to be aware of the shortcomings of that policy even though one has chosen it (Tetlock, Skitka, and Boettger 1989).

For certain purposes, the distinction between these interpretations may be irrelevant (Tetlock and Manstead 1985). Decreasing complexity in international crises may signal the imminence of war, regardless of whether simplification reveals changes in underlying thought or influence strategies that have been more or less deliberately selected; increases may predict eventual compromise, again regardless of the "true nature" of the construct that determines the complexity of the text. But for other purposes, the distinction may be highly consequential. It does make a difference, both psychologically and politically, whether leaders truly do not recognize legitimate alternative perspectives on a problem or whether they are strategically feigning nonrecognition (or, in the opposite direction, merely pretending to recognize the legitimacy of the adversary's view without any real intention to accommodate it).

In one sense, the impression management hypothesis is untestable because it is impossible to ascertain what impression the source of a message wishes to establish. Both high and low complexity can be evaluated positively or negatively by observers (Tetlock, Peterson, and Lerner 1996; Tetlock 1998; Tetlock, Peterson, and Berry 1993), so that there is no across-the-board advantage to either image. In specific cases, leaders often do not communicate at the level that would seem optimal for impression management. For instance, a show of complexity would seem to have been a good strategy for national leaders planning a strategic surprise attack, for Saddam Hussein as the UN Security Council's deadline for imposing sanctions approached, and for Mikhail Gorbachev as his economic and political problems at home grew steadily more threatening; but, in fact, all of these leaders showed lower complexity (Suedfeld and Bluck 1988; Suedfeld, Wallace, and Thachuk 1993; Wallace, Suedfeld, and Thachuk 1996). To rescue the impression management hypothesis, it could be argued that in desperate circumstances leaders might have expected that the projection of a determined "I shall not be moved" stance would discourage opponents or lead them to make more concessions. Without seeing into the mind of the leader, this is an unanswerable question.

Two research procedures that might disentangle intrapsychic from impression management explanations are reviewed by Tetlock and Manstead (1985). One is to compare private and public documentation: the disruptive stress hypothesis would predict simplification in both, the impression management only in the second, preceding war or other uncompromising conflict. The public-private difference predicted by impression management was found in two studies (Levi and Tetlock 1980; Guttieri, Suedfeld, and Wallace 1995), but not in three others (Suedfeld and Rank 1976; Tetlock and Tyler 1996; Wallace, Suedfeld, and Thachuk 1996).

Another approach is to study circumstances where impression management is unlikely to be relevant. Significant stress-related drops in complexity have been found in an experiment using a noise stressor with university students (Loewen and Suedfeld 1992) and in a field study of students as they drew temporally nearer to a stressful examination (S. Coren, personal communication, March 1997). Marked reductions in complexity during periods of acute societal stress have also been found in nonspecific archival materials—those dealing with topics other than the crisis and those produced by societal elites not involved in crisis resolution, such as novelists, scientists, and presidents of the American Psychological Association (Porter and Suedfeld 1981; Suedfeld 1981, 1985, 1992b).

One option open to impression management theorists is to reconsider what counts as a truly "private" setting. Even in confidential meetings of elite decision makers, the level of complexity may be chosen with an eye to its effect; and important figures may want to impress the recipient of personal letters or, anticipating that even their private notes and diaries may eventually become public, write with future readers in mind. At the extreme, we are concerned with favorably impressing ourselves, and thought itself becomes a presentation. This formulation makes the impression management hypothesis completely immune from disconfirmation.

Intrapsychic explanations, too, can be applied post hoc. Pre- to postelection shifts in presidential rhetoric may reflect changing impression management goals and strategies, just as individual presidents who do not show such a shift may be revealing their own unchanged goals (Suedfeld 1994; Tetlock 1981b). But low complexity can also be interpreted as caused by the disruptive stress of a grueling election campaign, followed by recovery once the election has been decided (as in Lee's military campaigns; Suedfeld, Corteen, and McCormick 1986), or successful candidates for high office may gain immediate access to information that broadens their perspective and acquaints them with alternate viewpoints and novel possible solutions to problems.

In short, the intrapsychic and impression management explanations are fuzzy sets with overlapping boundaries. The two may interact, or each may become dominant in particular situations. Some types of predictions—disruptive stress, value conflict, correlations with stable personality constructs such as dogmatism—flow more naturally from intrapsychic perspectives, while others—the impact of the anticipated audience or of power and political role—are more clearly derivable from an impression management model. More general explanations, such as the cognitive manager model, can subsume both. A reasonable conclusion at this stage is that integrative complexity has the attributes not only of both a state and a trait but also of both cognitive processes and social influence tactics.

Source Position and Status

Another factor that influences complexity, sometimes related to impression management goals, is the status of the source of the utterance. People and groups who are criticizing an established policy or attacking opponents who hold power generally express themselves at lower levels of complexity than do those who are in power and who are defending their policies or proposing new ones. This pattern has been found in election campaigns (Tetlock 1981b) and environmental controversies (Lavallee and Suedfeld 1997). Previously mentioned complexity differences between liberal and conservative politicians may have been affected by the fact that, during most of the past five decades, liberal parties have dominated the legislatures of the countries included in these studies: Canada, the United States, and the United Kingdom.

A Canadian study (Pancer et al. 1992) found that MPs who belonged to the governing party gave more complex speeches than members of the opposition party. When a minority government was in place, MPs of both parties showed higher complexity, reflecting a greater need to reach mutually agreeable policy solutions. As the next election approached, but *before* it was called, complexity increased among the governing party—contrary to Tetlock's (1981b, 1985a) findings in American presidential elections—and decreased among the opposition. Once under way, Canadian election campaigns are much more distinct from the "business as usual" activities of elected legislators than is the case in the United States—in fact, Parliament is dissolved when the election is called. However, speeches given *during* Canadian electoral campaigns are characterized by substantially lower complexity than parliamentary speeches (Pancer et al. 1992; Suedfeld et al. 1990).

When the status of an individual changes from being in opposition to being in power, success and long-term esteem accrue to those who move from relatively low to higher levels of complexity, while those who fail to make this change are more likely to lose their position or the respect of posterity. This is true among both revolutionary leaders (Suedfeld and Rank 1976) and elected ones (Tetlock 1981b; Suedfeld et al. 1990). No study has yet appeared that tracks the equivalent change as people lose power and move into opposition.

Other Factors

Another relevant social factor is the nature and perceived opinions of the audience in a persuasion situation (Guttieri, Suedfeld, and Wallace 1995; Suedfeld and Wallbaum 1992; Tetlock 1985b), which influences perceived *accountability* for one's position (Tetlock and Boettger 1989, 1994). In several experiments, integrative complexity was found to increase when students were expected to have to discuss their ideas later with another student, whose opinions on the topics they did not know (Tetlock, Skitka, and Boettger 1989), or with an expert who might judge the quality of their responses (Tetlock and Boettger 1994; Tetlock and Kim 1987). Incidentally, accountability also enhances other cognitive maneuvers such as passing the buck to other decision makers, procrastinating, and paying increased attention to irrelevant information (Tetlock and Boettger 1989). In these studies, the opinion of the eventual audience was unknown to the subject; it is interesting to note that when students were made accountable to an audience either known to agree with them or known to disagree, the former condition evoked higher complexity—perhaps because of disruptive stress in the latter (Suedfeld and Wallbaum 1992).

Not much research has been conducted on the effects of *groupthink* on integrative complexity. One could reasonably predict that groupthink—with its emphasis on in-group solidarity, delusions of infallibility, conformity guardians, and identification with an admired leader (Janis 1972, 1982, 1989)—would lead to simplification. Comparing international crises in which Janis had characterized American decision making as either groupthink or nongroupthink, Tetlock (1979) found that the latter had produced significantly more complex public statements from the U.S. president and secretary of state. However, given recent critiques of the groupthink model and the reclassification of some of the crises previously studied (e.g., Tetlock et al. 1992), further exploration of this relationship is warranted. In an interesting variant, Walker and Watson (1994) found an increase in complexity as British leaders shifted away from groupthink to multiple advocacy in deciding on a continental policy vis-à-vis Nazi Germany.

One other social variable that calls for more study is the question of individual differences within leadership groups. Tetlock (1979) reported that Dean Rusk retained a stable level of complexity across both groupthink and nongroupthink crises, but this study (like similar interleader comparisons of Wallace and Suedfeld 1988) did not examine ongoing interactions among the leaders. Guttieri, Suedfeld, and Wallace (1995), in an intensive analysis of the documents of the inner circle of the Kennedy administration, traced changes in complexity during the course of the 1962 Cuban Missile Crisis. This was a decision-making process that had been extolled by Janis as the epitome of nongroupthink approaches. There were no complexity differences between so-called hawks and doves in either public or private communications, but Guttieri, Suedfeld, and Wallace found evidence of cognitive management and disruptive stress: complexity first increased as the importance of the problem was fully recognized and solutions were weighed and then decreased as no resolution appeared and options were closed off. It is interesting to note that the Kennedy brothers—who, alone in the group, knew of a secret agreement to trade the withdrawal of Soviet missiles from Cuba for a later withdrawal of American missiles from Turkey—did not show the decreased complexity of exhausted cognitive resources. Individual differences were also found in British cabinet discussions in the late 1930s (Walker and Watson 1989, 1994), but this whole intriguing issue remains lamentably underresearched.

Problem Characteristics

The nature of the problems being faced or the decisions having to be made is important. As the cognitive manager model predicts, greater complexity is brought to bear on tasks that are both important and difficult. Maoz and Shayer (1987), for example, showed that Israeli prime ministers used more complex arguments when trying to persuade the Knesset to adopt a conciliatory rather than a bellicose stance toward Arab adversaries. This may be viewed as a rhetorical strategy as well as the prime ministers' perception of the conciliatory persuasion task "as more difficult and demanding" (Maoz and Shayer 1987, 575). As Ceci and Ruiz (1992) have pointed out, tasks that are not highly motivating lead to underestimations of the person's capacity for complexity.

Different problems being addressed in the same time period may evoke different complexity levels. Tetlock (1985a, 1988) found that Soviet leaders varied in the complexity with which they approached a variety of foreign and domestic issues, the level varying with (among other factors) the severity of difficulties at a given time. Mikhail Gorbachev, in particular, was consistently more complex in foreign policy contexts than in regard to internal economics and politics (Wallace, Suedfeld, and Thachuk 1996).

Personal crises, such as a marital breakup, the death of someone close, occupational setbacks, and illness, seem to evoke a different pattern from societal hazards such as actual or impending war. It may be that the latter are seen as less amenable to the individual's control or coping strategies. At least among men, personal crises are accompanied by increases in complexity (Suedfeld and Bluck 1993; Suedfeld and Granatstein 1995), which disappear after the crisis ends. Women's complexity has not shown such variability in response to personal problems.

Some interesting data have been collected concerning materials that deal with either past or future events. One case study showed that retrospection about stressful events reveals higher complexity than material produced at the time of the event (Suedfeld and Granatstein 1995) and that retrospective accounts of life events that were intense, unpleasant, undesirable, and neither controlled nor predicted by the person are more complex than the accounts of events that had the opposite characteristics. This pattern shows no sex-related differences (de Vries, Blando, and Walker 1995). Similarly, both men and women show a significant decrease in complexity as they temporally approach their last and most powerful crisis: death (Porter and Suedfeld 1981; Suedfeld 1985; Suedfeld and Piedrahita 1984), although, in a research setting, thinking about death itself—especially one's own death—produces higher complexity than thinking about the process of dying (de Vries, Bluck, and Birren 1993).

Technical Aspects

A number of technical issues raised in critiques of the integrative complexity approach have not yet been fully settled.

Source Identity

It is sometimes difficult to establish how completely the material being scored is actually the product of the supposed source. The two most frequently encountered questions are whether the material may have been generated by an assistant, such as a ghostwriter, speech writer, or public relations specialist, and whether the material translated from another language into English can be trusted to reflect the complexity of the source rather than of the translator.

The answer to the first question can only be tentative. In studies that scored both personal letters and public statements of the same political leader, issued in the same time period, no significant complexity differences have been found (e.g., Suedfeld and Rank 1976). Many of the documents scored for complexity either have been holographs or showed extensive editing and annotation in the hand of the named source; the conclusion has generally been that, at least in the case of important statements, leaders either write much of the material themselves (although they may allow others to "polish" the product), set firm guidelines for the writer that embody their own cognitive approach, modify the final product to be compatible with how they think about the issue, or select writers whose thinking closely matches their own (Suedfeld, Tetlock, and Ramirez 1977; Suedfeld, Tetlock, and Streufert 1992). Last, no consistent differences have been found as a function of whether the material appears in personal or public communications, the latter including those directed to a small group of colleagues as well as those intended for widespread dissemination. On the other hand, as indicated previously, it has been argued that, among eminent people, the realization that even diaries and personal letters may someday be published erodes the border between public and private utterances. The net result of these factors should be a good fit between the information-processing complexity of the named source and the integrative complexity reflected in the product. It is important, however, to be aware of individual and cultural differences: for example, even today some eminent statesmen always write their own material (e.g., Vaclav Havel), and in some cultures a person in a prominent position merely delivers utterances written by functionaries (e.g., the British and Canadian Speeches from the Throne and the speeches of Japanese prime ministers).

The matter of translations is easier to deal with. In a number of studies where both the original statement (in Russian, German, Hungarian, French, or Spanish) and an "official" English translation have been scored, no significant difference has ever been found in the complexity of the two versions. It may be that such differences could emerge if the original were in a non-European language, but there is no a priori reason to expect this to happen. In the absence of evidence to the contrary, we may assume that professional translators are able to reproduce the complexity level of the original statement.

Scorer Knowledge

Another issue is how much background or contextual information a scorer should have (see, e.g., Suedfeld and Bluck 1996). This is particularly problematic when dealing with historical, biographical, and political materials. There is no universal answer to this question, because it is quite feasible for scorers who know nothing about context nevertheless to score passages validly; the problem arises when the scorer's understanding or ignorance of allusions or connotations in the text might alter the score. We have conducted tests with both informed and naive scorers and so far have found no significant or major differences; but the possibility of this type of confounding should be borne in mind. Incidentally, it is interesting to see that completely naive people—university students serving as research participants—appear to have a good implicit understanding of integrative complexity and of how various endogenous and situational factors affect it (Suedfeld et al. 1996).

Measurement

The material in this section is excerpted from "The Conceptual/Integrative Complexity Scoring Manual" (Baker-Brown et al. 1992).

Integrative complexity scoring proceeds on a 1–7 scale (see table 10.1). Scores of 1 indicate no evidence of either differentiation or integration. The author relies on unidimensional and evaluatively consistent rules for processing information. Scores of 3 indicate moderate or even high differentiation, but no integration. The passage shows recognition of at least two distinct dimensions of judgment but fails to consider possible conceptual connections between these dimensions. Scores of 5 indicate moderate to high differentiation and moderate integration. The author notes the existence of conceptual connections between differentiated dimensions of judgment. These integrative cognitions can take a variety of forms: the identification of a superordinate category linking two concepts, insights into the shared attributes of differentiated dimensions, the recognition of conflicting goals or value trade-offs, the specification of interactive effects or causes for an event, and the elaboration of possible reasons why reasonable people view the same event in different ways. Scores of 7 indicate high differentiation and high integration. A general principle provides a conceptual framework for understanding specific interactions among differentiated dimensions. This type of systemic analysis yields second-order integration principles that place in context, and perhaps reveal, limits on the generalizability of integration rules that operate at the scale value of 5. Scores of 2, 4, and 6 represent transitional levels in conceptual structure. Here the dimensions of differentiation or integration that would, if clearly stated, justify the next higher score are implicit and emergent rather than explicit and fully articulated.

In integrative complexity scoring, the basic unit is a section of material that focuses on one idea. Usually, but not always, this scorable unit consists of a single paragraph. Occasionally the scorer may divide a long paragraph into two or more scorable units, with each centering on a single idea. On the other hand, several short paragraphs in the original material may be collapsed into one scorable unit. Throughout the manual we refer to the scorable unit as a paragraph.

The first step in sampling paragraphs from archival material is to identify the complete pool of available and scorable paragraphs (some materials, such as quotations, proverbs, or ironic remarks, are not scorable and are omitted). From this pool, at least five paragraphs are randomly chosen for each entry into the data set (e.g., for each person studied at each time period or situation). The mean complexity score of the 5 or more passages represents the datum typically used in further statistical analyses.

A variety of approaches exist for the generation (or the designation) of material that may be coded for integrative complexity. In essence, these approaches fall along a continuum of experimenter control and range from high (i.e., the Paragraph Completion Test [PCT]) to low (archival documents).

TABLE 10.1. ILLUSTRATIVE PASSAGES AT VARIOUS LEVELS OF COMPLEXITY

Score of 1	I'd just use one of the messages he sent us and I'd send it right off, now. I wouldn't even talk to anybody about it. I'd tell him we're going to conduct surveillance, as announced by the president, and one shot and in we come, and he can expect it. If he wants to sit down and talk about this thing, he can call off his gunfire and do it right away.
Score of 3	We are working on that. We don't have the answer. We will have to talk with the provinces—what is the extent of the program, the cost, the savings in the hospital in relation to the cost outside the hospital.
Score of 5	If we act now to prevent global warming, we can win on both counts. We can win in respect to jobs and we can win in respect to a cleaner environment. If we get on with it, we can lay the cornerstone for a new, dynamic, and cleaner economy.
Score of 7	The present discussion will benefit our party's work a great deal. It will enable us to turn the passive situation into an active one in certain respects, to further understand the economic laws of socialism, to readjust in time imbalances that always exist, and to correctly understand the meaning of "positive balances."

The PCT (Schroder et al. 1967) was the method of choice in the conceptual complexity research. For the PCT, research participants were asked to complete six sentence stems (i.e., write six paragraphs) addressing important domains of the social cognition: interpersonal conflict (e.g., "When I am criticized . . ."), uncertainty (e.g., "When I don't know what to do . . ."), and orientation toward authority (e.g., "Rules . . ."). Typically one to two minutes were allocated per completion. Subsequent variations on these instructions modified the specific topics, as well as the number of paragraphs to be written, and significantly lengthened the amount of time allowed per stem to as much as ten minutes, in order to use the PCT as a power test rather than as a speed test.

A significant variation, originated by Claunch (1964), has been to present participants with a single topic on which they are asked to write an essay. De Vries and Walker (1987) had participants write an essay on capital punishment, and de Vries (1988) had individuals respond to the question, "Who am I?" More recently, Streufert (e.g., Streufert and Swezey 1986) has used a lengthy guided interview as the basis for the assessment of complexity. Tasks of this sort, when material is being generated specifically in the course of the study, require careful instructions both to ensure that respondents evaluate the materials on which they are writing and do not merely provide descriptive accounts, which are unscorable, and to ensure that the format does not bias the responses in the direction of either low or high complexity.

Comparisons of data-generating techniques such as the PCT, essays, or guided interviews show only minor variations in mean complexity scores. In general, higher complexity scores are found in material that has been generated after some thought or planning has taken place and under conditions of little or no time constraint. Lower complexity scores are found in material that was generated with little prior thought and under strict time-limiting conditions. Written accounts tend to have higher scores than oral material (i.e., transcriptions of interviews), probably because the latter are more spontaneous (less carefully thought out in advance) as well as subject to shorter time schemata.

The basic qualification for becoming a trained complexity coder is to reach a correlation of at least $r = 0.85$ with an expert coder. This criterion has proven difficult to meet without repeated practice and feedback from trained coders over a period of time. Learning to score texts for integrative complexity has traditionally occurred in training workshops lasting several days and involving detailed examination of problematic cases and group discussion of scoring decisions. More recently, a manual has been prepared to enable people to learn how to score integrative complexity without attending a workshop (Baker-Brown et al. 1992). Several candidates have used it and successfully reached a level of agreement with the expert scores to qualify as independent coders, but so far we have not had enough experience to know whether it will be generally adequate as a substitute for face-to-face training sessions.

Part III. Applications: William Jefferson Clinton and Saddam Hussein— An Introduction

The Construction of Causal Stories about Political Leaders

Jerrold M. Post and Stephen G. Walker

In this part, each of the previous methods of personality assessment is applied to William Jefferson Clinton as a Western democratic leader and to Saddam Hussein as a leader from a closed Arab society to illustrate the complementary contributions of these approaches to understanding political leaders. Each leader is the subject of a comprehensive portrait focusing on the deep structure of his personality followed by analyses of different features of the leader's personality. Drawing on his Neustadt Award–winning book *High Hopes,* Stanley A. Renshon constructs and interprets a psychoanalytic portrait of Clinton. Jerrold M. Post's psychobiographic/psychodynamic profile of Saddam Hussein's political personality is updated and revised here from his testimony before the House Armed Services and House Foreign Affairs Committees. These analyses provide a formulation of each leader's core personality structure along with an account of the formative experiences that shaped it and the externalization processes that displace private motives on public objects.

The remaining analyses of each leader are organized according to their focus on one of the kinds of causal mechanisms identified earlier as the processes of ego defense and externalization, mediation of self and other, and object appraisal. Weintraub's structural analyses of each leader's spontaneous speech patterns reveal each one's characteristic style of coping with stress as a pattern of ego defense. The profiles by Winter focus on motivational mechanisms that specify differences in how Clinton and Hussein engage in ego defense and mediate self-other relationships. Hermann's analyses of cognitive, affective, and stylistic personality traits identify their cumulative effects on each man's leadership style for mediating self-other relationships in their respective institutional settings. The analyses by Walker, Schafer, and Young and by Suedfeld and Tetlock concentrate on the beliefs and the cognitive style of each leader that act as mechanisms of object appraisal.

The authors of these analyses also follow a rough division of labor in which one presents a more intensive analysis of selected personality traits and the other identifies the leader within the context of a typology or a particular configuration of personality characteristics. Weintraub's identification of several personality traits for each leader complements Renshon's dimensional analysis of Clinton's character and Post's diagnosis of Hussein's clinical type. Winter's analysis of their respective needs for power, affiliation, and achievement resonates with Hermann's location of the two leaders within a typology of leadership styles. Suedfeld presents an analysis of each leader's style of processing information from the decision-making environment while Walker, Schafer, and Young classify them within a set of ideal types of operational code belief systems.

These different modes of analysis are captured by Greenstein (1987, 66–68), who identifies phenomenological, dynamic, and genetic analyses. *Phenomenological* analyses are represented by the cognitive models of object appraisal mentioned previously, which explore the link between observed behavior and relatively overt personality traits presented by the leader as symptoms of deeper personality dynamics. *Dynamic* analyses include models of the mediation of self-other relationships mentioned previously and "cover a host of rather disparate explanatory operations . . . [ranging] . . . from relatively atheoretical descriptions of the contingencies under which different aspects of phenomenology are manifested, though explanation in terms of inner events that can only be characterized in terms of the concepts of the various schools of personality theory." *Genetic* analyses are represented in the psychobiographical portraits discussed previously, which look "for the aspects of inborn structure, maturation, and experience that culminated in the observed presenting features and the inferred underlying dynamics."

Overall, a focus on leaders explains social phenomena, such as political decisions and outcomes, by reference primarily to the properties of the leaders as social agents. Such a focus comes at the expense of excluding an extended analysis of how the decision-making environment evolved and, depending on the analytical model, may not even account for how the leader came to be who he or she is at the point of decision. This strategy of explanation is consistent with a position that assumes that human events and social institutions are the end products of long and complex causal histories involving actions by human agents that cannot be easily reconstructed. That is, "faced with a world consisting of causal histories of nearly infinite length, in practice we can only hope to provide information on their most recent history" (Hedstrom and Swedberg 1998, 12–13).

Collectively, the following profiles tell a pair of causal stories about each leader. Renshon and Post provide an account of how the personalities of Clinton and Hussein were formed. The other authors identify particular causal mechanisms and ask what the likely consequences are in the form of decisions and actions under external conditions either taken as givens or specified by others. The application of these personality profiles to particular decision-making situations, therefore, requires the user to supply information about the macrolevel environment in which the particular leader operates along with data about the leader. We shall address this knowledge gap and other issues associated with profiling political leaders in the conclusion.

A. William Jefferson Clinton

11. William Jefferson Clinton's Psychology

Stanley A. Renshon

Emphasizing the organizing concept of character, as presented in chapter 5, this profile focuses on three key elements: ambition, character integrity, and relatedness. The relationship between William Jefferson Clinton's psychology (his character and related psychological characteristics) and his performance in the domains of leadership and judgment in decision making (the twin pillars of executive role performance)—first as governor and then as president—is traced.

The Development of President Clinton's Psychology

Every person's psychology contains both dynamic and developmental elements. That is, individual elements of a person's psychology are both related to each other, have coalesced through a series of developmental experiences. A brief narrative of the developmental experiences that seem most crucial in the development of President Clinton's character elements (ambition, character integrity, and relatedness) is presented, followed by a characterization of the dynamic elements of Clinton's psychology.

The Clinton Family: A Basic Annotated Chronology

William Jefferson Clinton was born William Jefferson Blythe in Hope, Arkansas, on August 19, 1946. His father, William Blythe, a traveling salesman, was killed in an automobile accident three months before his son was born.

His mother, Virginia Kelley, twenty-three years old at the time of his birth, widowed and a single parent, lived with her parents in Hope and worked as a nurse until the spring of 1947. In that period, two important events occurred for her and young Bill Clinton. First, she met and began to date Roger ("Dude") Clinton, a seemingly well-heeled man about town whose family owned a Buick dealership in Hot Springs. Then, in the fall of 1947, Mrs. Kelley left Hope for New Orleans to train to become a nurse-anesthetist. She was gone from Hope for approximately two years, during which time young Bill Clinton was left in the care of his grandparents, Edith and Eldridge Cassidy. Thus young Bill Clinton not only lost his father before he was born but was psychologically abandoned by his mother during the crucial developmental period between the ages of one and three.

Mrs. Kelley returned to Hope and her family's home after completing her training and settled into a work and social life that increasingly revolved around Roger Clinton. They were married on June 9, 1950, at which time young Bill was just shy of his fourth birthday, his mother was twenty-seven, and Roger was forty. The marriage was tempestuous. A major reason was Roger Clinton's alcoholism, but there were other problems as well.

The Clinton Family: A Psychologically Framed Narrative

Bill Clinton spent his early years with his grandmother and grandfather, who gave him his first introduction to reading and writing. He visited his mother once in New Orleans, a trip that made a lasting impression on him. In 1953, when Bill was six, the family moved to a farm just outside of Hot Springs, but they had difficulty making a go of it. After the first winter, the family moved to Hot Springs proper, where Roger took a job in his brother's thriving Buick dealership. Roger Cassidy Clinton, Bill's half brother, was born on July 25, 1956, just before Bill turned ten.

In Hot Springs, Bill attended a Catholic school for two years and began to distinguish himself academically. In class he raised his hand so often that one of his teachers gave him a poor grade for deportment (Maraniss 1995, 35; Levin 1992, 11). He started at a new school in fourth grade, "and within days seemed to be running the place" (Maraniss 1995, 35). Ronnie Cecil, a student at the school when Bill was there, recalled that "[h]e just took over the school. He didn't mean to, but he just took the place over" (36).

By the time Bill had completed Little Rock High School, he was the school's golden boy. Gifted in his studies, an accomplished participant in extra-curricular activities ranging from music to student politics, and surrounded by a large circle of admiring friends, Bill Clinton experienced an adolescence that was in most outward respects a developmental success.

But outward appearances obscured a tempestuous family life that was to leave lasting wounds. The marriage between Bill's mother and stepfather continued to deteriorate into a series of drunken fights. Roger Clinton was verbally and sometimes physically abusive. In 1962 Virginia Kelley filed for divorce. Mrs. Kelley by that time was thirty-nine, Bill was sixteen, and his brother was six. The divorce, like the marriage, was messy. Mrs. Kelley requested a court order to keep Roger from the family home (Oakley 1994, 29). Then, three months after their divorce, the Clintons reconciled and were remarried on August 6, 1962. The marriage lasted until Roger died in 1967 of a cancer that had been diagnosed shortly before his remarriage.

Approximately six months after Roger died, Mrs. Kelley received a call from George J. "Jeff" Dwire, her former hairdresser, and they began to see each other. In 1961, Dwire had been indicted on twenty-five counts of stock fraud and had served nine months in prison (Kelley 1994a, 22). In 1969, they were married. Five years later, in 1974, Dwire died. In January 1982, Virginia Kelley married a retired food broker, Richard W. Kelley, and remained married to him until her death in January 1994.

Developmental experiences help to account for and explain the character elements that are so evident in the adult Bill Clinton: his ambition, his ideals and sense of himself, and the nature of his relationships with others.[1] Since character and psychological development begin in the family, this requires us to focus in large part on his mother, Virginia.

It is clear that Virginia Kelley was a critically important emotional center of Bill Clinton's life both as a child and as an adult. That emotional centrality persisted past childhood well into adulthood, indeed, until her death. When the news about Gennifer Flowers broke and Clinton's presidential campaign went into free fall as he campaigned in New Hampshire in 1992, "Mr. Clinton excused himself from a critical strategy meeting . . . and disappeared. Later, his aides found him hunched over a pay phone in the lobby calling his mother" (Renshon 1996a).

Clearly, Clinton was very emotionally connected to his mother. But what of Virginia Kelley's relationship to her son? What kind of mother was she to young Bill? How did their relationship appear to affect him? In writing her autobiographical memoir, Mrs. Kelley observed the crisis-ridden quality of her life.

> I've wondered why there are so many hills. Is there something about our family, some built-in need to live life as if it were a StairMaster? Hillary says her family . . . didn't have crises every four minutes. What then explains our turbulence? (1994a, 276)

One cannot help but note the similarity of Mrs. Kelley's sense of her own life as crisis driven to that of her son, whose private and especially public life and presidency have also been substantially driven by crises. While the specific dynamics that help to explain and account for their crises-driven lives differ, the overall dynamic process seems remarkably parallel.

Her character had a direct effect on his, because her character helped to create the circumstances of his childhood and adolescence that played an important role in shaping his own character. What were Mrs. Kelley's ideals and values? What things were important to her? What guided her as she made the decisions that would shape her life and the lives of her sons? She gives many clues in her autobiography, but they can be organized around the twin themes of being noticed (narcissism) and putting pleasure before responsibility (the boundary problem). Charmed by appearance, especially in the men to whom she was drawn, she ignored behaviors that ultimately would prove destructive for her and her son. This was the model of relationships she provided for Bill Clinton.

Virginia Kelley in Psychological Perspective

Virginia Kelley has been characterized as "an American original" (Oakley 1993, 14). Of herself she says, "I'm a character, a cut up, a kook" and notes that "Even before Bill became a public official, I had what might be called a 'public persona'" (1994a, 16, 157). Perhaps the best brief summary of her life and persona is the portrait of her as a woman who

> worked hard and played hard, with an affinity for the night-clubs and the thoroughbred horse-racing tracks. . . . In later years, her flightiness and raucous laughter coupled with her love of flashy and multiple pieces of jewelry and colorful ensembles gave her an Auntie Mame quality as surely as her jutting jaw, spidery false eyelashes, and quarter- moon grin gave her an uncanny resemblance to Bette Midler. (Oakley 1994, 23)

Mrs. Kelley had ambition and possessed the ability and determination to accomplish her purposes. A major purpose early on was to find a way out of her mother's home and the tensions that existed in it. She seems to have identified strongly with her gentle, people-loving father and rebelled against any identification with a mother she saw as angry and vindictive (especially toward her father).[2]

A central feature of her psychology was her narcissism. One form this took was her great concern with appearances—hers and others. From the vision of how she would look in the crisp white uniform of the profession she chose in part because of this image, to her concern with the outward appearance of the men she married and the woman her son brought home from Yale, appearance, not substance, seemed to play a major role.

Another form her narcissism took was her desire to be noticed, indeed, to be the center of attention and doing whatever was necessary to ensure that position. From carefully constructing her Auntie Mame persona to joining entertainers on stage, Mrs. Kelley liked the spotlight. As she says of her partying in Hot Springs, "I was obviously born with a flashy streak inside me, just waiting to burst out, and Hot Springs let me be me with a vengeance" (1994a, 107).

Her narcissism was also reflected in the men she chose, men whose own narcissistic charm masked questionable character and behavior. Mrs. Kelley found Roger Clinton's

> vast vanity charming. I like a man who likes himself, and Roger Clinton certainly seemed to approve of Roger Clinton. He was always trying to catch his reflection in a mirror or a window. And when he was playing host, you've never seen such strutting in your life. (1994a, 81)

She was drawn to men who tended to skirt legality, convention, and ethics. Her first husband had several wives and a number of children she didn't know about. Her second husband, Roger, was a sometimes violent man whose behavior got him in trouble with the police. He was also a bootlegger, gambler, and bookie. Her third husband was a convicted swindler. Even her beloved father, it turns out, had a problem with alcohol,[3] and she learned while doing research on her autobiography that her mother sold bootleg whiskey from their house (1994a, 94).

Mrs. Kelley had a robust sense of self-worth, one she characterized as supreme self-confidence. However, her ambition was substantially shaped by her narcissism and her concern with her own pleasure. How did these characteristics play out in the context of Bill Clinton's early life?

Virginia Kelley as Mother: A Psychological Perspective

Clinton, in an interview with Charles Allen, said of his mother,

> She was, I thought, a good role model in three ways. She always worked, did a good job as a parent; and we had plenty of adversity in our lives when I was growing up and I think she handled it real well, *and I think she . . . gave me a high pain threshold,* which, I think, is a very important thing to have in public life. You have to be able to . . . take a lot of criticism—suffer defeats and get up and fight again. (Allen 1991, 20, emphasis added)

In many respects the evidence points to the fact that Mrs. Kelley's own emotional needs took precedence over those of her children. It is plausible to argue that in choosing to go to New Orleans for several years she might well have thought the short-term sacrifices for her and her son were worth the long-term benefits associated with furthering her career, but the same cannot be said for her immersion in partying and nightlife. Her disinclination or inability to moderate her party life calls into question the altruistic justification she provides for having left Hope. More important, her excessive partying was a constant reminder to her son, once she returned, of exactly what her priorities were.

Her partying and nightlife were not necessarily more important to her than her children, but in terms of her allocation of time and

282

energy, they were certainly strong rivals. The effect of her attachment to partying must also be considered in the context of the loss of Clinton's father. Given that one effect of losing a parent at an earlier age is a tendency to turn more forcefully to the remaining parent, Mrs. Kelley needed to be all the more available to her son. Yet she neglected him for her own pursuits.

Mrs. Kelley recalls that her son "never gave any overt indication that he didn't approve of my gambling, or of our social drinking; he just simply moved quietly in the other direction" (1994a, 138). What she doesn't mention is that she apparently tried to reduce her conflict between partying and mothering by bringing her son with her on her nocturnal rounds. There were a number of local "nightclubs[,] like the Vapors Supper Club, the Southern Club and the Pines, [which] were among the most popular watering holes, and Bill Clinton's mother, Virginia, made the rounds whenever possible, *occasionally dragging her son Billy on the night's merriment*" (Oakley 1994, 27, 96, emphasis added; see also Sheehy 1992, 214). Mrs. Kelley said she only took her son "to nightclubs to listen to jazz, [but] he was offended by the smoke and the drinking" (Wills 1992, 63).

A similar conflict between her own pleasures and her responsibilities was found in her professional life. Mrs. Kelley recalls that she went to the track every day it was in session (1994a, 109). Both the gambling and the scene attracted her. The problem was that, as a nurse, she was frequently on call. As a solution to this problem, she scheduled her cases in the mornings during racing season so she could go to the track in the afternoons. This is assuredly a dramatic reflection of the relative weight that Mrs. Kelley gave to her profession and her personal pleasure.

Mrs. Kelley's narcissism raises the question of her adoration for her son: What portion stemmed from her own needs and how much was a real appreciation of his accomplishments? The children of narcissistic adults are often viewed by the parent as extensions of themselves, reflective of their own sterling qualities. In doing well, the child reflects positively on the specialness of the parent. When Mrs. Kelley notes, "I'm a shameless reveler in my son's careers and accomplishments," her words suggest something more than just pride (1994a, 14).

The Primacy of Others: The Question of Fidelity

The interpersonal style of both Virginia Kelley and her son Bill is characterized by a movement toward people. Mrs. Kelley has characterized herself as a person who trusted others and was, if anything, too trusting. She and others have characterized Clinton in the same way.

However, one important lesson of Clinton's early experiences was that it was unwise to invest too much of oneself in individual relationships and to turn to a broad range of others to seek personal confirmation. The origin of Clinton's turn toward others can be traced to the loss of his biological father and the loss of his mother when she went to New Orleans for two years to study, a fact that his traumatic memories of their infrequent visits attest was an important early experience.

A child who loses a parent often longs for him or her and can become "object hungry" (Neubauer 1960, 68). That is, they search for persons (objects) able to provide what is missed in the absent parent (in this case *parents*). Clinton's growing realization that he didn't have a father, coupled with the simultaneous absence of his mother, was a powerful inducement for him to seek out other people.[4]

As powerful as they were, these early lessons do not, in and of themselves, fully account for the nature of Clinton's interpersonal relationships and the low levels of trust that underlie them. To do so, we must examine the relationship among Clinton, his mother, and his stepfather.

Parental irregularity, lack of reliability, and concern with pleasures at the expense of a commitment to a firmly rooted family life can be seen by a child as a form of betrayal. Clinton's stepfather was no more reliable than his mother. He often went out and left his stepson at home alone in the evening or all night (1994a, 111, 124). Clinton could count on neither parent, individually or as a couple. By the mid-1950s, when Bill Clinton was in adolescence, Mrs. Kelley's husband was drunk "nearly every single day" (1994a, 117). The fights between them escalated: verbal abuse sometimes turned physical. Mrs. Kelley began to secretly put away money. It is from this period that the dramatic stories date about Clinton standing up to his stepfather to protect his mother and young brother. Even Clinton's (then) four-year-old brother tried to protect his mother one evening by dragging into the house a large stick he could hardly carry (1994a, 135).

Mrs. Kelley and her children moved out of the house, and she filed for divorce. Once again coming to her aid, Clinton gave a deposition to his mother's attorney to support her case. He has said elsewhere that his stepfather "genuinely did love me, and I genuinely did love him" (Cliff and Alter 1992, 37). Mrs. Kelley reports that, through everything, "Bill never stopped loving Roger Clinton" (1994a, 169). Given those feelings for his stepfather, testifying against him must have been a very difficult emotional task for Clinton.[5]

The divorce was finalized in May, but Mrs. Kelley began to relent almost immediately. She did so, she says, because her then ex-husband came around, acted so pitiful, and promised that this time he would *really* change. Understandably, Clinton was against his mother's remarriage; she quotes him as telling her, "that would be a mistake" (1994a, 149). After a short period, she did change her mind, and they were remarried three months after the divorce was finalized.

Consider what effect these events and his mother's behavior must have had on Clinton and his ability to trust. Roger Clinton had struck his wife on a number of occasions and had threatened her children.[6] She had at last separated from this abusive situation, seeking her son's help to do so by having him submit an affidavit against the only father he had known. Then, impulsively, she returned herself and her children to the same dangerous and unpleasant situation. In returning herself and her children to a set of circumstances in which all had suffered emotionally (and she physically), she betrayed her own and her family's emotional well-being and sense of physical security (cf. Kelley 1994a, 134). She specifically betrayed the commitments her son had made to help her and his family, first by repeatedly standing up to his stepfather at some risk to himself and second by submitting an affidavit against him. Her remarriage subjected them all again to the situation they had escaped and rendered Clinton's stands against his father both at home and in the courts null and void. Clinton made an important, sincere, and difficult emotional commitment to his mother, and she responded by first making use of it and then disowning it.

A basic lesson of Clinton's early life experiences was that even those on whom you should be able to count are often unreliable. These experiences are consistent with Clinton's adult behavior, specifically his lack of fidelity in his commitments to others, such as supporters, colleagues, and voters, and his admission that he has "caused pain in his marriage" (Brook 1996). Clinton's early experiences are consistent with his willingness to ask others to walk the political plank with (or for) him and then reversing himself when it is to his advantage to do so, a model provided by his mother.

The Draft Controversy

On February 6, 1992, the *Wall Street Journal* published a long article asserting that Bill Clinton had secured a draft deferment during the Vietnam War by promising to enroll in the Reserve Officer Training Corps (ROTC) program at the University of Arkansas but had then reneged on that promise. In answer to the charge, Clinton said he had received a student deferment as an undergraduate and, though he was eligible for induction while a Rhodes Scholar in England, had been fortunate enough never to have received the call. He asserted that he had never asked for or received special treatment from his draft board, claiming, "I certainly had no leverage to get it" (Ifill 1992a, A16).

Subsequent reports revealed that Clinton's late uncle, Raymond Clinton, had led a successful effort to provide special protection for Clinton from being inducted during a ten-month period in 1968 when he was reclassified 1-A (*Los Angeles Times,* Sept. 2, 1992) and that Clinton himself had asked for help from Senator J. W. Fulbright's office (for whom Clinton had worked as an intern while in college) in securing a spot in the ROTC program (Suro 1992).

In both cases, Clinton first denied any knowledge of the events but shortly thereafter admitted he was qualified for the draft by asserting that he had never received special treatment.

Ambition, Ideals, and Clinton's Resolution of Quandaries

The elements selected for public presentation allowed Clinton to present himself in the best light or interpret his behavior in that manner.

Elements of a story that might contradict this somewhat self-idealized view of his behavior were simply omitted or else interpreted in a way that further stretched the bounds of common understanding. One example of that tact occurred when Clinton was forced to admit that powerful others, like Senator Fulbright, had interceded on his behalf. In response Clinton said, "when people ask you about special treatment, they mean did you leverage power or money, or something to get something that other people wouldn't have gotten, and the answer to that is no" (Bruck 1994).

A Life's Choice: Hillary Rodham Clinton

Ordinarily, a president's spouse receives only passing attention except if she becomes involved in a directly political way (as Edith Wilson did when she became the guardian of her husband's presidency after he suffered a severe stroke while in office) or if she breaks new ground in her public activities (as Eleanor Roosevelt did). The Clintons, however, are unique. They have been true, but troubled, political partners for decades.

Marriage reflects, at a basic psychological level, the attempt to blend together two separate but ideally complementary psychologies. Under favorable circumstances both partners complement and compensate each other at a core psychological level, particularly each person's character domains—ambition, ideals and character integrity, and relatedness. Development within a marriage is also crucial. Individuals do not simply come together with two separate psychologies that remain static and separate. Rather, in any long-term relationship, the two psychologies develop *in relation to each other*, as well as in relation to experiences with the outside world.

The idealism that one partner may bring to a marriage can be deepened or damaged by the other's behavior. A partner's ambitions can be dampened or enlarged. And the opportunities that marriage brings to realize one's ambitions also shape how spouses come to view themselves, their partner, and their marriage. Many analyses have examined the fit between the Clintons, but none has examined the ways in which their psychological relationship has evolved over time.

By all accounts to date, Bill and Hillary Clinton started their marriage with a remarkably good fit, given their basic psychologies, personalities, and larger interests. They were "an evenly matched romance and a fair fight . . . Two strong willed personalities" (Maraniss 1995, 247). Hillary Rodham's "intellect, resilience, and ambition were . . . equal to his" (426).

Hillary Rodham's approach to life, unlike her husband's, is "focused, pragmatic, and aggressive" (Oakley 1994, 89). Clinton, on the other hand, was, and in many respects remains, unfocused, with an aversion to boundaries, preferring charm to conflict. While Bill was somewhat sporadic in his attention to his studies, Hillary was much more focused: "Her focused intellect was . . . a perfect counterpoint to his restless diffuse mind" (Maraniss 1995, 247). Interpersonally, too, both differed from and complemented each other: "Hillary required less company than Clinton. . . . constant fellowship was not her style" (Oakley 1994, 102).

The Clintons as Political Partners: Two Psychologies, One Presidency

The Clintons are two highly intelligent people who want to make their mark and who share some definite ideas about how to do so. Each has a distinctive psychology. Bill Clinton is smart, charming, and unfocused. Hillary Rodham Clinton is smart, very focused, but less able and willing than her husband to move toward others.[7] In these ways, each provides more of what the other might benefit from having.

In addition to their shared high intelligence, both are very ambitious and display high levels of confidence in both themselves and the policies and approaches they propose. A critical issue, however, is not in what ways they are alike and different, but how these similarities and differences affected the Clinton presidency.

Hillary Rodham Clinton's ambition trumps her husband's. Senior presidential advisers have suggested that it was Hillary Clinton who came to Washington with a very ambitious view of the administration's goals (Drew 1994). At a meeting of the entire cabinet and senior White House staff at Camp David on January 30–31, 1993, the discussion turned to what items should be in the president's agenda. Some cabinet officials suggested limiting the large agenda because many of the items were difficult issues. However, Hillary Clinton "then gave a ringing speech in favor of just the opposite—

doing everything. 'Why are we here if we don't go for it?' she asked at the end" (Woodward 1994, 110–11).

It was Hillary Clinton who championed the large, mismanaged, and many believed unnecessary, government program to purchase vaccines for children. It was also Hillary Clinton who was the chief architect and strategist for the administration's complex health care proposal that went down to ignominious defeat.

> The problem of who will say no to the president is compounded by the problem of who can say no to his wife. Given her capacity to be sarcastic and angry with those who disagree with her, her tendency to retain her anger, and her obvious power in the administration, her views and recommendations are rarely challenged. A congressional aide who has dealt with her has said her staff is "terrified of her. . . . they are very loyal . . . but they are scared to death . . . she will fire them if they tell her the truth. (Bruck 1994, 88)

Becoming More Alike

In some ways Hillary Clinton has begun to resemble her husband—in their shared sense of the basic purity of their motivations and their somewhat idealized view of their own behavior; in their sense that they ultimately know what is right and best; in their conviction that their intentions are only to do good for others; in their confidence that they ultimately know what is best; and in their belief that others who don't share their views are misguided at best or, more likely, are driven by base motives. They have also come to share a view that they can't win, no matter how good their motives, no matter how competent their policies. Others—such as special interests, Republicans, the far right, journalists, commentators, and some segments of the public—have been named at one time or another as "out to get them."

It is Hillary who has provided the primary fuel for this view.

> Hillary's contribution . . . was the way in which—because her personality is so different than Clinton's—she complimented [*sic*] him. Bill sees the light and sunshine about people, and Hillary sees their darker side. She has much more ability than

he does to see who's with you, who's against you, and to make sure they don't take advantage of you. He's not expecting to be jumped, but she always is. So she's on the defensive. (Bruck 1994, 63)

She "has long been inclined toward bunker mentality. She tolerates critics much less graciously than her husband. . . . she assigns partisan evil to most detraction" (Brummett 1994, 244).

Ideals versus Politics

Like her husband, Hillary Clinton has often faced the dilemma of having to choose between her (and her husband's) political interests and her personal ideals. Sometimes the Clintons' political interests have been in direct conflict with Hillary Clinton's long-standing personal commitments. For example, though she has long been associated with children's causes, Arkansas was sued in 1991 for underfunding the state's child welfare system. For both Hillary and Bill, time and experience have provided a more realistic appraisal of the other's character and a fuller appreciation of the implications of that character on their hopes for the relationship. This realization does not mean that there are not continuing strong emotional ties between them, although the nature of these ties may have changed. At this point they may reflect mutual interests, shared experience, common fate, respect, and perhaps even admiration for the other's talents and skills.

The President's Character

The theory of character developed in *The Psychological Assessment of Presidential Candidates* (Renshon 1996a) and presented at length in chapter 5 is quite straightforward. It defines character in terms of three key domains: ambition, character integrity, and relatedness. Ambition simply refers to a candidate's or president's level of desire to achieve his or her purposes and the depth of the skills he or she can bring to bear on accomplishing them. Character integrity refers to the ideals and values by which a candidate says he or she lives and his or her fidelity to them. Both are important, but the latter is crucial. Character integrity is to be found in those circumstances where sticking to one's convictions entails the possibility of real loss, political or otherwise. Finally, relatedness refers to the basic nature of the candidate's interpersonal relationships, that is, how he or she relates to and treats others.

High Ambition

There could be little mistaking Bill Clinton's substantial level of ambition (used here in a purely descriptive sense). His path from Hope, a small town in rural Arkansas, to 1600 Pennsylvania Avenue in Washington, DC, is a chronicle of, and a testament to, his personal and political ambitions.

There was also little doubt that Clinton had the skills to accomplish his ambition—a great reserve of energy, strong intelligence, and a capacity to persist in his investment in his success and work. Historically there are numerous accounts of Clinton's high level of activity, beginning with his high school years and extending through college at Georgetown University; Oxford University, which he attended as a Rhodes Scholar; and Yale Law School. The energy to fund his psychological investments was evident during his presidential campaign. Describing Governor Clinton's frenetic schedule during the presidential campaign, Senator David Pryor, a good friend, noted that he had

> enormous energy. . . . His schedule defied human tolerance. . . . On February 17, the day before the New Hampshire primary vote, he made 17 stops over the state. At 11:30 that night, schedule completed, he asked, "Isn't there a bowling alley that's open all night? We need to shake some hands." (in Levin 1992)

Character Integrity

The second basic element of character—integrity—requires us to ask of Bill Clinton, What is the relationship between the ideals and values that truly define who he is and the person he presents himself to be?

There was evidence in the campaign that Clinton entertained few doubts about his motives, values, and candor. Plagued by questions about his integrity and honesty during the campaign, he responded by presenting himself as a man of conviction, determination, and principle. Critical to his self-image (as well as to his campaign strategy) was a view of himself as a victim.

These characteristics reflect a strong component of *self-idealization*. Most people wish to think well of themselves. However, Bill Clinton appears to believe the *best* of himself and to either avoid or discount evidence from his own behavior that indicates all is not as he believes it to be. Any attention called to a number of discrepancies between his real behavior and his view of it, as was done by the press during the campaign and the first two years of his presidency, was met with denial, exculpatory explanations, mostly long but sometimes short answers that did not deal directly with the point, and, when all else failed, unconcealed frustration and anger.

Relatedness

On the face of it, it seems clear that Clinton's interpersonal style reflects movement toward people. Much has been made of his empathy and natural friendliness, and to a substantial degree (with some very important caveats) these characterizations appear accurate.

Much has also been written about Clinton's difficulty in saying "no" and his eagerness to please. Both are often attributed to "Clinton's well-known need to be liked." Indeed, the brief biography of Governor Clinton that appeared on the front page of the *New York Times* (Kelly 1992) on the day of his election was entitled "A Man Who Wants to Be Liked and Is."

But the idea of a "need to be liked" does not fully come to grips with another psychological tributary of Clinton's political style—his tendency to build up and then lash out against institutions or groups who oppose his policies. The press is one example of such a group, but there are others, including lobbyists, special interests, "profiteering drug companies," "greedy doctors," "muscle-bound labor unions," and so on. Presidents, like others, can be known by, and can benefit from, having certain kinds of enemies. However, for a man who is said to have such a strong need to be liked, his list of enemies is rather long and inclusive, and the characterizations are often somewhat harsh. It appears that Clinton does not want to be liked so much as be validated. He wants others to accept the view of himself that he holds, and when they don't, he disowns them and turns against them angrily.

President Clinton's Character: Patterns of Psychology

A president's psychology is not synonymous with his character. A president, like any other person, develops characteristic psychological patterns. Built in part on the foundation of character, these patterns represent the related package of qualities that help define a person's psychological resources and limitations.

Persistence

Persistence, an excellent example of a character-based trait, reflects a capacity to tolerate disappointments, frustrations, and setbacks to one's plans and not to be deterred from continuing attempts to achieve them. Persistence is partially a function of an individual's desire to achieve his or her purposes (ambition). The greater a president's ambition, the more likely he or she is to continue trying to realize it. Persistence is also related to self-confidence. The greater one's self-confidence, the more capacity one has to persist. A no less powerful association is to be found in the reverse; namely, the more important success becomes to maintaining or validating one's self-regard or identity, the more determined a person may become to obtain that which success provides.

President Clinton is both determined and resilient. His persistence has been a great political asset. As governor and president, Clinton has had a number of serious setbacks from which he has recovered and from which he has gone on to new achievements. Going back to his student politics days, he lost in his bid for student council president at Georgetown during his junior year but won it his senior year (Levin 1992, 51). In his early political career he narrowly lost his first run for public office for a congressional seat in Arkansas in 1974 but went on to win the election for attorney general in 1976 and for governor in 1978. He lost his reelection bid in 1980 but ran again in 1982 and won. In the 1992 presidential campaign, he recovered from major questions raised about his character that would have led many candidates to withdraw.

Clinton's capacity to recover is obvious. But an important question is, Why does he have to do it so often? This relates to the crisis-pocked landscape of his life described by his mother and, in part, to his characteristic impatience and associated impulsivity.

Impatience

Bill Clinton is a man in a hurry. When asked by Dan Rather what his biggest disappointment in the presidency had been, he responded, "How hard it is to do everything I want to do as quickly as I want to do it. . . . I [still] get frustrated. . . . I'm an impatient person by nature, and I want to do things" (1993c, 479).

David Mathews, who has known Clinton for over twenty years, observed of his first term as governor, "When he began his administration in 1979, Bill was like a man in a hurry to accomplish many things in a short time. . . . I think somehow Bill felt that, through his sheer energy, he could change our state overnight" (in Levin 1992, 133).

In his presidency, a large number of public deadlines were self-imposed and unnecessary. For example, Clinton had publicly vowed to pick his whole cabinet by Christmas, a promise that led to a "mad scramble" (Drew 1994, 31). Appearing on *Larry King Live* on June 4, 1992, Clinton said, "I know I can pass a sweeping package of legislation during the first hundred days of my administration." In a May 1992 *Fortune* magazine article, Clinton is quoted as saying he will "put together a transition team to 'hit the ground running,' resulting in one of those great 100 days in which Congress would adopt my health care and education policies, my energy and economic initiatives."

The point here is not to criticize Clinton because of delays or slippages in the schedules he announced but rather to underscore that the time limits placed on him were of his own making and, strictly speaking, were not necessary. It seems clear that the president's time frame was unrealistic, given the complexity of what he was undertaking. It was also unnecessary and counterproductive to make such commitments publicly and prematurely. There is no evidence that the public expected or demanded that he produce detailed legislation in a variety of areas, some of which would be complex and contentious, and that it be passed or submitted to Congress within his first one hundred days in office.

The Need to Be Special

Bill Clinton was a very public president and most likely will continue to be a very public ex-president. For him to be appreciated, others, especially the public, *must* know all he is doing. Clinton is a man with strong analytic capacities and a mastery of facts that comes from decades of immersion in policy, and he *wants the public to know it.*

Consider in this regard the economic conference staged by the newly elected president and his staff in December 1992 in Little Rock during the transition period. Some advisers argued against it, believing (correctly, it turned out) that it would take time away from other important matters of planning and implementation. However, soon-to-be president Clinton wanted to make a strong impression as someone who had mastered the complexity of the American economy. "Professor" Clinton demonstrated at length his grasp of policy detail, putting his intelligence on display in a setting structured to be supportive of ideas he had presented during the campaign. "Clinton got to do what he loves most: talk policy and show off his knowledge" (Drew 1994, 27).

It is not surprising that someone with Clinton's large and successful ambitions, sometimes realized against great odds, would come to think of himself as somewhat special and unique. And I believe that he did see himself as uniquely experienced and qualified to provide this country with leadership. Both views, of course, had their origins in Clinton's early experience with his mother's view of him.

The sense of being special can also be reflected in the view that one has been singled out and treated differently, whether for good or for bad. For Clinton, this often takes the form of pointing out the impossible standards to which he is held. For example, when the issue of his marital fidelity was raised during the campaign, Clinton was suffused with a sense of his own victimization and a sense of being singled out for martyrdom. He complained loudly to his traveling companions, "No one has ever been through what I've been through in this thing" (Goldman et al. 1994, 118). In the famous *Rolling Stone* interview (Wenner and Greider 1993, 81), he complained of being held to "an impossible standard" and of "never" getting credit for his accomplishments in spite of having "fought my guts out." He conveys a sense of being above the law because of his special gifts.

The sense of having been singled out *because of* the important, major, or unusual nature of what one is trying to accomplish calls attention to one's efforts and to the valiant struggle one is waging. It has the effect of underscoring the unique and selfless nature of one's efforts. Both of these views are consistent with Clinton's idealized view of his own behavior, motives, and policy ambitions.

The Wish to Have It Both Ways and the Dislike of Boundaries

Due largely to his idealized view of himself, Clinton often seems unaware of the discrepancies between what he says and what he does. In matters large and small, there is an element in Clinton of not wishing to, or perhaps thinking that *he does not have to,* make the ordinary choices that individuals and presidents do.

His leadership behavior gives the unmistakable impression of a president who has difficulty following through on his professed commitments. Furthermore, his behavior suggests a president who wishes to give the appearance of following through on commitments while acting in a manner that is not wholly consistent with adhering to them. This behavioral tendency comes from the sense of not wanting to be limited in any way personally or politically (itself a manifestation of grandiosity) and from a sense of being special and therefore entitled to operate differently. However, in ordinary developmental experience, an individual's grandiose wish to "have it all" becomes modified by the acceptance and appreciation of realistic limits.

Taking Risks

Clinton's risk taking, like his character, contains inconsistent elements. In some areas he is not reckless and many of his risks are hedged. His frequent attempts to have it both ways are one strategy for managing these larger risks. On the other hand, the combination of strong ambition, high self-confidence, and feelings of being special and above the rules that govern others frequently pushes him toward substantial risk taking, often of a self-absorbed type.

On occasion, Clinton's belief that he can accomplish what has eluded others leads him to take large risks and to attempt to mask rather than hedge them. One prime example is the president's ambitious and complex health care plan. It should be kept in mind that this plan represented a risk, not only for President Clinton but for the public. He was willing to take a large policy gamble that his untried plan would work as promised, that it would not result in damaging consequences, and that it would function in a way that is fair.

Many of the president's aides and allies were not as confident as he was. Yet he and his wife overrode a number of his aides' concerns and went ahead with the plan anyway. Why? One answer lay

> in their sense that they were smarter than anyone else. For people who considered themselves masterly politicians with a fine feel for the public, and people who were of considerable political talents, they misjudged probable public reaction. (Drew 1994, 305)

In other words, strong ambition and high levels of self-confidence can lead to poor judgment. President Clinton and his wife not only underestimated the public's response to their health care plan but overestimated their ability to overcome it. Moreover, the method President Clinton chose to help him win acceptance of the plan, emphasizing security (which became the selling point after polling indicated it would be effective) instead of dealing directly with the many complex and difficult issues his plan raised, exacerbated the difficulties.

There is one other area of risk taking that requires mention: those in his personal life who are indulgent and reckless. This risk taking has publicly emerged in connection with his extramarital relationships,[8] with his dealings with the Whitewater real estate venture, and most famously with his relationship with Monica Lewinsky. In each of these cases, Clinton clearly engaged in behavior that was extremely risky from the standpoint of his personal and political ambitions.

In these circumstances, Clinton experiences difficulties with impulse control, apparently believing that, if caught, he can always find some way to defuse the situation. All of these behaviors are elements that emanate from character. From ambition comes the sense that he will achieve what he wants to go after. From the domain of character integrity comes the highly idealized view of oneself, a view he believes he can convince others to hold. And from the domain of relatedness comes the sense that he can and will do what it takes to get others to see things his way.

Taking Responsibility

Admitting error does not come easily to Clinton. While he is some-times able to simply claim it is his responsibility when something goes wrong, this is by far the exception to a more general pattern. That pattern, evident in the marijuana, draft, and fidelity controver-sies during the 1992 campaign, consists of denying; avoiding; blam-ing others; and misrepresenting or not fully disclosing information that, if disclosed, would put a different and less benign cast to his behavior.

During the 1992 campaign when he was first asked whether he had used marijuana, his response, not quite forthcoming, was that he had not broken the laws of this country. It then turned out that he had experimented with marijuana while in England, thus his answer was accurate while simultaneously unresponsive and evasive. He fur-ther tried to downplay what he thought would be a damaging admission by claiming that, while he had tried marijuana, he had not inhaled. This effort might have been more amusing than troubling had it been an isolated incident, but it was not: that pattern repeat-edly appeared in the course of his presidency.

A president who sees his own behavior in a somewhat idealized manner, who believes that he has been unfairly held to high or incon-sistent standards, and who wants to be publicly validated for his accomplishments would have difficulty acknowledging his mistakes in a direct and straightforward way.

In responding to the mishandling of the White House travel office investigation, Clinton said, "I had nothing to do with any decision, except to try and save the tax payers and the press money. . . . that's all I knew about it" (1993b, 942). In this statement President Clin-ton both takes credit for the investigation and disclaims responsibil-ity for the event itself. Later he said, "Ultimately, anything that hap-pens in the White House is the responsibility of the President" (Friedman 1993a, 1993b, A1). In the absence of a more specific statement, that aphorism, meant to recall the political courage of Harry Truman, is at once both an acknowledgment and a disclaimer.

Even when he appears to take full and unequivocal responsibility for a problem, further information sometimes emerges that casts a different light on his behavior. For example, in discussing his deci-sion to pull the controversial nomination of Lani Guinier, President

Clinton seemed to be unequivocal when saying, "I want to again say that I take full responsibility for what has happened here" (1993a, 1028). What was he taking responsibility for? He was taking responsibility for the fact that, among other matters, he hadn't read, and by implication was not aware of, Guinier's controversial racial views.

Competition

Clinton's psychology combines an intense desire to accomplish with a highly competitive nature. This trait has been part of his behavior from childhood and has been observed over many years of Clinton's life in differing contexts.

Individuals vary substantially in the degree to which they derive satisfaction from triumphing over others, from winning, or from accomplishing the goal itself. For some people, the enjoyment of what they accomplish outweighs whatever satisfaction they receive from winning or beating others. For others the reverse is true. In Clinton's psychology the three types of satisfaction are closely linked. His desire to win by having things done totally his way suggests that his reputation as a man too ready to compromise is not always deserved.

Achievement

By a number of different measures, Clinton is highly motivated to achieve. Ambition is the foundation of achievement but is not synonymous with it. There must be a match between the level of one's ambition and the level and applicability of the skills one has to accomplish it. Ordinarily, a strong need for achievement is a desirable trait in a president. A president who lacks a desire to achieve will also lack a strong sense of what he wants to accomplish and the conviction to follow through, resulting in presidential drift. There are, however, costs involved in having too much achievement motivation (Winter 1995, 127–28).

One of the most important questions here is how a president defines accomplishment. How much is "good"? How much is "enough"? What functions does accomplishment serve in the president's overall psychology?

The combination of intense ambition, high self-confidence, and strong self-regard leads Clinton to be very directed toward achievement, but it is achievement of *a particular type.* Modest successes are not sufficient; they are not what he has in mind. His achievement is self-defined at extremely high—even grandiose—levels of attempted accomplishment. Nor is the passage of *some* major policy initiatives enough. Some, even many, can be too few, given Clinton's definition of success.

Conclusion: The Ultimate Elusiveness of Certainty

Training, care with evidence, and theoretical prudence can add substantial measures of validity to the psychological analysis of leaders. Yet measured prudence seems a more useful stance than theoretical enthusiasm, stemming from the limits of our theories, our data, and also the complexity of what we are attempting. Whatever traction can be gained by a combined use of specific psychological theories, typological generalizations, and immersion in the biographical facts of a leader's personal and political life, it is necessary to recognize the limits of what can be accomplished.

Understanding and predicting the behavior of smart, highly functioning individuals, who are acutely aware of their circumstances and what may be needed to surmount them, make it a very tricky undertaking. It is possible that, in spite of their own psychological inclinations, such persons will overcome their impulses, if not alone, then certainly with the help of many advisers, whose only occupational purpose is to help the leaders pursue their own personal and political self-interest.

Notes

1. This is not simply a matter of working backward from the present in a post hoc, therefore proper, analysis. I take up the more technical methodological concerns in constructing a developmental analysis elsewhere (Renshon 1996b, 62–65).

2. There are obviously oedipal overtones to this situation. One could view this as Clinton's unconscious attempt to replace his father and win his oedipal victory. Several aspects of the situation, however, weigh against such an interpretation. First, at the time these events occurred Clinton was sixteen, not four or five. At best, these circumstances might retain some *echo* of an oedipal situation. Second, in some respects, if there are oedipal echoes in this situation, Clinton had already done something much more directly relevant to that issue: he had physically (and emotionally) stood up to his father when he was drunk and

abusive and provided legal papers that helped his mother get divorced. At any rate, to whatever extent his behavior represented some aspect of an oedipal situation his victory was short lived. Clinton's real rival during the oedipal period (roughly four through six) was not only his stepfather but his mother's immersion in Hot Springs nightlife.

3. Since Hempsted County, in which Hope was located, was a dry town, Roger's whiskey making was illegal (Kelley 1994a, 80). He also apparently ran a bookie joint in Hope (76).

4. It is also possible that there is some biologically based aspect to Clinton's early sociability; however, the only (inconclusive) data his mother presents that is relevant to this possibility is that he slept a lot in the first year or so of his life (Kelley 1994a, 70).

5. There are obviously oedipal overtones in this situation. One could view it as Clinton's unconscious attempt to replace his father and win his oedipal victory.

6. In Clinton's court affidavit, he wrote that his stepfather threatened "to mash my face in if I took her [his mother's] part" (Kelley 1994a, 147).

7. This is one primary trait that creates an interpersonal mismatch in the Clinton relationship: he wants validation and the emotional support of others, but she is not able to easily give it to him. There are, throughout the materials analyzed in conjunction with this book, a number of instances that reflect this basic psychological mismatch (Brummett 1994, 37, 50; see also Bruck 1995, 72). One friend who had known Clinton a long time said:

> Clinton needs reinforcement all the time . . . [and] looks for affirmation in even the smallest things. Sometimes you can see that Clinton needs this affirmation and Hillary doesn't give it to him. During the campaign you could see her be aloof when he needed . . . just a little warmth. She can be very cold. He's alone a lot. Hillary isn't the one to provide approval. (Drew 1994, 233)

The other side of that issue is that joining together two very smart, very ambitious people who are highly self-confident about the virtues of their particular views—one who tends to be very disorganized and one who doesn't—can also create strains. In Arkansas, to protect her husband, Hillary Clinton, along with two other Clinton aides—Betsey Wright and Joan Roberts—put up a protective cordon around him, which had the effect of not only protecting Clinton but limiting him. For a person who dislikes boundaries, the result was predictable. When Wright insisted that a policeman accompany the governor on his early morning jogs, Clinton shouted, "I won't have it! I won't have it!" (Maraniss 1995, 427).

Over the years, Hillary Clinton has had to take on many roles in their life, some no doubt less congenial to her than others. Before Leon Panetta became chief of staff, she had been the one in charge of organizing her husband's time and staff (Drew 1994, 49, 137, 254). Since their time in the governor's mansion, she had become his gatekeeper, especially after his 1980 reelection defeat, and she increasingly took on the role in the Clinton family of breadwinner.

8. The issue of Clinton's extramarital relationships came up several times during the presidential campaign and again after Clinton was in office. Extramarital relationships occur for many reasons and take many forms. The issues involved in such behavior ordinarily go well beyond the simple question of whether or not a president or candidate had a sexual relationship outside of his marriage (Renshon 1996a).

Did Clinton have extramarital relationships? A substantial body of evidence suggests he did. Betsey Wright, long-time aide to Clinton over several decades, recalls having felt in 1988, before Clinton was set to announce his plan to run that year for president, that

> the time had come to get past what she considered his self-denying tendencies and face the issue squarely. For years, she told friends later, she had been covering up for him. She was convinced that some state troopers were soliciting women for him. . . . "Okay," she said to him . . . then started listing the names of women he had allegedly had affairs with and the places where they were said to have occurred. "Now, I want you to tell me the truth about each one." She went over the list twice with Clinton, according to her later account, the second time trying to determine whether any of the women might tell their stories to the press. At the end . . . she suggested that he should not get into the race. (quoted in Maraniss 1995, 440–41)

Roger Starr, managing editor of the *Arkansas Democrat* for most of Clinton's tenure as governor, recalls: "We were talking about the Gary Hart factor in politics, and I asked him something to the effect of 'well, you haven't done anything like that, have you?' You know (I was) expecting a negative answer, be it a lie or the truth. And he said, 'Yes'" (Oakley 1994, 150).

Woodward (1994, 22) reports a similar discussion between Clinton and another friend in 1987 when Clinton decided against running for president. He quotes Clinton as asking his friend if he knew why Clinton had chosen not to run. The friend guessed it had something to do with the infidelity issue that forced Gary Hart to withdraw from the race. In response Clinton agreed and acknowledged he had strayed. And, of course on *Sixty Minutes* Clinton admitted in response to a question about his marital fidelity that he had "caused pain in his marriage" (Brook 1996).

Assuming there is sufficient evidence to make this case, what does it reveal? In the case of Clinton not much more than we could learn by examining his fidelity in other areas. For that reason, I do not deal at any length on these matters. Whatever useful information they might reveal about Clinton is more than adequately found in behavior that is more publicly accessible.

12. William Jefferson Clinton: Personality Traits and Motivational Biases

The following analyses of William Jefferson Clinton focus successively on his general personality traits and his motivational biases. The authors in each of the following sections apply their respective methods of content analysis to construct a profile of the causal mechanisms associated with the processes of ego defense and the mediation of self-other relationships.

General Personality Traits and Ego Defense

Walter Weintraub

Our verbal analysis of Bill Clinton's general personality is based upon 5,759 words gathered from answers to reporters' questions during extemporaneous press conferences. Table 12.1 compares Clinton's use of our categories with the speech habits of post–World War II presidents. Clinton's use of the pronoun *I* is the highest and his use of the pronoun *we* is the lowest among post–War II presidents. The president presented himself not as the leader of a cause but rather as a successful politician with a track record of getting things done. Clinton's passivity score (*I/me* ratio) was also the highest of post–World War II presidents. As we shall see, Clinton's frequent use of the pronoun *me* may be associated with his assuming the victim's role when attacked.

Clinton's moderate use of *qualifiers* and *retractors* indicates that he is spontaneous during press conferences and comfortable with reporters. He does not have a need to control interviews, which suggests that the president is probably not controlling in his relationships with others. Moderate qualifiers and retractors scores suggest that Clinton can make decisions and reconsider when necessary. His verbal profile is that of a flexible leader. Clinton has a moderate *explainers* score, suggesting that he is not excessively didactic when presenting his point of view. Indeed, he more often states rather than explains his point of view.

Clinton's *expressions of feeling* and *nonpersonal references* scores place him among the more emotionally expressive post–World War II presidents. His rather low *direct references* score indicates a tendency to avoid direct confrontation. It is somewhat surprising to learn that Clinton rarely addresses reporters by name, a favorite verbal habit of Ronald Reagan. During his press interviews, Clinton generally limits himself to a discussion of issues; he avoids personal interactions with reporters. Clinton has a rather high *adverbial intensifiers* score. The president has been called an "actor" and a "preacher." His high score in a category measuring histrionic behavior seems to confirm his reputation as an actor-politician. Of the post–World War II presidents, only Eisenhower had a higher adverbial intensifiers score. Clinton has a rather high *negatives* score. A careful scrutiny of the manner in which Clinton uses negatives indicates a tendency to become defensive when attacked.

Compared to other leaders, Clinton's speech reveals few creative or colorful remarks. His responses to reporters' questions show few attempts at humor, almost no metaphorical language, and no unusual juxtaposition of words. Clearly, with respect to his publicly displayed

TABLE 12.1.   BILL CLINTON VERBAL INDICATORS

Category	Clinton (5,759 words)	U.S. Presidents (20,000 words)
Personal pronouns		
I	54.8	31.6
We	10.4	18.3
Me	5.6	2.2
Qualifiers	11.0	11.2
Retractors	6.6	7.6
Negatives	18.4	13.7
Explainers	5.0	5.0
Feelings	3.8	3.3
Direct references	1.2	2.5
Adverbial intensifiers	18.6	14.1
Creative expressions	1.4	2.0
Nonpersonal references	469.5	742.2

wit, he is not John Kennedy. If the absence of creative language reflects a paucity of creative thinking, Clinton's effectiveness as a leader may lie in his ability to transmit other people's ideas. Clinton's main problem as a candidate and elected official has been the so-called character issue. He has been unable to put to rest allegations that he was a draft dodger and a womanizer. It is not so much that the president may have been guilty of the accusations that have hurt him but rather his manner of responding to them, a combination of denial, admission, and foul crying. Listeners come away doubting Clinton's integrity, a problem that continues to plague him.

Other leaders have dealt more successfully with similar attacks. Franklin Roosevelt was able to ignore personal attacks or to ridicule them, as in the famous "Fala" speech. Perhaps the most successful strategy of responding to personal attacks has been developed by former governor of Louisiana Edwin Edwards. He has handled charges of gambling and womanizing by denying nothing, admitting nothing, and changing the subject as quickly as possible. When questioned by reporters about gambling and relationships with women during the campaign against David Duke, Edwards stated that, yes, he had had problems, everybody knew about them, and now it was time to go about solving Louisiana's problems. Edwards never stated exactly what wrongdoing he was guilty of. He did not stir the public's curiosity. By denying nothing, he did not run the risk of being accused of lying, should ethical issues arise in the future.

Let us look now at how Clinton attempted to deal with allegations of unethical behavior. How were his responses to reporters' questions reflected in his grammatical choices? The following excerpt from a reply to a question by David Frost about Clinton's avoidance of military service shows exaggerated denial (negatives and adverbial intensifiers) and a tendency to assume the role of victim (frequent use of the personal pronoun *me*).

I *didn't willfully* fail to disclose anything in the draft thing. I *really* didn't. I've since that time—and I should have done this I guess before I started running for president, but because no one had ever criticized me, including the authorities—*I didn't.*

I have written to everybody in the world who might have any of these records. I said, "Send *me* the records. Let *me* get all the facts. Please let *me* see." (original emphasis)

It is likely that many Americans remained unconvinced by Clinton's response, believing that he "protested too much" and tried to shift responsibility from himself to others.

To sum up, Clinton's high *I/we* ratio suggests that he is more interested in being president than in leading a crusade that will accomplish specific goals. His passivity score (*I/me*) indicates that he assumes the victim's role when aggressively challenged about unethical behavior. His negatives score is rather high, suggesting a need to deny unpleasant realities about his behavior. The president's moderate qualifiers and retractors scores indicate that he is reasonably spontaneous and comfortable with reporters; he can make decisions and reconsider them without becoming paralyzed. There is no evidence of impulsivity, a trait that is usually accompanied by a high retractors score. Clinton shows little need to control interview situations.

A moderate explainers score suggests that Clinton is more categorical than didactic when presenting his positions on issues. He states rather than explains his point of view. This trait, combined with a high adverbial intensifiers score, is characteristic of a preacher's style of communication. Clinton's frequent use of expressions of feeling, personal references, and adverbial intensifiers establishes him as one of the more expressive presidents. His infrequent use of direct references suggests a tendency to avoid confrontation. Clinton's lack of verbal creativity suggests a possible dependence on others for innovative ideas.

Motivations and Mediation of Self-Other Relationships

David G. Winter

For assessing Clinton's power, achievement, and affiliation motivations, there is an enormous amount of material of every kind available: speeches, press conference statements and responses, and informal remarks. In fact, every "official" word that Bill Clinton has spoken or written since his 1993 inauguration is recorded in the *Weekly Compilation of Presidential Documents* series (published by the Office of the Federal Register), later to appear in the *Public Papers of the Presidents* volumes. Most presidential speeches are now also available on the World Wide Web. The researcher's problem is to select from this abundance an appropriate and manageable amount of material to score.

In studying Clinton, the need to identify a comparison group or groups (see chapter 7) quickly reduces the volume of verbatim material to two obvious and major standard speeches. For profiling Clinton the 1992 presidential candidate, his official announcement speech on October 3, 1991, can be compared to those of the other eight major candidates in the 1992 primary campaign. As president, Clinton's first inaugural address on January 20, 1993, can be compared to the first inaugural addresses of other presidents from George Washington through George Bush (see Winter 1987a, 1995), in the same way that Winter and Carlson (1988) assessed Richard Nixon's motive profile based on his first inaugural address in 1969. Moreover, Clinton's presidential speeches could be compared with themselves to determine whether and how his motives have changed over time.[1] Such an intrapersonal comparison could use, for example, the president's yearly State of the Union message. Typically, the speech is a broad summary of the condition of the country, focusing on topics and goals of the president's choosing and given to the same audience (Congress and invited dignitaries) under the same circumstances (national prime-time television) at the same time (late January) every year. Thus Clinton's State of the Union messages from 1993 through 1996 could be taken as a time-series of his motive levels during his first term.

Clinton as Candidate

In his announcement speech for the 1992 campaign, Clinton scored a little above average in achievement and affiliation and a little below average in power, as shown in table 12.2. The following sentence from Clinton's announcement speech illustrates the combination of these two motives: "I believe with all my heart that together [affiliation], we can make this happen. We can usher in a new era of progress [achievement], prosperity and renewal." The high achievement/high affiliation pattern also fits much of Clinton's rhetoric and performance before, during, and after the campaign: high goals and aspirations tinged with warmth and compassion (e.g., his oft-quoted remark, "I feel your pain"). However, Clinton's relatively low power motive score suggests that, for all his experience as governor of Arkansas, he might be neither comfortable nor effective in the quicksands of Washington federal politics.

Clinton as President

Clinton's inaugural address shows a motive profile similar to that of his announcement speech but with all three scores elevated, especially those of achievement and power. Still, achievement was higher than power (both in raw and standardized scores), as shown in the far right column of table 12.2. What do these scores mean for understanding and predicting Clinton's performance in office? One approach is to use Clinton's standardized scores, in conjunction with the information assembled in table 7.2 in chapter 7, to make predictions (or "retrodictions"). For example, Clinton's high achievement motivation scores in 1992 and 1993 were certainly consistent with his many first-term programs and actions directed toward improvement (e.g., health care reform), as well as his energetic personal style. Even his "Slick Willie" image (referring to his tendency to change views and modify positions) can be seen as reflecting the tendency of achievement-motivated people to modify their performance on the basis of the results of previous actions. His retreats on health care, withdrawals of contested appointments, acceptance of the Republican framework for welfare reform, and centrist agenda in 1995–96 all reflect the avoidance of extreme risks and the use of feedback, which are also characteristics of achievement motivation.

Although Clinton's affiliation motive score was relatively high in his inaugural, it was still a good deal lower than his achievement score. This suggests that his changes of position and policy were based more on calculations of risk and results than on the influence

TABLE 12.2. MOTIVE PROFILE OF BILL CLINTON IN 1992–93

Speech	Raw Scores (images per 1,000 words)				Standardized Scores[a]			
	Ach	Aff	Pow	Pow minus Ach	Ach	Aff	Pow	Pow minus Ach
1992 campaign announcement[b]	8.69	4.50	8.04	−.65	55	54	45	−10
1993 Inaugural[c]	10.23	5.75	9.59	−.64	71	60	65	−6

Source: Data from Winter 1998b.

[a]Mean of comparison sample = 50, SD = 10.

[b]Standardized in comparison to campaign announcement speeches of other major 1992 candidates.

[c]Standardized in comparison to first inaugurals of other U.S. presidents.

of close associates or the putative "trying to be loved by everybody" that is a staple of journalistic portraits of Clinton (e.g., Purdum 1996). Such a score is also consistent with Clinton's avoidance of war and search for peace in Haiti, Bosnia, and the Middle East, as well as the numerous scandals and rumors of scandals in his administration.

Another way to interpret Clinton's motive profile is to compare him to previous U.S. presidents. (With the motives of Clinton and all previous presidents standardized on the same scales, and with the three motives assumed to be independent and orthogonal, the "most similar" president can be defined as that president whose score has the smallest Pythagorean or three-dimensional distance from Clinton's.) Based on his 1992 announcement speech, Clinton most closely resembled Lyndon Johnson.[2] Based on his 1993 inaugural, he had become more like Jimmy Carter.

What does it mean to say that Clinton "resembled" Johnson or Carter? Obviously it does not imply that he has the same personality, would take the same actions, or would have the same outcomes. Rather, it suggests possible similarities of goals and goal-setting styles; of reactions to the political process; and of personal strengths, weaknesses, opportunities, and vulnerabilities. Both Johnson and Carter had achievement motive scores that were high and greater than their power motivation. Similarly, both entered office with ideals and visions, only to depart several years later mired in frustration and defeat. Like Clinton in 1993, Carter in 1977 also approached Washington as an outsider, full of ideas for improvement. By the summer of 1979, however, he retreated to Camp David, his presidency sunk by economic problems and the malaise of the political process. (Chapter 7 discusses the importance of balance between the achievement and power motives in democratic politics and the difference between politics and business, in which high achievement motivation typically leads to success.)

On the other hand, Clinton's inaugural power motive score was a considerable increase over that of his announcement speech and even approached the level of his achievement motivation. *From a motivational perspective, therefore, the most critical question of Clinton's first term was whether his power motive would be high enough to balance his achievement motive.* In everyday language, would Clinton's capacity to "enjoy power"—to take pleasure from the political scrimmages of the pres-

309

idency—be sufficient to allow him to navigate through the morass of politics: compromise, frustration, gridlock, independent power centers, difficulties in implementing policy, and so forth?

After the 1994 midterm elections, it looked as though Bill Clinton's presidency was indeed going to end in a single-term frustration of Carteresque proportions. His political obituaries were being prepared by journalists and pundits who were confident that his very ability to govern, let alone his chances of reelection, had been permanently disabled by the Republican juggernaut. Eighteen months later, during the 1996 campaign, it was the Republican forces that were in disarray. Through deft handling of the 1995–96 budget debates and the government closings, the Clinton administration rolled the advance guard of the Gingrich "revolution" back upon itself. Meanwhile, the Republicans emerged from the 1996 primary season with an aging, lackluster candidate who may have trouble holding his party together with its platform. As a result, Clinton was reelected by a substantial margin.

What happened? Drawing on stock political clichés, we could say that Bill Clinton repeated his 1992 success as the "Comeback Kid." But this does not tell us the kind of comeback he made or how he came to make it. However, a *New York Times* analysis by Alison Mitchell (1996) provides a clue. Drawing on four major Clinton speeches during 1995–96, Mitchell concluded that Clinton changed from a policy wonk "bogged down in particulars" into the "man in the bully pulpit," willing and able to use the full rhetorical powers of the presidency. In motivational terms, such a change suggests an increase in the power motive, relative to achievement.

To track changes in Clinton's motive profile, I scored his four State of the Union messages, along with four "landmark" speeches identified by Mitchell (1996) as prototypical of the "new Clinton" (Dallas, April 7, 1995; Georgetown University, July 6, 1995; Houston, October 17, 1995; and Long Beach, February 24, 1996). Because this analysis considers only a single leader over time, in which different speeches by the same person are compared with each other, there is no need for an external control or comparison sample. However, by itself such an intrapersonal study cannot tell us much about the leader in comparison to other people.

As shown in figure 12.1, Clinton's four State of the Union mes-

sages during his first term show a steadily increasing trend away
from the "frustration" pattern (achievement greater than power),
reminiscent of Carter, toward the "pleasure of politics" pattern
(power greater than achievement) that characterized Presidents
Franklin Roosevelt, Truman, and Kennedy. Clinton's 1993 inaugural address had 0.64 more achievement images, per one thousand
words, than power images. His first State of the Union message, a
few weeks later, reversed this trend slightly: 1.23 more power
images than achievement images. In 1995 there were 5.84 more
power images than achievement images, and in January 1996, well
into the 1996 presidential campaign, the difference climbed to 7.02.

The power-greater-than-achievement motive profile also appeared
in each of the four speeches cited by Mitchell. A close reading of
Clinton's landmark speeches shows that the similarity to Harry Truman (and the 1948 campaign) involved more than abstract psychological indicators. His first landmark speech in Dallas, for example,
contained the phrase "I will veto" seven times. And during his January 1996 State of the Union message, Clinton issued thirteen direct
challenges to the Congress ("I challenge you" or "I challenge the
Congress") and fifteen other direct challenges to various other
groups. Still, Clinton continued to wave an olive branch wrapped in

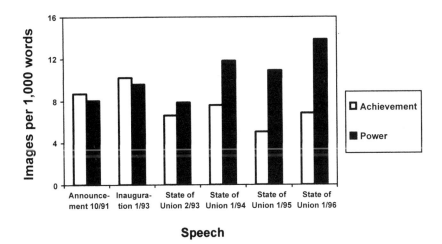

Fig. 12.1. Images of power and achievement in Clinton's
speeches

the images of achievement and affiliation that characterized his earlier motive profile: "But if Congress will just sit down with me and work out a reasonable solution . . . we can create an historic achievement."

Of course the 1995–96 transformation in Clinton's political fortunes involved many factors other than Clinton's motives: for example, good advice about strategy and tactics, opportunities furnished by Republican miscalculations and mistakes, and plain luck. But good advice, opportunities, and luck do not automatically effectuate themselves. My point here is that the changes in Clinton's motive profile increased his readiness to *take advantage of* these opportunities, to *use* the good advice, and to *feel comfortable with* the new directions. Another president, with an unchanged high achievement/low power profile, might have ignored the advice and maintained a self-defeating course.

The two analyses of Bill Clinton show how motive profiles can be used in different ways to understand political leaders: (1) to predict initially the broad outlines of the leader's performance—especially vulnerabilities and opportunities—in office, and (2) to understand the underlying psychological basis of changes in the leader's behavior over time.

Notes

1. Motives are generally conceptualized as relatively fixed dispositions. On the other hand, no motive operates at the same level of strength or intensity all the time. (Consider the case of hunger, for which even the highest levels can be satisfied, temporarily, with food.) Thus apparent "changes" or fluctuations in observed levels of motive imagery can be thought of as reflecting *different amounts of arousal* of a *stable dispositional motive* (see Atkinson 1982). However, there is also evidence that motives can change over time, either as a result of developmental and aging processes (see Veroff 1983; Veroff, Reuman, and Feld 1984; Veroff and Smith 1985) or in response to certain extraordinary events or influences (see McClelland and Winter 1969).

2. The following example, from Johnson's inaugural address, illustrates his achievement and affiliation motives in combination:

> For the hour and the day and the time are here to achieve progress [achievement] without strife, to achieve change without hatred—not without difference of opinion, but without the deep and abiding divisions which scar the union [affiliation] for generations.

13. William Jefferson Clinton's Leadership Style

Margaret G. Hermann

This leadership profile of Bill Clinton, forty-second president of the United States, is based on an analysis of his responses to the domestic and international press in fifty-four interviews between 1992 and 1998. The description that follows is derived from an at-a-distance assessment of some 36,750 words. The words were examined for evidence of seven different characteristics that have implications for how political leaders will behave, the kinds of actions they are likely to urge on their parties and governments, and the way they structure and interact with their advisory groups. An individual leader's traits are put into perspective by comparing them with similar scores for other political leaders from their region and around the globe. The characteristics are contextualized further by exploring how stable they are across issues, audiences, and time. The attributes that define the profile are those that historians, journalists, political scientists, and other students of leadership have found to be influential in shaping what leaders will do politically. The traits that are examined are (1) the belief that one can influence or control what happens, (2) the need for power and influence, (3) conceptual complexity (the ability to differentiate among things and people in one's environment), (4) self-confidence or self-esteem, (5) in-group bias, (6) general distrust of others, and (7) the tendency to focus on problem solving and accomplishing something versus maintenance of the group and dealing with others' ideas and sensitivities. The at-a-distance technique is described in more detail in chapter 8.

Several types of verbal material were available on Clinton:

speeches, public statements, memorandums, messages, and interviews with the press. Since the first four types of material can be written or crafted for the leader by others, some caution must be exercised in examining such statements to ascertain what the leader is like. Care and thought have often gone into what is said and how it is said. Interviews with the media, however, are generally more spontaneous. During the give-and-take of a question-and-answer period, the leader must respond quickly without props or aid; what he or she is like can influence the nature of the response and how it is worded. Although there may be some preparation of leaders prior to an interview with the press, during the interview they are on their own to respond. For these reasons, the following profile is based only on Clinton's responses to media questions in an interview setting.

Leadership Profile in General

Table 13.1 reports the average trait scores for Clinton across 105 interview responses. The scores represent the percentage of time Clinton used words that are indicative of a particular characteristic where the criteria for coding the trait were present. The percentages can range from zero to one hundred. Table 13.1 also presents what would be considered low and high scores on a specific characteristic based on the scores of 18 North American leaders, as well as those of 122 political leaders from forty-six countries around the globe. Low and high scores are one standard deviation below and above the average score for a particular trait for the group of leaders with whom Clinton is being compared and differentiate him from these others. Clinton is considered moderate in the characteristic if his score is *not* one standard deviation above or below the mean of the particular group of leaders; in other words, he resembles the comparison set of leaders on that trait. As the reader will note, when Clinton's scores are close to being low or high, I have noted that he leans toward being one or the other.

Bill Clinton is different from the two samples of leaders on four of the seven traits (57 percent). He differs from the other leaders on conceptual complexity, self-confidence, in-group bias, and distrust of others. The similarities and differences between Clinton and these other leaders have implications for his leadership style. The discussion that follows details these implications. It is based on extensive research in the social sciences on how these characteristics affect leadership, elaborated in chapter 8.

Does the Leader Respect or Challenge Constraints in the Political Environment?

In considering leaders' responsiveness to political constraints, we are interested in how important it is for them to exert control and influence over the environment in which they find themselves, as opposed to being adaptable to the situation and remaining open to responding to the demands of domestic and international constituencies and circumstances. Scores on the *belief one can control events* and on the *need for power* provide us with information with which to

TABLE 13.1. CLINTON'S SCORES ON SEVEN TRAITS

Characteristic	Clinton's Average Profile Score	Compared to	18 American Leaders	122 World Leaders
Belief can control events	.47	Moderate	Mean = .41 Low < .28 High > .55	Mean = .45 Low < .33 High > .57
Need for power	.52	Moderate	Mean = .49 Low < .35 High > .64	Mean = .50 Low < .38 High > .62
Conceptual complexity	.62	Leans high (18 North American leaders); high (122 world leaders)	Mean = .52 Low < .39 High > .66	Mean = .45 Low < .32 High > .58
Self-confidence	.72	Leans high	Mean = .56 Low < .36 High > .75	Mean = .57 Low < .34 High > .80
Task vs. interpersonal focus	.61	Moderate	Mean = .61 Low < .50 High > .72	Mean = .62 Low < .48 High > .76
In-group bias	.32	Leans low (18 North American leaders); low (122 world leaders)	Mean = .38 Low < .30 High > .47	Mean = .43 Low < .34 High > .53
Distrust of others	.27	Leans low	Mean = .42 Low < .20 High > .63	Mean = .38 Low < .20 High > .56

decide whether a leader will challenge or respect constraints. Leaders who are high on both traits work to take charge of any situation in which they find themselves and to test the limits of what is possible; those who are low in both traits perceive the importance of working within the constraints in their environments to build consensus and to accommodate constituents' interests.

Clinton's scores on these traits indicate that he is moderate in comparison to other leaders. He is like these leaders; he does not stand out on either characteristic from leaders in his region or around the globe. Such moderate scores suggest the leader will generally respect constraints but under certain circumstances can challenge what appear to be inappropriate or unfounded limitations on his role. Most of the time leaders with moderate scores like Clinton's will work within the parameters they perceive to structure their political environment. Because of the limitations within which they perceive they have to work, building consensus and achieving compromise are important skills for a politician to have and to exercise.

Such leaders are more likely to be reactive than to take the initiative; they want to wait to see how the situation will probably play out before acting. They prefer to let others take the lead and responsibility for anything too daring and out of the ordinary; they want to lead in contexts where there is at least a 50 percent or better chance of success or where compromise is possible. Leaders like Clinton will want to test out their ideas before making decisions—to "run ideas up the flagpole and see who salutes them." Polling data, particular constituents' opinions, and discussions with affected groups are important in providing the basis for knowing what will work. Such cautious behavior makes it possible to blame others if something goes wrong but also reduces the likelihood of action unless it will already receive support.

As will become evident in the discussion when we contextualize Clinton's profile, there are some times when leaders with his scores will challenge the constraints put in their path. Threats to policies that undergird their leadership positions, what appear to them to be unfair charges, and national crises are some situations in which leaders with moderate scores on the belief that they can control what happens and on the need for power will be more likely to take charge and become highly manipulative in moving toward their goals. The situations require action, and the person will be viewed as lacking leadership if he or she does not do something.

Is the Leader Open or Closed to Contextual Information?

Political leaders have been found to differ in their degree of openness to contextual information based on their levels of *self-confidence* and *conceptual complexity*. These two traits interrelate to form a leader's self-other orientation—how open they will be to input from others in the decision-making process and from the political environment in general. Leaders like Clinton whose scores on these two traits are relatively equal and higher than other leaders are generally open to information. Indeed, they are likely to be quite strategic in their behavior, focusing their attention on what is possible and feasible at any point in time. Their high self-confidence facilitates having patience in the situation and taking their time to see what will succeed, while their high conceptual complexity pushes them to search for information from a variety of constituents and perspectives. These leaders combine the best qualities of both these traits—a sense of what they want to do but the capability to check the environment to see what will work.

These leaders seek both confirmatory and disconfirmatory information from the context to know what is feasible. They want to become the center of any information network that will provide them with a sense of what is happening and who is supporting or opposing what options and activities. In their minds, information is power. If they can maintain themselves as the hubs of such networks, they know more than any other member. Such a role allows them to be in the middle of all decisions.

One dilemma such leaders have is that their behavior can seem erratic and opportunistic to the outside observer. If one does not know the goals or understand how such leaders are perceiving the situation, their decisions and actions may seem indecisive and chameleonlike as they try to decipher what is doable at any point in time. To gather information, these leaders may lead particular constituents and groups to believe that their position is supported when, indeed, all that the leaders were doing was considering options and getting reactions.

Political leaders like Clinton who are high in conceptual complexity attend to a wider array of stimuli from their environment than do those who are low. They have a sense that issues are more gray than black or white and seek a variety of pieces of information through which to organize the situation in which they find themselves. These leaders remain highly attuned to contextual information since they do not necessarily trust their initial response to an event. In order to understand a situation and to plan what to do, such individuals perceive that there is always room for one more piece of data or point of view. Thus, such leaders often take their time in making decisions and touch base with a large number of actors in the decision-making process. Flexibility is seen as the key to being effective in politics.

Is the Leader Motivated by Problem or Relationship?

In politics, the literature suggests that leaders have certain reasons for assuming their positions of authority that have to do with them and with the relevance of the groups with whom they identify. Leaders are driven, in general, either by an internal focus—a problem, cause, specific set of interests—or by the desire for a certain kind of feedback from those in their environment—relationship, be it acceptance, power, support, or acclaim. They also appear to be activated by needs to protect their own kind. Whereas leaders who are more closely identified with particular groups work to ensure such entities' survival, those who are less strongly tied to a specific group view the world as posing potential opportunities for working with others for mutual or their own benefit. *Task versus interpersonal focus* indicates the former type of motivation, and a combination of *in-group bias* and *distrust of others* indicates the latter type.

Leaders like Clinton who have moderate scores on task versus interpersonal focus have the facility to direct their attention to the problem when that is appropriate to the situation at hand or to build relationships when that seems more relevant. Such leaders sense when the context calls for each of these functions and focus on it at that point in time. Depending on the circumstances, they can push toward their goals or center their attention on keeping the loyalty and morale of important constituencies high. In effect, they can fulfill both functions considered important to governance—accomplishing something and maintaining coalitions. With the ability to move between a concern for solving a problem and a sensitivity to what it will take to keep people allied to a cause, these leaders are likely to monitor the environment for cues that indicate the demand for a particular focus of attention. For Clinton, such a capability augments his more general openness to information, enhancing the strategic nature of his proposals and activities. Situations are judged, and actions are taken, based on what he has to do to keep his position and move toward his goals, be it to become a taskmaster or to rally the troops around the flag.

Clinton's relatively low scores on in-group bias and distrust of others indicate that he tends to see politics as more cooperative than conflictual. Indeed, there are certain times when cooperation with others is both feasible and appropriate. The political environment contains opportunities as well as threats and the possibility for win-win agreements. In fact, Clinton views the political process as a large game board, where all players must sacrifice some things so that they can advance toward the general goal. The desirable end is a solution that is mutually beneficial to all—or a compromise in which all gain some of what they want while only having to give up a little. Compared to leaders with an adversarial or zero-sum view of politics, where there should always be a clear winner and loser, such tactics make Clinton seem as if he has no principles or, at the least, is wishy-washy and weak.

For Clinton, politics is the art of the possible. There will generally be another chance, another time to try to get more. In effect, there is forever next year. Some observers have described Clinton as similar to a child's "Bobo clown"—when hit down in one place, it pops back up; no matter how many times the clown is pushed down, it comes right back up again. The toy, in a similar manner to Clinton, seems to say, "You didn't like that; well let's try another way to do it." There are always opportunities to be taken advantage of and relationships to be built.

One downside of this more optimistic view of life and politics is that threats may have to be major before they are registered as threatening. Clinton may miss what to others would be obvious signs of a brewing confrontation because he is working on what is positive in the situation rather than seeing the negative. Thus, at times he is figuratively interested in negotiating a settlement, not perceiving that the other party is not ready to go to the bargaining table. Some have called this behavior of Clinton's an "artichoke" reaction to stress, peeling off one layer at a time and in bits and pieces. But his scores on in-group bias and distrust of others suggest that it may take a number of times for the threat quality of the situation to be perceived.

Leadership Style

Clinton's pattern of scores on the seven traits helps us determine the kind of leadership style he will exhibit. By ascertaining that he is likely to (1) generally respect constraints in his political environment, (2) be open to, and to search out, information in the situation, (3) be motivated by both solving the problem and keeping morale high, and (4) view politics as the art of the possible and mutually beneficial, we know from extensive research that Clinton will exhibit a collegial leadership style. His focus of attention is on reconciling differences and building consensus, on retaining power and authority through building relationships and taking advantage of opportunities to work with others toward specific ends. Clinton's leadership style predisposes him toward the team-building approach to politics. Like the captain of a football or basketball team, the leader is dependent on others to work with him to make things happen. Such leaders see themselves at the center of the information-gathering process. With regard to the advisory process, working as a team means that advisers are empowered to participate in all aspects of policy-making but also to share in the accountability for what occurs. Members of the team are expected to be sensitive to and supportive of the beliefs and values of the leader.

Given Clinton's ability to move between building relationships and solving problems, he can, at times, evidence a more opportunistic leadership style as he takes advantage of a situation to move toward his goals. Although his predispositions lean toward the collegial style of leadership, when circumstances call for it, Clinton can become more focused on the task and what needs to be done, using the event to accomplish something on his agenda.

Among the 122 leaders from around the world who formed the comparison group for this profile, Clinton's pattern of scores is closest to those of Mikhail Gorbachev (Soviet Union) and Chou En-Lai (China). Both these leaders retained their positions because they understood the constraints under which they had to operate but were sensitive to what was feasible and doable in the situation at hand. For each, information was power, and they sought to be at the center of any information network. Both took advantage of what they perceived to be opportunities in their political environments to build relationships and viewed politics as requiring consensus and compromise. Mutually beneficial solutions were possible in the right circumstances and with the right negotiating partners. They believed that being politically effective required flexibility and openness.

Leadership Profile in Context

An important question with any leadership profile centers around the stability of the traits. Do Clinton's scores remain basically the same across his tenure in office, when he is being interviewed by the domestic and foreign press, and when he is discussing different substantive topics? We can be assured that we are assessing what the leader is like if there is little change in the scores as the context changes; at the least, we know that the leader does not seem to be responding to the situation. It is easier to suggest what a leader is likely to do politically when the trait scores are more stable; with changes in scores, the researcher or analyst must consider contextual factors in deciding both how to influence the leader and what he or she is likely to do.

A statistical procedure (analysis of variance) can be used to determine whether Clinton's scores are stable across time, audience, and topic. Table 13.2 presents the results of such an analysis and the traits where there were statistically significant differences among the scores across the various types of context. Of the twenty-one possible changes (seven traits times three contextual factors), six (29 percent) were statistically significant. In other words, the leadership profile described previously for leaders like Clinton is applicable for him in most circumstances. The statistically significant differences, however, do amplify the portrait of Clinton as leader and, thus, will be discussed subsequently in some detail.

Effects of Time Period

A comparison of Clinton's scores during interviews held during his first administration with those occurring in the second administration suggests that he has changed his style somewhat since being reelected. In the second administration, Clinton has shown more willingness to challenge the constraints in his environment—to work both directly and indirectly to move toward his goals. His scores for the belief that he can control what happens and for the need for power become higher during the second administration. He evidences more interest in guiding and manipulating what is occurring than he did during the first administration. Consensus and compromise have to, at times, be pushed and coerced into place. If other parties are not forthcoming, then the leader has the right to force the issue.

In the second administration Clinton also shows more tendency to focus on solving problems rather than attending to others' feelings and desires. He becomes more of a taskmaster, taking the initiative to push his agenda. Moreover, his environment becomes more suspicious and threatening by the second administration. It is no longer enough to take advantage of opportunities, but he must be vigilant to deal with potential enemies and threats to his position. The world is a little less rosy in the second administration than it was during the first.

Clinton's leadership style in the second administration is more actively independent—he begins to act out the part of the "new

TABLE 13.2. CLINTON'S SCORES IN CONTEXT (STATISTICALLY SIGNIFICANT DIFFERENCES)

Characteristic	Mean Score
Time	
Belief can control events	First administration = .42
	Second administration = .52
Need for power	First administration = .48
	Second administration = .56
Task vs. interpersonal focus	First administration = .54
	Second administration = .68
Distrust of others	First administration = .16
	Second administration = .38
Audience	
Belief can control events	Domestic = .53
	International = .41
Need for power	Domestic = .58
	International = .46

Democrat." Although still highly sensitive and responsive to stimuli from the political arena, Clinton is now ready to challenge what he perceives as growing constraints on his role and activities; to push his agenda, albeit in subtle and strategic ways; and to be prepared to contain an adversary if he is threatened himself or if his programs are attacked. He is interested in maintaining his flexibility and maneuverability. In the second administration, there is the perception that these two important characteristics of the political game are being taken away from him. How to gain them back and be able to show some movement on his agenda become focal points for him and his administration.

Effects of Audience

The data in table 13.2 suggest that Clinton is much more willing to challenge constraints in the domestic than the international arena. His scores on the belief that he can control events and on the need for power lean high when he is talking to the domestic press; these two scores are moderate for discussions with the international media. Given Clinton's lack of experience in foreign policy before taking office, these differences may reflect his own greater degree of comfort with domestic than foreign policy issues. As observers have commented, even when Clinton has become involved in foreign policy, it has been with a domestic orientation. But the domestic center of his attention has meant that Clinton has been learning foreign policy on the job and has been only as good at it as the sources and information at his disposal. He has known where to search for data and people to help him on the domestic front; he has been less skillful in the international domain. His scores suggest this willingness to be more reactive and to let others take the leadership in international affairs. As a result, it is possible to shift the blame when something goes wrong or to accuse others of making it difficult for him to act.

14. William Jefferson Clinton:
Beliefs and Integrative Complexity

The profiles of Bill Clinton in this chapter focus on his beliefs and cognitive style during his tenure in office. The content and structure of his cognitions are two aspects of the process of object appraisal, which both represent reality and express the leader's personality. In the following sections, the authors identify diagnostic and choice propensities in Clinton's operational code beliefs and examine the integrative complexity of his thought processes to assess their likely impact on his behavior as the president of the United States.

Operational Code Beliefs and Object Appraisal

Stephen G. Walker, Mark Schafer, and Michael D. Young

The following analysis of President Clinton's operational code is based on a sample of sixteen speeches from public sources for three months (January–March 1994) during his first term. Each speech was machine-coded with Profiler+, an automated content analysis software package, using the VICS coding procedures described in chapter 9 (see also Young 2001; Schafer and Walker 2001). The reliability of the results is very high because the coding process was automated and, therefore, perfectly reproducible. The following analysis of Clinton's beliefs is in terms of their direction and intensity compared to the average VICS scores for a norming group of twenty world leaders from different regions and eras.

The validity of the results is subject to the degree of generalizability from the sample to the population of speeches and other public statements by President Clinton. Since the sample does not cover an extended time period, its generalizability is limited unless one assumes that operational code beliefs are personality traits and not cognitive states of mind (Walker 1995). Research dealing with this problem has revealed enough variability to issue a cautionary notice that the following profile may apply only to the time period in which the data were gathered (Schafer 2000).

Index scores for Bill Clinton's general operational code, found in table 14.1, are reported as standard deviations from the norming group's scores for each VICS index. Their interpretation in table 14.1 is in terms of the number of standard deviations above and below the average VICS score for each element in the operational code construct. The anchoring points for each VICS index in chapter 9, expressed as "Somewhat, Definitely, Very, and Extremely," are

TABLE 14.1.   THE GENERAL OPERATIONAL CODE OF BILL CLINTON

	Std Dev	Descriptor
Philosophical Beliefs		
P-1. Nature of the political universe	**+2.63**	**Extremely friendly**
P-2. Prospects for realization of political values	+2.13	Extremely optimistic
P-3. Predictability of Political Future	−1.33	Very low
P-4. Belief in Historical Control		
a. Self's Control	+1.40	**Very high**
b. Other's Control	-1.40	**Very low**
P-5. Role of Chance	±0.00	Average
Instrumental Beliefs		
I-1. Approach to goals (direction of strategy)	**+2.95**	**Extremely cooperative**
I-2. Pursuit of goals (intensity of tactics)	+3.07	Extremely cooperative
I-3. Risk orientation (averse/acceptant)	±0.00	Average
I-4. Timing of action		
a. Flexibility of coop/conf tactics	−3.47	Extremely low
b. Flexibility of word/deed tactics	+0.20	Average
I-5. Utility of Means		
a. Reward	+2.40	Extremely high
b. Promise	+1.33	Very high
c. Appeal/support	+2.29	Extremely high
d. Oppose/resist	−2.57	Extremely low
e. Threaten	−2.00	Extremely low
f. Punish	−1.20	Definitely low

Source: Data from Foreign Broadcast Information Service.

   Note: Key VICS indices are in bold. Indices are expressed as standard deviations above and below the mean for a sample of twenty world leaders from a variety of regions and eras.

applied in table 14.1 to half-standard-deviation intervals above and below the mean score of the norming group for each VICS index.

The VICS scores for Clinton's philosophical beliefs in table 14.1 show that he views the nature of the political universe (P-1) as extremely friendly, greater than two standard deviations above the average leader. He is also extremely optimistic about the prospects for realizing fundamental political goals (P-2). Clinton sees the political future (P-3) as very low in predictability, but he believes that he has a very high degree of control over historical development compared to others (P-4). Finally, Clinton's assessment of the role of chance in politics is average (P-5).

The VICS scores for Clinton's instrumental beliefs in table 14.1 indicate that Clinton believes that an extremely cooperative direction is the best strategy (I-1) in the political universe, coupled with extremely cooperative tactics (I-2). His general risk orientation (I-3) is average, meaning he is no more risk acceptant or risk averse than other leaders. Clinton's propensity to shift between cooperative and conflictual tactics (I-4a) is extremely low, and his propensity to shift between word and deed tactics is average (I-4b). The utility of means indices (I-5) show that his reliance on appeal/support and reward tactics is extremely high, along with a very high reliance on promises. His reliance on oppose/resist and threaten tactics is extremely low, and his propensity to punish is definitely low compared to other leaders.

Overall, the key VICS scores for Self and Other in table 14.1 indicate that Clinton believes in an extremely cooperative approach to strategy (I-1) and attributes a very high level of control (P-4a) to himself in the political universe. He sees the political universe as extremely cooperative (P-1) and attributes a very low level of control (P-4b) to others in the political universe. These dual images of Self and Other and a low propensity to shift between conflict and cooperation (I-4a) suggest that his strategies and tactics will be relatively consistent.

The standard deviation scores for the key indices in table 14.1 also allow us to locate Clinton in Holsti's revised typology of operational codes and to extrapolate some predictions about his likely strategic and tactical interaction patterns. The strategies and tactics in the four quadrants in figure 14.1 represent the likely interaction patterns

TYPE A QUADRANT   **TYPE C QUADRANT**

P-1/I-1
Axis
+2.0

Appease   Reward   Reward   Exploit
DED   DDD   DDD   DDE

+1.5

FOLLOW/COOPERATE   COOPERATE/LEAD
STRATEGIES   STRATEGIES

+1.0

Bluff   Deter   Punish   Compel
EED   DEE   EEE   EDD

+.50

P-4   -2.0 -1.5 -1.0 -.50 0.00 +.50 +1.0 +1.5 +2.0 P-4
Axis   Axis

-.50

Bluff   Deter   Punish   Exploit
EED   DEE   EEE   DDE

-1.0

SUBMIT/CONFLICT   CONFLICT/DOMINATE
STRATEGIES   STRATEGIES

-1.5

Bully   Punish   Compel   Bully
EDE   EEE   EDD   EDE

-2.0
P-1/I-1
Axis

TYPE DEF QUADRANT   **TYPE B QUADRANT**

Note: Key indices of beliefs in the leader's operational code are scaled in standard deviations along the vertical and horizontal axes of the revised Holsti typology. Reward, Deter, Punish and Compel tactics are variants of a general strategy of reciprocity in which Self initiates either an escalatory (E) move or de-escalatory (D) move and then responds in kind to whether Other escalates (E) or de-escalates (D) in response to Self's initial move. Appease, Bluff, Exploit, and Bully tactics are variants of a general strategy of cooperation or conflict in which Self initiates either an escalatory (E) move or de-escalatory (D) move and then violates the norm of reciprocity after Other escalates (E) or de-escalates (D) in response to Self's initial move.

Fig. 14.1.   Prediction template for key VICS indices. (Data from Walker, Schafer, and Marfleet 2001.)

with Other that we hypothesize are associated with the four types of operational codes in the revised Holsti typology of belief systems discussed in chapter 9. The vertical axis in figure 14.1 is the continuum of standard deviations for a leader's image of the political universe (P-1) and approach to political strategy (I-1). The horizontal axis is the continuum of standard deviations for a leader's attribution of historical control to Self (P-4a) and Other (P-4b). These axes provide coordinates for a leader's location within each quadrant.

Clinton's I-1 score for approach to goals and his P-4a score for self's control over historical development place his generalized image of Self in the type C quadrant in figure 14.1. His P-1 score for nature of the political universe and P-4b score for other's control over historical development locate his generalized image of Other in the type A quadrant. The strategic and tactical interaction implications in figure 14.1 for Bill Clinton's general operational code as a type C leader are that his extremely cooperative strategic orientation and very high sense of historical control are likely to lead him to initiate the reciprocity tactics of reward and punish and to tempt him to employ exploit and compel tactics if he encounters opposition.

However, the American leader's diagnostic propensity to view Other as a friendly type A is likely to generate a cooperative outcome unless Other directs hostility toward him. Because of his very high sense of historical control, President Clinton is more likely to diagnose a hostile Other as a type DEF than as a type B opponent. If Clinton takes the strategic initiative against a hostile Other, he is less likely to use bluff or appease tactics and more likely to employ reciprocity or compel and exploit tactics.

President Clinton: Cognitive Manager in Trouble

Peter Suedfeld and Philip E. Tetlock

While the content of a leader's beliefs may dispose him toward different decisions, it also seems reasonable to hypothesize that a president's cognitive style in decision making and decision implementation has an important influence on the fate of his proposals. The following analysis of President Clinton's leadership is based on a relatively parsimonious and, to some extent, even simplistic model. This is the assessment of the president as a cognitive manager. The cognitive manager model (Suedfeld 1992a) proposes that the psychological resources that a good decision maker will devote to solving a particular problem are commensurate with the importance of the problem. Vigilance, information search and processing, reexamination of alternatives, and the other components of ideal decision making exact a cost; when the potential benefit is worth the cost, these processes will be utilized.

It is also important to bear in mind that problems do not come singly, nor are they solved by perfect machines. It is the importance of a problem in relation to others and the resource repertoire of the problem solver at that time that determine resource allocation. The resource repertoire, in turn, varies with time, personality, health, the situation, and so on. Thus, for example, leaders under severe prolonged stress will have fewer cognitive resources to allocate to the solution of even important problems. Our research focuses on how, within that limited pool, the available resources are allocated.

The good cognitive manager will use shortcuts to solve less important problems and will reserve high levels of cognitive effort for more important ones. Furthermore, once all of the criteria of cognitive preparation have been met, the decision itself may be made in a simple or a complex fashion—for example, either as a final and unchangeable answer to the problem or as a proposition open to further adjustment—depending on the situation. In other words, we can expect flexibility in response to resource availability, on the one hand, and to the challenge being confronted, on the other. We use integrative complexity scoring to measure these characteristics.

It is important to remember that integrative complexity scoring assesses the structure, not the content, of thought. Any specific policy or view of the source can be chosen, explained, defended, or criticized at any level of complexity. So, for example, there is no reason to expect general complexity differences between pro- and antiabortion policies, pro- and anti-immigration policies, liberal and conservative policies, and so on. The content-structure distinction may be particularly important in the case of President Clinton. Watching him deal with political issues, many journalists and political scientists—using content variables—have described him as flexible, information oriented, and responsive to others, in other words, what we would term *high complexity*. Based on such evalua-

329

tions, this is in fact what we expected to find when scoring Clinton's utterances.

In two successive studies (Suedfeld 1994; Suedfeld and Wallace 1995) we scored a large number of Clinton's statements made during his first presidential election campaign (spring 1992) and up to the end of his first year in office (1994). We started with the hypothesis, based on the consensus of the media, that Clinton's problems arose out of an excessively high level of complexity and an inability or unwillingness to take a simple, firm, and uncompromising stand when such a stand was needed. Much to our surprise, we found President Clinton's mean complexity score to be quite low. Both during the election campaign and in the first year of the administration, it reached only the level of moderate differentiation (scores around 2.0–2.5). Although this level was not unusual for the campaign speeches of presidential *candidates* during the past eighty years or so, it was lower than that of any sitting *president* except for Ronald Reagan and was at about the same level as the second-lowest, George H. W. Bush.

Another striking datum was a small but consistently downward trend in complexity from the time of the presidential campaign to the period after the inauguration and throughout Clinton's first year in office. There was relatively little variation across topics, although he exhibited somewhat higher complexity in his campaign speeches on economic policy and in his presidential speeches on health care and the environment. This pattern is thought to identify areas that are of special concern and in which success is perceived as possible. There were no changes as a particular presidential initiative moved toward congressional approval or rejection (e.g., the health care bill, the North American Free Trade Agreement [NAFTA]).

We had expected to find a consistent increase in complexity as the president gained more experience in office and learned the complications of developing and then selling his policies. This pattern had been found in most twentieth-century American presidents and in all of those whom current judgment considers to have been good at the job (Tetlock 1991). (Incidentally, the first study to apply integrative complexity scoring to archival materials [Suedfeld and Rank 1976] found exactly the same pattern among successful revolutionary leaders.) We had also thought that there would be complexity increases as Clinton's proposals encountered opposition and as he mustered his cognitive resources to obtain victory, with perhaps a decrease as their future was resolved, and that important topics such as the national health care policy would engage substantially higher complexity than such secondary issues as homosexuals in the military. None of these hypotheses was supported.

Most recently, we looked at the president's speeches during and after his second election campaign. The absolute level of his complexity still had not changed much, although this time there was a pre- to postelection increase; but both the increase and his postelection level of complexity were still among the lowest of all twentieth-century presidents. Another researcher has reported results highly similar to ours: Panos (1998) found Clinton's complexity in the 1992 and 1996 campaign debates to be 1.5 and 1.9 respectively, and the annual mean score of his presidential speeches between 1993 and 1997 ranged from 1.8 to 2.6. In 1998, during the first two months after the Lewinsky scandal broke, his speeches (including the State of the Union address) were scored at a mean of 2.0.

It appears that, contrary to the implications of some other analyses, President Clinton deals with policy issues at a consistently low level of integrative complexity. We may ask, So what? After all, the cognitive manager model argues that simple decision strategies are not necessarily worse than more complex ones. As we have said, different kinds of problems are particularly amenable to complex or simple decision making. There is general agreement that simple strategies are optimal when, for example, a decision must be made quickly, one is confronting an implacably hostile opponent, crucial values are at significant risk, and it is important to project an image of decisiveness and strength. These situations have not been typical of the ones with which President Clinton has had to deal.

Conceptual complexity theorists would propose that Clinton may be operating at a low level of trait, not merely state, complexity. This would explain his strikingly consistent scores across time periods and issue domains. Subjects low in (trait) conceptual complexity have been found to function inadequately in many situations requiring the processing of high levels of changing information, a condition that must be the prototype of most presidential decision making. The cognitive manager model suggests that people differ in their ability to recognize the need to change their level of complexity in response to environmental demands and/or in their ability to effect the change once the need to do so is recognized. President Clinton's very restricted range of complexity scores, regardless of audience, topic, proximity to a decision, and so on, indicates that his cognitive strategies are unresponsive to the environment.

Clinton may not recognize when circumstances indicate the desirability of moving to higher levels of complexity—perhaps his famous optimism hampers his ability to foresee the possibility of failure—or, even if he realizes the need, he may be unable to formulate a more complex approach. Some observers have referred to his frequent changes of policy or image in response to poll results and similar influences (e.g., Morris 1997; Renshon 1996b). This pattern is reflected in a comment by George Stephanopoulos that Clinton was like a kaleidoscope: he "could change in an instant" (in Renshon 1996a, 82). The successive abandonment and replacement (as opposed to modification) of strategies are scored as a series of undifferentiated inclusions/exclusions: a score of 1.

We have not yet addressed the complexity aspects of Clinton's habitual use, when under pressure, of language that "while technically accurate, [is] unresponsive and evasive" (Renshon 1996a, 138). This tendency has surfaced on many occasions, both before and since he attained national prominence. In the latter period, it reappears from his first presidential campaign (e.g., the controversies about his avoidance of military service and his use of marijuana) right through to his handling of the Lewinsky scandal.

The painstaking selection of words that seem to answer a question categorically but upon closer examination do not meet some technical definition necessary for a full response may be an example of impression management in that content is effectively and subtly manipulated. However, the choice of particular words over others is not a criterion for differentiation and therefore does not affect structural complexity. Previous studies have found that particularly successful leaders are more likely to show significant complexity increases when faced with important, but not overwhelming, challenges. President Clinton shows very little situation-specific change of *any sort*. This unresponsiveness to environmental conditions is disquieting.

B. Saddam Hussein

15. Saddam Hussein of Iraq: A Political Psychology Profile

Jerrold M. Post

Identified as a member of the "axis of evil" by President George W. Bush, Saddam Hussein's Iraq continues to pose a major threat to the region and to Western society.[1] Saddam has doggedly pursued the development of weapons of mass destruction, despite UN sanctions imposed at the conclusion of the Gulf crisis. To deal effectively with Saddam Hussein requires a clear understanding of his motivations, perceptions, and decision making. To provide a framework for this complex political leader, a comprehensive political psychology profile has been developed, and his actions since the crisis have been analyzed in the context of this political psychology assessment.

Saddam Hussein, president of Iraq, has been characterized as "the madman of the Middle East." This pejorative diagnosis is not only inaccurate but also dangerous. Consigning Saddam to the realm of madness can mislead decision makers into believing he is unpredictable when in fact he is not. An examination of the record of Saddam Hussein's leadership of Iraq for the past thirty-four years reveals a judicious political calculator who is by no means irrational but is dangerous to the extreme.

Saddam Hussein, "the great struggler," has explained the extremity of his actions as president of Iraq as necessary to achieve "subjective immunity" against foreign plots and influences. All actions of the revolution are justified by the "exceptionalism of revolutionary needs." In fact, an examination of Saddam Hussein's life and career reveals that this is but the ideological rationalization for a lifelong pattern in which all actions are justified if they are in the service of furthering Saddam Hussein's needs and messianic ambitions.

Painful Beginnings: The "Wounded Self"

Saddam Hussein was born in 1937 to a poor peasant family near Tikrit, some hundred miles north of Baghdad, in central-north Iraq. But the central lines of the development of Saddam Hussein's political personality were etched before he was born, for his father died of an "internal disease" (probably cancer) during his mother's pregnancy with Saddam and his twelve-year-old brother died (of childhood cancer) a few months later, when Saddam's mother, Sabha, was in her eighth month of pregnancy. Destitute, Saddam's mother attempted suicide. A Jewish family saved her. Then she tried to abort herself of Saddam but was again prevented from doing this by her Jewish benefactors. After Saddam was born, on April 28, 1937, his mother did not wish to see him, which strongly suggests that she was suffering from a major depression. His care was relegated to Sabha's brother (his maternal uncle) Khayrallah Talfah Msallat in Tikrit, in whose home Saddam spent much of his early childhood. At age three Saddam was reunited with his mother, who in the interim had married a distant relative, Hajj Ibrahim Hasan. Hajj Ibrahim, his stepfather, reportedly was abusive psychologically and physically to young Saddam.

The first several years of life are crucial to the development of healthy self-esteem. The failure of the mother to nurture and bond with her infant son and the subsequent abuse at the hands of his stepfather would have profoundly wounded Saddam's emerging self-esteem, impairing his capacity for empathy with others, producing what has been identified as "the wounded self." One course in the face of such traumatizing experiences is to sink into despair, passivity, and hopelessness. But another is to etch a psychological template of compensatory grandiosity, as if to vow, "Never again, never again shall I submit to superior force." This was the developmental psychological path Saddam followed.

From early years on, Saddam, whose name means "the one who confronts," charted his own course and would not accept limits. According to his semiofficial biography, when Saddam was only ten, he was impressed by a visit from his cousin, who knew how to read and write. He confronted his family with his wish to become educated, and when they turned him down, since there was no school in his parents' village, he left his home in the middle of the night, making his way to the home of his maternal uncle Khayrallah in Tikrit in order to study there. It is quite possible that in the approved biography Saddam somewhat embellished his story, but there is no mistaking his resentment against his mother and stepfather that emerges from it.

Khayrallah Inspires Dreams of Glory

Khayrallah was to become not only Saddam's father figure but also his political mentor. Khayrallah had fought against Great Britain in the Iraqi uprising of 1941 and had spent five years in prison for his nationalist agitation. He filled the impressionable young boy's head with tales of his heroic relatives—his great-grandfather and two great-uncles—who gave their lives for the cause of Iraqi nationalism, fighting foreign invaders. He conveyed to his young charge that he was destined for greatness, following the path of his heroic relatives and of heroes of the radical Arab world. Khayrallah, who was later to become governor of Baghdad, shaped young Hussein's worldview, imbuing him with a hatred of foreigners. In 1981, Saddam republished a pamphlet written by his uncle entitled "Three Whom God Should Not Have Created: Persians, Jews, and Flies."

Khayrallah tutored his young charge in his view of Arab history and the ideology of nationalism and the Baath party. Founded in 1940, the Baath party envisaged the creation of a new Arab nation that would defeat the colonialist and imperialist powers and achieve Arab independence, unity, and socialism. Baath ideology, as conceptualized by its intellectual founding father, Michel Aflaq, focuses on the history of oppression and division of the Arab world, first at the hands of the Ottomans, then the Western mandates, then the monarchies ruled by Western interests, and finally by the establishment of the "Zionist entity." Thus inspired by his uncle's tales of heroism in the service of the Arab nation, Saddam has been consumed by dreams of glory since his earliest days, identifying himself with Nebuchadnezzar, the king of Babylonia who conquered Jerusalem in 586 B.C., and Saladin, who regained Jerusalem in 1187 by defeating the crusaders. But these dreams of glory, formed when he was so young, were compensatory, for they sat astride a wounded self and profound self-doubt.

✗ Saddam was steeped in Arab history and Baathist ideology by the time he traveled with his uncle to Baghdad to pursue his secondary education. The school, a hotbed of Arab nationalism, confirmed his political leanings. In 1952, when Saddam was fifteen, Gamal Abdel Nasser led the Free Officers' revolution in Egypt and became a hero to young Saddam and his peers. As the activist leader of Pan Arabism, Nasser became an idealized model for Saddam. Only by courageously confronting imperialist powers could Arab nationalism be freed from Western shackles.

✗ At age twenty, inspired by Nasser, Saddam joined the Arab Baath socialist party in Iraq and quickly impressed party officials with his dedication. Known as a "street thug," he willingly used violence in the service of the party, and he was rewarded with rapid promotion. Two years later, in 1958, apparently emulating Nasser, Army General Abd Karim Qassem led a coup that ousted the monarchy. But unlike Nasser, Qassem did not pursue the path of socialism and turned against the Baath party. The twenty-two-year-old Saddam was called to Baath party headquarters and given the mission to lead a five-man team to assassinate Qassem. The mission failed, reportedly because of a crucial error in judgment by Saddam. But Saddam's escape to Syria, first by horseback across the desert and then by swimming a river, has achieved mythic status in Iraqi history. During his exile, Saddam went to Egypt to study law, rising to the leadership ranks of the Egyptian Baath party. He returned to Iraq after 1963, when Qassem was ousted by the Baaths, and was elected to the National Command. Michel Aflaq, the ideological father of the Baath party, admired young Hussein, declaring the Iraqi Baath party the finest in the world and designating Saddam Hussein as his successor.

Rivalry with Assad to be Supreme Arab Nationalist Leader

Despite—or rather because of—fellow Baathist Hafez al-Assad's success in taking control of Syria, Saddam confronted the new Syrian Baath leadership in a party meeting in Iraq in 1966. The split and rivalry persist to this day, for there can be only one supreme Arab nationalist leader, and destiny has inscribed his name as Saddam Hussein.

With the crucial secret assistance of military intelligence chief Abdul Razzaz al Nayef, Saddam mounted a successful coup in 1968. In "gratitude" for services rendered, within two weeks of the coup,

Saddam arranged for the capture and exile of Nayef and subsequently ordered his assassination.

This act was a paradigm for the manner in which Saddam has rewarded loyalty and adhered to commitments throughout his career. He has a flexible conscience: commitments and loyalty are matters of circumstance, and circumstances change. If an individual, or a nation, is perceived as an impediment or a threat, no matter how loyal in the past, that individual or nation will be eliminated violently without a backward glance, and the action will be justified by "the exceptionalism of revolutionary needs." Nothing must be permitted to stand in "the great struggler's" messianic path as he pursues his (and Iraq's) revolutionary destiny, as exemplified by this extract from Saddam Hussein's remarkable "Victory Day" message of August 8, 1990.

> This is the only way to deal with these despicable Croesuses who relished possession to destroy devotion . . . who were guided by the foreigner instead of being guided by virtuous standards, principles of Pan-Arabism, and the creed of humanitarianism. . . . The second of August . . . is the legitimate newborn child of the struggle, patience and perseverance of the Kuwaiti people, which was crowned by revolutionary action on that immortal day. The newborn child was born of a legitimate father and an immaculate mother. Greetings to the makers of the second of August, whose efforts God has blessed. They have achieved one of the brightest, most promising and most principled national and Pan-Arab acts.
>
> Two August has come as a very violent response to the harm that the foreigner had wanted to perpetrate against Iraq and the nation. The Croesus of Kuwait and his aides become the obedient, humiliated and treacherous dependents of that foreigner. . . . What took place on 2 August was inevitable so that death might not prevail over life, so that those who were capable of ascending to the peak would not be brought down to the abysmal precipice, so that corruption and remoteness from God would not spread to the majority. . . . Honor will be kept in Mesopotamia so that Iraq will be the pride of the Arabs, their protector, and their model of noble values.

Capable of Reversing His Course

Saddam's practice of revolutionary opportunism has another important characteristic. Just as previous commitments must not be permitted to stand in the way of Saddam's messianic path, neither should he persist in a particular course of action if it proves to be counterproductive for him and his nation. When he pursues a course of action, he pursues it fully; if he meets initial resistance, he will struggle all the harder, convinced of the correctness of his judgments. But should circumstances demonstrate that he has miscalculated, he is capable of reversing his course. In these circumstances, he does not acknowledge that he has erred but rather that he is adapting to a dynamic situation. The three most dramatic examples of his revolutionary pragmatism and ideological flexibility are in his ongoing struggle with his Persian enemies.

Yields on Shatt al Arab to Quell the Kurdish Rebellion

Saddam had forced a mass relocation of the Kurdish population in 1970. In 1973, he declared that the Baath party represented all Iraqis, that the Kurds could not be neutral, and that the Kurds were either fully with the people or against them. Indeed, this is one of Saddam's basic principles: "He who is not totally with me is my enemy." The Kurds were therefore seen as insidious enemies supported by foreign powers, in particular the Iranians. In 1973, the Kurdish minority, supported by the Shah of Iran, rebelled. By 1975, the war against the Kurds had become extremely costly, having cost sixty thousand lives in one year alone. Demonstrating his revolutionary pragmatism, despite his lifelong hatred of the Persians, Saddam's urgent need to put down the Kurdish rebellion took (temporary) precedence. In March 1975, Saddam signed an agreement with the Shah of Iran, stipulating Iranian sovereignty over the disputed Shatt al Arab waterway in return for Iran's ceasing to supply the Kurdish rebellion.

The loss of the Shatt al Arab waterway continued to rankle, and in September 1980, sensing weakness and confusion in the Iranian leadership, Saddam invaded Khuzistan Province, at first meeting little resistance. One of his first acts was to cancel the 1975 treaty dividing the Shatt al Arab waterway. After Iraq's initial success, Iran stiffened and began to inflict serious damage not only on Iraqi forces but also on Iraqi cities. It became clear to Saddam that the war was counterproductive.

Attempts to End the Iran-Iraq War

In June 1982, Saddam reversed his earlier militant aggression and attempted to terminate hostilities, offering a unilateral cease-fire. Khomeini, who by now was obsessed with Saddam, would have none of it, indicating that there would be no peace with Iraq until Saddam no longer ruled Iraq, and the Iran-Iraq War continued for another bloody six years, taking a dreadful toll, estimated at more than one million lives. In 1988, an indecisive cease-fire was agreed upon, with Iraq sustaining an advantage, retaining control of some seven hundred square miles of Iranian territory and retaining control over the strategic Shatt al Arab waterway. Saddam, who maintained five hundred thousand troops in the disputed border, vowed that he would "never" allow Iran sovereignty over any part of the waterway until Iran agreed to forgo its claim to the disputed waterway. Saddam declared that he would not agree to an exchange of prisoners nor would he withdraw from Iranian territory. But revolutionary pragmatism was to supersede this vow, for he desperately needed the five hundred thousand troops that were tied up in the dispute.

Reverses Policy on Disputed Waterway

On August 15, 1990, Hussein agreed to meet Iranian conditions, promising to withdraw from Iranian territory; agreeing to an exchange of prisoners; and, most important, agreeing to share the disputed Shatt al Arab waterway. Never is a short time when revolutionary pragmatism dictates, which is important to remember in evaluating Saddam's vow of 1990 never to relinquish Kuwait and his continued intransigence to Western demands.

Reversal of Hostage Policy

The decision to release all foreign hostages fits this pattern. As with other misdirected policies in the past, Saddam initially pursued his hostage policy with full vigor, despite mounting evidence that it was counterproductive. When it became clear to him that it was not protecting him from the likelihood of military conflict, as initially conceived, but was actually unifying the international opposition, he reversed his policy. His announcement followed an especially strong statement by Secretary of State James Baker concerning the use of "decisive force," but the anger of his former ally, the Soviet Union, was undoubtedly important as well. Moreover, the timing was designed not only to play on perceived internal divisions within the United States but also to magnify perceived differences in the international coalition, a demonstration of his shrewdly manipulative sense of timing.

A Rational Calculator Who Often Miscalculates

The labels "madman of the Middle East" and "megalomaniac" are often affixed to Saddam, but in fact there is no evidence that he is suffering from a psychotic disorder. He is not impulsive, he acts only after judicious consideration, and he can be extremely patient; indeed, he uses time as a weapon. While he is psychologically in touch with reality, he is often politically out of touch with reality. Saddam's worldview is narrow and distorted, and he has scant experience outside the Arab world. His only sustained experience with non-Arabs was with his Soviet military advisers, and he reportedly has only traveled outside of the Middle East on two occasions—a brief trip to Paris in 1976 and a trip to Moscow. Moreover, he is surrounded by sycophants, who are cowed by Saddam's well-founded reputation for brutality and who are afraid to contradict him. He has ruthlessly eliminated perceived threats to his power and equates criticism with disloyalty.

In 1979, when he fully assumed the reins of Iraqi leadership, one of his first acts was to meet with his senior officials, some two hundred in number, of which there were twenty-one officials whose loyalty he questioned. The dramatic meeting of his senior officials in which the twenty-one "traitors" were identified while Saddam watched, luxuriantly smoking a Cuban cigar, has been captured on film. After the forced "confession" by a "plotter" whose family had been arrested, the remaining senior officials were complimented for their loyalty by Saddam and were rewarded by being directed to form the execution squads.

In 1982, when the war with Iran was going very badly for Iraq and Saddam wished to terminate hostilities, Khomeini, who was personally fixated on Saddam, insisted there could be no peace until Saddam was removed from power. At a cabinet meeting, Saddam asked his ministers to candidly give their advice, and the minister of health suggested that Saddam temporarily step down, to resume the presidency after peace had been established. Saddam reportedly thanked him for his candor and ordered his arrest. His wife pleaded for her husband's return, indicating that her husband had always been loyal to Saddam. Saddam promised her that her husband would be returned. The next day, Saddam returned her husband's body to her in a black canvas bag, chopped into pieces. This incident powerfully concentrated the attention of the other ministers, who were unanimous in their insistence that Saddam remain in power, for it emphasized that to be seen as disloyal to Saddam is not only to risk losing one's job but could lead to forfeiting one's life. Thus Saddam is deprived of the check of wise counsel from his leadership circle. This combination of limited international perspective and a sycophantic leadership circle has in the past led him to miscalculate.

Saddam's Psychological Characteristics: Malignant Narcissism

Exalted Self-Concept: Saddam Is Iraq; Iraq Is Saddam

Saddam's pursuit of power for himself and Iraq is boundless. In fact, in his mind, the destinies of Saddam and Iraq are one and indistinguishable. His exalted self-concept is fused with his Baathist political ideology. Baathist dreams will be realized when the Arab nation is unified under one strong leader. In Saddam's mind, he is destined for that role.

No Constraint of Conscience

In pursuit of his messianic dreams, there is no evidence that he is constrained by conscience; his only loyalty is to Saddam Hussein. When there is an obstacle in his revolutionary path, Saddam eliminates it, whether it is a previously loyal subordinate or a previously supportive country.

Unconstrained Aggression in Pursuit of His Goals

In pursuing his goals, Saddam uses aggression instrumentally. He uses whatever force is necessary and will, if he deems it expedient, go to extremes of violence, including the use of weapons of mass destruction. His unconstrained aggression is instrumental in pursuing his goals, but it is at the same time defensive aggression, for his grandiose facade masks underlying insecurity.

Paranoid Orientation

While Hussein is not psychotic, he has a strong paranoid orientation. He is ready for retaliation and, not without reason, sees himself as surrounded by enemies. But he ignores his role in creating those enemies and righteously threatens his targets. The conspiracy theories he spins are not merely for popular consumption in the Arab world but genuinely reflect his paranoid mind-set. He is convinced that the United States, Israel, and Iran have been in league for the purpose of eliminating him, and he finds a persuasive chain of evidence for this conclusion. His minister of information, Latif Jassim, who was responsible for propaganda and public statements, probably helped reinforce Saddam's paranoid disposition and, in a sense, was the implementer of his paranoia.

It is this political personality constellation—messianic ambition for unlimited power, absence of conscience, unconstrained aggression, and a paranoid outlook—that makes Saddam so dangerous. Conceptualized as *malignant narcissism,* this is the personality configuration of the destructive charismatic, who unifies and rallies his downtrodden supporters by blaming outside enemies. While Saddam is not charismatic, this psychological stance is the basis of Saddam's particular appeal to the Palestinians, who see him as a strongman who shares their intense anti-Zionism and will champion their cause.

Views Self as One of History's Great Leaders

Saddam Hussein genuinely sees himself as one of the great leaders of history, ranking himself with his heroes: Nasser, Castro, Tito, Ho Chi Minh, and Mao Zedong, each of whom he admires for adapting socialism to his environment, free of foreign domination. Saddam sees himself as transforming his society. He believes that youth must be "fashioned" to "safeguard the future" and that Iraqi children must be transformed into a "radiating light that will expel" traditional family backwardness. Like Mao, Saddam has encouraged youth to inform on their parents' antirevolutionary activity. As godlike status was ascribed to Mao, and giant pictures and statues of him were placed throughout China, so too giant pictures and statues of Saddam abound in Iraq. Asked about this cult of personality, Saddam shrugs and says he "cannot help it if that is what they want to do."

Probably Overreads Degree of Support in Arab World

Saddam Hussein is so consumed with his messianic mission that he probably overreads the degree of his support in the rest of the Arab world. He assumes that many in the Arab world, especially the downtrodden, share his views and see him as their hero. He was probably genuinely surprised at the nearly unanimous condemnation of his invasion of Kuwait.

Saddam at the Crossroads in 1990–91

It is not by accident that Saddam Hussein has survived for more than three decades as his nation's preeminent leader in this tumultuous part of the world. While he is driven by dreams of glory, and his political perspective is narrow and distorted, he is a shrewd tactician who has a sense of patience. He is able to justify extremes of aggression on the basis of revolutionary needs, but if the aggression is counterproductive, he has shown a pattern of reversing his course when he has miscalculated, waiting until a later day to achieve his revolutionary destiny. His drive for power is not diminished by these reversals but only deflected.

Saddam Hussein is a ruthless political calculator who will go to whatever lengths are necessary to achieve his goals. But he is not a martyr, and his survival in power—with his dignity intact—is his highest priority. Saddam has been characterized by Soviet foreign minister Yevgeny Primakov and others as suffering from a "Masada complex," preferring a martyr's death to yielding. This is assuredly not the case, for Saddam has no wish to be a martyr and survival is his number one priority. A self-proclaimed revolutionary pragmatist, he does not wish a conflict in which Iraq will be grievously damaged and his stature as a leader destroyed.

While Saddam's advisers' reluctance to disagree with Saddam's policies contributes to the potential for miscalculation, nevertheless his advisers are able to make significant inputs to the accuracy of Saddam's evaluation of Iraq's political/military situation by providing information and assessments. Moreover, despite their reluctance to disagree with him, the situation facing the leadership after the invasion of Kuwait was so grave that several officials reportedly expressed their reservations about remaining in Kuwait.

As the crisis heightened in the fall of 1990, Saddam dismissed a number of senior officials, replacing them with family members and known loyalists. He replaced Petroleum Minister Issam Abdulra-heem Chalabi, a highly sophisticated technical expert, with his son-in-law Hussein Kamal. Moreover, he replaced Army Chief of Staff General Nizar Khazraji, a professional military man, with General Hussein Rashid, commander of the Republican Guards and a Tikriti. Tough and extremely competent, Rashid is both intensely ideological and fiercely loyal. It was as if Saddam were drawing in the wagons. This was a measure of the stress on Saddam, suggesting that his siege mentality was intensifying. The fiercely defiant rhetoric was another indicator of the stress on Saddam, for the more threatened Saddam feels, the more threatening he becomes.

While Saddam appreciated the danger of the Gulf crisis, it did provide the opportunity to defy the hated outsiders, a strong value in his Baath ideology. He continued to cast the conflict as a struggle between Iraq and the United States and even more personally as a struggle between the gladiators Saddam Hussein and George Bush. When the struggle became thus personalized, it enhanced Saddam's reputation as a courageous strongman willing to defy the imperialist United States.

When President George H. W. Bush depicted the conflict as the unified civilized world against Saddam Hussein, it hit a tender nerve for Saddam. Saddam has his eye on his role in history and places great stock in world opinion. If he were to conclude that his status as a world leader was threatened, it would have important constraining effects on him. Thus the prospect of being expelled from the UN and of Iraq being castigated as a rogue nation outside the community of nations would be very threatening to Saddam. The overwhelming majority supporting the Security Council resolution at the time of the conflict must have confronted Saddam with the damage he was inflicting on his stature as a leader, despite his defiant rhetoric dis-missing the resolutions of the UN as reflecting the United States' control of the international organization.

Defiant rhetoric was a hallmark of the conflict and lent itself to misinterpretation across cultural boundaries. The Arab world places great stock on expressive language. The language of courage is a hallmark of leadership, and there is great value attached to the act of expressing brave resolve against the enemy in and of itself. Even though the statement is made in response to the United States, when Saddam speaks it is to multiple audiences; much of his language is solipsistic and designed to demonstrate his courage and resolve to the Iraqi people and the Arab world. There is no necessary connection between courageous verbal expression and the act threatened. Nasser gained great stature from his fiery rhetoric threatening to make the sea red with Israeli blood. By the same token, Saddam probably heard the Western words of President Bush through a Middle Eastern filter. When a public statement of resolve and intent was made by President George H. W. Bush, Saddam may well have discounted the expressed intent to act. This underlines the importance of a private channel to communicate clearly and unambiguously. The mission by Secretary of State Baker afforded the opportunity to resolve any misunderstandings on Saddam's part concerning the strength of resolve and intentions of the United States and the international coalition.

Gulf Crisis Promotes Saddam to World-Class Leader

Throughout his twenty-two years at the helm of Iraq, Saddam Hussein had languished in obscurity, overshadowed by the heroic stature of other Middle Eastern leaders such as Anwar Sadat and Ayatollah Khomeini. But with the Gulf crisis, for the first time in his entire career, Saddam was exactly who and where he believed he was destined to be—a world-class political actor on center stage commanding world events, with the entire world's attention focused upon him. When his rhetoric was threatening, the price of oil rose precipitously and the Dow Jones average plummeted. He was demonstrating to the Arab masses that he is an Arab strongman with the courage to defy the West and expel foreign influences.

Now that he was at the very center of international attention, his appetite for glory was stimulated all the more. The glory-seeking Saddam would not easily yield the spotlight of international attention. He wanted to remain on center stage but not at the expense of his power and his prestige. Saddam would only withdraw if he calculated that he could do so with his power and his honor intact and that the drama in which he was starring would continue.

Honor and reputation must be interpreted in an Arab context. Saddam had already achieved considerable honor in the eyes of the Arab masses for having the courage to stand up to the West. It should be remembered that, even though Egypt militarily lost the 1973 war with Israel, Sadat became a hero to the Arab world for his willingness to attack—and initially force back—the previously invincible forces of Israel. Muammar Qaddafi mounted an air attack when the United States crossed the so-called line of death. Even though his jets were destroyed in the ensuing conflict, Qaddafi's status was raised in the Arab world. Indeed, he thanked the United States for making him a hero. Thus Saddam could find honor in the 1990 confrontation. His past history reveals a remarkable capacity to find face-saving justification when reversing his course in very difficult circumstances. Nevertheless, it would be important not to insist on total capitulation and humiliation, for this could drive Saddam into a corner and make it impossible for him to reverse his course. He would—could—only withdraw from Kuwait if he believed he could survive with his power and his dignity intact.

By the same token, he would only reverse his course if his power and reputation were threatened. This would require a posture of strength, firmness, and clarity of purpose by a unified civilized world, demonstrably willing to use force if necessary. The only language Saddam Hussein understands is the language of power. Without this demonstrable willingness to use force, even if the sanctions are biting deeply, Saddam is quite capable of putting his population through a sustained period of hardship.

It was crucial to demonstrate unequivocally to Saddam Hussein that unless he withdrew, his career as a world-class political actor would be ended. The announcement of a major escalation of the force level was presumably designed to drive that message home. The UN resolution authorizing the use of force unless Iraq withdrew by January 15 was a particularly powerful message because of the large majority supporting the resolution.

The message almost certainly was received. In the wake of the announcement of the increase in force level, Saddam intensified his request for "deep negotiations," seeking a way out in which he could preserve his power and his reputation. That President Bush sent Secretary of State Baker to meet one-on-one with Saddam was an extremely important step. In the interim leading up to the meeting, the shrewdly manipulative Saddam continued to attempt to divide the international coalition.

Considering himself a revolutionary pragmatist, Saddam is at heart a survivor. If in response to the unified demonstration of strength and resolve he did retreat and reverse his course, this would only be a temporary deflection of his unbounded drive for power. It would be a certainty that he would return at a later date, stronger than ever, unless firm measures were taken to contain him. This underlines the importance of strategic planning beyond any immediate crisis, especially considering his progress toward acquiring a nuclear weapons capability. If blocked in his overt aggression, he could be expected to pursue his goals covertly through intensified support of terrorism.

Saddam will not go down in the last flaming bunker if he has a way out, but he can be extremely dangerous and will stop at nothing if he is backed into a corner. If he believes his very survival as a world-class political actor is threatened, Saddam can respond with unrestrained aggression, using whatever weapons and resources are at his disposal, in what would surely be a tragic and bloody final act.

Why Saddam Did Not Withdraw from Kuwait[2]

In the political psychology profile prepared for the congressional hearings on the Gulf crisis in December 1990, recapitulated in the preceding material, it was observed that Saddam was by no means a martyr and was indeed the quintessential survivor. The key to his survival in power for twenty-two years was his capacity to reverse his course when events demonstrated that he had miscalculated. We believed that he could again reverse himself if he concluded that unless he did so his power base and reputation would be destroyed and if by so doing he could preserve his power base and reputation.

How can it be, then, that this self-described revolutionary pragmatist, faced by an overwhelming array of military power that would surely deal a mortal blow to his nation, entered into and persisted in a violent confrontational course? Cultural factors probably contributed to his calculation and miscalculation. As mentioned previously, Saddam may well have heard President Bush's Western words of intent through a Middle Eastern filter and calculated that he was bluffing. It is also possible he downgraded the magnitude of the threat, likening it to the characteristic Arab hyperbole. Even though he expected a massive air strike, he undoubtedly was surprised by the magnitude of the destruction wrought on his forces.

But more important, the dynamic of the crisis affected Saddam. What began as an act of naked aggression toward Kuwait was transformed into the culminating act of the drama of his life. Although he had previously shown little concern for the Palestinian people, the shrewdly manipulative Saddam had wrapped himself and his invasion of Kuwait in the Palestinian flag. The response of the Palestinians was overwhelming. They saw Saddam as their hope and their salvation, standing up defiantly and courageously to the United States to force a just settlement of their cause. This caught the imagination of the masses throughout the Arab world, and their shouts of approval fed his already swollen ego as he went on a defiant roll.

Intoxicated by the elixir of power and the acclaim of the Palestinians and the radical Arab masses, Saddam may well have been on a euphoric high and may have optimistically overestimated his chances for success, for Saddam's heroic self-image was engaged as never before. He was fulfilling the messianic goal that had obsessed him—and eluded him—throughout his life. He was actualizing his self-concept as leader of all the Arab peoples, the legitimate heir of Nebuchadnezzar, Saladin, and especially Nasser.

His psychology and his policy options became captives of his rhetoric. He became so absolutist in his commitment to the Palestinian cause and to not yielding Kuwait until there was justice for the Palestinian people and UN Resolutions 242 and 338 had been complied with that it would have been extremely difficult for him to reverse himself without being dishonored. To lose face in the Arab world is to be without authority. Unlike past reversals, these absolutist pronouncements were in the full spotlight of international attention. Saddam had, in effect, painted himself into a corner. The Bush administration's insistence on "no face-saving" only intensified this dilemma.

Not only, then, had Saddam concluded that to reverse himself would be to lose his honor, but he also probably doubted that his power base would be preserved if he left Kuwait. Saddam doubted that the aggressive intention of the United States would stop at the border of Iraq. For years he had been convinced that a U.S.-Iran-Israeli conspiracy was in place to destroy Iraq and remove him from power.

Earlier, foreign minister Tariq Aziz had indicated that "everything was on the table," but by late December the semblance of diplomatic flexibility had disappeared, and Saddam seemed intent on challenging the coalition's ultimatum. It is likely that Saddam had concluded that he could not reverse himself and withdraw without being dishonored and that he needed to enter the conflict to demonstrate his courage and to affirm his claim to pan-Arab leadership.

Saddam expected a massive air campaign and planned to survive it. In the succeeding ground campaign, he hoped to engage the U.S. "Vietnam complex." As he had demonstrated in the Iran-Iraq War, he believed that his battle-hardened troops could absorb massive casualties, whereas the weak-willed United States would not have the stomach for this, and a political-military stalemate would ensue. By demonstrating that he had the courage to stand up against the most powerful nation on earth, Saddam would consolidate his credentials as pan-Arab leader, and he would win great honor. In the Arab world, having the courage to fight a superior foe can bring political victory, even through a military defeat. Sadat, for example, won great honor in 1973 by leading the attack against previously invincible Israel, even though Egypt lost the military conflict. Indeed, his enhanced prestige permitted him to approach Israel as an equal negotiating partner and ultimately led to the Camp David Accords. Saddam's political hero and model, Nasser, gained great honor for attacking the imperialists in the 1956 Suez campaign, even though he lost.

Saddam hoped to consolidate his place in Arab history as Nasser's heir by bravely confronting the U.S.-led coalition. On the third day of the air campaign, his minister of information, Latif Jassim, declared victory. To the astounded press he explained that the coalition expected Iraq to crumble in two days. Having already survived the massive air strikes for three days, the Iraqis were accordingly victorious, and each further day would only magnify the scope of their victory.

It was revealed in January that under Saddam's opulent palace was a mammoth bunker, fortified with steel and prestressed concrete. The architecture of this complex is Saddam's psychological architecture: a defiant, grandiose facade resting on the well-fortified foundation of a siege mentality. Attacked on all sides, Saddam remains besieged and defiant, using whatever aggression is necessary to consolidate his control and ensure his survival.

Saddam after the Conflict[3]

Iraqi domestic support for Saddam Hussein was drastically eroded after the Gulf War. By late 1996, a series of betrayals, failures, and disappointments had left him in a more precarious domestic position than at any time since March 1991. There have been three main areas of change for Saddam since the conflict:

- increased security vulnerabilities
- strengthening international support
- increased importance of the weapons of mass destruction program

Increased Security Vulnerabilities

A principle of Saddam's leadership that has always been true—ensuring his domestic stability and eliminating internal threats to his regime—has intensified in the postwar period and is Saddam's central concern. The three greatest threats to Saddam's domestic stability have come from a dramatically weakened military, fractures in tribal loyalties, and fault lines in his family.

Weakened Military

Immediately after the conflict was terminated in March 1991, Saddam's major source of support, the Iraqi army, was gravely weakened. Once the fourth largest army in the world, the Iraqi army, its proud reputation as the most powerful military force in the Gulf shattered, its ranks and materiel depleted, and its morale destroyed, now represented a grave threat to Saddam's survival.

- The Iraqi armed forces, including the Republican Guard, became disillusioned with Saddam's regime.

- The standard of living for soldiers had reached the lowest level ever.
- The no-fly zone over the north/south was seen as a humiliating affront to the once powerful military. Moreover, Kurdish control over the north was a painful reminder that Iraq was powerless and at the mercy of the United States.
- The UN-sponsored weapons inspections were a continuing humiliation and demonstration of Saddam's lack of control over Iraq's sovereignty.
- A rising tide of disillusionment, desertion, and resentment led to repeated coup attempts by different military factions against Saddam.
- In March 1995, two regular army brigades suffered severe losses from clashes with the Kurds and Iraqi National Congress (INC), further humiliating Saddam and the military.

Fractures in Tribal Loyalty

Within the larger Sunni tribal system there were signs of weakening solidarity. Of the five most important Sunni tribes that had been the core of Saddam's support, and were in leadership roles throughout the military, three were involved in coup attempts against Saddam. A 1990 plot involved Jubbur members of the Republican Guards and regular army units. Officers of the 'Ubayd tribe were involved in coup plotting in 1993–94. Al-Bu Nimr (of the Dulaym tribe) revolted against Saddam in 1995. Frictions within Saddam's al-Bu Nasir tribe also compounded problems—by late summer in 1996, five "houses" within the tribe had grievances with Saddam or his family. While Dulaymis and 'Ubaydis continue to serve in Republican Guard and key security positions, they have been removed from most sensitive positions and are closely watched. Overall, the threat of a large-scale tribal uprising remains remote, though Saddam is no longer able to trust his once loyal tribes.

Fault Lines in the Family

Uday. The temperament and unconstrained behavior of Saddam's older son, Uday, thirty-eight, have been a continuing issue. He has a reputation as the "bad boy" of Iraq and is greatly feared among the population of Baghdad. He has been involved in several widely publicized incidents, but Saddam has regularly either overlooked Uday's excesses or, if the event was too public to ignore, dealt with it in the mildest of manners. Prior to the conflict in the Gulf, there were reports of violent excesses involving Uday. In one incident in 1988, Uday, drunk at a party, used an electric carving knife to kill one of his father's aides. In a second dramatic public event that year, Uday, angry with Saddam's personal valet for his role in facilitating an affair Saddam was having with a married Iraqi woman (whose husband was rewarded for not objecting with the presidency of Iraqi Airlines), crashed a party being held in honor of Suzanne Mubarak, the wife of the Egyptian president Hosni Mubarak. Uday beat the valet to death in full view of all the guests. As a result of this, Saddam put Uday on trial for murder, but in response to the family members of the victim who "pleaded for leniency," Saddam exiled Uday to Switzerland. A year later, after having been declared persona non grata by Swiss authorities, Uday returned to Iraq, where he began reintegrating himself into Iraqi society.

In 1995, Uday reportedly shot one of his uncles in the leg and killed six "dancing girls" at a party, not coincidentally the night before his brother-in-law Hussein Kamal defected. It is believed that Uday played a major role in causing the defection of Kamal, whom he saw as threatening his relationship with his father.

In 1996, an assassination attempt on Uday left him bedridden for at least six months with both his legs shattered. He was reportedly temporarily paralyzed following the assassination attempt. There have been some reports that he was left paraplegic from the injury and continues to be paralyzed from the waist down. There are rumors that he was left impotent, which, given the nature and location of the paralyzing spinal cord injury, may well be true. He remains in general poor health.

Hussein Kamal's Defection and Assassination: A Major Turning Point. Hussein Kamal, a cousin of Saddam, married Saddam's favorite daughter, Rghad. Kamal rose through the ranks of Saddam's inner circle with meteor-like speed, garnering him the resentment of the military core as well as other insiders. After having held several sensitive security positions, Kamal went on to found the Republican Guard and eventually became one of the few insiders who had access to Saddam Hussein, magnifying Uday's feelings of rivalry and jealousy. In August 1995, reportedly after having been threatened by Uday, Hussein Kamal and his brother Saddam Kamal, who also had married a daughter of Saddam, fled to Jordan with their wives, where they received asylum. Hussein Kamal provided copious information concerning Iraq's special weapons program, of which he had been in charge, greatly embarrassing Saddam and setting back his goals of ending the sanctions regime. Six months later, in February 1996, in what might be characterized as "assisted suicide, Iraqi style," both men and their wives returned to Iraq after Saddam provided assurances that they would be safe and forgiven. Within forty-eight hours of their arrival back in Iraq, both men had been murdered. Uday reportedly played a key role in orchestrating the murder of Kamal and his brother.

Demotion of Uday. Saddam demoted and publicly humiliated Uday after Kamal's flight, demonstrating that he believed Uday was responsible for the conflicts in the family that led to the defection. Saddam torched Uday's collection of vintage cars and stripped him of his leadership role in restoring Iraq's military equipment. He forced Uday to abandon his command of Saddam's private army dedicated to Saddam's protection, the Fidaiyiin. And, most important, Saddam elevated his younger son, Qusay, to the regime's most powerful security position. This demonstrated to all that even being a member of the immediate family, indeed Saddam's favorite child, will not protect one from Saddam's wrath if one's actions threaten the regime.

Qusay. While Uday is part of Saddam's problem, Qusay is part of the solution. Since 1989, Saddam has been preparing Qusay for the duty of czar of internal security. Qusay has worked closely with the former head of internal security, General Abd Hamid Mahmud (or Ihmid Hmud). They are in charge of the Special Security Organization (SSO), the most formidable of all security bodies, and in charge of security inside all security bodies, including the Himaya and the Special Republican Guard (SRG). The president's security rests mainly on them, but they are also in charge of concealment and deployment of Iraq's nonconventional weapons.

Qusay is also the supreme authority when it comes to "prison cleansing," the execution of hundreds of political prisoners to make room for new ones in Iraq's crowded prisons. He is also the one who authorizes executions of military and security officers suspected of disloyalty. Starting in 2000, Qusay started receiving a great deal of coverage by the Baath party and is now referred to as "Warrior Qusay." Supplanting Uday in the succession, he has been named Saddam's deputy "in the event of an emergency." Since 2001, Qusay has also been a member of the Regional Leadership (RL) of the Baath party in Iraq and deputy secretary of its important Military Bureau (*al-Maktab al-'Askari*).[4] The promotion of Qusay to the RL is seen as the first step toward his inclusion in the Revolutionary Command Council (RCC) and, eventually, his promotion to the RCC chairmanship and presidency.

Strategic Shift. The family disarray culminating in the Hussein Kamal defection and assassination, and the decline of Uday and his replacement as director of security forces by Qusay, signaled a major change of strategy. No longer could the loyalty of Saddam's family be unquestioningly relied upon. Rather it was necessary for Saddam to strengthen the Baath party and rely more centrally on long-standing party loyalists.

Redemption and Restoration of Morale Courtesy of the Kurds

In late August 1996, Saddam Hussein authorized elements of the Republican Guard to attack the Kurdish city of Irbil following the securing of military assistance from Iran by the Patriotic Union of Kurdistan (PUK). The guard "smashed" the PUK and the U.S.-backed INC. The seizure of Irbil was a major success for Saddam. This triumph after a series of setbacks and reminders of their diminished status restored the morale of the Republican Guard (and their faith in Saddam). It demonstrated that the regime was still very much in control and was a major power throughout the country. It also showed the fractionalization and impotence of the opposition movements in Iraq and was a powerful demonstration of the risk of rising against Saddam. This was a major turning point for the regime in terms of restoring its power position—had the guard not taken Irbil, it is likely that Saddam's support would have been so undermined that his position would have been in grave jeopardy.

UN Resolution 986

Facing an imminent economic collapse in 1996, Saddam was forced to accept UN Resolution 986, the so-called oil-for-food deal. This represented a great humiliation because it glaringly infringed on the national sovereignty of Iraq and indirectly on Saddam's personal honor. Saddam also feared that it would undermine international pressure to lift the sanctions imposed on Iraq following the Gulf War: as long as the suffering of the Iraqi people could be alleviated through the resolution, the embargo could stay in effect forever. But eventually Saddam had no choice but to accept the recommendations of his economic advisers. On November 25, Iraq announced its acceptance of the resolution.

Considerable advantages resulted from accepting Resolution 986. The sale of oil greatly improved Iraq's international and regional standing. That the food and medicines distributed to the population alleviated the people's suffering was less important than the fact that, from now on, Saddam could save the sums he had had to spend on food for his impoverished people. The disadvantages were minor by comparison, for credit for the increase in supplies went mainly to the regime, not to the UN. The improved situation did diminish the regime's ability to trumpet as loudly as before the suffering of the Iraqi people. Thus, it may well be that the crisis Saddam provoked with the UN in October–November 1997 over UN Special Commission Observation Mission (UNSCOM) inspections was prompted by fears that the humanitarian issue would no longer be an issue and that the embargo would remain. (In reality, the Iraqi regime still emphasized the suffering with considerable success, with the help of Western humanitarian groups.)

Strengthening International Support

In the events leading up to the 1990 invasion of Kuwait and the subsequent Gulf crisis, Saddam had been extremely isolated, misjudging the impact of his actions not only upon his Arab neighbors, the so-called near abroad, but also on major international actors on whose support he had previously been able to count, especially Russia and France. He had regularly seriously miscalculated both the risks of his actions and the degree of his support. His foreign policy initiatives in the interim have demonstrated a much surer and more sophisticated hand. Having learned from experience, he has worked assiduously to strengthen identified vulnerabilities.

Near Abroad

In his diplomatic efforts toward the "near abroad," Saddam has been quite effective. Having been surprised by the lack of support for Iraq during the Gulf crisis, Saddam has worked assiduously to rebuild relations with his regional neighbors. Relying heavily on its increased economic power generated as a result of increased oil sales, Iraq has become a crucial partner for these nations. While in the past Iraqi politics were driven primarily by internal politics and factors, it has been external factors that have begun to open up new opportunities for Iraqi policies and help to ameliorate Saddam's domestic problems. His immediate neighbors (the near abroad) have had the greatest impact.

Syria. The most telling example of Saddam's modus operandi when he feels weak and under great threat is provided by his tremendous resolve to mend fences with his oldest living Middle Eastern rival, President Hafez al-Assad and his regime. The years 1997–98 saw the beginning of a new relationship between Iraq and Syria. Saddam extended an olive branch to Assad, and the latter reciprocated in kind. Although ties were mainly limited to economic and diplomatic areas, this relationship was the beginning of Iraq's reacceptance into Middle Eastern politics.[5]

The two countries signed a free trade agreement. As a result of this agreement, mutual trade volume grew from $500 million in 2000 to around $1 billion in 2001.[6] According to some reports, mutual trade in 2001 actually reached almost $2 billion.[7] By the middle of 2002, it was estimated that the annual value of trade exchange between the two countries would exceed $3 billion.[8]

Iran. After taking power in 1997, Iranian president Mohammad Khatami sought to improve relations with the United States and Saudi Arabia, something that worried Saddam a great deal. However, hindered by internal politics, those relationships have not had the expected impact, which left more room for an improvement of Iraqi-Iranian relations.

Turkey. Turkey's strong ties to the United States and insistence on working with the United States on Iraqi matters are a great source of frustration for Baghdad. Turkish military forays into autonomous Iraqi Kurdistan, too, elicit bitter condemnations from Baghdad. Even though Saddam is no longer in control of Kurdistan, such forays are seen in Baghdad as infringing on its sovereignty. Turkish-Iraqi economic ties saw a quantum leap since December 1996. Just before the invasion of Kuwait, Turkey's annual exports to Iraq amounted to around $400 million. In 2000, exports already had reached almost the same annual rate as in 1990, $375 million, and in 2001, exports almost doubled to $710 million.[9] By the end of 2001, it was estimated that Turkey would be exporting $2 billion worth of products to Iraq in 2002.[10]

Jordan. While it did not participate in the international anti-Iraqi war coalition and was unwilling to confront Iraq politically, Jordan has consistently distanced itself from Iraq since the early 1990s. Much like Turkey, Jordan is getting the best of both worlds: it maintains excellent relations with the United States and Israel, including receiving U.S. economic aid; it thwarts, as best it can, Iraqi attempts to smuggle weapons through its territory to the Palestinians; and it continues to receive cheap oil from Saddam and to trade with Iraq. Saddam is fully aware of this practice, but he does not seem to care; for him, Jordan is an important avenue to the outside world. Even more important, securing Jordan's objection to a U.S. attack against him is now his top priority. Jordanian compliance with a U.S. offensive will mean Saddam's immediate demise, as it will provide the United States with the most effective bridgehead from which to launch the attack and prevent him from launching his own missiles against Israel.

Saudi Arabia. Until March 2002, the Saudis remained opposed to the Iraqi regime and moved to improve relations with Iran as a counter to Iraq in the event that the United States could not live up to its commitments of security or if the Saudi regime were compelled to ask the U.S. forces to leave the country. The first deviation from this stance occurred in December 1997, when Prince Abd Allah called upon the Gulf Cooperation Council (GCC) states to "overcome the past with its events and pains."[11] This was interpreted as a call for rapprochement with Saddam's Iraq. Saudi Arabia, like other regional players, expected to boost exports to Iraq—from about $200 million in 2000 to about $600 million in 2001.[12]

Other Gulf States. In the spring of 2002, the United Arab Emirates (UAE) ratified a free trade agreement with Iraq that had been signed in November 2001. The most significant feature of this deal is that the six members of the GCC will merge their markets into a customs union in 2003. This will give Iraq open access to the entire GCC market. By mid-2002, the UAE was already one of Iraq's biggest economic partners in the region.

The only Gulf state that, by mid-2002, was still hostile to Saddam's regime was Kuwait: despite Iraq's alternating offers of "friendship" and undisguised threats, Kuwait has steadfastly refused to improve bilateral relations. Kuwaiti officials refused an Iraqi offer to visit Iraqi prisons to prove there are no Kuwaiti POWs being held, and they continue to be highly critical of the Iraqi regime. It seems that Kuwait is also sympathetic to the idea of a U.S.-inspired violent regime change in Baghdad. If so, Kuwait is the only Arab state to support such a military operation.

Egypt. Egypt was the main Arab participant in the anti-Iraqi coalition of 1990–91. And yet Iraqi-Egyptian relations started to pick up significantly the moment Iraq's buying power surged. Trade became meaningful, and in January 2001, Iraq and Egypt signed a free trade zone agreement. According to statements made by Iraq's trade minister, Muhammad Mahdi Salih, during his visit to Cairo, the mutual trade in 2000 reached $1.2 billion, triple the 1999 figure. The minister expressed the hope that in 2001 the volume would go beyond $2 billion.[13] Egypt is the fourth largest trading partner for Iraq, after France, Russia, and China.[14]

Far Abroad

Saddam's patient diplomacy toward Russia and France, both of which have significant economic interests in an Iraq freed of economic shackles, with Iraq owing them a combined $11 billion, has permitted him to challenge the UNSCOM inspections regime with relative impunity, knowing that these permanent Security Council members with veto power could be counted upon to weaken reprisals against Iraq. China too has supported his beleaguered regime in international forums, as have Kenya and Egypt. These countries took the stance that the sanctions were hurting the Iraqi people more than the regime and that lifting the sanctions was the only way to alleviate the suffering of the Iraqi people—creating a sense that Washington, not Iraq, was increasingly isolated.

Weapons of Mass Destruction

To Saddam, nuclear weapons, and weapons of mass destruction in general, are important—indeed critical. After all, world-class leaders have world-class weapons. Especially since the military was grievously wounded by the 1991 conflict, with a marked reduction in conventional strength, unconventional weapons have become all the more important. Moreover, defying the international community on this matter is a regular reminder to the military of his courage in defying the superior adversary and that he has not and will not capitulate.

Weapons Inspections

Despite tactical retreats in October–November 1997 and January–February 1998, Iraq succeeded in winning important concessions on the sanctions front relating to weapons inspections. This was crucial in continuing to build Saddam's support among the Iraqi people—it was seen as a victory. The embargo is dissipating slowly, and yet Saddam did not have to give up his weapons of mass destruction. Today the Iraqi people have a better standard of living, many aspects of the embargo are gone, Saddam has his weapons of mass destruction, and his power elite feels more empowered—resulting in solidifying Saddam's position in Iraq.

Indeed, when UNSCOM left Iraq in December 1998 and was not allowed back, this was a major victory for Saddam in the eyes of the Iraqi people. The United Nations had been forced out of Iraq, and Saddam was unscathed. The challenge of the UNSCOM inspections regime strengthened Saddam's internal support, diminishing the internal threat as he demonstrated his ability to weaken and challenge the international coalition while retaining the coveted weapons of mass destruction program and weakening support for the sanctions regime. The divisions within the UN that Saddam helped promote were so deep that Saddam concluded that he was essentially immune to UN reprisals for pursuing unconventional weapons programs, which have become all the more important to him given the weakening of his military in terms of personnel, conventional weaponry, and materiel. Since 1999, there have been no meaningful coup attempts; those who might have challenged a leader perceived to be a loser did not dare challenge a leader who had successfully challenged the UN and the United States.

Return to International Community/Change of Image

Saddam has continued to work to increase his standing in the international community, seizing on opportunities to change his image, including bolstering his image within the Arab community:

- Starting in the early 1990s, Saddam began working to change his image as a secular leader. This "return to Islam" can be seen in the increased Islamic language used by Saddam; the introduction into Iraq of the Qur'anic punishment of severing the right hand for the crime of theft; forbidding the public consumption of alcohol; and decapitation with a sword for the "crimes" of prostitution, homosexuality, and providing a shelter for prostitutes to pursue their occupation. On the cultural level, a few million Qur'an books were printed in Iraq and distributed without charge, and people in many walks of society, starting with students, are being forced to attend Qur'an courses. In the same vein, a law issued in the late 1990s made it possible to release Muslim prisoners who learned the Qur'an in jail.[15] Another component of the "Islamization" campaign is the construction of extravagant mosques. The new Saddam Mosque (construction began in 1999) is one of the largest in the Middle East after the mosque in Mecca.
- Saddam has also fashioned himself as the patron of the Palestinian cause. He has increased the original "reward" that was paid to families of suicide bombers from $10,000 to $25,000. In addition, Iraq informed the Palestinian

Authority and public that it had asked permission from the Security Council to dedicate one billion Euros (around $940 million) from its New York escrow to the Intifadah.[16] There are other forms of support that, while not substantial, are still serving Saddam's propaganda machine. For example, a few of the Palestinians wounded in the Intifadah have been hospitalized in Baghdad.[17] Also, Iraq sent a number of trucks through Jordan and the Jordan River bridges to the West Bank full of humanitarian goods. Israel allowed these trucks to cross over.

Other Signs of Iraq's Growing Acceptance in the International Community

In August 2000, Venezuelan president Hugo Chavez bucked international convention and traveled to Iraq to meet with Saddam Hussein. He was the first head of state to visit Iraq since the Gulf War, signaling Iraq's growing acceptance in the international community. Two months later, Iraq was invited to attend the Arab Summit for the first time since the start of the Gulf crisis, indicating a thawing in Arab attitudes toward Iraq. In another sign of normalcy, Baghdad's international airport reopened in the fall of 2000. When a hijacked Saudi airliner landed in Baghdad in October 2000 and all passengers were released unharmed, there was a great deal of international praise for Saddam Hussein.

In January 2001, humanitarian flights began arriving daily from abroad, and Iraqi airlines began operating (even in the no-fly zones). As oil production recovered to prewar levels, food rations increased, power cuts became less severe, and drinking water and sewer services began to improve dramatically. In a calculated step to garner international favor, Saddam offered to allow Kuwaiti officials to inspect Iraqi prisons in January 2002; this offer was rejected. Finally, in March 2002, at the Beirut Arab Summit, Saudi crown prince Abd Allah hugged and kissed Izzat Ibrahim al-Duri, Saddam's deputy chairman of the RCC, in front of the world's TV cameras. This ended more than a decade of bitter hostility and was a visible symbol that Saddam's Iraq had been fully welcomed back into the community of Arab nations.

Saddam continues to strengthen his reputation both by his re-Islamization program and by his ostentatious support for the Palestinian people, further endearing him to his Arab neighbors. Saddam has pledged U.S.$881 million from oil revenues for the Palestinian people.

The Use of International Crisis

Saddam has found that international crises are helpful to him in retaining power in his country, and his string of foreign policy successes has allowed him to stunt the growth of internal opposition. For Saddam, success is not limited to the elimination of domestic opposition; such elimination is only a precondition to achieve his continuing ambition to be recognized as the preeminent leader in the region and a worthy successor to Nasser. However, in order to be able to become a world-class leader, he needs, in the first place, to control the domestic scene, and in his mind, control means absolute control, namely, the complete elimination of any opposition. To achieve that, Saddam has always been ready to confront anybody, including world powers. The most damaging outcome of any crisis is one that shows him as a failure as a leader. Thus Saddam regularly promotes international crises to shore up his internal position.

While assuredly Saddam's position today is much weaker than it was on the eve of the invasion of Kuwait in 1990, he has demonstrated a more sophisticated leadership both in terms of internal security vulnerabilities and in terms of diplomacy with his Arab neighbors and Turkey, the "near abroad," as well as with his "far abroad." He has patiently and assiduously worked to reduce his vulnerabilities and to strengthen his position, both internally and internationally.

Conclusion

Saddam's survival in power is his continuing goal. A rational calculator who can bob and weave and is astutely Machiavellian, he has shrewdly managed to sustain the loyalty of his military and to weaken international opposition. That he has been sophisticated and better attuned to the context of his leadership both internally and internationally does not however lessen a still persistent danger—

that when Saddam is backed into a corner, his customary prudence and judgment are apt to falter. On these occasions he can be dangerous to the extreme—violently lashing out with all resources at his disposal. The persistent calls for regime change may well be moving him into that dangerous "back against the wall" posture. The setting afire of the Kuwaiti oil fields as he retreated in 1991 is an example that might well be repeated with his own Iraqi oil fields, as if to say, "If I can't have them no one will." Moreover, with his back to the wall it is probable that he would attempt to use chemical/biological weapons against Israel and against U.S. armed forces in the region. The question then will be the degree to which he can continue to sustain the loyalty of his senior military commanders or whether they can be induced to disobey Saddam in extremis in order to safeguard their own futures. Of one thing we can be sure, this is a man who "will not go gentle into that good night, but will rage, rage against the dying of the light."

Notes

1. This assessment is an updated and expanded version of a profile "Saddam Hussein of Iraq: A Political Psychology Profile" by Jerrod M. Post, M.D., presented in testimony to hearings on the Gulf crisis by the House Armed Services Committee on December 5, 1990, and of the House Foreign Affairs Committee on December 12, 1990.

2. This section, "Why Saddam Did Not Withdraw from Kuwait," is drawn from "Saddam Hussein: Afterword," *Political Psychology* 12, no. 4 (1991): 723–25.

3. This section, "Saddam after the Conflict," draws extensively from Amatza Baram, *Building toward Crisis: Saddam Husayn's Strategy for Survival* (Washington, DC: Institute for Near East Policy, 1998).

4. *Al-Hayat* (London), June 18, 2001, 2, in Foreign Broadcast Information Service, FBIS-NES GMP 2001 061800048, June 18, 2001.

5. For details of the period 1991–98 see Baram, *Building toward Crisis,* 87–96.

6. *HaAretz,* February 1, 2001.

7. *MENA Report* (Middle East and North Africa business report), May 27, 2002, MENAreport.com.

8. *Iraq Press,* June 25, 2002.

9. *Turkish Daily News,* June 26, 2002.

10. *Anatolia,* November 2, 2001.

11. *Jordan Times,* December 24, 1997.

12. Reuters newsgroup, January 24, 2001, in Washington Kurdish Institute, January 24, 2001.

13. Xinhua (the official Chinese news agency), February 14, 2001, in Washington Kurdish Institute, February 14, 2001. *MENA Report* (in English), January 18, 2001, in Foreign Broadcast Information Service, FBIS-NES GMP 2001 01180000178, January 18, 2001.

14. Muhammad Mahdi Salin, interview in *MENA Report,* Cairo, January 18, 2001 (in English), in Foreign Broadcast Information Service, FBIS-NES GMP 2001 0118000028, January 18, 2001.

15. *Al-Quds al-Arabi,* January 10, 2001, 3, in Foreign Broadcast Information Service, FBIS-NES GMP 2001 0110000146, January 10, 2001.

16. Agence France-Press (AFP) news agency, January 24, 2001.

17. *Christian Science Monitor,* February 2, 2001.

16. Saddam Hussein:
Personality Traits and Motivational Biases

The following analyses of Saddam Hussein focus successively on his general personality traits and his motivational biases. The authors in each of the following sections apply their respective methods of content analysis to construct a profile of the causal mechanisms associated with the processes of ego defense and the mediation of self-other relationships.

General Personality Traits and Ego Defenses

Walter Weintraub

The analysis of Saddam Hussein's general personality from his speech habits is based upon 9,461 words gathered randomly from responses to foreign reporters' questions during three interviews in 1990. Table 16.1 compares the Iraqi leader's use of different categories with that of U.S. presidents since World War II. Of twelve verbal categories, Hussein's scores are low in the following categories: the personal pronouns *I, we,* and *me; qualifiers; expressions of feeling;* and colorful or *creative speech.* His scores are high in the following categories: *explainers, adverbial intensifiers, direct references,* and *nonpersonal references.* The paucity of personal pronouns together with low scores in the expressions of feeling and personal references categories gives the Iraqi leader's speech a cold, detached, impersonal quality. A rather high adverbial intensifiers score imparts a certain dramatic flavor to Hussein's speech.

If Hussein's speech lacks warmth, it is not without a certain engaging quality. A high direct references score reflects a confrontational quality to his speech. Hussein's responses to aggressive questions tend to be equally aggressive. The following excerpt from an interview with Dan Rather illustrates Hussein's aggressive engagement of the interviewer.

> *Rather:* You invaded a weak neighbor who is no threat to you.
>
> *Hussein:* Do you realize how wicked those in authority in that country, which you call weak, were? As a U.S. citizen who should honor his U.S. citizenship by telling the truth, you must know how wicked the al-Sabah family were.

Hussein's low qualifiers score indicates careful preparation for his interviews. Careful preparation reflects a need to control the human environment, a fear of being caught in an unfamiliar situation. The Iraqi leader's low qualifiers score also suggests an unimpaired ability to make decisions. His moderate retractors score indicates an ability to reconsider decisions. A moderate retractors score also suggests an absence of impulsivity. Hussein's low *me* score indicates an active temperament, a proclivity to master situations rather than to react passively to events. A moderate negatives score indicates an ability to withstand pressure but does not suggest a paralyzing stubbornness.

Hussein has a rather high explainers score. His responses to reporters' questions have a certain didactic flavor. A high explainers

TABLE 16.1. COMPARISON OF SADDAM HUSSEIN'S AND U.S. PRESIDENTS' USE OF VERBAL CATEGORIES

Category	Hussein (9,461 words)	U.S. Presidents (20,000 words)
Personal Pronouns		
I	5.6	31.6
We	11.9	18.3
Me	0.6	2.2
Qualifiers	2.5	11.2
Retractors	6.4	7.6
Negatives	14.0	13.7
Explainers	8.5	5.0
Feelings	0.5	3.3
Direct references	4.8	2.5
Adverbial intensifiers	17.5	14.1
Creative expressions	1.3	2.0
Nonpersonal references	793.6	742.2

score also reflects a rationalizing tendency, a disinclination to face unpleasant realities. Indeed, many of Hussein's explainers were used to justify Iraq's aggressive behavior in the Middle East. In the category of creative or colorful speech, Hussein's score is rather low. There is almost no wit in his responses, few metaphors, and little in the way of idiosyncratic juxtaposition of words. The lack of color, together with low scores in the feelings categories, reinforces the impression of a cold and detached speaker. If creative speech reflects creative thinking, we may conclude that the Iraqi leader lacks the capacity for innovative reflection.

How are we to understand Hussein's minimal use of the personal pronouns *I* and *we?* Western leaders tend to use more *I's.* If a Western leader is a crusader, a leader who presents himself as the leader of a movement, his or her use of the pronoun *we* will increase. Eastern autocratic leaders, particularly those who are the heads of political parties, often make little use of personal pronouns. Communist party leaders, for example, try to present themselves as representatives of a collective leadership. In such cases, an excessive use of personal pronouns would be considered to be in bad taste. One indication that Mikhail Gorbachev was a new kind of Soviet leader was his frequent use of personal pronouns during his press conferences. It is likely that Hussein's avoidance of personal pronouns is due partly to a detached speaking style and partly to his need to present himself as the leader of a political party.

What is the impact on a listener of a speaking style that combines few expressions of feeling with the frequent use of adverbial intensifiers and direct references? We suggest that the effect of such a verbal pattern would be one of cold, aggressive intrusiveness. This is the speech pattern of a menacing speaker, a bully. In my experience, this use of the verbal categories is unusual among American political leaders. Listeners in a democratic society do not easily tolerate such forceful speaking styles. Candidates with intrusive and aggressive speaking styles usually do not win free elections.

Of all the political leaders I have studied in the United States, only Pat Buchanan possesses the speaking style of a bully. Buchanan, however, possesses a verbal quality absent in Hussein's speech—creative expressions. Many of Buchanan's creative remarks are humorous, a verbal characteristic that softens the intrusive nature of his remarks and provides an element of disarming entertainment to his verbal style.

To sum up, Saddam Hussein's use of verbal categories includes high scores in the following categories: explainers, adverbial intensifiers, direct references, and nonpersonal references. His scores in the following categories are low: the personal pronouns *I, we,* and *me;* qualifiers; expressions of feeling; and creative expressions. As measured by this system of verbal behavior analysis, Saddam Hussein emerges as a cold, impersonal, intrusive speaker. An autocratic ruler possessing such speaking habits would be perceived by his people to be dangerous and menacing—a bully.

To some extent Hussein preserves some of the speaking habits of an Eastern leader whose official position depends upon control of the ruling political party. This is particularly true of his sparse use of personal pronouns. Hussein's use of qualifiers and retractors suggests an ability to make decisions and to reconsider them when appropriate. A low frequency of occurrence of qualifiers indicates a controlling speaker, one who is not comfortable in a setting where surprises may occur. The Iraqi leader shows a rationalizing tendency by his frequent use of explainers. A low *me* score suggests an active leadership style. With respect to verbal creativity, as reflected in the use of wit, metaphors, and unusual juxtaposition of words, Hussein shows little evidence of the capacity to think and act in an original or innovative style.

Motivations and Mediation of Self-Other Relationships

David G. Winter

For assessing Saddam Hussein, there is very little verbal material available. What is available has probably been selected, edited, and otherwise controlled to an unknown but considerable extent. The researcher's problem is thus to find any usable material at all. Some speeches are available in books (e.g., Bengio 1992; Hussein 1981; Matar 1981) or in the *Foreign Broadcast Information Service Daily Report,* but for assessing the motives of most world leaders, prepared speeches are not very useful because they are given on specific occasions to specific audiences, such that it is difficult to find much comparable material from other world leaders.[1]

However, most world leaders do give interviews and news conferences, and so researchers have usually scored transcripts to assess motive profiles (see Hermann 1980b; Winter 1980). Over the years, I have assembled an interview-based sample of twenty-two world leaders, drawn from a wide range of regions and political roles, as a generic comparison sample for assessing other leaders. There is a good deal of variation, in interlocutor, conditions, and intended audience, across leaders and across the comparison interviews, which introduces "noise" and error, thus making interview-based assessments of world leaders less precise than the speech-based assessments of Bill Clinton. However, this procedure does provide a basis for estimating the motive profile of any other individual world leader from the material available.

Even so, at the time I assessed Saddam Hussein's motives (shortly after the end of the Gulf War in the spring of 1991), he was somewhat of a "fugitive" subject for interviewers. The readily available material from books, magazines, and the *Foreign Broadcast Information Service Daily Report* consisted of only eleven English-language texts of interviews (only one was a true news conference), ranging over the period April 1974–January 1991 (see appendix). Many of these texts existed only as excerpts, and some showed signs of heavy editing. Six of these interview texts could be characterized as seemingly more spontaneous (or less edited), and five as less spontaneous or more edited.[2]

Table 16.2 presents the motive profiles of Saddam Hussein based on all eleven interviews, on the more spontaneous interviews, and on the less spontaneous interviews. All three profiles are quite similar: quite high power motivation, above average affiliation motivation, and very low achievement motivation. Saddam Hussein's power motive score is considerably higher than his achievement score.

In comparing Saddam Hussein's motive profile with that of Bill Clinton, it is important to focus only on the standardized scores, since the raw scores are undoubtedly affected by factors such as the format (speech versus interview) and occasion, which may obscure individual differences. Thus, for example, almost any leader would be likely to use more achievement imagery and less power imagery in announcing candidacy for the U.S. presidency than in being interviewed about foreign policy. Standardizing the raw motive imagery scores on comparable samples removes such effects, making it possible to discern individual differences.

Does the motive profile presented in table 16.2 fit with Saddam Hussein's actions? Post (1993b) outlined an interpretation of his personality and behavior that emphasized a general *unbounded drive for power and prestige,* with more specific components of extreme narcissism, exalted and extravagant rhetoric, aggression as an instrument of policy, and a paranoid fear of enemies. Each of these characteristics is associated with power motivation (see McClelland 1975; Winter 1973, 1996; Winter and Stewart 1978), especially in the absence of a sense of responsibility (Winter and Barenbaum 1985).

Saddam Hussein's high power motivation can also help us to understand specific aspects of his behavior, such as his repeated and rigid defiance in the face of his obvious misjudgments (see Renshon 1993). Laboratory research has demonstrated that power-motivated people take extreme risks in the pursuit of prestige but tend to confuse feelings of power and omnipotence with the reality of genuine social power and, as a result, overestimate their chances of success. They are vulnerable to ingratiation, such that they end up surrounded by sycophants who will not tell them the truth. Success breeds future creativity and further success, but failure drains their reserves of creative innovation (Fodor 1990).[3] Taken together, these behaviors add up to the ancient Greek concept of hubris, or overreaching ambition.

What are we to make of Saddam Hussein's above average score on affiliation motivation? At first this seems to contradict his behavior: can anyone point to many instances where he showed a "concern for

TABLE 16.2. MOTIVE PROFILE OF SADDAM HUSSEIN IN 1974–91

Material	Raw Scores (images per 1,000 words)				Standardized Scores[a]			
	Ach	Aff	Pow	Pow minus Ach	Ach	Aff	Pow	Pow minus Ach
All interviews	1.60	2.69	7.65	+6.05	39	55	57	+18
More "spontaneous" interviews (N = 6)	.74	2.36	8.59	+7.85	31	52	61	+30
Less "spontaneous" interviews (N = 5)	2.64	3.09	6.52	+3.88	32	56	57	+25

Source: Data from Winter 1993a.

[a]*Mean* = 50, and standardization = 10, based on a comparison group of interviews from twenty-two world leaders.

warm, friendly relationships"? As pointed out in chapter 6, however, laboratory research findings suggest a more complicated picture of the affiliation motive. People high in affiliation motivation *are* drawn into warm, friendly, and cooperative relationships, but *only* with people they perceive as similar to themselves and *only* when they feel safe. Under threat, they are often quite "prickly" and defensive. In the turbulent and dangerous world of Iraqi politics, Saddam Hussein has acted like an affiliation-motivated person under threat, surrounding himself with his own like-minded people (literally, people from his own village and family; see Renshon 1993) and fusing his affiliative concerns with his power motives in a messianic message of "brotherhood" directed with defiance but also (at least in 1990–91) with futility to the wider Arab community.

Summary: Major Dimensions of Political Motivation

Taken together, the Bill Clinton and Saddam Hussein cases suggest how the three major motives may interact to produce two underlying dimensions of political motivation.

(1) *The relationship between the achievement and power motives reflects the leader's underlying approach to politics: as an arena for accomplishment, as an arena for the expression of personal power, or both.* If the achievement motive predominates, as with Clinton during the 1992 campaign and the early years of his first term, then the leader is vulnerable to frustration as the political process chews up their carefully formulated and rationally framed goals and aspirations. (Ross Perot was an even more extreme example of such a profile; see Winter 1995.) On the other hand, if the power motive predominates, as with Saddam Hussein, then the leader may approach politics as an arena for untrammeled and ruthless exercise of personal will and whim. (Ayatollah Khomeini, in the 1970s, was a more extreme example of such a profile.) In contrast, a balance of these two motives, as in the case of Clinton in 1995–96, is associated with a more pragmatic and (in a democratic context, at least) effective approach to politics.

(2) *The affiliation motive has complex and varied political effects, depending on the leader's perceptions of comfort and threat.* While affiliation motives may temper power motivation and direct it away from aggression and violence (see McClelland 1975; Winter 1993b), it may also arouse a defensive, even bitter and aggressive, reaction to situations of threat.

Politics is a complicated arena, involving many situational forces in addition to individual personality factors and many other aspects of personality besides motives. Thus any individual leader's motive profile should be considered as only one aspect—a set of possibilities, biases, opportunities, and liabilities—from among the whole array of inner and outer forces affecting the leader in any concrete situation.

Appendix

INTERVIEWS WITH SADDAM HUSSEIN

April 8, 1974	Interview with Arab and foreign journalists
January 19, 1977	"Detente and the Zionist conflict" (interview with Sakina al-Sadat)
July 17, 1978*	*Newsweek* interview
July 17, 1979	Interview with Fu'ad Matar
October 13, 1979*	Interview with *Al-Mustaqbal* correspondent Fu'ad Matar
July 19, 1982*	*Time* interview
May 31, 1983	Interview with journalist Charles Saint-Prot
March 8, 1989*	Interview with 'Uthman al-'Umayr
July 25, 1990	Interview with U.S. Ambassador April Glaspie
August 30, 1990*	Interview with CBS anchor Dan Rather
January 28, 1991*	Interview with CNN reporter Peter Arnett

(*Judged to be more "spontaneous" interviews)

Notes

1. There are exceptions to this problem: Hermann (1980b) was able to assess motives of several Soviet Politburo members by scoring comparable speeches, and Schmitt (1990) was able to compare four general secretaries of the Communist party of the Soviet Union to each other by scoring their first political report to a party congress. Winter (1992a) compared British "Sovereign's Speeches" ("Speech from the Throne") to Parliament over a span of 380 years.

2. Those interviews appearing in books rather than in magazines or in broadcasts, plus the transcript of the July 25, 1990, interview with U.S. ambassador April Glaspie, of which there were only excerpts from an Iraqi-supplied transcript, were published by the *New York Times* on September 23, 1990, well into the Gulf Crisis.

3. In contrast, achievement-motivated people are able to learn from their mistakes by paying attention to negative results (McClelland and Winter 1969, chap. 1). As shown in table 16.2, Saddam Hussein's achievement motive score is almost two standard deviations below the mean for world leaders.

17. Saddam Hussein's Leadership Style

Margaret G. Hermann

This leadership profile of Saddam Hussein is based on an analysis of his responses to the domestic and international press in fifteen interviews between 1979 and the present. The description that follows is derived from an at-a-distance assessment of some twenty-one thousand words. The words are examined for evidence of seven different characteristics that have implications for how heads of state will behave, the kinds of actions they are likely to urge on their governments, and the way they structure and interact with their advisory systems. An individual leader's traits are put into perspective by comparing them with similar scores for other heads of state more generally and from the particular region. The characteristics are also contextualized by exploring how stable they are across issues, audiences, and time. The attributes that define the profile are those that historians, journalists, political scientists, and other students of leadership have found to be influential in shaping what leaders will do politically. The traits that are examined are (1) nationalism, (2) the belief that one can influence or control what happens, (3) the need for power and influence, (4) conceptual complexity (the ability to differentiate things and people in one's environment), (5) one's general distrust or suspiciousness of others, (6) one's self-confidence or self-esteem, and (7) the tendency to focus on problem solving and accomplishing something versus maintenance of the group and dealing with others' ideas and sensitivities. The at-a-distance technique is described in more detail in chapter 8.

Several types of verbal material were available on Saddam Hussein: speeches, proclamations, messages, and press interviews. Since the first three types of material can be written or crafted for the leader by others, some caution must be exercised in examining such statements to ascertain what the leader is like. Care and thought have often gone into what is said and how it is said. Interviews with the media are generally a little more spontaneous. During the give-and-take of a question-and-answer period, the leader must respond quickly without props or aid; what he or she is like can influence the nature of the response and how it is worded. Although there may be some preparation of leaders prior to an interview with the press, during the interview leaders are on their own to respond. For these reasons, the following profile is based only on Hussein's responses to media questions in an interview setting.

Leadership Profile in General

Table 17.1 reports the average trait scores for Hussein across sixty interview responses. The scores represent the percentage of time that Hussein used words that could have exhibited a particular trait where the criteria for coding the trait were present. The percentages can run from zero to one hundred. Table 17.1 also presents what would be considered a low and high score on a specific characteristic based on the scores of twelve Middle Eastern leaders from seven countries, as well as on the scores of eighty-seven heads of state from forty-six countries. The twelve Middle Eastern leaders are a more culturally focused subset of the eighty-seven. Low and high scores are one standard deviation below and above the average score for a particular characteristic for the group of leaders with whom Hussein is being compared and differentiate him from these others. Hussein is considered moderate in the trait if his score is *not* one standard deviation above or below the mean of the group; in other words, he resembles the comparison group of leaders on that trait. As the reader will note, when Hussein's scores are close to being low or high, I have noted that he leans toward being one or the other.

Saddam Hussein is different from the two samples of leaders on over half of the traits— nationalism, need for power, distrust of others, and self-confidence. He is like other leaders with regard to his belief that he can control events, conceptual complexity, and his focus on accomplishing something versus focusing on the people involved (the higher the score here, the more likely the focus on getting things done). These similarities with and differences from other leaders have implications for Hussein's leadership style. The discussion that follows is based on extensive research in the social sciences on how these characteristics affect leadership, elaborated in chapter 8.

Nationalism and Distrust of Others

The higher the score on nationalism, the more isomorphic the leader and the country; indeed, in the leader's eyes, he or she is the country. If something happens to the nation, it happens to the leader too, and vice versa. Such leaders are likely to internalize threats to the state as threats to their power and prestige. Moreover, leaders high in nationalism will perceive their political world as divided into friends and enemies ("us" versus "them") and will be quick to blame their enemies for the country's problems. They are prone to see only the

TABLE 17.1.   HUSSEIN'S SCORES ON SEVEN TRAITS

Characteristics	Hussein's Score	Hussein's Average Profile	Middle East Leaders	Compared to 87 Heads of State
Nationalism	.66	High	Mean = .49 Low < .47 High > .50	Mean = .42 Low < .32 High > .53
Belief can control events	.49	Moderate	Mean = .44 Low < .31 High > .57	Mean = .44 Low < .30 High > .58
Need for Power	.57	Moderate (ME) Leans high (87)	Mean = .54 Low < .42 High > .64	Mean = .50 Low < .37 High > .62
Conceptual complexity	.49	Moderate	Mean = .49 Low < .48 High > .50	Mean = .44 Low < .32 High > .56
Distrust of others	.53	High (ME) Leans high (87)	Mean = .44 Low < .43 High > .45	Mean = .41 Low < .25 High > .56
Self-confidence	.83	Leans high (ME) High (87)	Mean = .71 Low < .52 High > .88	Mean = .62 Low < .44 High > .81
Task vs. interpersonal focus	.56	Moderate	Mean = .54 Low < .49 High > .59	Mean = .59 Low < .46 High > .71

good aspects of their own nation and to deny or rationalize away any weaknesses. As a result, these leaders are likely to mobilize the support of their people through scapegoating or attributing the ills in society to an external threat. In the extreme, they may keep their country mobilized militarily indefinitely to deal with *the* external threat. Politics is a battle between good and evil, just and unjust, the noble and the degenerate; it is a zero-sum game where one side's loss is another side's gain. Therefore, a leader must be constantly vigilant to ensure that his or her nation wins, not loses—or be quick to interpret ambiguous events as wins. Highly nationalistic leaders generally choose to have around them advisers who are loyal and committed to the goals and interests of the leader; advisers who show any individual initiative risk becoming a scapegoat themselves for any failed policies.

Leaders who combine a strong sense of nationalism with a high distrust of others are likely to view politics as the art of dealing with threats. Everything that has just been said about leaders who are high in nationalism is accentuated by an intense distrust of others. Such leaders will always be suspicious of the intentions and actions of others, seeing ulterior motives and designs where there may be none. Moreover, the others—the enemies—are viewed as "pulling the strings" and being in charge of what happens; thus, these leaders can only react, so they must be highly vigilant and try to anticipate what is going to happen if they are to have any influence over events. And they will become hypersensitive to criticism, often perceiving that they have been criticized where others would not; such leaders are always on the watch for a challenge to their authority or self.

Given Hussein's high scores on nationalism and distrust of others, he is expected to reflect this type of leadership. As a consequence, he is likely to take most actions on his own—advisers are implementers of actions, not participants in the decision-making process—to act deliberately but often to interpret the environment as threatening and demanding when such was not the intention of those involved, to take bold actions in anticipation of what is going to happen, to be highly sensitive to criticism, and to be very controlling of those around him. He wants to be the winner in the game of chess that is politics; to do so requires vigilance, strategic behavior, and a willingness to take risks.

The Need for Power and Task Focus

Information on the characteristics of the need for power and task focus provides clues about the motives of leaders. A high score on task focus is suggestive of a high interest in achievement; a low score on task focus indicates a concern with the feelings and sensitivities of others and, thus, a need for affiliation/approval/support. Leaders who are moderate in their scores on the task focus trait have been found in the comparative politics literature to be charismatic. They can concentrate on solving problems when called for by the situation, but they can also switch to an interest in others' ideas and feelings when the context in which they find themselves changes. The charismatic leader has a certain degree of flexibility, matching motive to context in attempting to meet what he or she perceives are the people's needs. The need for power assesses leaders' desire to have control and influence over other persons and groups.

Leaders with Hussein's motive scores (moderate in task focus and leaning toward high in the need for power) often display a certain charismatic charm but are highly Machiavellian in their use of this charm. Whether or not they are sensitive to others or focus on solving a problem depends on the issue at hand and the goal of the leader. Such leaders work to manipulate the environment to stay in power and to appear a winner. They are good at sizing up situations and sensing what tactics will work to achieve their ends. In effect, other people and groups are viewed as instruments for the leader's ends; guile and deceit are perceived as part of the game of politics. These leaders are more skillful when they can directly interact with those involved than when they must deal with important constituencies at a distance. Without face-to-face interaction, they can misjudge the assumptions the other party is making and how far they are willing to go.

Leaders with Hussein's type of motive pattern can be very good to those who are loyal to them and facilitate them retaining power. But their attachments serve a purpose; these leaders are not emotionally invested in people nor necessarily guided by conventional morality or a conscience. To remain within the leader's inner circle, advisers must be willing to do what the leader wants without regard to the action's consequences. Moreover, they need to stay alert to when the leader has changed tactics and to move with him; any perceived challenges to the leader's authority provide reasons for dismissal, exile, or even death.

It can be very difficult to have an effect on leaders with this motive pattern because they appear to be one step ahead, always maneuvering in any situation to gain what they want—often at the other party's expense. At issue is how to frame proposals and information so that the offers appear in the self-interest of such leaders; they are likely to pursue and be attracted to overtures that are self-serving. But in framing proposals in this way, it is important to put oneself into the leader's shoes and consider how he is likely to view the current circumstances, given his need to retain control and influence over what is happening. In the vernacular of the bazaar merchant, an opponent will have to give something in order to get something in return; bartering and bargaining allow these leaders to sense what is possible and what the consequences will be of pushing further toward their goals. Leaders with this motive pattern will test the limits before adhering to a course of action.

Self-Confidence and Conceptual Complexity

Scores on the characteristics of self-confidence and conceptual complexity indicate how open leaders will be to input from others and the environment in the decision-making process, as well as the kinds of incentive systems leaders are likely to use with advisers, subordinates, and other leaders. In table 17.1, note that Hussein scores high in self-confidence and moderate in conceptual complexity in comparison to other heads of state.

When the trait score for self-confidence exceeds that for conceptual complexity, the leader tends to be more principled and less pragmatic in decision making and dealings with others. Such leaders know what they want and what should happen and spend their time persuading others of the appropriateness of their course of action. They are not above using coercion or devious tactics to ensure that their views are adopted. Indeed, threats are perceived as a legitimate incentive for prodding others into action. These leaders seek out information that will confirm their case and enhance their ability to convince others of what should be done. The focus is on developing a persuasive rationale for an already selected course of action, not considering what would be best, most cost effective, or most feasible given the situation and context. It will take a series of failures to convince this type of leader that a plan is faulty or will not work. But once convinced, such leaders can evidence a dramatic shift in behavior and can produce a persuasive argument for why the change was necessary, given the country's goal. *They* interpret the world and politics; learning about others' views only becomes important in order to sell one's position or to know who needs to be persuaded.

Leaders with this pattern of scores often organize the decision-making process in a hierarchical fashion so that they can maintain control over what happens. This type of organization means that they are the hub of the information wheel, able to withhold or share intelligence so that they will be the only person who knows everything. That they are moderate in conceptual complexity means that they are constantly monitoring the environment for data that facilitates them maintaining influence over the process and who is included in implementing actions. These leaders will not win any "most popular leader" contests, but they are often admired or feared for what they can do, and they stand out and cannot be discounted.

General Orientation to Politics

Hussein's pattern of scores suggests that he has an expansionistic orientation to politics. Leaders who are more expansionistic in their behavior have been found to be high in nationalism, the need for power, distrust of others, and self-confidence. In a similar fashion to such leaders, Hussein perceives the political world as highly anarchic and full of threats; the only way for him and Iraq to have any power and influence in this world is for him to maintain control over what he currently has and to work to increase his power and authority in his region through enterprises such as building and maintaining various types of weaponry, invading neighbors' territory, affecting world oil prices, challenging the world's superpower, or attempting to assume the mantle of leader of the Arab world. Hussein's profile is quite similar to those of Fidel Castro (Cuba), Kwame Nkrumah (Ghana), and Gamal Abdel Nasser (Egypt). Each of these leaders was interested in playing a larger role on the world's stage than their country's size or capabilities had dealt them. Each centralized power in his government, perceived himself as the government, was highly distrustful of others' intentions, skillfully used scapegoating to enhance the nationalistic fervor of their constituencies, was highly Machiavellian in dealing with the superpowers of the day, and appeared to the world to know where he was going and to be in charge of getting there. Pressure from the outside world only increased the challenge and raised the competitive stakes for these leaders—made the game of politics more fun and potentially more deadly. Engaging in the give-and-take of face-to-face bargaining or expressing willingness to grant them a momentary place on the major power stage appears to have been more successful in reigning in their behavior than threats. However, whenever they gave in, or were forced to accede, these leaders always pronounced themselves the winners to their people.

Leadership Profile in Context

An important question with any leadership profile centers around the stability of the traits. Do Hussein's scores remain basically the same across his tenure in office, when he is being interviewed by the domestic and foreign press, and when he is discussing different substantive topics? We can be assured that we are assessing what the leader is like if there is little change in the scores as the context changes; at the least, we know that he does not seem to be responding to the situation. It is easier to suggest what a leader is likely to do politically when the trait scores are more stable; with changes in scores, the researcher or analyst must consider contextual factors in deciding both how to influence the leader and what he or she is likely to do.

A statistical procedure (analysis of variance) indicated that generally Hussein's scores were stable across time, audience, and topic. Only five out of twenty-one (24 percent) possible changes (seven traits times three contextual factors) were statistically significant. Overall, the leadership profile described previously for leaders like Hussein is applicable for him in most circumstances. The statistically significant differences, however, do amplify the portrait of Hussein as leader and, thus, will be discussed in some detail. Table 17.2 presents the traits where there were significant differences across the various types of context.

The differences in Hussein's scores on conceptual complexity across time and audience suggest that he may appear more dogmatic and inflexible in the international arena and with regard to Iraq's position in the world in the aftermath of the Gulf War and UN inspections than is actually the case. He is capable of much more flexibility than these scores imply, given his scores for domestic press interviews across time from 1979 to 1990. Indeed, these latter scores would be considered high when compared with the conceptual complexity of other Middle Eastern leaders and eighty-seven heads of state (see table 17.1). The data intimate that, when Hussein wants or believes he needs more information in order to decide what to do or to maintain his power and influence, he can be quite complex and pragmatic. When, however, he has made up his mind or believes he is backed into a corner, his rhetoric will become very principled and

TABLE 17.2.   HUSSEIN'S SCORES IN CONTEXT (STATISTICALLY SIGNIFICANT DIFFERENCES)

Characteristic	Means
Time	
Conceptual complexity	Pre-Iran-Iraq War = .50
	Iran-Iraq War period = .55
	Gulf War period = .27
Audience	
Conceptual complexity	Domestic = .54
	International = .44
Topic	
Nationalism	Relations with Arabs = .58
	Relations with non-Arabs = .58
	Kurds = .80
	Domestic politics = .70
	Iran-Iraq War = .76
	Gulf War = .72
Need for power	Relations with Arabs = .69
	Relations with non-Arabs = .64
	Kurds = .53
	Domestic Politics = .39
	Iran-Iraq War = .65
	Gulf War = .39
Distrust of others	Relations with Arabs = .44
	Relations with non-Arabs = .49
	Kurds = .65
	Domestic politics = .39
	Iran-Iraq War = .66
	Gulf War = .68

dogmatic; he is doing what is right. He may, though, be merely posturing, proposing the "tough" bargaining position as his opening move, and testing the opposition. If the opposition does not counter, Hussein has proven his point; if they do counter, the bargaining has begun. In the course of the bargaining, the subtleties in Hussein's thinking and a certain pragmatism will become evident. To be most effective, given Hussein's Machiavellian impulses, any negotiations with him should be face-to-face or through highly trusted intermediaries. He is less likely to misinterpret or misconstrue toward his own ends what is possible in such settings than when the negotiations occur at a distance.

The data in table 17.2 suggest that Hussein is sensitive to issues and problems; three of the seven (43 percent) traits evidenced statistically significant differences by the topic under discussion. Given his proclivity to see the world as full of threats that must be dealt with, it is easier to understand his focus on problems. To maintain power and influence, he has to meet such threats head on and, thus, must be constantly vigilant. But this responsiveness implies that one way to know what Hussein is thinking about a problem is to code his discussions of that issue in speeches and interviews.

One of the traits that differed significantly by topic was nationalism. Although all the means for nationalism by topic were high when compared to Middle Eastern leaders and eighty-seven heads of state, Hussein clearly tempered and increased his emphasis on nationalism depending on the target. Although still high, his nationalism in discussions of relations with Arabic and non-Arabic countries is more focused on the positive qualities of Iraq and the payoffs of relationships with Iraq for the other government and state; it is more tempered and is "courting" in tone—whereas when he perceives trouble, his nationalism increases and his focus is on contrasting how good Iraq is with how bad the particular opposition is. Indeed, he tends to "rail" against those who are causing him trouble. In such cases, there are definite enemies, and they are in the wrong. His nationalism scores are above his own mean score for areas that are threatening to him and below his mean score when he perceives there is an opportunity to move ahead on his goals. This difference in scores may signal a potential indicator of what he perceives as threats and what he perceives as opportunities. Note that of the six topics, two-thirds are threats, which is likely to be the balance in any examination of his rhetoric, given his generally high nationalism.

Another of Hussein's traits that showed statistically significant differences across topics was the need for power. The literature on this motive suggests that individuals display this need when they are in situations where they, indeed, do seek power and believe they do not currently have it. Hussein's scores across topics tend to reflect this more general finding. He evidences less need for power in his discussions of domestic politics and the Gulf War. Both these need for power scores are low in comparison to Middle Eastern leaders and the eighty-seven heads of state. Hussein had and was wielding power in both these contexts. Where he sought more power and influence was in his responses to interviewers' queries about relations with other Arab as well as non-Arab states and in his responses regarding the Iran-Iraq War. All three of the need for power scores are high when related to the comparison groups of leaders. Here is where Hussein's Machiavellianism will be at its most pronounced. He is likely to attempt all sorts of tactics to gain more influence. He will be charming if such behavior seems likely to succeed; he will be a bully if such a strategy has a chance of working. In each case, Hussein will test the limits to see how far he can go before he starts to lose rather than maintain or win more power. The differences in the need for power scores suggest how ruthless Hussein is prepared to be and how much risk he is likely to take to gain what he wants. To some extent, the topics where the scores are highest also indicate the arenas over which Hussein seeks more control.

The last characteristic where there were significant differences across topics was distrust of others. Hussein's scores on distrust of others suggest whom he blames for his situation and the ills of Iraq. His scores for responses regarding the Kurds, the Iran-Iraq War, and the Gulf War are all high in comparison to the Middle Eastern leaders and the group of eighty-seven heads of state. Others are to blame for what is happening, for stirring up trouble, for making it hard for him to succeed. Because Hussein himself is responsible for domestic policy-making, he can remove those who he perceives do him ill. He can control what happens. Thus, note that the distrust of others score surrounding discussions of domestic politics is low. According to Hussein, outsiders are responsible for what goes wrong in Iraq; he is responsible for what goes right. Such a view of politics is hard to disrupt unless one does not mind Hussein's taking credit for what an outsider might view as something he or she did to help Iraq.

18. Saddam Hussein: Beliefs and Integrative Complexity

The profiles of Saddam Hussein in this chapter focus on his beliefs and integrative complexity during different periods of his tenure as the leader of Iraq. The content and structure of his cognitions are two aspects of the process of object appraisal, which both represent reality and express the leader's personality. In the following sections of this chapter, the authors identify diagnostic and choice propensities in Hussein's operational code and examine the integrative complexity of his thought processes to assess their likely impact on the Iraqi leader's behavior.

Operational Code Beliefs and Object Appraisal

Stephen G. Walker, Mark Schafer, and Michael Young

The following analysis of Saddam Hussein's operational code is based on a small sample of six speeches from public sources for three years during the late 1990s (1996, 1998, 1999). Each speech was machine-coded with Profiler+, an automated content analysis software package using the VICS coding procedures described in chapter 9 (see also Young 2001; Schafer and Walker 2001). The reliability of the results is very high because the coding process was automated and, therefore, perfectly reproducible. The following analysis of Hussein's beliefs is in terms of their direction and intensity compared to the average VICS scores for a norming group of twenty world leaders from different regions and eras.

The validity of the results is subject to the degree of generalizability from the sample to the population of speeches and other public statements by the Iraqi leader. Since the sample does not cover an extended time period, its generalizability is limited unless one assumes that operational code beliefs are personality traits and not cognitive states of mind (Walker 1995). Research dealing with this problem has revealed enough variability to issue a cautionary notice that the following profile may apply only to the time period in which the data were gathered (Schafer 2000).

Index scores for President Saddam Hussein's general operational code, found in table 18.1, are reported as standard deviations from the norming group's scores for each VICS index. Their interpretation in table 18.1 is in terms of the number of standard deviations above and below the average VICS score for each element in the operational code construct. The anchoring points for each VICS index in chapter

TABLE 18.1.   THE GENERAL OPERATIONAL CODE OF SADDAM HUSSEIN

	Std Dev	Descriptor
Philosophical Beliefs		
P-1. Nature of the political universe	−1.47	**Very hostile**
P-2. Prospects for realization of political values	−1.33	Very pessimistic
P-3. Predictability of political future	−4.67	Extremely low
P-4. Belief in historical control		
a. Self's control	−3.80	**Extremely low**
b. Other's control	+3.80	**Extremely high**
P-5. Role of chance	+4.00	Extremely high
Instrumental Beliefs		
I-1. Approach to goals (Direction of strategy)	−1.24	**Definitely conflictual**
I-2. Pursuit of goals (intensity of tactics)	−1.08	Definitely conflictual
I-3. Risk orientation (averse/acceptant)	−1.71	Very low
I-4. Timing of action		
a. Flexibility of coop/conf tactics	+2.40	Extremely high
b. Flexibility of word/deed tactics	+1.60	Very high
I-5. Utility of means		
a. Reward	+0.40	Somewhat high
b. Promise	−4.67	Extremely low
c. Appeal/support	+0.00	Average
d. Oppose/resist	+1.71	Very high
e. Threaten	−3.00	Extremely high
f. Punish	+0.60	Somewhat high

Source: Data from Foreign Broadcast Information Service.

Note: Key VICS indices are in bold. Indices are expressed as standard deviations above and below the mean for a sample of twenty world leaders from a variety of regions and eras.

9, expressed as "Somewhat, Definitely, Very, and Extremely," are applied in table 18.1 to half-standard-deviation intervals above and below the mean score of the norming group for each VICS index.

The VICS scores for Hussein's philosophical beliefs in table 18.1 show that he views the nature of the political universe (P-1) as very hostile, almost one and a half standard deviations below the average leader. He is also very pessimistic about the prospects for realizing fundamental political goals (P-2). Hussein sees the political future (P-3) as extremely low in predictability, and he believes that he has an extremely low degree of control over historical development compared to others (P-4). Finally, Hussein's assessment of the role of chance in politics is extremely high (P-5).

The VICS scores for Hussein's instrumental beliefs in table 18.1 indicate that he believes that a definitely conflictual direction is the best strategy (I-1) in the political universe, coupled with definitely conflictual tactics (I-2). His general risk orientation (I-3) is very low; that is, he is more averse to taking risks than other leaders. The Iraqi leader's propensity to shift between cooperative and conflict tactics (I-4a) is extremely high, and his propensity to shift between word and deed tactics is very high (I-4b). The utility of means indices (I-5) show that his reliance on threats is extremely high, along with a very high reliance on oppose/resist tactics. Hussein's reliance on both reward and punish tactics is somewhat high; however, his reliance on promises is extremely low compared to other leaders. He is average in his propensity to use appeal/support tactics.

Overall, the key VICS scores for Self and Other in table 18.1 indicate that Hussein believes in a definitely conflictual approach to strategy (I-1) and attributes an extremely low level of control (P-4a) to himself in the political universe. He sees the political universe as very conflictual (P-1) and attributes an extremely high level of control (P-4b) to others in the political universe. These dual images of Self and Other and an extremely high propensity to shift between conflict and cooperation (I-4a) suggest that his strategies and tactics will be relatively flexible and perhaps erratic.

The standard deviation scores for the key indices in table 18.1 also allow us to locate Hussein in Holsti's revised typology of operational codes and extrapolate some predictions about his likely strategic and tactical interaction patterns. The strategies and tactics in the four

TYPE A QUADRANT   **TYPE C QUADRANT**

P-1/I-1
Axis
+2.0

Appease   Reward   Reward   Exploit
DED   DDD   DDD   DDE

+1.5

FOLLOW/COOPERATE   COOPERATE/LEAD
STRATEGIES   STRATEGIES

+1.0

Bluff   Deter   Punish   Compel
EED   DEE   EEE   EDD

+.50

P-4   -2.0   -1.5   -1.0   -.50   0.00   +.50   +1.0   +1.5   +2.0   **P-4**
Axis   **Axis**

-.50

Bluff   Deter   Punish   Exploit
EED   DEE   EEE   DDE

-1.0

SUBMIT/CONFLICT   CONFLICT/DOMINATE
STRATEGIES   STRATEGIES

-1.5

Bully   Punish   Compel   Bully
EDE   EEE   EDD   EDE

-2.0
P-1/I-1
Axis

TYPE DEF QUADRANT   **TYPE B QUADRANT**

Note: Key indices of beliefs in the leader s operational code are scaled in standard deviations along the vertical and horizontal axes of the revised Holsti typology. Reward, Deter, Punish and Compel tactics are variants of a general strategy of reciprocity in which Self initiates either an escalatory (E) move or de-escalatory (D) move and then responds in kind to whether Other escalates (E) or de-escalates (D) in response to Self s initial move. Appease, Bluff, Exploit, and Bully tactics are variants of a general strategy of cooperation or conflict in which Self initiates either an escalatory (E) move or de-escalatory (D) move and then violates the norm of reciprocity after Other escalates (E) or de-escalates (D) in response to Self s initial move.

Fig. 18.1.   Prediction template for key VICS indices. (Data from Walker, Schafer, and Marfleet 2001.)

quadrants in figure 18.1 represent the likely interaction patterns with Other that we hypothesize are associated with the four types of operational codes in the revised Holsti typology of belief systems discussed in chapter 9. The vertical axis in figure 18.1 is the continuum of standard deviations for a leader's image of the political universe (P-1) and approach to political strategy (I-1). The horizontal axis is the continuum of standard deviations for a leader's attribution of historical control to Self (P-4a) and Other (P-4b).

The Iraqi leader's I-1 score for approach to goals and his P-4a score for self's control over historical development place his generalized image of Self in the type DEF quadrant in figure 18.1. His P-1 score for nature of the political universe and P-4b score for other's control over historical development locate his generalized image of Other in the type B quadrant. The strategic interaction implications in figure 18.1 for Saddam Hussein's general operational code as a type DEF leader are that his definitely conflictual strategic orientation and extremely low sense of historical control are likely to lead him to initiate bluffing tactics that will escalate to bully tactics if he does not encounter firm opposition from Other.

Due to his extremely low sense of historical control, however, Saddam Hussein is more likely to diagnose Other as a type B opponent rather than a type DEF adversary. This diagnostic propensity to view Other as a type B and his aversion to taking risks are likely to make him relatively flexible and cautious if Other responds with hostility toward him. This diagnosis of perceived power realities, however, is not likely to lead Hussein to an unequivocal shift toward a cooperative strategy. Instead, he is likely to implement a mix of bluff, bully, and punish tactics that make him appear erratic rather than pragmatic in his response to a stronger opponent.

Saddam Hussein's Integrative Complexity under Stress

Peter Suedfeld

The Persian Gulf Crisis—comprising the Iraqi invasion of Kuwait in the summer of 1990, a period of international negotiations, and the subsequent coalition air and ground attack on Iraq early in 1991—provided an uncommonly useful set of data for integrative complexity research on Saddam Hussein's cognitive style. There were a number of reasons why the Gulf Crisis was particularly suitable for such analysis:

1. The episode covered a long time period (from the Kuwait invasion [August 2] to the cease-fire [February 27], nearly eight months), giving the protagonists many opportunities to present and discuss their perceptions, motives, goals, interpretations, plans, reactions to other participants and to events, and so forth.

2. A wide range of diplomatic, economic, and military maneuvers emerged at various stages of the confrontation, with different individuals and nations taking active and reactive roles at different times.

3. Many nations and leaders, representing very different cultures, were involved, and the degree of involvement (for example, potential losses and gains) also varied.

4. Both cooperative and competitive strategies were tried, including armed attacks both with and without warning.

5. In a high proportion of the countries most closely involved, the leader speaks for the government; his statements represent his views on the topic, not merely the transmission of a group decision.

The University of British Columbia research group conducted two studies dealing with the integrative complexity of leaders during this set of events. One (Wallace, Suedfeld, and Thachuk 1993a, 1993b) included statements made by heads of state and relevant high officials of many of the nations that played a part in the Gulf Crisis in the forums of the UN and international diplomacy; the other (Suedfeld, Wallace, and Thachuk 1993) concentrated on the top leaders of Middle Eastern countries.

The following comparisons of integrative complexity levels were made in the two articles: leaders of more involved nations with leaders of less involved ones; heads of state versus other officials; and pro- and anti-Iraq leaders. We also conducted detailed comparisons of George H. W. Bush and Hussein and examined changes in the complexity of particular individuals as the crisis progressed toward a solution. Several interesting findings emerged; in relation to Hussein, the following were perhaps the most informative (the complexity scores of Saddam Hussein, of immediate concern in the present chapter, are shown in table 18.2).

1. On average, Saddam Hussein (and other highly involved leaders, such as President Bush) showed lower complexity during the Gulf Crisis than did the leaders of less involved nations. This finding supports the disruptive stress hypothesis, which states that severe and/or prolonged stress leads to reduced complexity because of a depletion of psychological and other resources (e.g., Suedfeld and Rank 1976; Suedfeld, Corteen, and McCormick 1986).

2. In the two months prior to Iraq's invasion of Kuwait, which precipitated the Gulf Crisis, Hussein's complexity was relatively high. It dropped noticeably prior to the invasion, as had been found in previous studies of surprise armed attacks (Suedfeld and Bluck 1988). His complexity increased after the invasion and rose even further once the invasion was successfully completed and his stress level decreased.

3. During the late summer, fall, and early winter of 1990, as history recorded worldwide public excitement regarding the situation in the Persian Gulf, condemnation of the invasion by the UN, international economic sanctions (embargo and blockade) against Iraq, attempts by the UN secretary general as well as individual nations to bring about Iraq's withdrawal through diplomatic means, and—later in the year—the gathering of coalition military forces and the issuing of a deadline for Iraqi withdrawal, Hussein's complexity levels were slightly above the level seen after the victorious invasion. There was less of an increase in complexity than would be predicted by the cognitive manager hypothesis for leaders involved in complicated negotiations (Suedfeld 1992a); one inference might be that Hussein was not negotiating very seriously (and/or he did not believe that the coalition was negotiating seriously) in the sense of actually intending or expecting to develop a compromise solution. A much later episode showed the same pattern: in 1998, Hussein precipitated a confrontation with the UN just when he had a seemingly good opportunity to achieve an end to the economic sanctions against Iraq. As *Newsweek* (1998) put it, Clinton "learned that it may be easier to punish Saddam than to negotiate with him" (8).

4. His complexity showed a larger increase as the Security Council's deadline for Iraq's withdrawal from Kuwait (January 15, 1991)

393

approached and, presumably, as the need for a peaceful resolution seemed more pressing. These findings were not compatible with our previous conclusions that the nearing of military conflict leads to disruptive stress and a consequent reduction in complexity (e.g., Suedfeld and Tetlock 1977); Hussein may have thought that he had a chance to break up the coalition and delay or even avoid the long-threatened attack.

TABLE 18.2.   CHRONOLOGY OF THE GULF CRISIS AND THE COMPLEXITY OF SADDAM HUSSEIN

| Event | Date | | Hussein Complexity |
	Dates	M Score	
1990			
Peace	May–July		2.1
Pre-Invasion	June 28–Aug. 1		1.2
Invasion of Kuwait begins	Aug. 2		
Invasion complete	Aug. 3	Aug. 2–9	1.3
Iraq consolidates conquest of Kuwait;			
UN negotiations and sanctions:		Aug.–Sept.	1.6
Security Council (SC) announces			
trade embargo	Aug. 6	Aug. 10–24	2.2
U.S. and Egypt announce they will			
defend Saudi Arabia if it is attacked	Aug. 6		
Iraq takes Westerners hostage	Aug. 25	Aug. 25–Sept. 24	1.5
SC authorizes naval interception			
to enforce embargo	Aug. 25		
Diplomatic attempts continue:		Oct.–Dec.	1.9
Secretary-General Perez de			
Cuellar's mission to negotiate			
withdrawal fails	Sept. 2		
Hussein offers free oil to Third World			
nations that break blockade	Sept. 10		
SC announces air embargo	Sept. 25	Sept. 25–Dec. 2	1.4
SC announces withdrawal deadline	Nov. 29		
Hussein frees Western hostages	Dec. 6	Dec. 3–31	1.2
1991			
U.S. Congress votes for armed action			
if SC deadline is not met	Jan. 12	Jan. 1–15	2.2
SC deadline (not met)	Jan. 15		
Coalition-Iraq war			
Coalition air attacks begin	Jan. 17	Jan 16–31	1.2
Air war continues	Feb. 1–22		3.1
Coalition air attacks suspended	Feb. 24		
Coalition ground attack begins	Feb. 24	Feb. 23–27	1.4
Iraq defeated	Feb. 27		
Postwar restructuring		Feb. 27–March 31	2.8

5. Hussein's complexity scores during the coalition counterattack were very interesting. There was a dramatic drop during the early days of the air attacks against Iraq and its forces, followed by a substantial increase after the attacks had continued for over a month with no widening of coalition actions. When the ground war began, there was another large drop. This pattern demonstrates that opposition initiatives, even devastating ones, failed to make Hussein become more flexible or submissive in the short run. Instead, they strengthened rigid adherence to his established course. However, as the damage to his forces continued to mount, and as his defenses increasingly proved ineffectual, he may have begun to search for a compromise solution. The coalition ground attack preempted such a solution; his reduced level of complexity at that point may have indicated a hardening of his position. Another explanation for the episodes of lowered complexity is that they reflected disruptive stress; but if so, Hussein's recovery was remarkably rapid.

In either case, a pattern of resilience may be related to Saddam Hussein's remarkable ability to survive opposition. It may also identify conditions under which he does or does not engage in attempts at complex problem solving. New actions against him, rather than motivating him to search for compromise, buttress a unidimensional strategy; more cognitive investment in a differentiated and integrated viewpoint occurs when it becomes obvious that the simple strategy is unavailing. Perhaps most telling in this regard is the fact that he found the psychological resources for increased complexity toward the end of a period during which overwhelming coalition air power was rapidly demolishing his capital city and his armed forces almost without resistance.

6. Hussein's complexity rose again after the cease-fire was put into effect. This may reflect the ending of a major period of stress (Suedfeld, Corteen, and McCormick 1986; Suedfeld and Granatstein 1995). It may also be related to his recognition, as an effective cognitive manager, that at this point he did have to engage in serious planning and negotiation to salvage his own political survival out of a total military defeat.

7. A recurring concern in complexity studies is whether the level of complexity found in the material reflects actual cognitive processes or mere rhetoric designed to present a preferred image of

the self (Tetlock 1981b; Tetlock, Hannum, and Micheletti 1984). Earlier research (e.g., Suedfeld, Tetlock, and Ramirez 1977) has identified situations where impression management efforts concentrated on content, not structure, which may be the general pattern. Otherwise, one would expect Saddam Hussein to project a picture of flexible willingness to consider options when there was a chance to avert an attack by what would doubtless be massive forces (October through December 1990) and, on the other hand, to radiate strength and single-minded determination while an attack was actually occurring (mid-January through the end of February 1991). His pattern was actually the opposite of these intuitively appealing hypotheses. In this instance, the data are more compatible with the hypothesis that complexity scores show how the individual actually thinks about the situation rather than being determined by how he wants to appear to others.

Although in one earlier study we followed the complexity pattern of a military field commander before, during, and after a major war (Suedfeld, Corteen, and McCormick 1986), we had never before continued the complexity scoring of governmental leaders throughout the military conflict that capped an international crisis. In the two Gulf War studies, this enabled us to discover interesting aspects of Saddam Hussein's cognitive style; in addition, comparisons among other leaders were relevant to a number of theoretical postulates of integrative complexity theory.

Part IV. Conclusion

19. Assessing Political Leaders in Theory and in Practice

Jerrold M. Post and Stephen G. Walker

The evolution of efforts to assess the impact of leaders upon the course of events continues to be the subject of lively debates inside academe and within the policy community. The post–cold war era has ushered in a world without the bipolar power structure of super-power rivalry and has raised questions about the predictability of the new strategic environment. Jervis (1994) has contrasted the strongly structured, cold war system with the uncertainties of the weakly structured post–cold war world and has argued that cognition and other psychological processes will be more important in the latter environment.

This judgment about the potential relevance of political leaders is consistent with the general conditions of "action dispensability" and "actor dispensability" identified by Greenstein (1987) as necessary for "personality" to be influential in explaining and predicting polit-ical outcomes. The focus in this volume on an American president and a key leader in the Middle East as case studies has extended this logic by selecting political leaders located in strategic positions in the post–cold war environment. Bill Clinton and Saddam Hussein are examples of political leaders whose respective actions are likely to be indispensable in explaining important outcomes in world poli-tics, because one was the chief executive of the last superpower dur-ing its unipolar moment following the cold war and the other is the head of a rogue state located at the crossroads of the main energy source for the rest of the world (Walker, Schafer, and Young 1999; Mastanduno 1997).

To the extent that the post–cold war environment is weakly structured and highly charged emotionally, the personalities of both leaders may also have a significant impact and demonstrate each actor's indispensability in the resolution of conflicts and the coordination of cooperation among states in the Middle East. Bill Clinton's efforts at the end of his administration to facilitate the peace process between Arabs and Israelis are emblematic of both the possibilities for a leader's significant impact and the difficulties facing leaders with strategic leverage. Saddam Hussein's continued intransigence in the face of pressure and sanctions exercised by the international community demonstrates the central role of one actor's political personality in shaping Iraq's relations with the rest of the world during and after the Persian Gulf conflict.

This kind of analysis of the strategic importance of political leaders and their personalities as important causal mechanisms for explaining and predicting world politics is an argument for investing academic talent and government resources in the assessment of political leadership. It is also a brief for the continuation of two strands of research identified earlier in chapter 1. In this view, the basic research represented in the academy by the interdiscipline of political psychology and the applied leadership research implemented inside the U.S. government are more important than ever for gaining a perspective on the possibilities for peace and progress in the twenty-first century. However, for this knowledge to influence the understanding of scholars and the deliberations of policymakers, there are several gaps to be addressed between and within the academic and policy communities.

The Gap between Theory and Practice

"Bridging the gap" is a metaphor associated with the influential book by the same title, by Alexander George (1993) under the auspices of the U.S. Institute for Peace (see also Lepgold 1998). George wrote about the gap between the academic and policy communities, characterizing it as the divide between knowledge and action. He argues that academic knowledge is organized along theoretical and generic lines in order to explain international relations, while policymakers need knowledge about specific actors and problems in foreign policy in order to take action. These organizational differences create a gap that needs to be bridged between the supply of academic knowledge and the demand for policy-relevant knowledge (George 1993, 115–34).

Accompanying this difference is a confidence gap between the two cultures of academic theory and policymaking practice. Occupants of each world have reservations about the activities of the other. According to George, practitioners object to the efforts of academics to put their research in general theoretical terms on a scientific basis, especially when presented in a quantitative form or developed under controlled laboratory conditions. Such efforts are viewed as weak generalizations based on inadequate data, which can lead to irrelevant predictions and a false sense of confidence in the ability to understand and control foreign policy (George 1993, 6–11).

In turn, academics have their reservations about the use by policymakers of an outdated realist theory of international relations, a focus on the exercise of power that leads to simplistic diagnoses of policy problems. Worse yet are atheoretical decisions based on tacit assumptions or unrepresentative historical analogies, such as lessons drawn from the British failure to appease Germany at Munich or the American failure to prevent a surprise attack on Pearl Harbor by Japan. Other intelligence failures stem from images of the external world not subjected to social scientific scrutiny due to the intrusion of political considerations into intelligence estimates, which perpetuate distorted images that serve the interests of the policymaker (George 1993, 11–15).

There is a certain irony about these gaps between academics and practitioners, because there are parallel differences among schools of thought within the academic field of international relations. Although it has some competition from liberalism and constructivism, realism is still one of the dominant paradigms for the organization of knowledge in this field (Katzenstein, Keohane, and Krasner 1998). The theories associated with each of these approaches share a structural bias, which is that the individual leader does not matter much in the conduct of international relations. Depending on the paradigm at hand, realists see leaders as rational calculators of the relationships between national goals and national power; liberals conceptualize them as conformists to rules embodied in international or domestic institutions; and constructivists characterize them as constrained by cultural norms generated within and between societies. These schools of thought do not have a strong theory of agency, which would allow for the possibility that individual differences among leaders may make systematic and important differences in world politics.

In response, the decision-making school of foreign policy theory has long argued on behalf of the need for a robust theory of agency. These theorists would limit universal structural propositions to contingent generalizations based on intervening causal mechanisms linking structural conditions with foreign policy decisions and international outcomes (Snyder, Bruck, and Sapin 1954; C. Hermann 1969; Allison 1971; Tetlock 1998; Hagan 2002). George (1993, 107–14) is also an advocate of this position within academic circles.

However, until very recently this argument has not received much attention from structural theorists of international relations. Some realists and their critics have begun to wrestle with the desirability of limiting neorealist knowledge claims to emergent processes and outcomes among states at the systemic level of analysis (Waltz 1979; Elman 1996; Christenson and Snyder 1997; Schweller 1998). Neoliberal institutionalists have also started to recognize the importance of processes and conditions at the individual level of analysis (Keohane and Martin 1999). Constructivists are currently divided into conventional and critical camps over the wisdom of whether and how to solve the agent-structure problem (Katzenstein, Keohane, and Krasner 1998; Wendt 1987, 1999). Even so, this attention has not bridged the gap between the decision-making approach and structural paradigms within the academy.

In sum, the irony is that decision-making theorists view structural theories as underspecified models that generate weak generalizations based on inadequate data. This knowledge can lead to irrelevant predictions and a false sense of confidence in the ability to understand and control foreign policy (Hagan 2002)—which is the same critique of academic work by practitioners noted earlier by George (1993). This shared view of the shortcomings of general international relations theory should provide common ground for a fruitful dialogue between decision-making theorists and actual decision makers about specific actors in world politics.

While many government practitioners grasp this insight intuitively, they tend to go further than their academic counterparts and want to abandon the task of explanation in favor of interpreting each leader and situation as sui generis. They are not interested in ideal types so much as in the real case that a model is attempting to explain. They thereby commit "the fallacy of misplaced concreteness" (Whitehead [1925] 1948, 52; cited in Hedstrom and Swedberg 1998, 15). Decision-making theorists who search for causal mechanisms join with adherents to the quest on behalf of structural-covering laws in rejecting this move. They argue that a given concrete representation of a case is just one of an infinite number of possible models, which only an abstract formulation of the interpretation susceptible to counterfactual reasoning can reveal (Hedstrom and Swedberg 1998, 13–21; see also Little 1998, 237–40).

So what are the implications of these debates within and between academics and practitioners for assessing the contents of this volume? The good news associated with a microfoundations approach to social science is that a focus on leaders as causal agents turns out to be a good bet for specifying strong explanations of social processes and outcomes. The bad news is that the prospects for making strong general predictions based on a universal structural theory are not so promising. Instead, middle-range theories informed by ideal types and the careful empirical examination of differences among cases within each type become the basis for fine-grained analyses and short causal stories of political processes and outcomes (Little 1998, 247–55; Hedstrom and Swedberg 1998, 11–13). In turn, a focus on individual differences may generate valid contingent generalizations and predictions about specific actors (George 1993, 125–45).

The Gap between Parts and Wholes

The contributions in this volume by political psychologists illustrate a range of analytical models and empirical tools for identifying causal mechanisms within a leader's personality that impact political decisions and outcomes. One question that immediately presents itself for examination is how these different analyses are related to one another. Asking this question is likely to point the way to future research directions and to illuminate both the possibilities and the limits for integrating these methods. Future efforts by academics and practitioners are likely to yield several kinds of responses to the challenge of bridging parts and wholes.

One response is a *triangulation strategy.* The same leader is likely to be the subject of more than one approach that predicts a common feature of a leader's behavior, for example, bargaining style or risk-taking propensity. The applications of each approach will determine the degree to which the predictions are the same. Comparisons of the predictions by each approach with the subsequent behavior of the leader will assess the degrees of fit between the prediction and the outcome. Where the results overlap, that is, triangulate, confidence in the prediction of future cases is likely to increase. This solution has already surfaced elsewhere in profiles of George H. W. Bush and Mikhail Gorbachev by some of the contributors to this volume (see Winter et al. 1991a, 1991b).

A second response is an *integration strategy* to fit the components of each approach along the contours provided by an overarching "map" of personality and political behavior (Smith 1968). This kind of strategy appears in varying degrees in the comprehensive contributions to this volume by Post and Renshon, which suggest a spatial and temporal hierarchy among the elements of a leader's personality. Post and Renshon stress that the range of cognitive states is constrained by a leader's constellation of personality or characterological traits. In turn, these features of the core personality are generated by formative experiences in the individual's life history.

A third response is a *comparative leader strategy* that identifies scope conditions under which different features of the leader's personality are likely to be politically relevant. This approach is represented especially in the contributions by Hermann and Weintraub, who emphasize the need to compare a leader with a norming group in order to assess when a leader's standardized score is above or below average for a particular personality trait. Deviations from the norm indicate an increased likelihood of potential impact on a leader's political behavior. A longitudinal extension of this strategy in Winter's contribution to this volume is to compare scores for the same leader over time against a norming group in an effort to anticipate changes in his behavior as different traits are aroused by changes in the leader's context for action.

A fourth response is a *context-contingent strategy* in which the interactive effects of a leader's personality and the context for action are identified. The contribution by Suedfeld, Guttieri, and Tetlock emphasizes the necessity to take into account changes in such conditions as stress, accountability, and value conflict in the arousal of different levels of integrative complexity and its consequences for information processing and behavioral choice. The analysis of beliefs by Walker, Schafer, and Young in this volume also emphasizes the interaction effects between a leader's philosophical diagnosis of the context and his or her instrumental propensities for action in choosing strategies, tactics, and moves. Renshon's emphasis on the contingent nature of the relationship between a leader's character and different leadership roles is another manifestation of this strategy of inquiry.

A fifth response is a *typological strategy* in which the different personality characteristics are subsumed or reduced to a set of types. The typologies may be inductive and pragmatic reductions based on previous empirical or clinical research, such as the creation of leader types by Hermann based on the psychological literature or the use of clinical types by Post from the DSM-IV manual of personality disorders (APA 1994). The operational code typology of belief systems developed by Holsti (1977) and integrated theoretically with motivations for power, achievement, and affiliation by Walker (1983) represents a deductive strategy for developing a typology.

A sixth response is a *temporal consistency strategy* marked by a search for behavior consistent with the leader's basic character acquired early in life and manifested in a variety of contexts over a long period of time. The classic exposition of this approach is the analysis by George and George (1956) of Woodrow Wilson, which rests heavily on an account of Wilson's early socialization within his family of origin and the continuity in his behavior during his terms of office, first as the president of Princeton University, then as the governor of New Jersey, and finally as the president of the United States. A similar focus in this volume by Renshon on Bill Clinton's family-of-origin experiences and by Post on Saddam Hussein's childhood socialization is carried forward by these authors to interpret consistent behavior patterns by each leader as an adult during their respective political careers.

All of these strategies will also produce some assessment of the degree of conceptual commensurability and empirical correlation among the various approaches where there are overlapping personality or behavioral features. Is the use of such concepts as risk orientation, cognitive style, needs for power, achievement, affiliation, control over historical development, and conceptual complexity by the contributors to this volume commensurable? That is, do they mean the same thing? If so, then do the indicators that measure them correlate highly? If the answers to these two questions are "yes," then that happy configuration will allow the indicators to be used interchangeably, depending upon the availability of data for a particular leader.

If one or both answers are "no," then the validity of the measures needs to be qualified. They are either measuring different features or different dimensions of the same feature. If it is the former, then the uses of the underlying concept are partly incommensurable. If it is the latter, then perhaps they may be fruitfully combined into an overall index. An example of these potential difficulties and previous attempts to wrestle with them is the discussion by Suedfeld, Guttieri, and Tetlock in this volume regarding the initial use of *conceptual complexity* to refer to a stable personality trait and the growing realization that it also varies across contexts. This empirical finding led to a distinction between conceptual complexity and integrative complexity to distinguish between the default value and the arousal value within the context of cognitive manager theory.

Future Applications

Future applications of these approaches to leadership analysis are going to face some challenges in relating their respective models to different aspects of a leader's political behavior. The single biggest challenge is to establish reliable and valid measures of that behavior. While the authors have devoted a great deal of attention to developing measures of personality, they have expended relatively little effort on the systematic observation of decision-making processes and actions by the leaders. Addressing this gap is important for assessing both academic research and practical applications. Unless the outcome is clearly specified and measured, it is difficult to determine the predictive and explanatory power of the causal mechanism that is supposed to have generated it. The magnitude of this task varies, depending on the scope of the causal claims made by the leadership model.

The cognitive models of object appraisal mechanisms focus primarily on the explanation and prediction of bargaining and problem-solving strategies with relatively simple characteristics. Is the leader more likely to adopt a cooperative or conflict strategy, conditional tactics of reciprocity or unconditional tactics of appeasement and brinkmanship (Walker, Schafer, and Young)? Is a leader's tenure in office going to be short or long? Is the performance of a role likely to be successful or unsuccessful (Suedfeld, Guttieri, and Tetlock)? These outcomes pose relatively simple problems as dependent variables and are susceptible to quantification at a level of measurement commensurate with the independent variables in the causal mechanisms that inform the analysis.

The personality models of Hermann and Winter focusing on the mediation of self and others have more scope, explaining the leader's selection of advisers and processing of advice, management style in dealing with subordinates, risk-taking propensity, and negotiation style, as well as the behavioral outcomes of decision-making processes. In his personality analysis, Weintraub identifies even more general personality traits—such as creativity, impulsivity, and indecisiveness—and emotional states—such as anxiety, moodiness, and anger—as the sources of potential political behaviors. This extension carries with it the challenge of developing measures for additional variables, adapting measures developed by others, or extrapolating relationships to behavioral variables from laboratory experiments and previous research.

As the scope of the analysis addresses the processes of externalization and ego defense at a holistic level, Post and Renshon make the case that a leader's core personality constrains and shapes other personality features, as well as political behavior. Their methodology takes the form of an interpretive analysis of narrative evidence instead of a quantitative analysis that yields indicators of personality or behavior. This analysis yields either a personality type—narcissistic, obsessive-compulsive, or paranoid—or a set of dimensions—ambition, integrity, relatedness—that is postulated as generating particular personality traits and behavioral characteristics. The heuristic value of the analysis becomes the basis for other observers of the leader to recognize the connections between personality and behavior without a quantitative measurement strategy.

However it is achieved, the importance of effective methods for profiling political leadership cannot be overestimated. It has been heightened by the unstable international climate in the post–cold war era. The frequency of threats arising from relatively unknown and unfamiliar sources increases the need for rapid and sophisticated profiling of a new range of adversaries. The occasions for leadership assessment are likely to take several forms in the twenty-first century, including the following contingencies.

The Rise of Rogue Leaders and Outlaw Nations

The end of the cold war has been destabilizing, producing not a "peace dividend" but an unpredictable international climate in which rogue leaders of outlaw nations frequently have precipitated major political crises. The relatively stable and predictable super-power rivalry has been replaced by a series of regional conflicts often precipitated by the actions of previously unknown or poorly understood leaders. There has been a proliferation of destructive power, with more destructive power in the hands of small, independent leadership with hostile agendas toward the United States. The most worrisome nations—Iran, Iraq, and North Korea—are ruled by unpredictable dictatorships. The headlines of the past few years have been dominated by such names as Saddam Hussein, Kim Jung-Il, Mohammad Farah Aideed, Radovan Karadzic, Slobodan Milosevic, and Osama bin Laden.

Several of these leaders either already have or are actively seeking weapons of mass destruction. During the Gulf Crisis, a nuclear-armed Saddam Hussein would have entirely changed the dynamics of the conflict. Former U.S. secretary of defense William Perry referred to the "nightmare scenario" of a nuclear-armed North Korea. Should an extremist nationalist have won the presidency of Russia—not entirely out of the question, given Yeltsin's failing health and his tenuous hold on power—as the political and economic instability mounted, the prospect of a Vladimir Zhirinovskiy-like figure with his finger on the nuclear button would have been truly terrifying.

Avoiding Deadly Conflict

In addressing the challenge of effective coercive diplomacy, Alexander George (1993) stressed the importance of having clear models of the adversaries' psychology. As with information campaigns, effective diplomacy in a conflictual situation cannot proceed effectively without clear and accurate models of leadership psychology. This theme was carried forward in the work of the Carnegie Commission on Preventing Deadly Conflict (Hamburg, George, and Ballentine 1999). They stressed the critical role of leadership, both in promoting deadly conflict and in avoiding it. To effectively counter leaders such as Saddam Hussein, Slobodan Milosevic, and Osama bin Laden as they promote deadly conflict, clear actor-specific models of their psychology and decision making are an absolute requisite.

The Requirement to Counter Low-Intensity Conflict

Despite the military conflicts in the Gulf and in Bosnia and Kosovo, many political-military experts are persuaded that low-intensity conflict—insurgencies and terrorism—will continue to be a prominent feature of the security environment of the twenty-first century and will increasingly occupy our attention. While the frequency of terrorist incidents has gone down, the lethality has increased, and the increased destructiveness of terrorist groups and organizations, including consideration of the use of weapons of mass destruction, makes effective countering of terrorism a major priority. Two vivid examples drive home this point. The poison gas attack on the Tokyo subways by Aum Supreme Truth transformed a feared nightmare into terrifying reality. For this apocalyptic millenarian cult, the personality and decision making of the guru, Shoko Asahara, was of determinative influence on the decision to mount a broad-based program to develop weapons of mass destruction—nuclear, biological, and chemical.

The horrific destruction of the World Trade Center in Manhattan, foreshadowed by the bombing of the American embassies in Kenya and Tanzania, demonstrates the dangers of the new face of terrorism. A new form of terrorism, transnational terrorism with a global reach, has emerged with a particularly dangerous movement under the leadership of Osama bin Laden. He has actively threatened to employ weapons of mass destruction in his attacks against U.S. targets. As the barriers to mass casualty terrorism have weakened, the prospects for terrorists engaging in nuclear, biological, or chemical terrorism have increased.

Countering this new level of threat requires in-depth understanding of such leaders as Osama bin Laden and Shoko Asahara. Psychological operations doctrine, developed and applied in conventional warfare, also has an important role to play in countering terrorism, but its powerful techniques have not been adapted to the changing battlefield of low-intensity conflict. To apply psychological operations effectively to terrorism, the attributes of the target must be specified, particularly leadership and pattern of decision making. One cannot effectively target a group without a clear understanding of its leaders and decision structures, which vary widely from group to group.

Information Warfare and the Revolution in Military Affairs

While low-intensity conflict will continue to be an important element of the security environment in the twenty-first century, in considering the changing face of warfare, information has been identified as the central element in the security environment. The centrality of information in its strategic considerations, both offensively and defensively, is being called a revolution in military affairs. The battle for control of the information battlefield following the Gulf War was largely left uncontested as Saddam Hussein effectively reframed the conflict for his radical Arab constituents and enhanced his reputation and leadership standing. By his control of the information environment, Slobodan Milosevic effectively countered the military superiority of the NATO air campaign in Kosovo to reframe the contest in such a manner as to increase his support and steel the will of the Serbian people. He did this by identifying himself with Marshall Tito and Clinton with Hitler and NATO with the Nazis. The ability of Saddam Hussein and Slobodan Milosevic adroitly and successfully to manipulate the information environment adversely affected the course of these asymmetric campaigns.

Consider also how rapidly the support of the American public changed for U.S. intervention in Somalia. Initially, the televised spectacle of starving Somali children deeply touched the heartstrings of the American public, which strongly supported the humanitarian intervention. But the sight of American soldiers' bodies being hauled behind a Somali warlord's jeeps rapidly led to pressure to withdraw, lest further loss of American life ensue. Whether purposeful or not, this assuredly was a highly effective psychological operation by the Somali warlord Mohammad Farah Aideed. It is similarly clear that Saddam Hussein believes that the United States suffers from a "Vietnam Complex" and that numerous American battlefield casualties can lead to domestic opposition and a stalemate.

As major resources are being devoted to information warfare, it is crucial to incorporate state-of-the-art techniques for specifying the behavioral attributes of the adversary's leadership. One cannot influence an adversary one does not understand. What deters one opponent may incite another. At heart, the goal is psychological and must incorporate both an understanding and significant psychological elements for maximal effectiveness. This requires the ability rapidly and accurately to model psychologically the adversary's leadership.

The profiling techniques described in this volume chart a pathway to this end. They have been used to assess the personalities of foreign political and military leaders to assist in summit meetings and other high-level negotiations, in crisis situations, and in estimative intelligence. These methods have been employed to evaluate the intentions of foreign political and military leaders, to evaluate the impact of foreign policy events on their psychological state and political attitudes, and to analyze changes in their threat potential.

The rapidity with which international conflicts can "go critical" and the catastrophic consequences of miscalculation make it imperative that accurate evaluations of leader psychology be developed swiftly and be monitored closely during crises. Encouraging progress is being made by a number of the authors represented in this volume in utilizing computer-assisted content analysis, so that the capacity to evaluate on-line the psychological states of key leaders is considered attainable in the near future. In a complex politico-military crisis, such as the crisis in the Gulf precipitated by Saddam Hussein's invasion of Kuwait, the capacity to closely monitor fluctuations in the leader's mental state can valuably inform crisis managers regarding what might be his or her own next move or likely response to others' initiatives. Similarly, in a terrorist hostage and barricade crisis, rapid changes in a leader's profile could signal a sharp increase in the hazard to the hostages' lives, suggesting a shift from hostage negotiations to a SWAT team intervention. Real-time measures could also identify crucial moments in international negotiations, predicting the adversary's readiness to compromise.

Finally, leaders themselves often see people as the essence of politics and are strongly interested in what makes their adversaries and allies tick. A more informed leadership will better negotiate the treacherous shoals of national and international waters, and sound methods of psychologically evaluating political leaders can assist in that important task. Such knowledge can inform and guide the policy process without replacing the political skills necessary to exercise effective leadership. As George (1993, 23) points out, even the best-informed leader still needs to be able to make judgments about the trade-offs among (1) searching for high-quality decisions, (2) bargaining for support of the decision, and (3) expending time and other resources on searching and bargaining. Applied to the analysis of a policy problem, knowledge of who the players are can at least help prevent the selection of a policy option so compromised by decision-making trade-offs as to be ineffective in dealing with the people targeted in the political process (George 1993, 25).

References

Adkins, R. 1994. Strategic Politician Theory and the Presidency: Why "First Tier" Candidates Rarely Win the Nomination. Paper presented at the annual meeting of the Southern Political Science Association, Atlanta.

Adorno, T. W., E. Frenkel-Brunswick, D. J. Levinson, and R. N. Sanford. 1950. *The Authoritarian Personality.* New York: Harper.

Akhtar, S., and J. A. Thompson. 1982. Overview: Narcissistic Personality Disorder. *American Journal of Psychiatry* 139:12–20.

Aliotta, J. M. 1988. Social Backgrounds, Social Motives, and Participation on the U.S. Supreme Court. *Political Behavior* 10:267–84.

Allen, C. F. 1991. Governor William Jefferson Clinton: A Biography with a Special Focus on His Education Contributions. Ph.D. diss., University of Missouri.

Allen, C. F., and J. Portis. 1992. *The Comeback Kid: The Life and Career of Bill Clinton.* New York: Birch Lane Press.

Allison, G. 1971. *Essence of Decision: Explaining the Cuban Missile Crisis.* Boston: Little, Brown.

Allport, G. 1961. *Pattern and Growth in Personality.* New York: Holt, Rinehart and Winston.

Altemeyer, R. 1996. *The Authoritarian Specter.* Cambridge, MA: Harvard University Press.

APA (American Psychiatric Association). 1994. *Diagnostic and Statistical Manual of Mental Disorders* (DSM-IV). American Psychiatric Association.

Aronson, H., and W. Weintraub. 1967. Verbal Productivity as a Measure of Change in Affective Status. *Psychological Reports* 20:483–87.

Atkinson, J. W. 1982. Motivational Determinants of Thematic Apperception. In A. J. Stewart, ed., *Motivation and Society,* 3–40. San Francisco: Jossey-Bass.

Axelrod, R. 1976. *Structure of Decision: The Cognitive Maps of Political Elites.* Princeton: Princeton University Press.

Babbie, E. 1995. *The Practice of Social Research.* 7th ed. Belmont, CA: Wadsworth.

Bakan, D. 1966. *The Duality of Human Existence.* Chicago: Rand McNally.

Baker-Brown, G., E. J. Ballard, S. Bluck, B. de Vries, P. Suedfeld, and P. E. Tetlock. 1992. The Conceptual/Integrative Complexity Scoring Manual. In C. P.

References

Smith, ed., *Motivation and Personality: Handbook of Thematic Content Analysis,* 400–418. Cambridge: Cambridge University Press.

Baker, J. 1999. Differing Views of McCain. *Arizona Republic,* October 31, A9.

Bales, R. F. 1958. Task Roles and Social Roles in Problem-Solving Groups. In E. E. Maccoby, T. Newcomb, and E. Hartley, eds., *Readings in Social Psychology,* 3d ed., 437–47. New York: Holt, Rinehart, and Winston.

Ballard, E. J. 1983. Canadian Prime Ministers: Complexity and Political Issues. *Canadian Psychology* 24:125–30.

Bandura, A. 1982. Self-Efficacy Mechanism in Human Agency. *American Psychologist* 37:122–47.

Bannister, D. 1962. Personal Construct Theory: A Summary and Experimental Paradigm. *Acta Psychologica* 20:104–20.

Baram, A. 1997. An Historical-Political Analysis of Saddam Hussein. Paper presented at George Washington University, Washington, DC, January 1997.

———. 1998. *Building toward Crisis: Saddam Husayn's Strategy for Survival.* Washington, DC: Washington Institute for Near East Policy.

Barber, J. D. 1965. *The Lawmakers.* New Haven, CT: Yale University Press.

———. 1977. *The Presidential Character.* Englewood Cliffs, NJ: Prentice-Hall.

———. [1972] 1992. *Presidential Character: Predicting Performance in the White House.* 4th ed. Reprint, Englewood Cliffs, NJ: Prentice Hall.

Bar-Siman-Tov, Y. 1995. Value-Complexity in Shifting from War to Peace: The Israeli Peace-Making Experience with Egypt. *Political Psychology* 16:545–65.

Bass, B. M. 1981. *Stogdill's Handbook of Leadership.* New York: Free Press.

Baudry, F. 1989. Character, Character Type, and Character Organization. *Journal of the American Psychoanalytic Association* 37:655–85.

Bengio, O., ed. 1992. *Saddam Hussein on the Gulf Crisis: A Collection of Documents.* Tel-Aviv: Moshe Dayan Center for Middle Eastern and African Studies, Tel-Aviv University.

Bennis, W., and B. Nanus. 1997. *Leaders: Strategies for Taking Charge.* 2d ed. New York: Harperbusiness.

Berke, R. L. 1993. Advisors Looking Askance at Pledge of 25% Staff Cut. *New York Times,* January 7, A18.

———. 1994. Survey Finds Voters in U.S. Rootless and Self-Absorbed. *New York Times,* September 21, A21.

Binder, J. 1975. Personal communication. September 15.

Binion, R. 1976. *Hitler among the Germans.* New York: Elsevier.

Blumenthal, S. 1993a. Letter from Washington: Rendezvousing with Destiny. *New Yorker,* March 8, 38–44.

———. 1993b. Letter from Washington: Dave. *New Yorker,* June 28, 36–41.

———. 1994. Letter from Washington: The Education of a President. *New Yorker,* January 24, 31–43.

Bonham, G. M. 1993. Cognitive Mapping as a Technique for Supporting International Negotiation. *Theory and Decision* 34:255–73.

References

Bracken, P. 1983. *The Command and Control of Nuclear Forces*. New Haven, CT: Yale University Press.

Brams, S. 1994. *Theory of Moves*. New York: Cambridge University Press.

Brewster-Smith, M. 1968. A Map for the Analysis of Personality and Politics. *Journal of Social Issues* 24:3.

Broder, D. S. 1999. For McCain, No Place Like Home for Controversy. *Washington Post*, November 28, A1.

Brook, D. 1996. *The Seduction of Hillary Rodham*. New York: Free Press.

Brown, R. W. 1965. *Social Psychology*. New York: Free Press.

Bruck, Connie, 1994. Hillary and the Pol. *New Yorker*, May 30, 58–96.

Brummett, J. 1994. *Highwire: From the Back Roads to the Beltway—The Education of Bill Clinton*. New York: Hyperion.

Bunge, M. 1967. *Scientific Research*. Vol. 3 of *Studies of the Foundations, Methodology, and Philosophy of Science*. Berlin: Springer-Verlag.

Burns, J. F. 2000. Methods of the Great Leader. *New York Times Book Review*, February 6, 6–7.

Burns, J. M. 1978. *Leadership*. New York: Harper and Row.

Bush, B. 1994. *Barbara Bush: A Memoir*. New York: Scribner.

Bush, B., and L. Bush. 1999. Transcript of Interview with Cokie Roberts on ABC's *This Week*, December 19.

Bush, G. W. 1999. *A Charge to Keep*. New York: Morrow.

Bushman, B. J., and R. F. Baumeister. 1998. Threatened Egotism, Narcissism, Self-Esteem, and Direct and Displaced Aggression: Does Self-Love or Self-Hate Lead to Violence? *Journal of Personality and Social Psychology* 75:219–29.

Buss, A. H. 1989. Personality as Traits. *American Psychologist* 44:1378–88.

Byars, R. S. 1972. The Task/Affect Quotient. *Comparative Political Studies* 5:109–20.

———. 1973. Small-Group Theory and Shifting Styles of Political Leadership. *Comparative Political Studies* 5:443–69.

Carter, J. 1975. *Why Not the Best?* New York: Bantam.

———. 1983. *Keeping Faith: Memoirs of a President*. New York: Bantam.

Ceci, S. J., and A. Ruiz. 1992. The Role of General Ability in Cognitive Complexity: A Case Study of Expertise. In R. R. Hoffman, ed., *The Psychology of Expertise: Cognitive Research and Empirical AI*, 218–32. New York: Springer-Verlag.

Chomsky, N. 1957. *Syntactic Structures*. The Hague, Netherlands: Mouton.

Christenson, T., and J. Snyder. 1997. Progressive Research on Degenerate Alliances. *American Political Science Review* 91:919–22.

Claunch, N. C. 1964. Cognitive and Motivational Characteristics Associated with Concrete and Abstract Levels of Conceptual Complexity. Ph.D. diss., Princeton University.

Cliff, E., and J. Alter. 1992. You Don't Reveal Your Pain: Clinton Reflects on the Turmoil of His Childhood. *Newsweek*, March 30, 37.

Clinton, W. J. 1993a. Remarks Announcing the Withdrawal of the Nomination of Lani Guinier and an Exchange with Reporters, June 3, 1993. *Weekly Compilation of Presidential Documents*, June 7, 29:22, 1027.

————. 1993b. Exchange with Reporters Prior to a Meeting with House Democratic Leaders, May 25, 1993. *Weekly Compilation of Presidential Documents*, May 31, 29:21, 942.

————. 1993c. Interview with Dan Rather of *CBS News*, March 24, 1993. *Weekly Compilation of Presidential Documents*, March 29, 29:12, 497.

————. 1994. *Public Papers of the Presidents of the United States.* Washington, DC: U.S. Government Printing Office.

————. 1995. Interview with Larry King in Culver City, Ca., September 21. *Weekly Compilation of Presidential Documents*, September 25, 38:1641–54.

Cocks, G., and T. L. Crosby. 1987. *Psycho-History: Readings in the Method of Psychology, Psychoanalysis, and History.* New Haven, CT: Yale University Press.

Colloff, P. 1999. The Son Rises: How Growing Up in West Texas Made Him Different from His Dad. *Texas Monthly,* June 1.

Coren, S., and P. Suedfeld. 1995. Personality Correlates of Conceptual Complexity. *Journal of Social Behavior and Personality* 10:229–42.

Crichlow, S. 1998. Idealism or Pragmatism? An Operational Code Analysis of Yitzhak Rabin and Shimon Peres. *Political Psychology* 19:683–706.

Crockett, W. H. 1965. Cognitive Complexity and Impression Formation. In B. A. Maher, ed., *Progress in Experimental Personality Research,* 2:47–90. New York: Academic Press.

Crosby, F., and T. L. Crosby. 1981. Psychobiography and Psychohistory. In S. L. Long, ed., *Handbook of Political Behavior,* 1:195–254. New York and London: Plenum.

Crown, J. T. 1968. *The Kennedy Literature: A Bibliographic Essay on John F. Kennedy.* New York: New York University Press.

de Vries, B. 1988. *The Concept of Self in a Life-Span: Life Perspective.* Ph.D. diss., University of British Columbia.

de Vries, B., J. Blando, and L. J. Walker. 1995. The Review of Life's Events: Analyses of Content and Structure. In B. Haight and J. Webster, eds., *The Art and Science of Reminiscing: Theory, Research, Methods, and Applications,* 123–37. Washington, DC: Taylor and Francis.

de Vries, B., S. Bluck, and J. E. Birren. 1993. The Understanding of Death and Dying in a Life-Span Perspective. *Gerontologist* 33:366–72.

de Vries, B., and L. J. Walker. 1987. Conceptual/Integrative Complexity and Attitudes toward Capital Punishment. *Personality and Social Psychology Bulletin* 13:448–57.

Diaz, A. J. 1982. An Empirical Study of the Effects of CEO Motives on Intra-Industry Performance with Examples Drawn from U.S. and Japanese Auto Manufacturers. Unpublished Thesis, Harvard University.

Dille, B. 2000. The Prepared and Spontaneous Remarks of Presidents Reagan and Bush: A Validity Comparison for at-a-Distance Measurements. *Political Psychology* 21:573–86.

Direnzo, G. J. 1967. *Personality, Power, and Politics.* Notre Dame, IN: University of Notre Dame Press.

Dole, R. J., and E. H. Dole, with R. N. Smith. 1988. *The Doles: Unlimited Partners.* New York: Simon and Schuster.

Dominowski, R. L., and L. E. Bourne Jr. 1994. The History of Research on Thinking and Problem Solving. In R. J. Stern, ed., *Thinking and Problem Solving.* San Diego: Academic Press.

Donley, R. E. 1968. Psychological Motives and the American Presidency. Thesis, Wesleyan University.

Donley, R. E., and D. G. Winter. 1970. Measuring the Motives of Public Officials at a Distance: An Exploratory Study of American Presidents. *Behavioral Science* 15:227–36.

Drew, E. 1994. *On the Edge: The Clinton Presidency.* New York: Simon and Schuster.

Driver, M. J. 1977. Individual Differences as Determinants of Aggression in the Inter-Nation Simulation. In Margaret G. Hermann, ed., *A Psychological Examination of Political Leaders.* New York: Free Press.

Druckman, D. 1968. Ethnocentrism and the Inter-Nation Simulation. *Journal of Conflict Resolution* 12:45–68.

———, ed. 1977. *Negotiations: Social-Psychological Perspectives.* Beverly Hills, CA: Sage.

Elman, C. 1996. Horses for Courses: Why Not Neorealist Theories of Foreign Policy? *Security Studies* 6:7–53.

Elms, A. C. 1976. *Personality in Politics.* New York: Harcourt, Brace, Jovanovich.

———. 1986. From House to Haig: Private Life and Public Style in American Foreign Policy Advisers. *Journal of Social Issues* 42 (2): 33–53.

———. 1994. *Uncovering Lives: The Uneasy Alliance of Biography and Psychology.* New York: Oxford University Press.

Entwisle, D. R. 1972. To Dispel Fantasies about Fantasy-Based Measures of Achievement Motivation. *Psychological Bulletin* 83:1131–53.

Erikson, E. H. 1942. Hitler's Imagery and German Youth. *Psychiatry* 5:475–93.

———. [1950] 1963. The Legend of Hitler's Childhood. In *Childhood and Society,* 326–58. Reprint, New York: Norton.

———. 1967. Review of *Thomas Woodrow Wilson: A Psychological Study. International Journal of Psycho-Analysis* 48:462–68.

Etheredge, L. S. 1978. *A World of Men: The Private Sources of American Foreign Policy.* Cambridge, MA: MIT Press.

Fazio, R. H. 1986. How Do Attitudes Guide Behavior? In R. Sorrentino and E. T. Higgins, eds., *Handbook of Motivation and Cognition: Foundations of Social Behavior.* New York: Wiley.

References

Fodor, E. 1990. The Power Motive and Creativity of Solutions to an Engineering Problem. *Journal of Research in Personality* 24:338–54.

Ford, K. M., and Chang, P. J. 1989. An Approach to Automated Knowledge Acquisition Founded on Personal Construct Theory. In M. Fishman, ed., *Advances in Artificial Intelligence Research*, 1:83–132. Greenwich, CT: JAI Press.

Foreign Broadcast Information Service, near East and South Asia. 1990a. 137, July 17, 23.

———. 1990b. August 10.

Freud, S. [1901] 1953. *The Interpretation of Dreams.* In J. Strachey, ed., *Standard Edition of the Complete Psychological Works of Sigmund Freud,* vols. 4–5. Reprint, London: Hogarth.

———. [1936] 1964a. A Disturbance of Memory on the Acropolis. In J. Strachey, ed., *Standard Edition of the Complete Psychological Works of Sigmund Freud,* 22:239–48. Reprint, London: Hogarth.

———. [1940] 1964b. Outline of Psycho-Analysis. In J. Strachey, ed., *The Standard Edition of the Complete Psychological Works of Sigmund Freud,* 23:144–207. Reprint, London: Hogarth.

Freud, S., and Bullitt, W. C. 1967. *Thomas Woodrow Wilson: A Psychological Study.* Boston: Houghton Mifflin.

Friedman, T. L. 1992. Professor Elect on T.V.: More Than Just a Talk Show. *New York Times,* December 18, B12.

———. 1993a. Clinton Aide Demurs on White House Staff Cuts and Recovery Plans. *New York Times,* January 13, 17.

———. 1993b. Clinton Trimming Lower-Level Aides. *New York Times,* February 10, A1.

Friedman, W. 1994. Woodrow Wilson and Colonel House and Political Psychobiography. *Political Psychology* 15:35–59.

Fromm, E. 1973. *The Anatomy of Human Destructiveness.* New York: Holt, Rinehart, and Winston.

Fursenko, A., and T. Naftali. 1997. *"One Hell of a Gamble": Khrushchev, Castro, and Kennedy, 1958–1964.* New York: Norton.

Gandhi, I., with E. Pouchpadass. 1982. *My Truth.* New York: Grove.

Gelderman, C. 1997. *All the President's Words: The Bully Pulpit and the Creation of the Virtual Presidency.* New York: Walker.

George, A. L. 1959. *Propaganda Analysis: A Study of Inferences Made from Nazi Propaganda in World War II.* Westport, CT: Greenwood.

———. 1968. Power as a Compensatory Value for Political Leaders. *Journal of Social Issues* 24 (3): 29–50.

———. 1969. The "Operational Code": A Neglected Approach to the Study of Political Leaders and Decision-Making. *International Studies Quarterly* 13:190–222.

———. 1971. Some Uses of Dynamic Psychology in Political Biography: Case

References

Materials on Woodrow Wilson. In F. I. Greenstein and M. Lerner, eds., *A Source Book for the Study of Personality and Politics*, 78–98. Chicago: Markham.

———. 1979. The Causal Nexus between Cognitive Beliefs and Decision-Making Behavior: The "Operational Code." In L. Falkowski, ed., *Psychological Models in International Politics*, 95–124. Boulder, CO: Westview.

———. 1980. *Presidential Decision Making and Foreign Policy: On the Effective Use of Information and Advice*. Boulder, CO: Westview.

———. 1991. *Forceful Persuasion: Coercive Diplomacy as an Alternative to War*. Washington, DC: United States Institute of Peace Press.

———. 1993. *Bridging the Gap: Theory and Practice in Foreign Policy*. Washington, DC: United States Institute of Peace Press.

George, A. L., and J. L. George. 1956. *Woodrow Wilson and Colonel House: A Personality Study*. New York: John Day.

———. 1981–82. Woodrow Wilson and Colonel House: A Reply to Weinstein, Anderson, and Link. *Political Science Quarterly* 96:641–65.

———. 1983. Comments on "Woodrow Wilson Re-Examined: The Mind-Body Controversy Redux and Other Disputations." *Political Psychology* 4:307–12.

———. 1998. *Presidential Personality and Performance*. Boulder, CO: Westview.

Glad, B. 1973. Contributions of Psychobiography. In J. N. Knutson, ed., *Handbook of Political Psychology*, 296–321. San Francisco: Jossey-Bass.

Goldman, P., et al. 1994. *Quest for the Presidency, 1992*. College Station: Texas A&M Press.

Goldstein, K. M., and S. Blackman, eds. 1978. *Cognitive Style: Five Approaches and Relevant Research*. New York: Wiley.

Goleman, D. 1991. Experts Differ on Dissecting Leaders' Psyches from Afar. *New York Times*, January 29.

Gottfried, K., and B. Blair. 1988. *Crisis Stability and Nuclear War*. New York: Oxford University Press.

Greenstein, F. I. 1969. *Personality and Politics*. Chicago: Markham.

———. 1987. *Personality and Politics*. 2d ed., with a new preface. Princeton: Princeton University Press.

———. 2000. *The Presidential Difference: Leadership Style from FDR to Clinton*. New York: Free Press.

Greenwald, A. G., and M. R. Banaji. 1995. Implicit Social Cognition: Attitudes, Self-Esteem, and Stereotypes. *Psychological Review* 102:4–27.

Guttieri, K., P. Suedfeld, and M. D. Wallace. 1995. The Integrative Complexity of American Decision-Makers in the Cuban Missile Crisis. *Journal of Conflict Resolution* 39:595–621.

Hagafors, R., and B. Brehmer. 1983. Does Having to Justify One's Decisions Change the Nature of the Judgment Process? *Organizational Behavior and Human Performance* 31:223–32.

References

Hagan, J. D. 1994. Domestic Political Systems and War Proneness. *Mershon International Studies Review* 38:183–207.

———. 1995. Domestic Political Explanations in the Analysis of Foreign Policy. In Laura Neack, Jeanne A. K. Hey, and Patrick J. Haney, eds., *Foreign Policy Analysis*. Englewood Cliffs, NJ: Prentice-Hall.

———. 2002. Does Decision Making Matter? Systemic Assumptions versus Historical Reality. In M. Hermann, ed., *Leaders, Groups, and Coalitions: Understanding the People and Processes in Foreign Policymaking*, 5–46. Special issue of *International Studies Review*. London: Blackwell.

Hamburg, D., A. George, and K. Ballentine. 1999. Preventing Deadly Conflict: The Critical Role of Leadership. *Archives of General Psychiatry* 56:971–97.

Hargrove, E. C. 1989. Two Conceptions of Institutional Leadership. In Bryan D. Jones, ed., *Leadership and Politics*. Kansas City: University of Kansas Press.

Harris, J. F. 1999. Top Adviser to Clinton Announces Departure: Begala Will Lecture at Georgetown, Write. *Washington Post*, February 25, A16.

Hart, J. A. 1977. Cognitive Maps of Three Latin American Policy Makers. *World Politics* 30:115–40.

Hart, J. A., and F. I. Greenstein. 1977. Cognitive Maps of Presidential Documents. Paper, Department of Politics, Princeton University.

Harvey, O. J., D. E. Hunt, and H. M. Schroder. 1961. *Conceptual Systems and Personality Organization*. New York: Wiley.

Hedstrom, P., and R. Swedberg. 1998. *Social Mechanisms*. Cambridge: Cambridge University Press.

Heifetz, R. A. 1994. *Leadership without Easy Answers*. Cambridge, MA: Harvard University Press.

Hermann, C. 1969. *Crises in Foreign Policy*. Indianapolis: Bobbs-Merrill.

Hermann, M. 1976. Circumstances under Which Leader Personality Will Affect Foreign Policy: Some Propositions. In J. Rosenau (ed.), *In Search of Global Patterns*, 326–32. New York: Free Press.

———. 1977. *A Psychological Examination of Political Leaders*. New York: Free Press.

———. 1979. Who Becomes a Political Leader? Some Societal and Regime Influences on Selection of a Head of State. In L. S. Falkowski, ed., *Psychological Models in International Politics*, 15–48. Boulder, CO: Westview.

———. 1980a. Explaining Foreign Policy Behavior Using the Personal Characteristics of Political Leaders. *International Studies Quarterly* 24:7–46.

———. 1980b. Assessing the Personalities of Soviet Politburo Members. *Personality and Social Psychology Bulletin* 6:332–52.

———. 1983. Assessing Personality at a Distance: A Profile of Ronald Reagan. *Mershon Center Quarterly Report* 7 (6). Columbus: Mershon Center of the Ohio State University.

———. 1984a. Personality and Foreign Policy Making. In Donald Sylvan and

References

Steve Chan, eds., *Perceptions, Beliefs, and Foreign Policy Decision Making.* New York: Praeger.

———. 1984b. *Validating a Technique for Assessing Personalities of Political Leaders at a Distance: A Pretest.* Report prepared for Defense Systems, Inc., as part of Contract DSI-84-1240.

———. 1984c. Personality and Foreign Policy Decision Making: A Study of 53 Heads of Government. In D. A. Sylvan and S. Chan, eds., *Foreign Policy Decision-Making: Perceptions, Cognition, and Artificial Intelligence,* 53–80. New York: Praeger.

———. 1985. *Validating a Technique for Assessing Personalities of Political Leaders at a Distance: A Test Using Three Heads of State.* Report prepared for Defense Systems, Inc., for Contract DSI-84-1240.

———. 1986a. The Ingredients of Leadership. In Margaret G. Hermann, ed., *Political Psychology: Contemporary Problems and Issues.* San Francisco: Jossey-Bass.

———. 1986b. *Effects of Speech and Interview Materials on Profiles of Leaders at a Distance: A Validation Exercise.* Report prepared for Defense Systems, Inc., as part of Contract DSI-85-1240.

———. 1987a. *The Effects of Translation on Profiles of Leaders at a Distance.* Report prepared for Defense Systems, Inc., as part of Contract DSI-86-1240.

———. 1987b. Assessing the Foreign Policy Role Orientations of Sub-Saharan African Leaders. In S. G. Walker, ed., *Role Theory and Foreign Policy Analysis,* 161–98. Durham, NC: Duke University Press.

———. 1987c. *Handbook for Assessing Personal Characteristics and Foreign Policy Orientations of Political Leaders.* Columbus: Mershon Center of the Ohio State University.

———. 1988a. Hafez Al-Assad, President of Syria: A Leadership Profile. In B. Kellerman and J. Rubin, eds., *Leadership and Negotiation in the Middle East,* 70–95. New York: Praeger.

———. 1988b. *Validating a Technique for Assessing Personalities of Political Leaders at a Distance: Profiles of 12 Leaders from the Same Culture.* Report prepared for Defense Systems, Inc., as part of Contract DSI-87-1240.

———. 1989a. Defining the Bush Presidential Style. *Mershon Memo* (spring): 1. Columbus: Ohio State University.

———. 1989b. Personality Profile Data on Gorbachev. Paper presented at the annual meeting of the International Studies Association, London, March.

———. 1993. Leaders and Foreign Policy Decision Making. In D. Caldwell and T. McKeown, eds., *Diplomacy, Force, and Leadership: Essays in Honor of Alexander George.* Boulder, CO: Westview.

———. 1995. Leaders, Leadership, and Flexibility: Influences on Heads of Government as Negotiators and Mediators. *Annals of the American Academy of Political and Social Science* 542:148–67.

References

Hermann, M. G., and J. D. Hagan. 1998. International Decision Making: Leadership Matters. *Foreign Policy* (spring): 124–37.

Hermann, M. G., and C. F. Hermann. 1989. Who Makes Foreign Policy Decisions and How: An Empirical Inquiry. *International Studies Quarterly* 33:361–87.

Hermann, M. G., and C. W. Kegley. 1995. Rethinking Democracy and International Peace: Perspectives from Political Psychology. *International Studies Quarterly* 39:511–33.

Hermann, M. G., and N. Kogan. 1977. Personality and Negotiating Behavior. In D. Druckman, ed., *Negotiations: Social-Psychological Perspectives.* Beverly Hills, CA: Sage.

Hermann, M. G., and T. Preston. 1994. Presidents, Advisers, and Foreign Policy: The Effect of Leadership Style on Executive Arrangements. *Political Psychology* 15:75–96.

Hermann, M. G., T. Preston, and M. Young. 1996. Who Leads Can Matter in Foreign Policymaking: A Framework for Leadership Analysis. Paper presented at the annual meeting of the International Studies Association, San Diego, April 16–20.

Holsti, O. 1967. Cognitive Dynamics and Images of the Enemy: Dulles and Russia. In D. Finlay, O. Holsti, and R. Fagen, *Enemies in Politics,* 25–96. Chicago: Rand McNally.

———. 1969. *Content Analysis for the Social Sciences and Humanities.* Reading, MA: Addison-Wesley.

———. 1970. The Operational Code Approach to the Study of Political Leaders: John Foster Dulles' Philosophical and Instrumental Beliefs. *Canadian Journal of Political Science* 3:123–57.

———. 1976. Foreign Policy Viewed Cognitively. In R. Axelrod, ed., *The Structure of Decision,* 18–54. Princeton: Princeton University Press.

———. 1977. The "Operational Code" as an Approach to the Analysis of Belief Systems. *Final Report to the National Science Foundation,* Grant SOC 75-14368, Duke University.

Horney, K. 1937. *The Neurotic Personality of Our Times.* New York: Norton.

House, R. J., W. D. Spangler, and J. Woycke. 1991. Personality and Charisma in the U.S. Presidency: A Psychological Theory of Leader Effectiveness. *Administrative Science Quarterly* 36:364–96.

Howe, M. J. A. 1997. Beyond Psychobiography: Towards More Effective Syntheses of Psychology and Biography. *British Journal of Psychology* 88:235–48.

Hussein, S. 1981. *On Iraq and International Politics.* Baghdad: Translation and Foreign Languages Publishing House.

Ifill, G. 1992a. Democrats Drop Donors Session with President. *New York Times,* May 2, A1.

———. 1992b. Questioned about Trust, Clinton Turns Angry. *New York Times,* April 24, A21.

References

————. 1992c. Vietnam War Draft Status Becomes Issue for Clinton. *New York Times,* February 17, A16.

Janis, I. L. 1972. *Victims of Groupthink.* Boston: Houghton Mifflin.

————. 1982. *Victims of Groupthink.* 2d ed. Boston: Houghton Mifflin.

————. 1989. *Crucial Decisions: Leadership in Policy-Making and Management.* New York: Free Press.

Jaques, E. 1986. The Development of Intellectual Capability: A Discussion of Stratified Systems Theory. *Journal of Applied Behavioral Science* 22:361–83.

Jaques, E., and K. Cason. 1994. *Human Capability: A Study of Individual Potential and Its Application.* Falls Church, VA: Cason Hall.

Jervis, R. 1976. *Perception and Misperception in International Politics.* Princeton: Princeton University Press.

————. 1994. Leadership, Post-Cold War Politics, and Psychology. *Political Psychology* 15:769–78.

————. 1997. *System Effects: Complexity in Social and Political Life.* Princeton: Princeton University Press.

John, O. P., and S. Srivastava. 1999. The Big Five Trait Taxonomy: History, Measurement, and Theoretical Perspectives. In L. Pervin and O. P. John, eds., *Handbook of Personality: Theory and Research,* 2d ed., 102–38. New York: Guilford.

Joll, J. 1968. *1914: The Unspoken Assumptions.* London: Weidenfeld and Nicolson.

Jones, E. 1953–57. *The Life and Work of Sigmund Freud.* 3 vols. London: Hogarth.

Jones, E. E., and R. E. Nisbett. 1972. The Actor and the Observer: Divergent Perceptions of the Causes of Behavior. In E. E. Jones, D. E. Janouse, H. H. Kelley, R. E. Nisbett, S. Valins, and B. Weiner, eds., *Attribution: Perceiving the Causes of Behavior,* 79–94. Morristown, NJ: General Learning Press.

Jonsson, C. 1982. The Ideology of Foreign Policy. In Charles W. Kegley and Patrick McGowan, eds., *Foreign Policy: USA/USSR.* Beverly Hills, CA: Sage.

Kaarbo, J., and M. G. Hermann. 1998. Leadership Styles of Prime Ministers: How Individual Differences Affect the Foreign Policymaking Process. *Leadership Quarterly* 9:243–63.

Katzenstein, P., R. Keohane, and S. Krasner. 1998. International Organization and the Study of World Politics. *International Organization* 52 (4): 645–86.

Kellerman, B. 1991. Political Leadership in Political Science: Toward a Cultural Approach. Paper presented at the George Washington University Political Psychology Seminar.

Kelley, V. 1992. Transcript of Interview with Katherine Couric on *NBC Today,* July 15, 33–36.

———— (with J. Morgan). 1994a. *Leading with My Heart: My Life.* New York: Simon and Schuster.

————. 1994b. Transcript of Interview with Connie Chung on *CBS Eye to Eye,* January 6, 20.

References

Kelly, G. A. 1955. *The Psychology of Personal Constructs.* New York: Norton.

Kelly, M. 1992. William Jefferson Clinton: A Man Who Wants to Be Liked and Is. *New York Times,* November 7, A1.

Kelman, H. C. 1983. Conversations with Arafat: A Social-Psychological Assessment of the Prospects for Israeli-Palestinian Peace. *American Psychologist* 38:203–16.

Keohane, R., and L. Martin. 1999. Institutional Theory as a Research Program. Paper presented at the annual meeting of the American Political Science Association, Atlanta, GA, September 1–4.

Kershaw, I. 1999. *Hitler, 1889–1936: Hubris.* New York: Norton.

Kohut, H. 1971. *The Analysis of the Self.* New York: International Universities Press.

————. 1977. *The Restoration of the Self.* New York: International Universities Press.

————. 1984. *How Does Analysis Cure?* Ed. A. Goldberg with P. Stepansky. Chicago: University of Chicago Press.

Kornadt, H.-J., L. H. Eckensberger, and W. B. Emminghaus. 1980. Cross-Cultural Research on Motivation and Its Contribution to a General Theory of Motivation. In H. C. Triandis and W. Lonner, eds., *Handbook of Cross-Cultural Psychology,* 3:223–321. Boston: Allyn and Bacon.

Kowert, P. A. 1996. Where *Does* the Buck Stop? Assessing the Impact of Presidential Personality. *Political Psychology* 17:421–52.

Kowert, P., and M. G. Hermann. 1997. Who Takes Risks? Daring and Caution in Foreign Policy Making. *Journal of Conflict Resolution* 41:611–37.

Krosnick, J. A., and D. Kinder. 1990. Altering the Foundations of Support for the President through Priming. *American Political Science Review* 84:497–512.

Labaton, S. 2000a. McCain Urged F.C.C. Action on Issue Involving Supporter. *New York Times,* January 6, A1.

————. 2000b. Issue for McCain Is Matching Record with His Rhetoric. *New York Times,* January 7, A16.

Laffal, J. 1965. *Pathological and Normal Language.* New York: Atherton Press.

Lalljee, M., and M. Cook. 1975. Anxiety and Ritualized Speech. *British Journal of Psychology* 66:299–306.

Langer, L. L. 1999. Satan's Biographers. *Atlantic Monthly* (February): 98–104.

Langer, W. 1972. *The Mind of Adolf Hitler: The Secret Wartime Report.* New York: Basic Books.

Lasswell, H. 1930. *Psychopathology and Politics.* Chicago: University of Chicago Press.

————. 1948. *Power and Personality.* New York: Norton.

Lau, R. R., and D. O. Sears. 1986. *Political Cognition.* Hillsdale, NJ: Lawrence Erlbaum.

Lavallee, L., and P. Suedfeld. 1997. Conflict in Clayoquot Sound: Using Thematic Content Analysis to Understand Psychological Aspects of Environmental Controversy. *Canadian Journal of Behavioural Science* 29:194–209.

Lefcourt, H. M. 1976. *Locus of Control: Current Trends in Theory and Research.* New York: Halstead.

Lehmann-Haupt, C. 1994. Low Shock Threshold in White House Exposé. *New York Times,* June 9, C18.

Leites, N. 1951. *The Operational Code of the Politburo.* New York: McGraw-Hill.

———. 1953. *A Study of Bolshevism.* New York: Free Press.

Leng, R. 1993. *Interstate Crisis Behavior, 1816–1980: Realism versus Reciprocity.* Cambridge: Cambridge University Press.

———. 2000. *Bargaining and Learning in Recurring Crises: The Soviet-American, Egyptian-Israeli, and Indo-Pakistani Rivalries.* Ann Arbor: University of Michigan Press.

Leng, R., and S. Walker. 1982. Crisis Bargaining: Confrontation, Coercion, and Reciprocity. *Journal of Conflict Resolution* 26:571–91.

Leonard, R. 1997. Theorizing the Relationship between Agency and Communion. *Theory and Psychology* 7:823–35.

Lepgold, J. 1998. Is Anyone Listening? International Relations Theory and the Problem of Policy Relevance. *Political Science Quarterly* 113:43–62.

Levi, A., and P. E. Tetlock. 1980. A Cognitive Analysis of Japan's 1941 Decision for War. *Journal of Conflict Resolution* 24:195–211.

Levin, R. E. 1992. *Bill Clinton: The Inside Story.* New York: S.P.I. Books.

Levine, R. A., and D. T. Campbell. 1972 *Ethnocentrism.* New York: Wiley.

Levinson, D. 1978. *The Seasons of a Man's Life.* New York: Knopf.

Lifton, R. J., and G. Mitchell. 1996. *Hiroshima in America: A Half Century of Denial.* New York: Avon Books.

Linville, P. 1982. The Complexity-Extremity Effect and Age-Based Stereotyping. *Journal of Personality and Social Psychology* 42:193–211.

———. 1985. Self-Complexity and Affective Extremity: Don't Put All of Your Eggs in One Cognitive Basket. *Social Cognition* 3:94–120.

Little, D. 1998. *Microfoundations, Method, and Causation.* New Brunswick, NJ: Transaction.

Loewen, L., and P. Suedfeld. 1992. Cognitive and Arousal Effects of Masking Office Noise. *Environment and Behavior* 24:381–95.

Lorenz, M. 1953. Language as Expressive Behavior. *Archives of Neurology and Psychiatry* 70:277–85.

Luck, D. 1974. A Psycholinguistic Approach to Leader Personality: Hitler, Stalin, Mao, and Liu Shao-Ch'i. *Studies in Comparative Communism* 7:426–53.

Mancuso, J. C., ed. 1970. *Readings for a Cognitive Theory of Personality.* New York: Holt, Rinehart, and Winston.

Maoz, Z., and A. Shayer. 1987. The Cognitive Structure of Peace and War Argumentation: Israeli Prime Ministers versus the Knesset. *Political Psychology* 8:575–636.

425

Maraniss, D. 1995. *First in His Class: A Biography of Bill Clinton.* New York: Random House.

Marcus, G. E., W. R. Neuman, and M. MacKuen. 2000. *Affective Intelligence and Political Judgment.* Chicago: University of Chicago Press.

Marfleet, G. 2000. The Operational Code of John F. Kennedy during the Cuban Missile Crisis: A Comparison of Public and Private Remarks. *Political Psychology* 21:545–58.

Marmor, M. F. 1982. Wilson, Strokes, and Zebras. *New England Journal of Medicine* 307:528–35.

———. 1983. Comments on "Woodrow Wilson Re-Examined: The Mind-Body Controversy Redux and Other Disputations." *Political Psychology* 4:325–27.

Mastanduno, M. 1997. Preserving the Unipolar Moment: Realist Theories and U.S. Grand Strategy after the Cold War. *International Security* 21:49–88.

Matar, F., ed. 1981. *Saddam Hussein: The Man, the Cause, and the Future.* London: Third World Centre.

Mazlish, B. 1972. *In Search of Nixon: A Psychohistorical Inquiry.* New York: Basic Books.

McAdams, D. P., and R. L. Ochberg. 1988. *Psychobiography and Life Narratives.* Durham, NC: Duke University Press.

McClelland, D. C. 1961. *The Achieving Society.* Princeton, NJ: Van Nostrand.

———. 1975. *Power: The Inner Experience.* New York: Irvington.

McClelland, D. C., J. W. Atkinson, R. A. Clark, and E. L. Lowell. 1953. *The Achievement Motive.* New York: Appleton-Century-Crofts.

McClelland, D. C., and D. G. Winter. 1969. *Motivating Economic Achievement.* New York: Free Press.

Mehrabian, A., and M. Weiner. 1966. Non-Immediacy between Communicator and Object of Communication in a Verbal Message: Application to the Inference of Attitudes. *Journal of Consulting Psychology* 30:420–25.

Miller, M. 1974. *Plain Speaking: An Oral Biography of Harry S. Truman.* New York: Putnam.

Mischel, W. 1968. *Personality and Assessment.* New York: Wiley.

———. 1984. On the Predictability of Behavior and the Structure of Personality. In R. A. Zucker, J. Aronoff, and A. I. Rabin, eds., *Personality and the Prediction of Behavior,* 269–305. Orlando, FL: Academic Press.

Mitchell, A. 1996. Now, It's the Rhetorical Presidency. *New York Times,* March 31, E1, 3.

———. 2000a. While Calling for a Positive Campaign, McCain Is Accused of Being Negative. *New York Times,* January 6, A22.

Monroe, R. T. (n.d.) Comments on "Woodrow Wilson's Neurological Illness" by Dr. E. A. Weinstein. Papers of Arthur Walworth. New Haven, CT: Yale University Library.

Morgan, C. D., and H. A. Murray. 1935. A Method for Examining Fantasies:

References

The Thematic Apperception Test. *Archives of Neurology and Psychiatry* 34:289–306.

Morris, D. 1996. *Inside the Oval Office*. New York: Simon and Schuster.

———. 1997. *Behind the Oval Office*. New York: Random House.

Murray, H. A. 1938. *Explorations in Personality*. New York: Oxford University Press.

Neubauer, P. B. 1960. The One-Parent Child and His Oedipal Development. *Psychoanalytic Study of the Child* 37:201–21.

Nicolson, H. 1930. *Portrait of a Diplomatist*. Boston: Houghton Mifflin.

Nisbett, R. E., and T. D. Wilson. 1977. Telling More than We Can Know: Verbal Reports on Mental Processes. *Psychological Review* 84:231–59.

Nixon, R. M. 1982. *Leaders*. New York: Warner Books.

Noonan, P. 1990. *What I Saw at the Revolution: A Political Life in the Reagan Era*. New York: Random House.

Oakley, M. L. 1994. *On the Make: The Rise of Bill Clinton*. Washington, DC: Regnery.

Ohmann, R. 1967. Prolegomena to the Analysis of Prose Style. In S. Chatman and S. R. Levin, eds., *Essays on the Language of Literature*, 398–411. Boston: Houghton Mifflin.

One Step Forward, Two Back. 1998. *Newsweek*, January 5, 8.

Pancer, S. M., B. Hunsberger, M. W. Pratt, S. Boisvert, and D. Roth. 1992. Political Roles and the Complexity of Political Rhetoric. *Political Psychology* 13:31–43.

Panos, P. 1998. A Test of Integrative Complexity in Political Rhetoric. Unpublished master's thesis, North Carolina State University.

Payne, J., O. Woshinksky, E. Veblen, W. Coogan, and G. Bigler. 1984. *The Motivation of Politicians*. Chicago: Nelson-Hall.

Perceptions of Saddam Husayn. 1990. Report prepared for Defense Systems, Inc. November 13.

Porter, C. A., and P. Suedfeld. 1981. Integrative Complexity in the Correspondence of Literary Figures: Effects of Personal and Societal Stress. *Journal of Personality and Social Psychology* 40:321–30.

Post, J. 1973. On Aging Leaders: Possible Effects of the Aging Process on the Conduct of Leadership. *Journal of Geriatric Psychiatry* 6.

———. 1979. Personality Profiles in Support of the Camp David Summit. *Studies in Intelligence* (spring): 1–5.

———. 1980. The Seasons of a Leader's Life: Influences of the Life Cycle on Political Behavior. *Political Psychology* 2 (3/4): 35–49.

———. 1983a. Reply to the Three Comments on "Woodrow Wilson Re-Examined: The Mind-Body Controversy Redux and Other Disputations." *Political Psychology* 4:329–31.

———. 1983b. Woodrow Wilson Re-Examined: The Mind-Body Controversy Redux and Other Disputations. *Political Psychology* 4:289–306.

References

————. 1984. Dreams of Glory and the Life Cycle: The Life Course of Narcissistic Leaders. *Journal of Political and Military Sociology* 12 (1).

————. 1986. Narcissism and the Charismatic Leader-Follower Relationship. *Political Psychology* 7 (4).

————. 1991a. Saddam Hussein of Iraq: A Political Psychology Profile. *Political Psychology* 12 (2).

————. 1991b. Saddam Hussein of Iraq: Afterword. *Political Psychology* 12 (4): 723–25.

————. 1992. Current Concepts of Narcissism: Implications for Political Psychology. *Political Psychology* 13 (1): 99–121.

————. 1991c. Perspective on Saddam Hussein: Crazy Like a Fox. *Los Angeles Times,* January 25, 1991, Metro, part B, 7.

————. 1993. The Defining Moment of Saddam's Life: A Political Psychology Perspective on the Leadership and Decision Making of Saddam Hussein during the Gulf Crisis. In S. A. Renshon, ed., *The Political Psychology of the Gulf War: Leaders, Publics, and the Process of Conflict,* 49–66. Pittsburgh: University of Pittsburgh Press.

Post, J., and R. Robins. 1993. *When Illness Strikes the Leader: The Dilemma of the Captive King.* New Haven: Yale University Press.

Post, J., and P. Rogers. 1988. Bridging Troubled Waters: Personality and Belief Systems. Paper presented at the annual scientific meeting of the International Society of Political Psychology, July.

Purdum, T. S. 1996. Facets of Clinton. *New York Times Magazine,* May 19, 35–41, 62, 77–78.

Pye, L. W. 2000. The Elusive Concept of Culture and the Vivid Reality of Personality. In S. A. Renshon and J. Duckitt, eds., *Political Psychology: Cultural and Crosscultural Foundations.* Macmillan: London.

Ramirez, C. E., and P. Suedfeld. 1988. Nonimmediacy Scoring of Archival Materials: The Relationship between Fidel Castro and "Che" Guevara. *Political Psychology* 9 (1): 155–64.

Raphael, T. D. 1982. Integrative Complexity Theory and Forecasting International Crises: Berlin, 1946–1962. *Journal of Conflict Resolution* 26:423–50.

Redlich, F. 1998. *Hitler: Diagnosis of a Destructive Prophet.* New York: Oxford University Press.

Reich, R. B. 1997. *Locked in the Cabinet.* New York: Knopf.

Reich, W. 1933. *Character Analysis.* New York: Orgone Institute.

Renshon, S. A. 1993. Good Judgment, and the Lack Thereof, in the Gulf War: A Preliminary Psychological Model with Some Applications. In S. A. Renshon, ed., *The Political Psychology of the Gulf War: Leaders, Publics, and the Process of Conflict,* 67–105. Pittsburgh: University of Pittsburgh Press.

————. 1996a. *High Hopes: The Clinton Presidency and the Politics of Ambition.* New York: New York University Press.

References

———. 1996b. *The Psychological Assessment of Presidential Candidates.* New York: New York University Press.

———. 1998. Analyzing the Psychology and Performance of Presidential Candidates at a Distance: Bob Dole and the 1996 Presidential Campaign. *Journal of Leadership Studies* 3:253–81.

———. 2002. *America's Second Civil War: Dispatches from the Political Center.* New Brunswick, NJ: Transaction.

Ritzler, B., and M. Singer. 1998. MMPI-2 by Proxy and the Rorschach: A Demonstration Assessment of the Commandant of Auschwitz. *Journal of Personality Assessment* 71:212–27.

Robins, R., and J. Post. 1987. The Paranoid Political Actor. *Biography* 10 (1).

———. 1997. *Political Paranoia: The Psychopolitics of Hatred.* New Haven: Yale University Press.

Rokeach, M. 1960. *The Open and Closed Mind.* New York: Basic Books.

Rosenbaum, R. 1998. *Explaining Hitler: The Search for the Origins of His Evil.* New York: Random House.

Rosenberg, M. 1979. *Conceiving the Self.* New York: Basic Books.

Ross, D. 1982. Review Essay: Woodrow Wilson and the Case for Psychohistory. *Journal of American History* 69:659–68.

Rubenzer, S. J., T. R. Faschingbauer, and D. S. Ones. 2000. Assessing the U. S. Presidents Using the Revised NEO Personality Inventory. Paper presented at the annual meeting of the American Psychological Association, Washington, DC, August.

Runyan, W. M. 1981. Why Did Van Gogh Cut off His Ear? The Problem of Alternative Explanations in Psychobiography. *Journal of Personality and Social Psychology* 40:1070–77.

———. 1982. *Life Histories and Psychobiography: Explorations in Theory and Method.* New York: Oxford University Press.

———. 1983. Idiographic Goals and Methods in the Study of Lives. *Journal of Personality* 51:413–37.

———. 1984. *Life Histories and Psychobiography: Explorations in Theory and Method.* New York: Oxford University Press.

———. 1988a. A Historical and Conceptual Background to Psychohistory. In W. M. Runyan, ed., *Psychology and Historical Interpretation,* 3–60. New York: Oxford University Press.

———. 1988b. Progress in Psychobiography. *Journal of Personality* 56:295–326.

———. 1990. Individual Lives and the Structure of Personality Psychology. In A. I. Rabin, R. A. Zucker, R. A. Emmons, and S. Frank, eds., *Studying Persons and Lives,* 10–40. New York: Springer.

———. 1997. Studying Lives: Psychobiography and the Conceptual Structure of Personality Psychology. In R. Hogan, ed., *Handbook of Personality Psychology,* 41–69. San Diego, CA: Academic Press.

References

Sachs, H. 1913. Ein Traum Bismarcks [A dream of Bismarck.]. *Internationale Zeitschrift Für Psychoanalyse* 1:80–98.

Safire, W. 1975. *Before the Fall: An Inside View of the Pre-Watergate White House.* New York: Belmont Tower Books.

Satterfield, J. 1997. Cognitive Predictors of Resilience: A Content Analysis of Churchill, Hitler, Roosevelt, and Stalin. Manuscript.

———. 1998. Cognitive-Affective States Predict Military and Political Aggression and Risk Taking. *Journal of Conflict Resolution* 42:667–90.

Satterfield, J. M., and M. E. P. Seligman. 1994. Military Aggression and Risk Predicted by Explanatory Style. *Psychological Science* 5:77–82.

Schafer, M. 2000. Issues in Assessing Psychological Characteristics at a Distance: An Introduction to the Symposium. *Political Psychology* 21:511–27.

———. Forthcoming. Assessing Psychological Characteristics in Foreign Policy Analysis. *Political Psychology.*

Schafer, M., and S. Crichlow. 2000. Bill Clinton's Operational Code: Assessing Source Material Bias. *Political Psychology* 21:559–72.

Schafer, M., and S. Walker. 2001. The Operational Code of Vladimir Putin: Analyzing a New Global Leader with a New Automated Coding System. Prepared for the annual meeting of the International Studies Association, Chicago, February 21–24.

Schafer, M., M. Young, and S. Walker. 1995. U.S. Presidents as Conflict Managers: The Operational Codes of George Bush and Bill Clinton. Paper presented at the annual meeting of the International Society of Political Psychology, Vancouver, BC.

Schmitt, D. P. 1990. *Measuring the Motives of Soviet Leaders and Soviet Society: Congruence Created or Congruence Reflected?* Paper presented at the annual meeting of the International Society of Political Psychology, Washington, DC, July.

Schmitt, D. P., and D. G. Winter. 1998. Measuring the Motives of Soviet Leadership and Soviet Society: Congruence Reflected or Congruence Created? *Leadership Quarterly* 9:181–94.

Schroder, H. M., and P. Suedfeld, eds. 1971. *Personality Theory and Information Processing.* New York: Ronald.

Schroder, H. M., M. J. Driver, and S. Streufert. 1967. *Human Information Processing.* New York: Holt, Rinehart, and Winston.

Schulte Nordholt, J. W. 1991. *Woodrow Wilson: A Life for World Peace.* Berkeley: University of California Press.

Schweller, R. 1998. *Deadly Imbalances.* New York: Columbia University Press.

Scott, W. 1993. Walter Scott's Personality Parade. *Parade,* October 24, 2.

Scott, W. A., D. W. Osgood, and C. Peterson. 1979. *Cognitive Structure: Theory and Measurement of Individual Differences.* Washington: Winston.

Seeyle, K. 2000. Gore Would Quiz Nominee for Pentagon on Obedience. *New York Times,* January 11, A1.

Shapiro, D. 1967. *Neurotic Styles.* New York: Basic Books.

References

Shaw, E. 1990. The Impact of Sanctions on the Psychological State and Political Perceptions of Saddam Husayn. November 13. McLean, VA: Defense Systems, Inc.

———. 1998. A Political Psychological Profile of Saddam Hussein: Contributions from Self Psychology and Empirical Evaluation. Paper presented at the Institute for Contemporary Psychotherapy Scientific Meeting, Washington, DC, October 9.

Shaw, M. L. G., and B. R. Gaines. 1987. An Interactive Knowledge-Elicitation Technique Using Personal Construct Technology. In A. L. Kidd, ed., *Knowledge Acquisition for Expert Systems*, 109–36. New York: Plenum.

Sheehy, G. 1992. What Hillary Wants. *Vanity Fair*, May 10, 140–47, 212–17.

———. 2000. *Hillary's Choice*. New York: Putnam.

Simon, H. 1957. *Models of Man*. New York: John Wiley.

Simonton, D. K. 1986. Presidential Personality: Biographical Use of the Gough Adjective List. *Journal of Personality and Social Psychology* 51:149–60.

———. 1988. Presidential Style: Personality, Biography, and Performance. *Journal of Personality and Social Psychology* 55:928–36.

———. 1999. Significant Samples: The Psychological Study of Eminent Individuals. *Psychological Methods* 4:425–51.

Smith, C. P., ed. 1992. *Motivation and Personality: Handbook of Thematic Content Analysis*. New York: Cambridge University Press.

Smith, M. 1968. A Map for the Study of Personality and Politics. *Journal of Social Issues* 24:15–28.

Snare, C. E. 1990. At-a-Distance Personality Assessment of Iranian Leaders since the Shah. Paper presented at the annual meeting of the International Society for Political Psychology, Washington, DC, July.

———. 1992a. Applying Personality Theory to Foreign Policy Behavior: Evaluating Three Methods of Assessment. In E. Singer and V. Hudson, eds., *Political Psychology and Foreign Policy*, 103–34. Boulder, CO: Westview.

———. 1992b. *Personality and Political Postures: The Case of the Clerical Rules of Iran: I and II*. Ph.D. diss., Ohio State University.

Snow, P. J. 1972. *Hussein: A Biography*. Washington, DC: R. B. Luce.

Snyder, J. 1991. *Myths of Empire: Domestic Politics and International Ambition*. Ithaca, NY: Cornell University Press.

Snyder, M. 1987. *Public Appearances, Private Realities: The Psychology of Self-Monitoring*. New York: W. H. Freeman.

Snyder, R., H. Bruck, and B. Sapin. 1954. *Foreign Policy Decision-Making as an Approach to the Study of International Politics*. Foreign Policy Analysis Project Series, no. 3. Princeton: Princeton University Press.

Steingart, I., and N. Freedman. 1972. A Language Construction Approach for the Examination of Self/Object Representations in Varying Clinical States. In R. R. Holt and E. Peterfreund, eds., *Psychoanalysis and Contemporary Science*, vol. 1. New York: Macmillan.

References

Stephanopoulos, G. 1999. *All Too Human: A Political Education.* Boston: Little, Brown.

Stewart, P. D., M. G. Hermann, and C. F. Hermann. 1989. Modeling the 1973 Soviet Decision to Support Egypt. *American Political Science Review* 83:35–59.

Stoessinger, J. D. 1979. *Crusaders and Pragmatists: Movers of Modern American Foreign Policy.* New York: W. W. Norton.

Stone, W. F., and P. E. Schaffner. 1988. *The Psychology of Politics.* 2d ed. New York: Springer-Verlag.

Streufert, S., and S. C. Streufert. 1978. *Behavior in the Complex Environment.* Washington, DC: Winston.

Streufert, S., and R. W. Swezey. 1986. *Complexity, Managers, and Organizations.* New York: Academic Press.

Strickland, B. R. 1977. Internal-External Control of Reinforcement. In T. Blass, ed., *Personality Variables in Social Behavior,* 219–79. Hillsdale, NJ: Erlbaum.

Stuart, D., and H. Starr. 1981–82. The "Inherent Bad Faith Model" Reconsidered. Dulles, Kennedy, and Kissinger. *Political Psychology* 3:1–33.

Suedfeld, P. 1981. Indices of World Tension in the *Bulletin of the Atomic Scientists. Political Psychology* 2:114–23.

———. 1985. APA Presidential Addresses: The Relation of Integrative Complexity to Historical, Professional, and Personal Factors. *Journal of Personality and Social Psychology* 49:1643–51.

———. 1992a. Cognitive Managers and Their Critics. *Political Psychology* 13:435–53.

———. 1992b. Bilateral Relations between Countries and the Complexity of Newspaper Editorials. *Political Psychology* 13:601–11.

———. 1994. President Clinton's Policy Dilemmas: A Cognitive Analysis. *Political Psychology* 15:337–49.

Suedfeld, P., and S. Bluck. 1988. Changes in Complexity prior to Surprise Attacks. *Journal of Conflict Resolution* 32:626–35.

———. 1993. Changes in Integrative Complexity Accompanying Significant Life Events: Historical Evidence. *Journal of Personality and Social Psychology* 64:124–30.

———. 1996. Cognitive Concomitants of Life Events—Finding a Balance between Generalizability and Contextualization: Reply to Pennell (1996). *Journal of Personality and Social Psychology* 71:781–84.

Suedfeld, P., S. Bluck, E. J. Ballard, and G. Baker-Brown. 1990. Canadian Federal Elections: Motive Profiles and Integrative Complexity in Political Speeches and Popular Media. *Canadian Journal of Behavioural Science* 22:26–36.

Suedfeld, P., S. Bluck, L. Loewen, and D. J. Elkins. 1994. Sociopolitical Values and Integrative Complexity of Student Political Groups. *Canadian Journal of Behavioural Science* 26:121–41.

References

Suedfeld, P., and S. Coren. 1990. A Power Test of Conceptual Complexity: Textual Correlates. *Journal of Applied Social Psychology* 20:357–67.

———. 1992. Cognitive Correlates of Conceptual Complexity. *Personality and Individual Differences* 13:1193–99.

Suedfeld, P., R. S. Corteen, and C. McCormick. 1986. The Role of Integrative Complexity in Military Leadership: Robert E. Lee and His Opponents. In G. Y. Nogami, ed., Special Issue on Military Psychology, *Journal of Applied Social Psychology* 16:498–507.

Suedfeld, P., B. de Vries, S. Bluck, A. B. C. Wallbaum, and P. W. Schmidt. 1996. Intuitive Perceptions of Decision-Making Strategy: Naive Assessors' Concepts of Integrative Complexity. *International Journal of Psychology* 31:177–90.

Suedfeld, P., and Y. M. Epstein. 1973. Attitudes, Values, and Ascription of Responsibility: The Calley Case. *Journal of Social Issues* 15:1–15.

Suedfeld, P., and J. L. Granatstein. 1995. Leader Complexity in Personal and Professional Crises: Concurrent and Retrospective Information Processing. *Political Psychology* 16:509–22.

Suedfeld, P., and L. E. Piedrahita. 1984. Intimations of Mortality: Integrative Simplification as a Precursor of Death. *Journal of Personality and Social Psychology* 47:848–52.

Suedfeld, P., and A. D. Rank. 1976. Revolutionary Leaders: Long-Term Success as a Function of Conceptual Complexity. *Journal of Personality and Social Psychology* 34:169–78.

Suedfeld, P., and P. E. Tetlock. 1977. Integrative Complexity of Communications in International Crises. *Journal of Conflict Resolution* 21:169–84.

———. 1991. Psychological Advice about Foreign Policy Decision Making: Heuristics, Biases, and Cognitive Defects. In P. Suedfeld and P. E. Tetlock, eds., *Psychology and Social Policy,* 51–70. New York: Hemisphere.

Suedfeld, P., P. E. Tetlock, and C. Ramirez. 1977. War, Peace, and Integrative Complexity. *Journal of Conflict Resolution* 21:427–42.

Suedfeld, P., P. E. Tetlock, and S. Streufert. 1992. Conceptual/Integrative Complexity. In C. P. Smith, ed., *Motivation and Personality: Handbook of Thematic Content Analysis,* 393–400. Cambridge: Cambridge University Press.

Suedfeld, P., A. B. C. Wallbaum. 1992. Modifying Integrative Complexity in Political Thought: Value Conflict and Audience Disagreement. *Interamerican Journal of Psychology* 26:19–36.

Suedfeld, P., and M. D. Wallace. 1995. President Clinton as a Cognitive Manager. In S.A. Renshon, ed., *The Clinton Presidency: Campaigning, Governing, and the Psychology of Leadership,* 215–33. Boulder, CO: Westview.

Suedfeld, P., M. D. Wallace, and K. L. Thachuk. 1993. Changes in Integrative Complexity among Middle East Leaders during the Persian Gulf Crisis. *Journal of Social Issues* 49:183–99.

References

Sullivan, A. 1994. All the President's Problems. *New York Times Book Review,* July 3, 2, 11.

Suro, R. 1992. Senate Office Helped Clinton on Draft, Aides Acknowledge. *New York Times,* September 19, A1.

Tartakoff, H. 1966. The Normal Personality in our Culture and the Nobel Prize Complex. In R. M. Lowenstein, L. M. Newman, and A. J. Solnit, *Psychoanalysis: A General Psychology,* 222–52. New York: International University Press.

Taylor, A. J. P. 1961. *The Origins of the Second World War.* London: Hamish Hamilton.

Tellegen, A., J. Kamp, and D. Watson. 1982. Recognizing Individual Differences in Predictive Structure. *Psychological Review* 89:95–105.

Tetlock, P. E. 1979. Identifying Victims of Groupthink from Public Statements of Decision-Makers. *Journal of Personality and Social Psychology* 37:1314–24.

———. 1981a. Personality and Isolationism: Content Analysis of Senatorial Speeches. *Journal of Personality and Social Psychology* 41:737–43.

———. 1981b. Pre- to Post-Election Shifts in Presidential Rhetoric: Impression Management or Cognitive Adjustment? *Journal of Personality and Social Psychology* 41:207–12.

———. 1983a. Cognitive Style and Political Ideology. *Journal of Personality and Social Psychology* 45:118–26.

———. 1983b. Policy-Makers' Images of International Conflict. *Journal of Social Issues* 39:67–86.

———. 1983c. Accountability and Complexity of Thought. *Journal of Personality and Social Psychology* 45:285–92.

———. 1984. Cognitive Style and Political Belief Systems in the British House of Commons. *Journal of Personality and Social Psychology* 46:365–75.

———. 1985a. Integrative Complexity of American and Soviet Foreign Policy Rhetoric: A Time-Series Analysis. *Journal of Personality and Social Psychology* 49:1565–85.

———. 1985b. Accountability: The Neglected Social Context of Judgement and Choice. *Research in Organizational Behavior* 7:297–332.

———. 1986. A Value Pluralism Model of Ideological Reasoning. *Journal of Personality and Social Psychology* 50:819–27.

———. 1988. Monitoring the Integrative Complexity of American and Soviet Policy Rhetoric: What Can Be Learned? *Journal of Social Issues* 44:101–32.

———. 1991. An Integratively Complex Look at Integrative Complexity. Paper presented at the annual meeting of the American Psychological Association, San Francisco, CA, August.

———. 1998. Social Psychology and World Politics. In D. Gilbert, S. Fiske, and G. Lindzey, *Handbook of Social Psychology,* 869–912. New York: McGraw-Hill.

———. In press. Trade-Off Reasoning: Psychological Constraints and Political

References

Implications. In S. Popkin, S. McCubbins, and S. Lupia, eds., *Political Reasoning*. Berkeley: University of California Press.

Tetlock, P. E., D. Armor, and R. Peterson. 1994. The Slavery Debate in Antebellum America: Cognitive Style, Value Conflict, and the Limits of Compromise. *Journal of Personality and Social Psychology* 66:115–26.

Tetlock, P. E., and R. Boettger. 1989. Accountability: A Social Magnifier of the Dilution Effect. *Journal of Personality and Social Psychology* 57:388–98.

———. 1994. Accountability Amplifies the Status Quo Effect When Change Creates Victims. *Journal of Behavioral Decision Making* 7:1–23.

Tetlock, P. E., K. Hannum, and P. Micheletti. 1984. Stability and Change in Senatorial Debate: Testing the Cognitive versus Rhetorical Style Hypotheses. *Journal of Personality and Social Psychology* 46:979–90.

Tetlock, P. E., and J. I. Kim. 1987. Accountability and Judgment Processes in a Personality Prediction Task. *Journal of Personality and Social Psychology* 52:700–709.

Tetlock, P. E., and A. S. R. Manstead. 1985. Impression Management versus Intrapsychic Explanations in Social Psychology: A Useful Dichotomy? *Psychological Review* 92:59–77.

Tetlock, P. E., C. McGuire, R. S. Peterson, P. Feld, and S. Chang. 1992. Assessing Political Group Dynamics: A Test of the Groupthink Model. *Journal of Personality and Social Psychology* 63:403–25.

Tetlock, P. E., R. Peterson, and J. Berry. 1993. Flattering and Unflattering Personality Portraits of Integratively Simple and Complex Managers. *Journal of Personality and Social Psychology* 64:500–511.

Tetlock, P. E., L. Skitka, and R. Boettger. 1989. Social and Cognitive Strategies for Coping with Accountability: Conformity, Complexity, and Bolstering. *Journal of Personality and Social Psychology* 57:632–40.

Tetlock, P. E., R. Peterson, and J. Lerner. 1996. Revising the Value Pluralism Model: Incorporating Social Content and Context Postulates. In C. Seligman, J. Olson, and M. Zana, eds., *Ontario Symposium on Social and Personality Psychology: Values.* Hillsdale, NJ: Erlbaum.

Tetlock, P. E., and A. Tyler. 1996. Winston Churchill's Cognitive and Rhetorical Style: The Debates over Nazi Intentions and Self-Government for India. *Political Psychology* 17:149–70.

Tucker, R. C. 1965. The Dictator and Totalitarianism. *World Politics* 17:55–83.

Vaillant, G. E. 1992. *Ego Mechanisms of Defense: A Guide for Clinicians and Researchers.* Washington, DC: American Psychiatric Press.

Vasquez, J. 1993. *The War Puzzle.* Cambridge: Cambridge University Press.

Veroff, J. 1983. Contextual Determinants of Personality. *Personality and Social Psychology Bulletin* 9:331–43.

Veroff, J., D. Reuman, and S. Feld. 1984. Motives in American Men and Women across the Adult Life Span. *Developmental Psychology* 20:1142–58.

435

Veroff, J., and D. A. Smith. 1985. Motives and Values over the Adult Years. *Advances in Motivation and Achievement* 4:1–53. Greenwich, CT: JAI Press.

Volkan, M. 1980. Narcissistic Personality Organization and Reparative Leadership. *International Journal of Group Psychotherapy* 30:131–52.

———. 1988. *The Need to Have Enemies and Allies.* New York: Jason Aronson.

Volkan, V. D., N. Itzkowitz, and A. W. Dodd. 1997. *Richard Nixon: A Psychobiography.* New York: Columbia University Press.

Waite, R. G. L. 1977. *The Psychopathic God: Adolf Hitler.* New York: Basic Books.

Walker, S. G. 1977. The Interface between Beliefs and Behavior: Henry Kissinger's Operational Code and the Vietnam War. *Journal of Conflict Resolution* 21:129–68.

———. 1983. The Motivational Foundations of Political Belief Systems: A Re-Analysis of the Operational Construct. *International Studies Quarterly* 27:179–201.

———. 1986. Woodrow Wilson's Operational Code. Paper presented at the annual meeting of the International Society of Political Psychology, Amsterdam, July.

———. 1990. The Evolution of Operational Code Analysis. *Political Psychology* 11:403–18.

———. 1995. Psychodynamic Processes and Framing Effects in Foreign Policy Decision-Making: Woodrow Wilson's Operational Code. *Political Psychology* 16:697–717.

———. 2000. Assessing Psychological Characteristics at a Distance: Symposium Lessons and Future Research Directions. *Political Psychology* 21:597–601.

———. 2002. Operational Code Analysis as a Scientific Research Program: A Cautionary Tale. In C. Elman and M. Elman, eds., *Progress in International Relations Theory,* 245–76. Cambridge, MA: MIT Press.

Walker, S., and L. Falkowski. 1984a. The Operational Codes of U.S. Presidents and Secretaries of State. *Political Psychology* 5:237–66.

———. 1984b. The Belief Systems and Crisis Behavior of U.S. Leaders. Paper presented at the annual meeting of the International Society of Political Psychology, Toronto.

Walker, S., and M. Schafer. 2000. The Political Universe of Lyndon B. Johnson and His Advisors. *Political Psychology* 21:529–44.

Walker, S., M. Schafer, and G. Marfleet. 2001. The British Strategy of Appeasement: Why Did Britain Persist in the Face of Negative Feedback? Paper presented at the annual meeting of the Political Science Association, San Francisco, CA, August 29–September 2.

Walker, S., M. Schafer, and M. Young. 1998. Systematic Procedures for Operational Code Analysis: Measuring and Modeling Jimmy Carter's Operational Code. *International Studies Quarterly* 42:175–90.

436

References

————. 1999. Presidential Operational Codes and the Management of Foreign Policy Conflicts. *Journal of Conflict Resolution* 43:610–25.

Walker, S. G., and G. L. Watson. 1989. Groupthink and Integrative Complexity in British Foreign Policy-Making: The Munich Case. *Cooperation and Conflict* 24:199–212.

————. 1992. The Cognitive Maps of British Leaders, 1938–1939: The Case of Chamberlain-in-Cabinet. In E. Singer and V. Hudson, eds., *Political Psychology and Foreign Policy*, 31–58. Boulder, CO: Westview.

————. 1994. Integrative Complexity and British Decisions during the Munich and Polish Crises. *Journal of Conflict Resolution* 38:3–23.

Wallace, M. D. 1991. Preventing Accidental Nuclear War: Risks and Remedies in a Post-Cold War World. *Disarmament* 14:74–96.

Wallace, M. D., and P. Suedfeld. 1988. Leadership Performance in Crisis: The Longevity-Complexity Link. *International Studies Quarterly* 32:439–451.

Wallace, M. D., P. Suedfeld, and K. L. Thachuk. 1993a. Political Rhetoric of Leaders under Stress in the Gulf Crisis. *Journal of Conflict Resolution* 37:94–107.

————. 1993b. Information Processing among Leaders under Stress: Findings from the Gulf Crisis. *Journal of Conflict Resolution* 37:94–107.

————. 1996. Failed Leader or Successful Peacemaker? Crisis, Behaviour, and the Cognitive Processes of Mikhail Sergeyevitch Gorbachev. *Political Psychology* 17:453–72.

Waltz, K. 1979. *Theory of International Politics.* Reading, MA: Addison-Wesley.

Watson, C. B., and D. G. Winter. 1997. Motivation and Leadership Performances: An Archival Study of Woodrow Wilson. Paper presented at the annual meeting of the International Society of Political Psychology, Kraków, Poland, July.

Wedge, B. 1968. Krushchev at a Distance—A Study of Public Personality. *Trans-Action* 5 (October): 24–28.

Weinberger, J., and D. C. McClelland. 1990. Cognitive versus Traditional Motivational Models: Irreconcilable or Complementary? In E. T. Higgins and R. M. Sorrentino, eds., *Handbook of Motivation and Cognition*, 2:562–97. New York: Guilford.

Weinstein, E. A. 1970. Woodrow Wilson's Neurological Illness. *Journal of American History* 57:324–51.

————. 1981. *Woodrow Wilson: A Medical and Psychological Biography.* Princeton: Princeton University Press.

————. 1983. Comments on "Woodrow Wilson Re-Examined: The Mind-Body Controversy Redux and Other Disputations." *Political Psychology* 4:313–24.

Weinstein, E. A., J. W. Anderson, and A. S. Link. 1978–79. Woodrow Wilson's Political Personality: A Reappraisal. *Political Science Quarterly* 93:585–98.

References

Weintraub, W. 1981. *Verbal Behavior: Adaptation and Psychopathology.* New York: Springer.

————. 1986. Personality Profiles of American Presidents as Revealed in Their Public Statements: The Presidential News Conferences of Jimmy Carter and Ronald Reagan. *Political Psychology* 7:285–95.

————. 1989. *Verbal Behavior in Everyday Life.* New York: Springer.

Weintraub, W., and H. Aronson. 1964. The Application of Verbal Behavior Analysis to the Study of Psychological Defense Mechanisms. II: Speech Patterns Associated with Impulsive Behavior. *Journal of Nervous and Mental Disease* 139:75–82 .

————. 1965. The Application of Verbal Behavior Analysis to the Study of Psychological Defense Mechanisms. III: Speech Patterns Associated with Delusional Behavior. *Journal of Nervous and Mental Disease* 141:172–79.

————. 1969. Application of Verbal Behavior Analysis to the Study of Psychological Defense Mechanisms. IV: Speech Patterns Associated with Overeating. *Archives of General Psychiatry* 21:739–44.

————. 1974. Verbal Behavior Analysis and Psychological Defense Mechanisms. VI: Speech Patterns Associated with Compulsive Behavior. *Archives of General Psychiatry* 30:297–300.

Weintraub, W., and M. S. Plaut. 1985. Qualifying Phrases as a Measure of Spontaneity in Speech. *Journal of Nervous and Mental Disease* 173:694–97.

Wendt, A. 1987. The Agent-Structure Problem in International Relations Theory. *International Organization* 41:335–70.

————. 1999. *Social Theory of International Politics.* Cambridge: Cambridge University Press.

Wenner, J. S., and W. Greider. 1993. President Clinton: The Rolling Stone Interview. *Rolling Stone Magazine,* December 9, 40–45, 80–81.

White, R. W. 1959. Motivation Reconsidered: The Concept of Competence. *Psychological Review* 66:297–333.

Whitehead, A. [1925] 1948. *Science and the Modern World: Lowell Lectures, 1925.* Reprint, New York: New American Library.

Wicker, F. W., F. B. Lambert, F. C. Richardson, and J. Kahler. 1984. Categorical Goal Hierarchies and Classification of Human Motives. *Journal of Personality* 52:285–305.

Wilkenfeld, J., S. Kraus, T. E. Santmire, K. M. Holley, and T. E. Santmire. 1996. Cognitive Structure and Crisis Decision Making. Paper presented at the annual meeting of the International Studies Association, San Diego, April.

Wills, G. 1992. Mr. Clinton's Forgotten Childhood. *Time,* June 8, 62–63.

Wines, M. 1993. Clinton, Who Opposed "Soft Money," Got Plenty. *New York Times,* March 19, 19.

Winter, D. G. 1973. *The Power Motive.* New York: Free Press.

References

————. 1980. Measuring the Motives of Southern Africa Political Leaders at a Distance. *Political Psychology* 2 (2): 75–85.

————. 1982. Motives and Behavior in the 1976 Presidential Candidates. In A. J. Stewart, ed., *Motivation and Society,* 244–73. San Francisco: Jossey-Bass.

————. 1987a. Leader Appeal, Leader Performance, and the Motive Profiles of Leaders and Followers: A Study of American Presidents and Elections. *Journal of Personality and Social Psychology* 52:196–202.

————. 1987b. Power Motive Distortion in British and German Newspapers and Diplomatic Dispatches at the Outbreak of World War I. Paper presented at the annual meeting of the Eastern Psychological Association, Arlington, VA, April.

————. 1991. Measuring Personality at a Distance: Development of an Integrated System for Scoring Motives in Running Text. In A. J. Stewart, J. M. Healy Jr., and D. Ozer, eds., *Perspectives in Personality: Approaches to Understanding Lives,* 59–89. London: Jessica Kingsley.

————. 1992a. Content Analysis of Archival Materials, Personal Documents, and Everyday Verbal Productions. In C. P. Smith, ed., *Motivation and Personality: Handbook of Thematic Content Analysis,* 110–25. New York: Cambridge University Press.

————. 1992b. Personality and Foreign Policy. In E. Singer and V. Hobson, eds., *Political Psychology and Foreign Policy,* 79–101. Boulder, CO: Westview.

————. 1993a. Personality and Leadership in the Gulf. In S. A. Renshon, ed. *The Political Psychology of the Gulf War: Leaders, Publics, and the Process of Conflict,* 107–17. Pittsburgh: University of Pittsburgh Press.

————. 1993b. Power, Affiliation, and War: Three Tests of a Motivational Model. *Journal of Personality and Social Psychology* 65:532–45.

————. 1995. Presidential Psychology and Governing Styles: A Comparative Psychological Analysis of the 1992 Presidential Candidates. In S. A. Renshon, ed., *The Clinton Presidency: Campaigning, Governing, and the Psychology of Leadership,* 113–34. Boulder, CO: Westview.

————. 1996. *Personality: Analysis and Interpretation of Lives.* New York: McGraw-Hill.

————. 1997. Comparing War and Peace Crises: The Role of Motivation, Responsibility, and Integrative Complexity. Paper presented at the annual meeting of the International Society of Political Psychology, Kraków, Poland, July.

————. 1998a. Toward a Science of Personality Psychology: David McClelland's Development of Empirically Derived TAT Measures. *History of Psychology* 1:130–53.

————. 1998b. A Motivational Analysis of the Clinton First Term and the 1996 Presidential Campaign. *Leadership Quarterly* 9:253–62.

————. 1999. Origins of Power Motivation in Males: Data from a Longitudinal

Study. Paper presented at the annual meeting of the American Psychological Association, Boston, August.

———. 2002. Motivation and Political Leadership in American Presidents. In O. Feldman and L. Valenty, eds., *Political Leadership for the New Century: Personality and Behavior among American Leaders.* Westport, CT: Praeger.

Winter, D. G., and N. B. Barenbaum. 1985. Responsibility and the Power Motive in Women and Men. *Journal of Personality* 53:335–55.

Winter, D. G., and L. Carlson. 1988. Using Motive Scores in the Psychobiographical Study of an Individual: The Case of Richard Nixon. *Journal of Personality* 56:75–103.

———. 1991b. The Personalities of Bush and Gorbachev at a Distance: Follow-up on Predictions. *Political Psychology* 12:457–64.

Winter, D. G., M. G. Hermann, W. Weintraub, and S. G. Walker. 1991a. The Personalities of Bush and Gorbachev Measured at a Distance: Procedures, Portraits, and Policy. *Political Psychology* 12:215–45.

Winter, D. G., O. P. John, A. J. Stewart, E. Klohnen, and L. E. Duncan. 1998. Traits and Motives: Toward an Integration of Two Traditions in Personality Research. *Psychological Review* 105:230–50.

Winter, D. G., and A. J. Stewart. 1977a. Content Analysis as a Method of Studying Political Leaders. In M. G. Hermann, ed., *A Psychological Examination of Political Leaders,* 27–61. New York: Free Press.

———. 1977b. Power Motive Reliability as a Function of Retest Instructions. *Journal of Consulting and Clinical Psychology* 45:436–40.

———. 1978. The Power Motive. In H. London and J. Exner, eds., *Dimensions of Personality,* 391–447. New York: John Wiley.

Winter, N. J. G. 1992. The Effects of the Hitler Relationship on Mussolini's Motive Profile. Paper presented at the annual meeting of the International Society of Political Psychology, San Francisco, July.

Witkin, H.A., R. G. Dyk, H. F. Faterson, D. R. Goodenough, and S. A. Karp. 1962. *Psychological Differentiation.* New York: Wiley.

Woodward, B. 1994. *The Agenda: Inside the Clinton White House.* New York: Simon and Schuster.

Wormley, W. P. 1976. Portfolio Manager Preferences in an Investment Decision-Making Situation: A Psychological Study. Ph.D. diss., Harvard University.

Woshinsky, O. H. 1973. *The French Deputy: Incentives and Behavior in the National Assembly.* Lexington, MA: D.C. Heath.

Wriggins, W. H. 1969. *The Ruler's Imperative: Strategies for Political Survival in Asia and Africa.* New York: Columbia University Press.

Wright, J. C., and W. Mischel. 1987a. A Conditional Approach to Dispositional Constructs: The Local Predictability of Social Behavior. *Journal of Personality and Social Psychology* 53:1159–77.

References

———. 1987b. Conditional Hedges and the Intuitive Psychology of Traits. *Journal of Personality and Social Psychology* 55:454–69.

Young, M. 2001. Building WorldViews with Profiler+. In Mark D. West, ed., *Applications of Computer Content Analysis.* Progress in Communication Sciences 17. Westport, CT: Ablex Publishing.

Young, M. D. Forthcoming. *Profiler Software System.* Columbus, OH: Social Science Automation, Inc.

Ziller, R. C. 1973. *The Social Self.* New York: Pergamon.

Ziller, R. C., William F. Stone, Robert M. Jackson, and Natalie J. Terbovic. 1977. Self-Other Orientations and Political Behavior. In Margaret G. Hermann, ed., *A Psychological Examination of Political Leaders.* New York: Free Press.

Zillmer, E. A., M. Harrower, B. A. Ritzle, and R. P. Archer. 1995. *The Quest for the Nazi Personality: A Psychological Investigation of Nazi War Criminals.* Hillsdale, NJ: Erlbaum.

Zullow, H. M., G. Oettingen, C. Peterson, and M. E. P. Seligman. 1988. Pessimistic Explanatory Style in the Historical Record: Caving LBJ, Presidential Candidates, and East versus West Berlin. *American Psychologist* 43:673–82.

Contributors

KAREN GUTTIERI is a member of the Department of National Security Affairs, Naval Postgraduate School (NPS), in Monterey, California. Since joining NPS, Dr. Guttieri has been leading faculty development and other curricular issues for a new master of arts degree track and research portfolio, "Security Building in Post-Conflict Environments." From 1999 to 2001, she was a Social Sciences and Humanities Research Council of Canada postdoctoral fellow at the Center for International Security and Cooperation (CISAC) at Stanford University. Dr. Guttieri's current research focuses upon military operations in civilian environments. This focus includes studying the effectiveness of civil-military operations, military organizational learning from peace operations, and civil-military relations issues in peace implementation. Professor Guttieri earned her Ph.D. in political science from the University of British Columbia in Vancouver in 1999.

MARGARET G. HERMANN, Cramer Professor of Global Affairs in the Department of Political Science in the Maxwell School at Syracuse University and director of that school's Global Affairs Institute, conducts research on political leadership, foreign policy decision making, and comparative foreign policy. Former president of the International Society of Political Psychology and the International Studies Association, she has written *A Psychological Examination of Political Leaders* (1977); *Describing Foreign Policy Behavior* (1982); and *Leaders, Groups, and Coalitions: Understanding the People and Processes in Foreign Policymaking* (2001). She has been the editor of the journal *Political Psychology* and is an incoming editor of *International Studies Review*. As author of over one hundred articles, Hermann has applied her method of assessing leadership style at a distance to heads of state, terrorist leaders, and leaders of international institutions, as well as CEOs of nongovernmental organizations and multinational corporations.

Contributors

JERROLD M. POST, M.D., is Professor of Psychiatry, Political Psychology, and International Affairs and the director of the Political Psychology Program at the George Washington University. Dr. Post has devoted his entire career to the field of political psychology. He came to George Washington after a twenty-one-year career with the U.S. government, where he founded and directed the Center for the Analysis of Personality and Political Behavior, an interdisciplinary behavioral science unit that provided assessments of foreign leadership and decision making for the president and other senior officials to prepare for summit meetings and other high-level negotiations and for use in crisis situations. He played the lead role in developing the "Camp David profiles" of Menachem Begin and Anwar Sadat for President Jimmy Carter and initiated the U.S. government program in understanding the psychology of terrorism. Dr. Post received his B.A. and M.D. from Yale University. He is the coauthor of a study of the politics of illness in high office, *When Illness Strikes the Leader: The Dilemma of the Captive King* (1993), and of *Political Paranoia: The Psychopolitics of Hatred* (1997). A nationally recognized expert on the psychology of political leadership, Dr. Post has testified before Congress on his profiles of Saddam Hussein and Osama bin Laden and regularly provides commentary on national and international media.

STANLEY A. RENSHON is professor of political science at the City University of New York and a certified psychoanalyst. He is the author of eighty articles and eleven books, including his psychological biography of the Clinton presidency, *High Hopes,* which won both the 1997 American Political Science Association's Richard E. Neustadt Award for the best book published on the topic of the presidency and the National Association for the Advancement of Psychoanalysis's Gradiva Award for the best published work in the category of biography. His most recent book is *America's Second Civil War: Political Leadership in a Divided Society* (2002).

MARK SCHAFER is associate professor of political science at Louisiana State University. His research focuses primarily on political psychology and conflict resolution, with particular emphases on political leadership and decision-making dynamics. He has published articles in the *Journal of Politics, International Studies Quarterly, Journal of Conflict Resolution, International Interactions,* and several edited volumes.

Contributors

PETER SUEDFELD is dean emeritus of graduate studies and professor emeritus of psychology at the University of British Columbia in Vancouver. The development of the integrative (state) model of complexity and the method of scoring complexity from archival materials began as part of his long-term research program on coping and adaptation during and after critical decision situations, traumatic experiences, and extreme and unusual environments.

PHILIP E. TETLOCK is professor of organizational behavior at the Haas School of Business at the University of California, Berkeley. He has received scientific achievement awards from a variety of professional societies, including the National Academy of Sciences, the American Association for the Advancement of Science, the American Political Science Association, and the American Psychological Association. He has contributed to a wide range of professional journals and books. His current interests include the study of social and political cognition and the problems of assessing rationality in organizational contexts.

STEPHEN G. WALKER, professor of political science at Arizona State University, had done research on leaders and decision making funded by the National Science Foundation. His publications have appeared in *International Studies Quarterly, World Politics, Journal of Politics, Journal of Peace Research,* and *Political Psychology.* He is currently vice president of the International Studies Association and has also served as vice president of the International Society of Political Psychology.

WALTER WEINTRAUB, M.D., is clinical professor in the Department of Psychiatry of the University of Maryland School of Medicine. A psychoanalyst, teacher, and clinical investigator, he is the author of *Verbal Behavior: Adaptation and Psychopathology* (1981) and *Verbal Behavior in Everyday Life* (1989). Dr. Weintraub is a member of the American Psychoanalytic Association and the International Psychoanalytic Association and a fellow of the American Psychiatric Association. As a consultant to the U.S. government, he has developed procedures for analyzing the speech patterns of world leaders.

DAVID G. WINTER is professor of psychology at the University of Michigan. He was educated at Harvard and Oxford Universities. Within the subjects of personality and social psychology, his research interests focus on power and power motivation, the motivational bases of leadership, and the psychological aspects of conflict escalation and war. He is past president of the International Society of Political Psychology.

MICHAEL D. YOUNG is the president of Social Science Automation, Inc., a consulting firm providing remote leader assessment and automated text coding tools to government agencies, commercial businesses, and university researchers. He earned his Ph.D. in political science from the Ohio State University and is particularly interested in cognitive approaches to foreign policy analysis.

Index

Index

Index

450

Index

Index

455

Index

Index

"The only language Saddam Hussein understands is the language of power. Without this demonstrable willingness to use force, even if the sanctions are biting deeply, Saddam is quite capable of putting his people through a sustained period of hardship . . . this is the personality configuration of the destructive charismatic, who unifies and rallies his downtrodden supporters by blaming outside enemies."

Dr. Jerrold M. Post's prophetic description of Saddam's likely course of action, written over ten years ago, now rings with a terrible truth. And the Saddam of today, as an anxious world attests, is more than ever the subject of an intense campaign to divine not only his inner mechanisms, but what he might do next.